JFK:

THE FRENCH CONNECTION

Peter Kross

Adventures Unlimited Press

Books by Peter Kross:

Spys, Traitors and Moles
The Encyclopedia of World War II Spies
Oswald, the CIA and the Warren Commission
JFK: The French Connection

JFK:

THE FRENCH CONNECTION

Adventures Unlimited Press

JFK: The French Connection

by Peter Kross

ISBN 13: 978-1-935487-82-1

Published by:
Adventures Unlimited Press
One Adventure Place
Kempton, Illinois 60946 USA
auphq@frontiernet.net

www.adventuresunlimitedpress.com

JFK with Governor John Connelly and LBJ: A fateful day.

To Eric Eisenstein and Walter Barnes.

JFK:

THE FRENCH CONNECTION

Peter Kross

JFK with Jackie and Governor John Connelly.

Table of Contents

In the car, right before the assassination. It happened on Elm Street…

COMMISSION EXHIBIT 237

Mexico City Mystery Man: This was the man whom the CIA said was Lee Oswald in Mexico City in 1963. Steve Rivele believed he was Edmond Meunier, but he proved not to be the man he was seeking.

Above: Badgeman: Photo taken of a man with what looked like a gun flash coming from behind the fence on the grassy knoll. Possibly one of the shooters in Dealey Plaza. *Right*: Steve Rivele: American writer and reporter who first believed in the French Connection theory to the Kennedy assassination. He traveled the world looking for the "Men Who Killed Kennedy."

Above: Mary Moorman photo: Photo taken from across Dealey Plaza of the shot that killed Kennedy, most likely coming from the grassy knoll behind the picket fence.

Charles de Gaulle: President of France in the 1960s, and the target of numerous assassination attempts on him by the OAS. Also linked to the assassination attempts on de Gaulle were Jean Souetre and Michael Mertz.

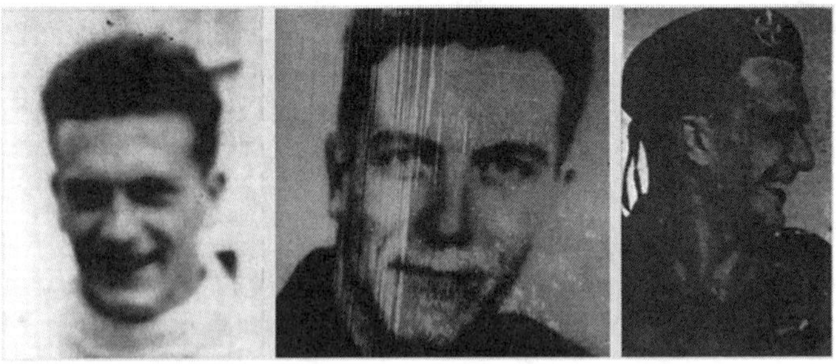

Jean Souetre: Former member of the OAS who was believed to have been in Dallas on the day of the assassination and deported to either Canada or Mexico after the assassination.

JFK:

THE FRENCH CONNECTION

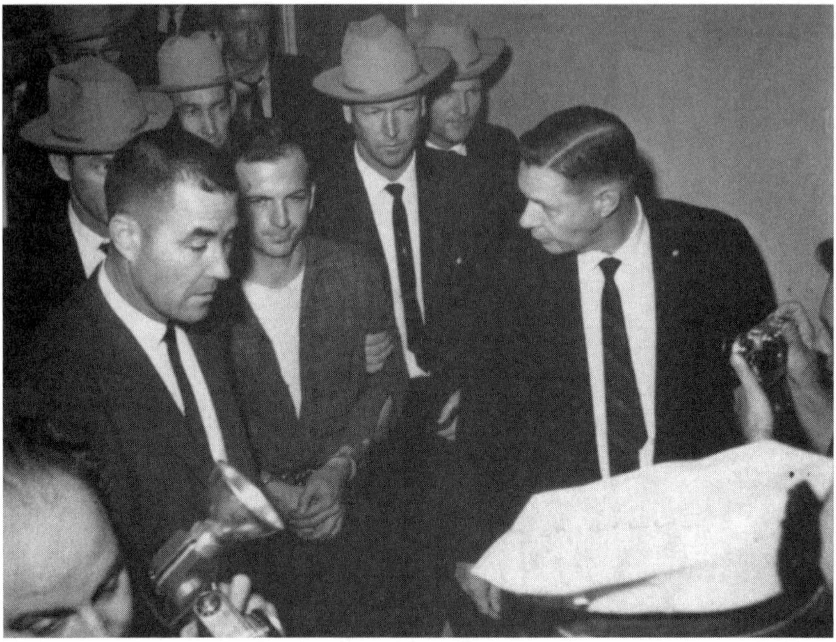

Lee Harvey Oswald was questioned by the Dallas Police, the FBI and the press for two days until gangster and nightclub owner Jack Ruby shot Oswald while he was being transferred from the Dallas jail.

Jack Ruby and some of the strippers at his club.

All men dream, but not equally. Those who dream by night in the dusty recesses of their minds wake in the day to find that it was vanity; but the dreamers of the day are dangerous men, for they may act their dream with eyes wide open, to make it possible.

—*T.E. Lawrence*
"The Seven Pillars of Wisdom"

Introduction

Two hours after the president was killed in Dealey Plaza on November 22, 1963, Dallas police arrested a 24-year-old, ex-Marine by the name of Lee Harvey Oswald at the Texas Theater on charges of killing a Dallas police officer name J. D. Tippit. After a scuffle in the almost empty movie house, Oswald was taken by the police downtown for questioning into the officer's murder. Oswald spent the next two days being interrogated by a slew of law enforcement officers, federal and local, without being given the right to an attorney.

In those two days, Oswald was subsequently charged with both the killing of Officer Tippit, as well as the president of the United States. Under interrogation, Oswald never revealed any pertinent information relating to both events. However, two days later, on Sunday, November 24, 1963, Oswald was killed while being transferred by the Dallas police to a waiting armored car to a more secure location by a local night club owner, Jack Ruby, with known mob ties.

One week later, the new president, Lyndon Johnson, ordered a federal investigation into the president's murder, headed by Chief Justice of the Supreme Court, Earl Warren. Warren, at first, did not want to accept the position but was cajoled into doing so by the new president.

Ten months later, in September 1963, after a slipshod, and rather selective investigation, the Warren Commission came up with the following conclusions: 1) Oswald alone killed President Kennedy had no confederates, foreign or domestic, 2) Three bullets were fired at the president's limousine, one of which, missed, 3) Jack Ruby did not know Oswald prior to his murder and, 4) there was no conspiracy, either foreign or domestic. Case closed.

But what the American public did not know about that terrible day in Dallas, Texas was that the day after the assassination, the FBI deported a French assassin by the name of Jean Souetre (or possibly two others), to either Mexico or Canada. It is not known just why Souetre, a member of the OAS, a French resistance movement which was violently against the government of French Prime Minister Charles de Gaulle, was doing in Dallas at the precise moment JFK was killed. The FBI did not interrogate this man, for reasons known only to them.

In February 1964, a French journalist was attending a party in Montreal, Canada. At the party was an OAS veteran who, after drinking too much, told the writer the following story. He was in Dallas on November 22, 1963 and he tried to recruit the journalist who had both French and Mexican citizenship, to help him in a plot to kill President de Gaulle when he was scheduled to visit Mexico in March of that year. The writer wisely declined the offer.

The so-called "French Connection" to the murder of JFK has been a staple in Kennedy assassination literature, but no major study has been done to tell the complete story. This book will attempt to tell that story, using documents and other written sources that were not available years ago. The book will delve into three major sections; the investigation of the French Connection by writer Steve Rivele who traveled Europe in the hope of finding the "Men Who Killed Kennedy," the investigation of the identities of two European assassins, both who were associated with the CIA-code named QJ/WIN and WI/ROGUE (whose true identities are still not known), and, the connection between the CIA and its predecessor, the OSS, in the illegal heroin trade that took place after World War 2, up to today. The major distribution point in the illegal heroin smuggling was centered in Marseilles, France, the home of many of the former OAS agents, and possibly the focal point of the plot to kill the president of the United States.

After digesting the story, the reader will have to make up, his or her own mind, as to how accurate the French Connection really is.

Chapter 1

The First Assassin

The French people, like most Europeans, are more attuned to the possibility of conspiracy theories in history as their American cousins. Political violence in Europe has plagued the old monarch's since the French Revolution where plots to overthrow the various governments (be it in England, France, or Russia during the Czars) was an almost monthly occurrence.

In America, political assassinations were the work of lone gunmen, not any organized plot to kill our president's. Even though the evidence points to an organized plot to kill President Abraham Lincoln with John Wilkes Booth at the center of the action, he had a number of confederates whose tentacles went back to the Confederate government in Richmond, The assassins of President's McKinley and Garfield were the work of one person, with no other confederates in sight.

However, that was not the popular view in Europe after the assassination of John Kennedy. It didn't take too long before popular opinion in Europe came down harshly on the findings of the Warren Commission and their view that Lee Oswald was the lone assassin of the much admired, John F. Kennedy. It would take longer for Americans to view the killing of JFK as a possible conspiracy than their European brethren. Skeptics of the Warren Commission's findings found a popular venue among Europeans (especially college aged people), as critics of the Warren Commission discussed their findings in front of packed audiences and left a vivid impression when they were finished. However, in time, the skepticism about the events in Dallas would percolate back in the United States.

The first crack in the armor of the Warren Commission came in an article published in 1972 by a French newspaper called

"L'Aurore" that was picked up by the Associated Press in the United States. The article in question was written by two journalists, Camille Gilles and Philippe Bernet. The Associated Press wrote that, "The newspaper L'Aurore published yesterday an account of a former French resident of Algeria who said that in 1961 he had been hired to kill President Kennedy, but had withdrawn from the assignment at the last moment. The newspaper said Jose Luis Romero, who now lives at an undisclosed place in South America, had signed a contract with a French book publisher for the story of his life. The article, written by Philippe Bernet and Camille Gilles, quoted Romero as saying that attempt on Kennedy's life was to have been made during the American president's visit to France to visit with President Charles de Gaulle. Romero said that he had been offered $460,000 through a man only identified as "Mike," who "visibly worked for certain secret service of the United States." He said after he got to Paris he got worried. He checked with the Secret Army Organization in Algiers and got orders to pull out of the deal."[1]

The Romero story was picked up on November 19, 1972 by the *National Insider,* which retold the story as originally published in "L'Aurore." Romero, according to the *National Insider,* was anti-De Gaulle and anticommunist. He was an OAS agent who, in the late 1950s, had served in the French military in Algeria and had loose ties with certain U.S. intelligence agencies. He said that when he joined the OAS, he retained his connections with the Americans and that the U.S. agencies gave the OAS intelligence, false passports as well as money and arms. The article went on to say that when Romero realized the implications of the plot, he knew that he was being set up to take the fall if JFK was killed in France. He said that he was chosen because of his prior medical condition—he had brain surgery after a land mine explosion. If he was captured after the attack on Kennedy, he would have been blamed for the shooting because of his mental instability.

Romero said he was first approached in May 1961 in Algeria by an American who was a high-ranking member of the American Embassy and a friend of his by the name of "Mike." They were supposed to have dinner together but that "Mike" did not show up.

---

1 JFK Assassination. www.theeldergeek.com/forum

Romero said that, "Two men entered and came up to my table. From their clothes I recognized them as Americans. They said they had come on behalf of my friend Mike. I realized something bigger must be up. We must fake an attempt on General de Gaulle's life during Kennedy's visit to France. They offered me $400,000 for the deal, half of it immediately and the other half after Kennedy was dead. He then outlined the details of the plot and its preparations involving conversion to Swiss citizenship, and an auto and a money belt given to him by Mike who had materialized to meet him in Spain."

Romero said that at that fateful meeting, the men told him that, "my interlocutors knew exactly whom they were talking to. They seemed to know my record as a sharpshooter... They offered me $400,000-half right away, the rest once the thing was over."

What happened next was right out of a spy novel. He went to Paris and went by taxi to the La Pairs café where he was met by a contact. The contact gave him his marching orders. The contact then went into the operational plans for the assassination attempt. He was offered two avenues of which he could carry out the assassination. He would use a Remington .280 with an infrared scope. He would pick up the rifle at the Northern Railroad Station and be given a locker key that contained the rifle in a valise.

However, before Romero took any further action, he began to have second thoughts about what he was about to do. It was obvious to him that if he did succeed in the assassination of the American president, the OAS (Secret Army Organization), would be blamed for the event. He had enough sense not to fall into their trap and he immediately contacted his OAS superior officer based in Algiers. The officer told him to drop the plan and have nothing more to do with the strange Americans.

Romero then made his way out of France, first going to Italy, Switzerland, and the Congo before winding up in South America with his half of the money. He later said of his strange encounter to possibly kill the American president, "I know my story has exceptional implications. It reveals that certain people were intent already in 1961 to murder Kennedy, using a revolutionary—me—as their patsy. Romero believes the same person or persons working closely with them who approached him about the assassination were possibly responsible for Kennedy's death later."

While this story has never been factually backed up, the article from "L'Aurore" was reprinted in the British newspaper the *Guardian* on December 1, 1972, written by reporter Martin Walker. The story went on to say that a book called "$400,000 Pour Abbatre Kennedy a' Paris" was published by a French publishing company called Julliard. It retells the Romero story with one huge addition. The man named "Mike" whom Romero who supposedly worked for the CIA, was indeed, E. Howard Hunt. However, there is no proof that the book was indeed published in France, as implied by the article.

In 1971 a book was published by thriller author Frederick Forsyth in the United States with the title *The Day of the Jackal.* It is a fictionalized account of an attempt on the life of French president Charles de Gaulle by a professional assassin who was given the contract by members of the OAS. Does this sound familiar?

The Day of the Jackal was an international hit, with a movie version of the book coming out some years later. The gist if the book was a historical event, based on the failed attempt on the life of de Gaulle that was carried out by Col. Jean-Marie Bastien-Thiry in the Paris suburb of Petit-Chamart. After the arrest of Bastien-Thiry, the French security service, the SDECE or Deuxieme Bureau mounted a no-holes barred operation to dismantle the plot against de Gaulle.

By 1954, the French colony of Algeria started a violent armed struggle against the French government seeking its independence. What followed was a decade long bloody fight between the French security forces and the FLN (Front de Liberation Nationale and their allies, the OAS (Organisation Armee Secrete) which began major attacks against French military forces in Algeria in 1958.

In the aftermath of the armed insurrection in Algeria, de Gaulle cracked down violently on both the dissident army officers whom he suspected were in league with the OAS, including many members of their own intelligence services. Many of these men believed that de Gaulle was a megalomaniac and wanted to see him removed from power any way possible, including assassination.

One of the most spectacular attacks on de Gaulle took place on August 22, 1962 while he was in a convoy with his wife heading for the town of Colombey. Sharpshooters from the OAS took up positions on the Avenue-Petit-Clamart at nightfall, waiting for the armed convoy to approach. Due to the pitch blackness of the night, they were delayed just a fraction and were not as well prepared as they should have been when the president's limousine approached. They fired at de Gaulle's car, hitting the front tire and the rear window, shooting it out. The president's car skidded out of control and almost collided with another car that was coming in the same direction. However, the chauffeur by the name of Marroux was able to steer the car away from the firefight and de Gaulle was unhurt, suffering only minor wounds.

On February 27, 1963, Antoine Argoud, a highly placed member, and a former colonel in the French army, was arrested in Paris after a tip was phoned in on his whereabouts. According the press reports of Argoud's arrest, the tipster said, "Argoud has betrayed us. He has failed in all the tasks which he should have organized-especially the attempt on the life of President De Gaulle at the Petit Clamart last August. You can pick him up now. He is very near you."

After another failed attempt on the life of De Gaulle by General Raoul Salan, took place in August 1961, Argoud was captured by French police and deported to the Canary Islands. He escaped in March disguised as a Spanish military officer. While he was on the lam, Argoud was sentenced to death in absentia.

The last attempt to kill De Gaulle took place on July 1, 1966, as he was being taken by car to Orly Airport in Paris en-route to the Soviet Union. Members of the militant organization called the National Resistance Council planted a car bomb that contained almost a ton of dynamite in the Boulevard Montparnasse very near where the president's caravan was to have passed. Fortunately, the explosives never went off due to the fact that some of these same students were arrested the previous night after a botched robbery to steal money for their escape out of France.

It seems that the OAS was not alone in seeking the death of President De Gaulle and they even tried to enlist the CIA to go along with their plans. And who was one of the men whom the CIA said approached in their desire to kill de Gaulle-none other than Jean Souetre.

A memo dated July 10, 1963 to the Deputy Director for

Coordination, Bureau of Intelligence and Research at the U.S. State Department was sent by the Deputy Director of Plans entitled "OAS Attempt to enlist the Government of the United States for its anti-de Gaulle activities." The memo reads in part:

1)"In May 1963, an attempt was made in Lisbon, Portugal by two members of the OAS to enlist the support of the United States Government (specifically the Central Intelligence Agency), although the name was never actually pronounced) in their operations against de Gaulle. The attempt was made by Captain Jean Rene Souetre and Captain Guerin. Captain Souetre identified himself in the OAS organization as coordinator of external affairs serving under Major Peirre Sergent. Souetre said that he foresaw the U.S. role as that of convincing other governments to cease supporting OAS activities in their respective countries, and later perhaps preventing monetary or material support. Souetre said he intends to provide some information about the activities of his organization that would be of interest to the U.S. In answer to a question on his status in Portugal, Souetre explained that he traveled on various passports, one of them being a U.S. passport. He claimed to be documented as a naturalized citizen from Martinique. He stated that he had U.S. contacts who could arrange documentation.

2) The CIA representative told Souetre that de Gaulle was the Chief of State of an old and respected ally of the U.S. and that the U.S. had absolutely no intention of working with any person or group against the duly-constituted government of France.

3) Available information from both press and official French sources indicates that Souetre is the name of a former French army captain who escaped from a detention camp in 1941. Subsequent to his escape he was alleged to have been involved in an assassination attempt against de Gaulle. Souetre was born on October 15, 1930, in the Girenade Department of France. Sargent is also a former French army captain who has been reported to be the successor to ex-Colonel Antoine Argoud, under whom he worked."[2]

While the CIA rightfully turned Souetre down, it would not be the last time that their paths would cross.

As mentioned in the introduction, journalist Steve Rivele

---

[2] RIF No. 102-620 JFK Records-National Archives.

scoured Europe and South America in the 1980s investigating the possible French Connection to the Kennedy assassination. In his work, he collected and wrote numerous articles and letters about his travels. A majority of his work was housed at the Assassinations Archives and Research Center that is located in Washington, D.C., and run by attorney Jim Lesar. In my capacity as editor of Back Channels Magazine, I traveled to Washington and was able to look at, and photocopy a large selection of the files in the center on Steve Rivele's investigation. His archives are a treasure trove of information on the people who had anything to do with the possible French Connection to the assassination, as well as descriptions of some of the major players in the story. (For the reader's information, I will note in the footnotes the designation "Rivele files," for the sources that I found as it pertains to this work.)

One of the research papers in the collection is an interview with a man named Jean-Claude Perez, a member of the OAS, which as conducted on November 20, 1982. In the interview, the name of Jean Souetre comes up.

Jean-Claude Perez said that there were various factions inside the OAS, of which he was one. Some were more willing to negotiate with the French, while others were not. When asked his opinion of de Gaulle, he said, "I held, and do so now, that De Gaulle was the gravest enemy of the Occident. I worked to see him assassinated." He said that he was arrested in Spain in 1962 and after his release he fled to South America.

He said that the OAS did not have any centers of operation in Rio de Janeiro, or Montreal, but that they centered a lot of their attention in Mexico City. Talking about OAS activity in Mexico City he said, "We knew that de Gaulle was going to visit Mexico City in March of 1964. We sent three men there to establish contacts, recruit assistance, and assassinate him; but they returned and reported we did not have any money. This was, after all, after the end of the war and the OAS was fragmented."[3]

Perez said that the never heard of Michel Victor Mertz, an alias that Souetre often times used. However, he did reveal that he had heard of Souetre. "Yeh, I know him. He was a member of a

3 Interview with Jean-Claude Perez, November 20, 1982. Rivele Files.

splinter. I think he worked for Pichon. You must remember that the OAS has lots of satellite groups not necessarily acting under OAS auspices and the intelligence gathering area, ORO."

Perez then expanded his comments on de Gaulle. "He was a communist. We could see it. No one else. De Gaulle pulled off the trick of the century; he moved the right to the left. No one but a nominal rightist could have got away with freeing our Algerian colony. If Mendes' France had tried it, would have been a revolution. De Gaulle was a wolf in sheep's clothing. He masqueraded as rightist, but was in fact the greatest enemy and for just that reason, of the west. Kennedy, on the other hand, although he occasionally made liberal noises, was a great thinker, understood a larger picture, was the West's greatest hope."

When asked why Kennedy was shot, he replied, "It was most likely by mistake. He appeared, as I have said, superficially liberal. We knew better, despite his statements for Algerian independence."

When told that JFK had made pro-Algerian independence speeches in congress, Perez said, "Yes, but it was his larger design that made him the hero of the Occident. De Gaulle embraced on every occasion the advantage of the East. His deception was the opposite of Kennedy's. There is the irony."

He then was asked if he knew Guy Banister, he said yes.

For those people who do not know who Guy Banister was, and how he fits into the Kennedy scenario, here is the short version.

At one time, Guy Banister was the head of the FBI's Bureau in Chicago. He was rabidly anticommunist, and anti-Kennedy in his political leanings. He was well connected with both the U.S. intelligence services and the criminal element at the same time. He was an associate of both Carlos Marcello, and big-time Mafia leader whose territory encompassed New Orleans, where, some believe, the plot to kill the president was hatched. Also, New Orleans was the home of Lee Oswald, the alleged assassin of the president.

In the summer of 1963, Banister ran a private detective agency out of his office at 544 Camp Street in New Orleans. From that office, guns and ammunition were funneled to the anti-Castro operatives who were training in the swamps near New Orleans in the hope of taking their fight to Cuba to oust Castro. One of the men closely associated with Banister was David Ferrie, a CIA asset, former airline pilot, a homosexual, and a close associate of mob boss, Carlos Marcello. Ferrie often times did paralegal work for Marcello and the two of them were very close. Ferrie ran a flight school for young cadets in New Orleans (Civil Air Patrol) and one of his young recruits was Lee Harvey Oswald.

After the president's assassination, New Orleans DA, Jim Garrison, began a quiet investigation of the Kennedy assassination. David Ferrie's name came up and he was one of the most important witnesses Garrison had. Unfortunately, before Ferrie could testify as to his knowledge of the assassination, he was found dead in his apartment, apparently a suicide.

Numerous witnesses in the summer of 1963 reported that Lee Oswald was working for Guy Banister out of his 544 Camp Street address in the summer of 1963. One time, Oswald handed out pro-Castro leaflets in the city with (FPCC-Fair Play for Cuba Committee) with the 544 Camp Street address printed on it. Banister, like other JFK assassination witnesses, died under mysterious circumstances (a heat attack), nine months after the president was killed.

Perez said about Banister, "Seems to me I once met a Banister, tall, older, said to be a former F.B.I. man. Met him in Madrid."

He said that he did not think Banister had any relations with the OAS. "Just met him. You must not assume from meeting that contact and support were the same thing."

Guy Banister's name also came up in connection with a shady, international conglomerate called Permindex, which was detailed during the Garrison investigation of the New Orleans connection to the Kennedy assassination. Garrison alleged that a former FBI agent who was employed by Banister, departed from New Orleans and delivered the sum of $100,000 of FBI money to unnamed French officers who were plotting to kill President De Gaulle.

The business entity behind Permindex was a company called CMC or "Centro Mondiale Commmerciale." CMC was a world trade organization located in Rome that was based on the Trade Mart in New Orleans.

By its own admission, CMC was a CIA front organization that funneled money to regular political parties, but also various right-wing political movements, especially in Europe. One of the groups which got CMC largess was the OAS. The Secret Army Organization whose main goal was the assassination of de Gaulle. Among the supporters on the OAS in New Orleans was Guy Banister.

Permindex was well known to the highest circles in France and one French newspaper, *Les Echos,* quoted de Gaulle as having said that Permindex was responsible for the attempt on his life.

The president of Permindex as the time was Ferenc Nagy. In 1945, he had been Prime Minister of Hungry. Nagy had been a CIA asset since the beginning of the cold war and had a longtime relationship with one of the founders of the CIA, Frank Wisner. Nagy was a financial supporter to Jacques Soustelle, a French professor, and former Algerian governor general and OAS supporter. In order to avoid being a target by French authorities in anti-de Gaulle activities, he went into exile in 1961. Writing in her book on Jim Garrison called "*A Farewell to Justice,*" author Joan Mellen says that Delphine Roberts who was Guy Banister's secretary, said that she had seen a photograph of Nagy and said he was once in Banister's office. To make matters worse for CMC, in 1962, the company was expelled from Italy on the grounds of financial irregularities.

The name of Clay Shaw also came up in a series of articles in a European magazine called *Paese Sera* that ran an exposé on CRC in March 1967. Coincidently for "Pase Sera," this was the same time that New Orleans businessman Clay Shaw, the head of the New Orleans Trade Mart, was arrested by Jim Garrison for his alleged participation in the Kennedy assassination. Like Banister, Clay Shaw was a CIA asset, having worked of the Company in a secret capacity for many years. Shaw was on the board of Permindex and his name has freely been associated with the ongoing machinations of the CRC since it began operations.

Shaw was very well known around New Orleans in the early 1960s, and was acquainted with both Guy Banister and David Ferrie. Shaw was regal looking in appearance, with a main of white hair. He was a respected businessman in the city due to his position as head of the Trade Mart. But Shaw also has a secret side to his life. He was a homosexual, frequenting many of the local bars that were common in the city. Years later, Shaw's CIA connections would come to light due to the release of papers from the JFK files and other researchers who doggedly followed his trail. Shaw had been on the CIA payroll since 1949, first staring out as a contract agent. His work for the agency took him to such varied places as East Germany, Peru, Argentina and Nicaragua. He filed thirty reports for the CIA from 1949-1956.

Shaw also went by the alias "Clay Bertrand," even giving that name to his arresting officer who took him in when he arrested for his alleged participation in the Kennedy assassination.

Shaw was the only person put on trial for his role in the Kennedy assassination. He was charged with the crime by New Orleans DA Jim Garrison but a jury found him not guilty of the charges. (While the jury found Shaw not guilty, they did say that they believed that there was a conspiracy to kill JFK but they couldn't prove Shaw's role in it).

If Shaw's relationship with Permindex isn't strange enough, there is one more event that directly ties in Shaw with Lee Oswald. In the summer of 1963, the Black organization, CORE-Congress of Racial Equality-was having a voter registration event in the small, Louisiana town of Clinton. Things were going normally until a large limousine suddenly pulled up in front of the place where the Negroes were lining up to register to vote. A tall, while haired man emerged from the car and spoke to the local sheriff, identifying himself as representing the New Orleans Trade Mart. That man was Clay Shaw. Along with Shaw was a man who remained inside the car, David Ferrie. There was a third man in the strange cavalcade, Lee Oswald.

Numerous witnesses in Clinton that day said they saw and talked with Oswald. Oswald was in Clinton trying to get a job at the local mental hospital. One of them was the local barber, Edward McGehee who gave Oswald a haircut. Oswald told him that he had recently been discharged from the Marines and was looking for work in the town. McGehee told Oswald to see the local state representative, Reeves Morgan who might be able to help. Morgan told Oswald that if he really wanted to get a job in town, he would have to register to vote. Oswald did not register to vote that day and left town, along with the men in the limousine.

The entire Clinton episode is ripe with mystery. Were Clay Shaw, David Ferrie and Lee Oswald really in Clinton that day, and if so, for what reason? If they were in Clinton, that proves that all three men, Shaw, Ferrie and Oswald knew each other prior to the assassination.

Another link to Permindex and its association with the OAS, was a small, but important department of the FBI called Division 5. It has been speculated that the money given to the OAS was funneled by Division 5 to the OAS for its planned attack on de Gaulle.

Division 5 was the counter-espionage branch of the Bureau that was headed by William Sullivan, a long time confidant of FBI Director J. Edgar Hoover. In 1961, Sullivan was appointed assistant director of the FBI's Intelligence Division and moved up the pecking order and eventually wound up being the third highest-ranking member of the FBI's triumvirate (behind Hoover and his assistant, Clyde Tolson). Like Hoover, Sullivan had a visceral dislike for the Rev. Martin Luther King and his civil rights movement, believing, (incorrectly), that the group was under communist influence. In January 1964, Sullivan wrote a scathing memo to Dr. King that was approved by Director Hoover. In part, the letter says, "It should be clear to all of us that King must, at some propitious point in the future, be revealed to the people of this country and to his Negro followers as being what he actually is-a fraud, demagogue, and scoundrel. When the true facts concerning his activities are presented, such should be enough, if handled properly, to take him off his pedestal and to reduce him completely in influence." This letter was supposed to have been written by someone in the Civil Rights movement and sent to King to discredit him.

As time went on, a rift began to grow between Sullivan and Hoover. Sullivan disagreed with Hoover about the threat posed by the American Communist Party and said that the FBI was devoting too much money and time investigating that organization. Sullivan even had the gall to suggest that Hoover retire as head of the FBI, something that the long-time director would never agree to by himself.

Things got so heated between Hoover and Sullivan that the director fired him in 1971.

But, that was not to be the end of the William Sullivan controversy. No November 9, 1977, William Sullivan was on a hunting trip with a few friends in the woods of New Hampshire.

Enroute to meet his friends, he was accidentally shot to death by the 18year old son of a state policeman. The young man later told police that while his gun had a telescopic sight, he mistakenly thought Sullivan was a deer and shot him. After an investigation, the young man in question was given a $500 fine and a ten-year suspension of his hunting license.

However, there were many questions asked about the circumstances surrounding the death of William Sullivan, after the fact. Sullivan was in the process of writing a damaging book on his years in the FBI (it was later published by his co-author under the title, *The Bureau).*

At the time of his death, the House of Representatives was in the process of conducting its own investigation of both the Kennedy and King assassinations. William Sullivan was supposed to be called as a witness shortly before his death. No one knows just what Sullivan would have told the eager congressman and senators about his years with Hoover at the FBI and what secrets he might have unveiled.

In 1975, however, when questioned by congressional panel investigating the Kennedy case about Lee Oswald, and the CIA, Sullivan said, "I think there may be something on that, but you asked me if I had seen anything. I don't recall having seen anything like that, but I think there is something on that point. It rings a bell in my head."[4]

While there is no concrete proof that Permindex or Division 5 had anything to do with the attempt on the life of de Gaulle, it is just another piece of a very intricate puzzle of intelligence agencies, and rouge operatives that make this story as intricate as it is.

If Division 5 was not a player in the attempts on the life of de Gaulle, history would tell another story when it came to the secret relationships between nations and individual members of intelligence organizations in their attempts to influence the great events that were taking place around them.

---

[4] Summers, Anthony, *Conspiracy*. McGraw Hill Book Company, New York, 1980, Pg. 507.

Chapter 2:

The Mafia and Uncle Sam

The use of shady individuals, as well as members of organized crime in the interests of U.S. foreign policy, did not begin in the 21st century. It has its origins in the beginning of the history of the United States and involved people right out suspense novels.

One of the men whom the United States government used in its battle against the British in the War of 1812 was a notorious pirate and brigand named Jean Laffite.

Lafitte's birth place is not known but he wound up in New Orleans in 1803.He told different tales about himself to different people, all of them verging in the ridiculous. Some people said he was the son of rich parents, others say he fled the slave revolts on the island of Haiti. What is clear is that he made his home amidst the wild dunes and marshes of the Gulf Coast, namely New Orleans.

In 1803, New Orleans became part of the United States due to the purchase of the vast territory by President Thomas Jefferson in what became known as the Louisiana Purchase. A rich diversity of people poured into New Orleans, including, French, Americans, soldiers-of-fortune, and traders of all stripes who wanted to get a piece of the rich action that lay in the land. The new governor of the territory, William Claiborne, had an immediate run in with Lafitte and he put a $1,500 dollar reward on his head, printing wanted posters to that effect. One day, the governor was shocked to find out that new wanted posters had been plastered around the city offering a $1,550 reward for anyone who brought Claiborne to Lafitte's hideout in the Barataria section of the country.

Barataria was a wild landscape about 100 miles south of New Orleans, and it was there that Lafitte made his home. He had over one thousand followers, mostly privateers and pirates who found any kind of government, too much to handle. However, Lafitte was a fair minded man who made rules that accommodated the people in the region and more surprisingly, was a devoted follower of the American Constitution which gave freedom to all men and women. He forbad his men from attacking American ships and any one caught doing so, faced the death penalty. Lafitte and his men operated as privateers, using Letters of Marque from Cartagena, a republic of Columbia that was fighting for its independence from Spain. This letter allowed anyone who had it to legally attack enemies of the mother country without being branded a pirate. Most of their attacks came against ships from both Spain and England,

When the War of 1812 broke out, two British naval officers came to Lafitte's camp and asked for his help. They wanted to pay him to aid the British war effort in the inlets and streams around Barataria and even offered to pay him in land and gold, and made available to him a commission in the Royal Navy. Due to his strong American loyalties, Lafitte turned down their offer.

In order to counter British covert activities in New Orleans during the War of 1812, Lafitte offered the services of he and his men to General Andrew Jackson whose job it was to protect New Orleans from attack by the British. Lafitte presented Jackson with 7,500 flints with powder and over one thousand of his men as a bulwark against the British force that was besieging the city. Granting the pirates pardons for any pervious crimes they may have committed, Lafitte's band spied on British fortifications in New Orleans and fought with the Americans when the British invaded the city. Unbeknownst to Jackson, a peace treaty between the United States and England had been signed at the time the battle of New Orleans took place.

When the battle was over, the British suffered huge losses, but by some miracle, Jackson's casualties were minimal. After the war ended, President James Madison pardoned Lafitte and his band for their heroic deeds in helping defeat the British.

A few years later, Lafitte and his men left New Orleans and made a new home at Galveston Island.

The use of mercenaries like Jean Lafitte was not the last time that the United States sought the help of members of the criminal element in the furtherance of its foreign policy. In World War 2, the Roosevelt administration hired members of the Mafia to help them in their efforts to defeat Nazi sabotage in New York harbor, and to aid the army when it invaded North Africa. Almost twenty years later, the CIA would hire the same members of the Mafia to help them in their covert efforts to kill Fidel Castro of Cuba.

* * *

As the year 1942 began, the United States was in the war for only a few months, but already the tide of battle was shifting away at a terrible rate. Along the Atlantic coast of France, German U-boats headed away from their docks and entered the teaming sea lanes toward the open Atlantic where convoys of allied ships, many originating from the United States, were ferrying much needed war supplies to beleaguered England. From the period of January to October 1942, 541 allied ships were sunk by the marauding U-boats that swarmed in wolf packs against the unsuspecting merchant ships. All along the east coast of the United States, from North Carolina to New Jersey, ships were sunk at a steady, dangerous rate with nothing the United States could do to stop them. In May 1942, alone, 102 ships were sunk. June was not much better with 11 going down.

If the U-boat threat went unchecked, there was no telling just how much destruction could be done by these invisible killers of the sea and the threat of a direct attack against the major cities of the east coast, New York, Baltimore, Boston and Washington was not out of the question. Something had to be done, and fast.

In order to ameliorate the ever-growing bad situation on the New York docks, an ingenious plan was hatched by the Office of Naval Intelligence to use certain members of the Mafia who just about ran the dock workers union in New York, to see if they could use their influence to try and stop the threat of Nazi penetration of the docks, and thus, stop any sabotage that the Nazi's were planning. By the time that "Operation Underworld," the code name that was given by the ONI in their secret alliance with the Mafia was over, a hidden pact between the highest members of the U.S. Navy, the Roosevelt administration, and the power brokers in New York State, would cement an alliance that would have roots far beyond the immediate threat.

The man whom the U.S. Navy turned to in order to quell the ever-growing threat to New York docks was Joseph "Socks"

Lanza. Lanza ran the highly lucrative Fulton Fish Market in lower Manhattan, the place where all the fish that was caught in the New York area was taken for sale by the hundreds of retailers who manned the huge warehouse. Lanza was one of the most powerful men in the local Teamsters Union, and even other, tough New York mobsters learned to stay away from him when he got mad. Lanza ran the Fulton Fish market like his own personal fiefdom, taking in a percentage of each sale. He received $10 from every boat that came in to the harbor, $50 from every truck that went out, and $2,000 from every trucking company that entered the market.

Lanza was well connected with the crime family of Charles "Lucky" Luciano, a major figure in Operation Underworld. As a young man, Lanza worked at the Fish Market, earning $12 a week. Now, years later, he was a multi-millionaire, doing the same, dirty work that he'done as a youngster, However, he was now in charge of the entire operation, and god forbid anyone who crossed hm.

Lanza's luck ran out in the decade of the 1930s, when he was sent to federal prison for a two-year sentence for the violation of the Sherman Anti-Trust Act. However, while in jail, his minions still extorted money from the Teamsters Union, making his reputation as a "made man," even that much more durable.

But in the grand scheme of things, "Socks" Lanza was not the final decision maker. The man whom U.S. officials asked Lanza to see was then serving time in a New York State prison for various and sundry criminal charges, Charles "Lucky" Luciano.

The U.S. Naval officer who was to be chosen as the intermediary between the Navy and the Mafia was Lt. Commander Charles Haffenden who was then in charge of the Third Naval District's investigation section, located in lower Manhattan.

Haffenden said of his task to find allies in the mob to undertake this rather unorthodox mission by commenting that: "I'll talk to anybody, a bank manager, a gangster, the devil himself, if I can get the information I need. This is a war. American lives are at stake. It's not a college game where we have to look up the rulebook every minute, and we're not running a headquarters office where regulations must be followed to the letter. I have a job to do."

If Commander Haffenden was the operations officer involved in running Operation Underworld, the brainchild was Captain Roscoe MacFall, the Chief Intelligence Officer of the Third Naval

District which included New York and New Jersey. It was Captain MacFall's idea to contact members of the mob in order to see if their plan could work. Captain MacFall got the go ahead from his superior officer, Admiral Carl Espe, Director of Naval Intelligence.

The man whom Captain MacFall turned to in the pecking order was Lt. Anthony Marsloe, who worked for the Third Naval District. Before joining the navy, Lt. Marsloe worked for the New York District Attorney's Office, under the supervision of Thomas Dewey (Dewey would play an intricate role in the upcoming events).

In a meeting on March 7, 1942, between Captain MacFall and Frank Hogan, the Manhattan DA, the rudimentary plan to use the mob was put in place. Also in the meeting was Murray Gurfein, who had been in charge of the DA's Office that ran the Rackets Bureau. DA Hogan had been working tiresely investigating the role of organized crime on the New York waterfront and he had an abiding interest in putting an end to the practice. Their discussion turned towards the threat that German submarines would be re-fueled by fishing boasts off New York, posing a threat to the city. Hogan said that the Mafia sometimes had advance warnings on all matters of illegal activity on the waterfront; maybe they could help in the war effort?

When the meeting broke up, all agreed to work with each other in trying to see if they could entice the mob to help. Gurfein was given the job of acting as the representative of the DA's office with Commander Haffenden. In subsequent meetings, it was Gurfein who recommended they meet with Socks Lanza.

A few days later, both Lanza and Gurfein met to work out details of their new arrangement. In the weeks that followed, Lanza gave Gurfein the names and telephone numbers of his top men on the waterfront whom he enticed to go along with their plan. As time went on, Lanza's fishing boat captains kept a watchful eye for any German submarines or other unusual naval traffic that they encountered on their regular fishing trips. They even communicated with the Navy via ship-to-shore radios provided by Commander Haffenden.

Lanza was not only working for the Navy in his new position. He also kept his two most important mob contacts, Meyer Lansky and Frank Costello up to date on what he was doing.

While Lanza was having a great deal of support from most of his assets, many of the Italian's whom he'd been trying to recruit were not cooperating. He then came up with an idea that changed the entire picture. He suggested to his Navy buddies that he be able to contact Charles Luciano, then serving time in a New York State prison for help in the project. This was a risky decision, one that might not go down very well with the major players in the game, especially the Navy brass who were supervising the entire show. Reluctantly, the ok was given to make discreet contacts with Luciano.

Charles "Lucky" Luciano was the most prominent Italian mobster in the United States at the time that he was recruited by the Navy in Operation Underworld. He was the Godfather of the modern American Mafia, even bigger in stature than the notorious hoodlum, Al Capone. He, along with Meyer Lansky, who was the moneyman behind the modern mob, were arguably the two most important Mafia figures of the time.

Hew was born Salvatore Luciana in Palermo, Italy and came to the United States in 1906. In his early years, he gravitated to a life of low-level street crime and met another youngster who would become his life long friend in crime; Meyer Lansky. By 1920, Luciano was a prominent member of the Five Points Gang and was a suspect in a number of murders. By the time the decade was over, he was a major figure in the bootlegging rackets and made friends with some of the most notorious criminals of the day; Vito Genovese, Frank Costello, among others.

In the late 1920s, Luciano had joined the gang that was run by Giuseppe "Joe the Boss" Masseria, who was the head of the biggest crime family in New York. Luciano did not take kindly to the way Masseria was running the mob, believing that in order for the mob to be successful, they had to open the door to other ethnic gangs, the Jews, etc. When open warfare broke out between the factions belonging to Masseria and Salvatore Maranzano, which left dozens of bodies strewn across the streets of the city, Luciano stayed on the sidelines, waiting for the carnage to end.

Masseria's bloody end came in 1931, when men associated with Luciano rubbed him out in a Coney Island restaurant. Maranzano was now the undisputed head of the Mafia and he made Luciano one of his top lieutenants. Unknown, to Luciano,

Maranzano had other ideas. He made secret plans to have Luciano killed, but Charles "Lucky" found out before hand and had Maranzano rubbed out in his own office.

With the death of Maranzano, the old Sicilian Mafia was for all intents and purposes dead. Luciano and his new cronies, namely Meyer Lansky, Dutch Shultz, Frank Costello, Joe Adonis, created a new Mafia, with its tentacles firmly situated in both New York and New Jersey, a 20th century Mafia, so to speak, with new rules and new bosses.

The duo of Lansky and Luciano broadened the scope of the new Mafia into areas such as narcotics, loan harking, gambling, labor racketeering, and prostitution.

In 1936, the tide turned dramatically for Luciano. He ran square into the powerful grip of Thomas Dewey, an ambitious New York prosecutor (Dewey would later become Governor of New York, and ran for President against Harry Truman in 1948—he lost). Luciano became Dewey's main target and he was able to have a jury convict him on "compulsory prostitution" charges. He was given one of the harshest sentences ever seen in New York criminal history, 30 to 50 years behind bars.

At the time that Sox Lanza and the Navy Department decided it was worth its while to contact Luciano, he was serving time in one of the most notorious prisons, Dannemora, in upstate New York.

In April 1942, Murray Gurfein got in touch with a man named Moses Polakoff, who served as Luciano's attorney in his trial for prostitution. Gurfein and Polakoff met and Gurfein pitched the story that the Italian community was interfering in their efforts to stop Nazi infiltration of the docks, etc. Could he use his good graces to seek Luciano's help? Polakoff called Luciano's good friend, Meyer Lansky, and told him of the Navy's offer. Much to his surprise, Lansky offered whatever help he could give.

In a most unusual meeting, Gurfein, Lansky and Polakoff met in New York and discussed the Navy's predicament. Luciano's name came up and Lansky proposed that he and Polakoff met with Luciano in Dannemora. Lansky said that he'd take no money; he, after all, was a patriot.

At the Astor Hotel in New York, Lansky and Polakoff met with Commander Haffenden. Haffenden explained to Lansky the predicament that the Navy found itself in. The New York docks were being infiltrated by German spies and the entire waterfront was in danger. He then told Lansky a secret; a convoy of U.S. troops would soon be heading overseas and the number one priority was the safety of the convoy. He also told Lansky about the U-boat refueling threat and asked if there was anything Lansky could do. Lansky agreed and put the word out to Lanza and Frank Costello to put the squeeze on any pending danger on the docks.

While all these covert dealings were going on vis-a-vi the New York docks, another secret arrangement was being implemented to get Lucky Luciano transferred out of his hellhole at Dannemora. With the intervention of Commander Haffenden and the Navy, New York prison authorities reluctantly agreed to transfer Luciano to another prison, Great Meadow. This was still a maximum-security jail, but the conditions were better for Luciano than what he'd been used to in Dannemora.

During the time period between May 15 and June 4, 1942, Luciano was visited by Lansky and Polakoff. Luciano was surprised to see his friends and knew immediately that something was up. As soon as they sat down, the two men briefed Luciano as to the purpose of their visit. After listening intently to what they had to say, Luciano said that he'd cooperate—however, there was one caveat.

As soon as he heard their proposal, Luciano knew he might have the government over a barrel. There was always a quit pro quo in life and Luciano was now ready to play his trump card. He realized that by helping with the war effort, he'd only be helping his own cause, which was now, a dire one. If he didn't help, he would not be released from jail until 1965, an incredibly long time.

For Luciano, the fact that he was not a citizen of the United States hung over his head like a lead balloon, one that might fall at any minute. There was also a deportation order waiting for him when he was eventually freed. He had no certainty where he'd be sent after leaving the United States, and he didn't want to take the chance that he'd be sent to a country that would not be favorable to his presence. Luciano made his secret deal with the Navy and he now began the process of delivering on his part of the bargain. Lucky passed the word to all his Mafia friends along the east coast that from then on, they were to cooperate with the Navy, no questions asked.

According to the Herlands Report, which told the complete story of the Luciano-Navy agreement, Luciano gave the following orders to the dockworkers, "There'll be no German submarines in the Port of New York. Every man down there who works in the harbor-all the sailors, all the fishermen, every longshoreman, every individual who has anything to do with the coming and going of ships to the United States-is now helping the fight against the Nazis."[5]

According to the Herlands Report, there were at least twenty meetings between Luciano, Polakoff and Lansky during the time period of May 15, 1942 and August 21, 1945. Luciano even conducted meetings in the warden's office at Great Meadow with his pals on the docks.

Meyer Lansky proved to be the main intermediary between Commander Haffenden and Luciano during the duration of Operation Underworld. What a strange arrangement that was. Here you had the number one mob figure in the country breaking bread on an on-going basis with a top member of Naval Intelligence. Lansky also persuaded his friends who owned restaurants in the predominately German speaking Yorkville section of New York, to hire German speaking U.S. Navy men to serve as waiters. Their job was to listen in to any unusual conversations that they might pick up when serving a meal.

The covert dealings between the U.S. Navy and the mob, lead by "Lucky" Luciano," proved to be a success. During the time that Operation Underworld was in effect, there were no attacks by German submarines or any sabotage along the New York docks. Unmistakably, this was a marriage of continence, one that ultimately aided both parties. While it was a fact that the Germans were able to successfully infiltrate two teams of men along the east coast of the United States-one in Florida and the other in Maine—they were all captured—there was no sabotage along the New York docks.

In 1946, Thomas Dewey, now the Governor of New York, paroled Charles Luciano for his secret wartime service for the United States. He was deported to Italy and then fled to Cuba where he establishment himself as one of the major drug kingpins

5 *Mafia Allies,* Tim Newark, Page 105.

of the time.

However, the Mafia's involvement in the war effort was not over, with the shutdown of Operation Underworld. There was still another area where they'd aid Uncle Sam—in Sicily.

By 1943, the Soviet Union was pleading with its allies, the United States and England, to open up a second front against the Germans. That decision was made in January 1943,when FDR and Churchill met at the summit at Casablanca, Morocco to plan future strategy. Joseph Stalin was not able to attend the conference, as his army was looking to defeat the Germans at the critical battle of Stalingrad. Prior to the Casablanca Conference, the tide had begun to slowly turn for the allies. The British and defeated the desert fox, German General Rommel's Africa Corps at the battle of El Alemein, a few months prior.

It was at Casablanca that both leaders decided to strike at Italy, the first road to Berlin and final victory for the allies. For his part, Winston Churchill was adamant that the allies' next goal was the invasion of Sicily and he persuaded the Combined Chiefs of Staff to go along with his plan.

Roosevelt realized that the American's had the upper hand in dealing with any possible invasion of Sicily, due to the large amount of Italian's living in the States, especially those of Sicilian decent, and he spoke to the president about that important fact. In that light, FDR wrote a letter to Churchill saying, "In view of the friendly feelings towards America entertained by a great number of citizens of Italy, and in consideration of the large number of citizens of the United States who are of Italian decent, it is my opinion that your military problem will be made less difficult by giving to the Allied Miliary Government (in Sicily) as much of an American character as is practicable."

Churchill agreed with Roosevelt's assessment of the situation, and his ambassador in the United States wrote home telling Churchill that certain elements of the Italian community in New York were already looking towards the day when they could play a positive role in the liberation of their homeland.

In that light, the Navy turned once again to it silent partner, the Mafia.

The Navy chose men from the Third Naval District in New York, veterans of the deal with Luciano, to aid the project. One of the men whom they turned to was Lt. Anthony Marsloe, one of four men who were going to be sent undercover to North Africa in May 1943 as prelude to Operation Husky, as the Sicilian operation was dubbed. The other men who'd be working with Lt. Marsloe were Lt. Joachim Titolo, Lt. Paul Alferi, and Ensign James Murray. Another familiar name was added to the ever-growing list of secret agents, that of Commander Haffenden who played such an important role in the Luciano-dock workers operation.

According to the Herlands Report, the authoritative narrative on the history of the Mafia-Navy connection during the war, Commander Haffenden believed that the Italian community in New York could be of immense help in the upcoming invasion. The report said in part, "Numerous Italians of Sicilian birth or background and their relatives were enlisted to provide Commander Haffenden and his assistants information about the terrain, harbors, etc., of Sicily in anticipation of the Allied invasion there. Through these contacts and informants, the names of friendly Sicilian natives and even Sicilian underworld and Mafia personalities who could be trusted were obtained and actually used in the Sicilian campaign."[6]

Prior to the invasion, Commander Haffenden turned to a familiar face; Meyer Lansky. Lansky had proved his mettle in the Navy's secret dealings with Luciano and he believed that Lansky would serve the Navy in this new assignment. Lansky agreed, and passed the word around in the Italian-American community to give any help that was asked of them. Under Lansky's tutelage, US. Navy officers began to interview many people who had just returned from private trips to Sicily. These people provided the Navy with an assortment of photographs they'd taken on their trips, maps of the region, including tide tables of the waters in the area of any possible American landing sites, and detailed photos of the entire Sicilian coastline.

Lansky also brought into the picture, Socks Lanza, and he used his considerable influence to provide as much information as he could. However, Lanza's role was put to a permanent end when he was arrested by the feds on extortion and conspiracy charges.

From his perch at Great Meadow, Luciano also put in the word

6 Ibid. Page 126.

to his men in the Italian-American community to assist the Navy as much as possible. When some people were reluctant to provide assistance, the word was given to them (discreetly) that if they failed to aid the cause, they'd pay the consequences. Needless to say, these people cooperated wholeheartedly.

All this intelligence was passed up the chain of command to Naval Intelligence in Washington where it was all collated and studied. The man responsible for collecting and evaluating all this important data was Captain Wallace Wharton, head of the Counter-Intelligence Section, Office of Naval Intelligence. Commander Haffenden provided Captain Wharton with numerous names of Mafia figures in Sicily who agreed to aid the Americans in the prelude to Operation Husky.

One of the wildest reports that passed Captain Wharton's desk was an offer by Luciano himself. He wanted to put himself on the front line of the upcoming American invasion of his homeland. He offered to go to Sicily with the invading Americans, even parachuting into the mainland by airplane. Meyer Lansky later said about Luciano's bid to be part of the invasion force, "He thought his presence would guarantee Sicilian cooperation. He didn't want anybody to think he was just trying to get out of prison; he was ready to risk his neck to prove his point. He said he was prepared to be parachuted into the island."

For his part, Commander Haffenden asked Captain Wharton to consider Luciano's offer. Haffenden said that he could try and persuade Gov. Tom Dewey to pardon Luciano and send him to a neutral country such as Portugal for the duration of the war.

Luciano also recommended that the U.S. forces land in the Golfo di Castellammare area of Sicily, a region that was known for his large contingent of Mafia figures, as well as a drug smuggling paradise for the mob.

In the end, Luciano's offer was rejected. How would it play out if America's number one Mafia figure was captured by the Germans or Italians as part of an invading American army? The public relations outcome of that scenario would be nothing less than a compete disaster.

However, the Navy did utilize the hundreds of tips and countless bits of intelligence provided to them by Luciano's behind the scenes work prior to the Husky landings.

In May 1943, Lt. Marsloe, Titolo, Alfieri and Murray, left the United States bound for North Africa where they were given training in commando type operations by members of the Counter-Intelligence Corps.

British intelligence officials were also instrumental in preparing Marsloe and his men for their clandestine role in the upcoming attack. MI-6 said that the Americans should try and make contact with a Sicilian Mafia figure named Vito La Mantia. La Manita according to the British, was anti-Fascist and ran an establishment that was a Mafia front in Palermo. MI-6 also recommended that at the time of the attack, that certain members of the Sicilian Mafia be armed and asked to carry out certain sabotage missions. These recommendations were even supported by the Joint Chiefs of Staff of the American military.

What is oblivious, as the eve of Operation Husky approached, was that the secret cooperation hatched earlier by a few members of Naval Intelligence in New York with Lucky Luciano was now known of, and approved by the highest-ranking members of the American military. The Mafia was now a full, cooperating partner with the American miliary in the up-coming battle. There was no turning back.

As preparations for Operation Husky took shape, the OSS assigned one of its top officers to act as a liaison with certain members of the Italian-American community, both here and in Sicily. The man whom Bill Donovan chose was Max Corvo, then 21 years old, of American-Sicilian origin. His first job was to make contact with certain members of the anti-Fascist movement in Chicago and New York. In his heated discussions with certain members of Naval Intelligence in Washington, Corvo persuaded them to allow him to draft detailed plans for a series of underground operations to take place in Sicily once the invasion got under way. One of his contacts was Girolamo Valenti, who was the editor of a newspaper called "La Parola."

Contrary to the Navy's use of the mob under Commander Haffenden, they decided not to use their services when dealing with Max Corvo and his new team. This new operation would strictly be a military operation, plain and simple.

The main objective was to recruit as many covert operatives into Sicily as possible, locate targets for sabotage, and find as many anti-Fascist's on the island as possible who'd aid the troops once they landed. In March 1943, Corvo and an eleven-man team of OSS operatives, under the command of Colonel William Eddy, arrived in North Africa.

Unbeknownst to Corvo, his plan to insert Italian-American agents into Sicily prior to D-Day was shot down by the top brass in Washington. It was even agreed that OSS agents would not take part in the initials landings in Sicily.

This job was given, instead, to members of the Army's Counter-Intelligence Corp (CIC). At least 80 CIC men went ashore and made initial contact with members of the Mafia. For Naval Intelligence, the heady days of their secret cooperation with the mob in the United States was now over, at least for the moment.

Operation Husky began on July 9-10, 1943, when over 160,000 allied troops began disembarking from their landing crafts on the southwestern shore of Sicily. The landing force consisted of troops from both the United States and England, commanded by Lt. Gen. George Patton and his extreme opposite, General Bernard Montgomery (Patton commanded the Seventh Army, while Montgomery lead the British and Canadian Eighth Army).

Accompanying the troops into Sicily were the members of the Naval Intelligence group consisting of Lieutenant Marsloe, Lt. Alfieri, Joachim Titolo and Ensign James Murray. Using information provided to them months before by Lucky Luciano, the ONI team began making contact with the numerous names given to them prior to leaving New York. Among those whom they linked up with, were certain individuals who were deported from the U.S. for crimes committed while in the States. One man whom they met was saved from being put to death by electrocution in the U.S. (he happened to be a cousin of Luciano's).

Using information provided by these men, Lt. Alfieri successfully raided a building that contained an office of the Italian naval command and killed a number of men guarding the base. Inside the room, they blew the safe and found valuable documents that contained information on both German and Italian defenses in Sicily. A second windfall from the raid was that it detailed data on German naval forces in the entire Mediterranean region.

Lt. Alfieri and his team recruited a number of local fishing captains in the area who provided them with food, as well as additional intelligence on the dispositions of Italian naval forces throughout Sicily. The local fishermen told the allies the locations of German mine fields on both land and water which were subsequently taken care of.

One of the most colorful stories coming out of Operation Husky took place on July 14, when an American plane flew over the village of Villalba, a center of Mafia power in Sicily. According to the story, the plane dropped a canvas sack that was addressed to "Zu Calo," who went by the name of Don Calogero Vizzini. Vizzini was the man to see in Mafia circles in Sicily and for all intents and purposes, was the head of the Sicilian Mafia. Inside the sack was a silk scarf with a Black letter L printed on it. The "L," was supposed to have stood for Lucy Luciano and when Don Calogero Vizzini received it, he automatically knew who sent it. Luciano was born in the town of Lercara Fridi, a mere fifteen miles from Villalba.

According to local custom, the use of a silk handkerchief was used as a symbol of greeting. While one can assume that Luciano was not in contact with Don Carlo Vizzini while he was serving his time in his New York prison cell, it is safe to assume that his influence made it safely to his old hometown.

After receiving his flying note from Luciano, Don Carlo sent a message to his second-in-command, Giuseppe Genco Russo. The note said, "Turi, the farm bailiff, will go to the fair at Cerda with the calves on Thursday 20th. I''ll leave on the same day with the cows, cart-oxen, and the bulls. Get the faggots ready for making the cheese, and provide folds for the sheep."[7]

According to their secret code, "Cows" was the U.S. Army, while "cart-oxen" was tanks, and the reference to "bull" was the U.S. commander (Patton).

A few days later, the first contingent of U.S. tanks rolled into Villalba, passing through enemy held territory without any difficulty. One American tank carried a yellow flag with a Black "L" on its top. At the sight of the welcome tank, Don Carlo himself walked triumphantly into the town square and greeted the American tank commander. Don Carlo boarded the tank, and is supposed to have spent the next several days traveling with the

---

7 Ibid. Page 159.

advancing American troops, bidding his jubilant townspeople to give all aid and comfort to the Americans as they could. Thanks to the good graces of Don Carlo and the use of his large contingent of Mafia soldiers, most German and Italian resistance in the area faded away, enabling the advancing American troops to push on to other strategic objectives.

To show just how much the allies appreciated the work Don Carlo had done for them, in July 1943, the American Civil Affairs Control Office, appointed him major of Villalba. As time went on, other local Mafia leaders were appointed as mayors of various towns in Sicily, becoming the trusted eyes and ears on the ground for the Americans.

On July 22, the strategic town of Palermo was captured by the Americans, a major success in winning the battle for Sicily. But the price of victory did not come cheap. The U.S. lost 9,213 killed and wounded. The British and Canadians lost over 12,000 men.

The successful allied campaign in Sicily had far-reaching consequences for the people of Italy. On July 24, 1943, the Fascist Grand Council in Rome passed a no confidence vote in the Italian dictator, Benito Mussolini. They asked King Victor Emmanuel to pick a new leader and he duly dismissed Mussolini and chose as the new Italian leader, Marshal Pietro Badoglio.

Mussolini was sent packing and the new government began negotiations with the allies for Italy's surrender. With Italy out of the war, Hitler ordered his army into the country and put Field Marshal Albert Kesselring in charge. Mussolini was taken by the Italian government to a hide-away location in the Italian Alps for safe keeping. However, in an audacious plan, Hitler ordered a crack team of commandos, lead by Otto Skorzeny, to mount a rescue operation. The operation was a success and a thankful Mussolini joined Hitler in Berlin.

The success of the Sicily invasion was the first step in the conquest of Germany. Once Italy had fallen, the allies spent the next two, bloody years advancing further into Germany proper, finally seizing Berlin in May 1945.

War makes strange bedfellows, and the United States, in the form of a secret alliance with the Mafia headed by men such as Meyer Lansky, Charles Luciano, Vito Genovese Sox Lanza, and others, made a precedent that they'd use as the cold war intensified.

The next step in their secret relationship with the mob came in 1960, as the Untied States looked toward its own hemisphere, and saw the rise of a young, charismatic, bearded revolutionary by the name of Fidel Castro.

* * *

The CIA-Mafia Plots

When John F. Kennedy was sworn in as the 35th president of the United States, he was immediately confronted by major cold war challenges. Among the hot spots were the situation in Laos, where the communists were threatening to take over that small, yet vital country. More importantly, as far as the United States was concerned, was Cuba, which lay 90 miles off the coast of Florida. By the time of his assassination, JFK would spend more time and energy on Cuban affairs than any other trouble spot in the world. Little did he know, that Cuba would play an important factor in the aftermath of his assassination, three years later.

During the Eisenhower administration, Cuba was run by the dictator, Fulgenio Batista who repressed his people, using the nations economy to divert millions of dollars to his personal use, and making the island a safe haven for the American mob who ran the lucrative casinos that attracted visitors from all over the world, Unknown to his fellow Cubans, Batista got a substantial cut of the casino profits, making a not so secret pact with such Mafia figures as Meyer Lansky (the same man who helped run Operation Underworld), Santos Trafficante, and others.

In the 1950s, Cuba served the anti-Communist purposes of the Eisenhower administration who saw in Batista's island, a safe place to fend off the rampant communist menace that was then spreading across the Atlantic. Ike knew of Batista's criminal past but chose to ignore it as long as he served our purposes. The CIA sent one of its top men, Lyman Kirkpartick, later to become the CIA's Inspector General, to Havana to break bread with Batista and assure him of continuing American support. After a period of time, Batista chose not to obey Washington's demands and the U.S. decided to end its support. Seeing the writing on the wall, Batista and his family fled Cuba on December 31, 1959. Shortly thereafter, Fidel Castro, fresh from his routing of what was left of Batista's army, made a triumphant march into Havana and took the reigns of power. For the United States, one dictator had taken the place of another. In time, we would regret the actions that we spawned.

In the last year of the Eisenhower administration, the president saw the writing on the wall as far as Castro was concerned. Over a short period of time, secret plans were put in place to facilitate his removal.

In March 1960, Ike's team began secret plans to topple the Castro regime. Richard Bissell was authorized to form a task force called "The Special Group," and later, "Operation 40", to devise an anti-Castro strategy. A Cuban Task Force was started, its members consisting of J.C. King of the CIA, CIA Inspector General Lyman Kirkpatrick, among others. A document was written that had the following points vis-a-vi the Castro problem. I) "The creation of a unified Cuban opposition to the Cuban regime located outside of Cuba, 2) the development of a means of mass communication to the Cuban people as part of a powerful propaganda effort, 3) the creation and development of a covert intelligence and action organization within Cuba which would be responsive to the orders and directions of the exile opposition, and 4) the development of a paramilitary force outside of Cuba for future guerilla action."

On March 17, 1960, President Eisenhower signed a secret National Security Council Directive giving "A Program of Covert Action Against the Castro Regime" the green light.

All this was going on during the hotly contested 1960 presidential election between Vice President Richard Nixon and Sen. John F. Kennedy. Eisenhower appointed Nixon as the point man in the administration's secret effort to oust Castro and he took on the job with relish. But Nixon was in a dammed if he did and dammed if he didn't situation. He saw the ouster of Castro as his ticket to the White House and he did all in his power to ensure that happened. But he was in a huge quandary. He couldn't tell the public about the secret plans to remove Castro, lest it be seen that the Eisenhower administration was creating an international incident in order to help Nixon's chances. When Kennedy began attacking Nixon for doing nothing as far as Castro was concerned, he had to bite his tongue and not respond to Kennedy's ever shrill charges.

Ike ordered the CIA to begin covert training of a number of Cuban exiles in the jungles of Guatemala under the agency's tutelage. Soon, a number of American military officers and staff were covertly sent to their jungle hideaway to train the raw, but eager troops for an eventual invasion of Cuba. The seeds that were planted in the jungles of Guatemala was the forerunner of the Bay of Pigs invasion.

By August 1960, two assassination plots against Castro and his brother Raul were approved by the CIA. The Air Force and the CIA had a hand in one of these plots in late 1959 or 1960 when the Air Force provided a plane that was used to fly two Cuban exiles into Cuba. "The witness was unable to provide names of these two Cuban exiles or names of any CIA personnel which he said were involved. However, at the time of the events the witness was an Air Force officer who had liaison functions between the Department of Defense and the CIA. He testified that he believes a plane was provided and that the two Cuban exiles were to carry with them one or more rifles with telescopic sites to be used in an attempt to assassinate Fidel Castro."[8]

When the HSCA (House Select Committee on Assassinations) began its investigation of the plots to kill Castro in the 1970s, they came across documentation regarding this, possible first attempt on Castro's life. Their records, dated May 15, 1975, said that in reviewing CIA operations during 1959-61, "a number of documents were found that referred to the intent on the part of some of the Cuban teams operating inside Cuba to attempt to assassinate Castro. Additionally, the files indicate that there was a considerable interest in procurement of Heilo Courier but there is no definite indication that they were intended for Cuban operations. Also, there is mention of the air drop of Springfield rifles with telescopic sights."

By the summer of 1960, at the time of the presidential election campaign, the first CIA-Mafia contacts were initiated using Robert Mahue as the go between. These contacts would eventually make up the CIA-Mafia-Giancana-Rosselli-Trafficante trio to kill Castro.

---

[8] RIF No. 178-10004-10116 Summary of Facts, Invest, CIA Involvement in Plans to Assassinate Leaders.

After winning the Democratic presidential nomination, Kennedy was given a briefing on world affairs by CIA Director Allan Dulles. Clearly, Cuba, and the worsening diplomatic relations between Washington and Havana were discussed.

In July 1960, shortly before accepting the nomination, Kennedy decided to cement his ties with a faction of the anti-Castro exiles then living in the United States. In a secret meeting in Washington, Kennedy met with four of the leading Cuban exiles; Manuel Artime, Tony Varona, Aureliano Sanchez Arrango, and Jose Mario Cardona. But this was no ordinary social chat. The meeting was set up by the CIA who were playing both sides of the political middle; they would either work with a President Kennedy or a President Nixon. Kennedy's most ardent supporter at CIA headquarters was the deputy director of plans, an Ivy League spook named Richard Bissell. In the 1950s, Bissell ran the CIA's most sensitive covert operation of the time; the U-2 spy planes that flew over both Russia and China. In Japan, a low level Marine named Lee Harvey Oswald was one of many men who monitored the take offs and landings of the U-2s from his location at Atsugi Air Base.

Kennedy was thus informed of the basic plans that the CIA had in preparation for action against Cuba. Limited though these discussions by Bissell and Dulles were, Kennedy was only given what they wanted him to know. Upon his election, he would be given a more thorough briefing on the Cuba Project. But by then, events had progressed far too long to stop the imminent exile invasion.

On electionday, Kennedy won the presidency by a little over 100,000 votes, one of the closets elections in modern American history. The problem of what to do about Cuba was now his.

It was only in the mid-1970s, that the American public were made privy to the secret dealings vis-a-vi Cuba that went on during the Eisenhower and Kennedy administrations. The revelations of CIA abuses at home, as well as the sordid tales of assassination planning against foreign leaders, led the congress to pass restrictive laws on the way the CIA could operate when it came to covert activities, as well as outlawing assassination as a tool of U.S. foreign policy.

The congressional committee that looked into CIA activities, as well as the Kennedy-King assassinations, was chaired by Idaho Democratic Senator Frank Church. Many of his hearings on the Kennedy case were televised and an eager nation, a huge majority of whom did not believe the "official' findings of the Warren Commission in 1964, listened eagerly to find out if new information was to be found on the Kennedy assassination.

The Church Committee began its investigation into the Kennedy administrations's efforts to kill Castro by looking into the background of three top Mafia dons who worked secretly for the CIA; Santos Trafficante, Johnny Rosselli, and Sam Giancana. An earlier CIA inquest into the Castro plots, the so-called Inspector General's Report (IG Report), also tried to find out, what, if anything, both Robert Kennedy and John Kennedy knew about the plots. Their report, of which only one copy was made, was placed in a safe at CIA headquarters where it languished in total secrecy for the next dozen years.

Both Sam Giancana, the mob boss of Chicago, and Santo Trafficante, as well as Johnny Rosselli, a dashing hoodlum out of Los Angeles, were, in the early 1960s, all being investigated by Robert Kennedy in his capacity as U.S. Attorney General. The so-called cut-out in the early Rosselli-Giancana-Trafficante efforts to kill Castro was Robert Mahue, a former FBI and CIA agent who had close ties to both organizations, even after his "retirement." The use of Mahue in the CIA-Mafia plots is a long, complicated story that has been gone over with a finetooth comb for the past 40 years.

As mentioned before, in August 1960, Richard Bissell approached Col. Sheffield Edwards to see if the CIA's Office of Security could find out if they had any "assets" who might be available to work in a "sensitive mission requiring gangster-type action." The target was Fidel Castro of Cuba.

These first plans were known to only a few, trusted officers at CIA headquarters, including the Director of the CIA, Allen Dulles, as well as J. C. King, The CIA station, that in only a few short years, would operate the largest CIA domestic operation to plan Castro's ouster was called JMWAVE, was not notified.

The CIA chose Robert Mahue who was a cleared source of the Office of Security, was briefed on the rudiments of the case and asked to find out if he could develop an entree into the so-called "gangster elements" as a first step in ousting Castro.

Robert Mahue was the owner of a private detective agency in Washington, D.C. and had high profile clients, not only in the city, but throughout the country. One of his most valued clients was Howard Hughes, the reclusive billionaire who had ties to the U.S. government and private industry, as well. In his early days, Mahue worked for both the FBI and CIA, from 1954-1960. In his secret line of work, Mahue came in contact with both sides of the law; his buddies at the CIA and FBI, as well as certain members of organized crime, notably, Johnny Rosselli. It was at this time (1960), that CIA officer, Jim O'Connell, (Mahue's "project officer" at the CIA), met with Mahue and asked him to recruit his Mafia pal, Johnny Rosselli in a clandestine plot to kill Fidel Castro. Mahue told Rosselli that at the same time that Castro was to be killed, an American sponsored invasion of Cuba was to be initiated. This must have been great news to Johnny Rosselli, whose mob colleagues had lost millions of dollars when the former Cuban dictator Batista, was overthrown by the young, brash, Fidel. Castro in turn, closed down the lush gambling casinos that brought in millions into Mafia coffers and also lined the pockets of Batista.

Mahue was paid $500 per month, but the real reason he took on the job was patriotism. In 1966, Robert Mahue told the following story that might have had some relevance at the time he was involved in the Castro plots. While he was working for Howard Hughes in Las Vegas, Hughes told Mahue to begin preparations for a large operation for the CIA. According to Mahue, Hughes wanted this kind of protection from the government in case he ever became involved in any serious problem with any agency of government."

Mahue had been in touch with Johnny Rosselli on various occasions during his trips to Las Vegas. They weren't the best of friends, but met through the intercession of other clients. Rosselli was described to Mahue as being a top ranking member of the "syndicate," a.k.a. Mafia. According to the CIA's long held "Family Jewels" document which was released a few years ago, "Mahue reasoned that if Rosselli was in fact a member of the clan, he undoubtedly had connections leading into the Cuban gambling interests."

When they first met, Rosselli believed Mahue to be a "personal relations executive" who handled clients at home and aborad. Rosselli was led to believe that Mahue had been contacted by a client who "represented several international business firms which were suffering heavy financial losses in Cuba as a result of Castro's action. They were convinced that Castro's removal was the answer to their problem and were willing to pay a price of $150,000 for its successful accomplishment. It was to be made clear to Rosselli that the United States government was not, and should not, become aware of this operation."

The original offer to Rosselli was made on September 14, 1960 at the Hilton Plaza Hotel in New York City. On hand was James O'Connell of the CIA's Office of Security. Rosselli was told that O'Connell was working for Mahue in an undisclosed capacity. O'Connell would serve as Rosselli's contact until May 1962 when he was placed on another assignment by the CIA. At first, Rosselli was not persuaded, but during the meeting, his mind was changed and he told O'Connell that he would introduce him to a friend named Sam Gold who was well connected with the "Cuban crowd… " Rosselli said that he did not want to be paid for his services.

At this point in their discussions, Rosselli did not know that O'Connell represented the CIA but he must have had some lingering feeling that O'Connell was not all he seemed to be. As time went on, and it became evident to Rosselli that his employers were indeed the CIA, he realized in the back of his mind that he now had a major trump card which he could play to blackmail the CIA if need be.

During the latter part of September 1960, Mahue met Sam Gold who was staying at the Fontainebleau Hotel in Miami Beach, Florida. Also at the meeting were Mahue and Santos Trafficante. "Sam Gold ", was in fact, Sam Giancana, and "Joe" was Santos Trafficante. "Joe" was described as a courier who operated between Havana and Miami. It must have been quite a shock to Mahue who learned in the Sunday supplemental *Parade* magazine in the local newspaper that "Sam Gold" was Sam Giancana, and that "Joe the courier" was Santos Trafficante, both of whom were identified as being on the 10 most wanted list put out by the U.S. Attorney General. The CIA's fist attempt to kill Castro came in the fall of 1960, when Castro, along with hundreds of other foreign heads of state, arrived in New York City to attend the annual General Assembly of the United Nations. While the dignitaries were delivering their speeches at the UN, uptown, the CIA was planning Castro's demise. In the safety of the Plaza Hotel, "Jim Olds" and his pals at the CIA's Technical Services Department, soon realized that Castro liked to smoke cigars and they sought to place poison in one of his smokes. This far-fetched scheme came to naught, along with another one that called for the CIA to spray Castro's broadcasting studio with lethal hallucinations.

At CIA headquarters, various schemes were discussed as to how to most effectively kill Castro. The use of firearms was rejected as being too risky, especially to the shooters who had a less than even chance of surviving such an attack. The "how to" was given to the CIA's Joseph Schneider of the TSD who made up a batch of pills that were tested on a monkey. After successful testing, the pills were given to Jim O'Connell in February 1961. O'Connell, in turn, gave them to Rosselli who turned them over to one of his agents in Cuba. The middleman in the poison plot caper was Santos Trafficante, who gave the pills to the CIA's man in Havana, Juan Orta, who was to be the one to actually plant the pills in Castro's food. Orta had served as the Office Chief and Director General of the Office of the Prime Minister (Castro). "The gangsters said that Orta had once been in a position to receive kickbacks from the gambling interests, had lost that source of income, and needed the money." Thus, the Orta channel was opened. After Orta received the pills, he apparently got cold feet and soon returned them to the CIA. On January 26, 1961, Orta lost his job in Castro's office, and in April, took refuge in the Venezuelan embassy. Orta stayed under the protection of the Venezuelan's until October 1964, when he was given a pass to leave the country. In February 1965, he returned to Miami.

As mentioned before, Santos Trafficante, the mob boss from Tampa, Florida, was one of the men whom the CIA asked to become part of the early plots to kill Castro. His testimony before the HSCA, clarifies some of his work in the plots.

He said that he was contacted by Rosselli in 1960 or early 1961 to serve as an interpreter between Rosselli and the Cuban exiles. He said that Rosselli told him that the job was to be a CIA operation. Robert Mahue worked for the CIA and represented the

U.S. government in their secret dealings.

At their first meeting, Trafficante said that Rosselli first brought up the name of a man named Gener who was to be a contact man for the operation. At that time, Mr. Gener was about 70 years old, and had been a former politician in the government of the late Cuban president, Carlos Prio. About three weeks later, Rosselli, Gener, Mahue and Trafficante met at the home of an influential Cuban exile by the name of Tony Varona, who lived on an island on the Venetian Causeway on Miami Beach. "The subject" said Trafficante, "was the destruction of Castro, the communists. Mr. Mahue told him he was going to get all the help he could get. After the second time I think, two or three times, Mr. Rosselli and Mr. Mahue told me that they didn't need my services."[9]

At this meeting, Trafficante served as the interpreter between Rosselli, Gener and Varona. Varona asked for supplies of guns, ammunition and machine guns be provided to him for his efforts to kill Castro. The possibility of his passing the poison pills to his contacts in Cuba were also discussed at the meeting. There were other Cuban's at the meeting, but they were not told the operation was sponsored by the CIA. Instead, Mahue was introduced as a representative of a New York business.

As mentioned before, after the meeting Trafficante was told by Rosselli that he was no longer needed to be part of the operation. It seems that they found another Cuban who could speak English. Trafficante said the only reason he took on the initial job was "that he became involved only out of friendship with Rosselli and his great dislike for Fidel Castro. Trafficante believed that Castro is a threat to this country and is quite capable of pulling off assassinations."[10]

In his testimony before the HSCA, Trafficante had this to say about Mr. Gener. He said that he had met Mr. Gener in Cuba and re-connected with him when he arrived in the United States. Trafficante said that Gener belonged to the same party as Tony Varona. "This is when Gener came back from Miami and he

---

9 RIF No. 180-10118-10137.

10 RIf No. 157-10014.10066: Testimony of Santos Trafficante, 1 October 1976.

thought his party was going to rule Cuba. Well, it didn't happen like that but I met him there. I think he is a nice man, I still do, and he was active in politics there. That is all I can tell you about him. I probably had dinner with him a few times in Cuba and in the States, too."

Trafficante elaborated further on how the CIA first brought Mr. Gener into the picture. He said that Rosselli had originally spoken with Mr. Gener about taking part in the conversations regarding killing Castro. "You see," said Trafficante, "the way I understand this, with hindsight, is that Mr. Rosselli had contacts inside the Cuban exile colony. Whether he got this through the CIA or by himself I don't know. He thought he had this contact with these people. He had them. I didn't give it to him, he had them. I just happened to know, I know Gener and he was glad that I could at least vouch for Gener. To me, he was an upright fellow and he was not a con artist or something like that."[11]

Another area that involved Trafficante and his possible links to the president's death was his meeting with Jose Aleman, a prominent Cuban exile leader. When the two men met in September 1962, it is alleged by Aleman that when discussing the Kennedy administration's foreign policy in general, and the Cuban situation in particular, Aleman said that it was likely that JFK would be re-elected in 1964. Trafficante, according to Aleman, said that JFK would not make it to the next election; he was gong to be "hit."

Aleman further said that he was certain Trafficante himself would not be the one to carry out the assassination, and stated that Jimmy Hoffa's name came up in the same conversation. According to Aleman, Hoffa said that Kennedy "would get what was coming to him," because of the Attorney General's ruthless pursuit of Hoffa.

Aleman further testified before the HSCA that it was his impression from his brief conversation with Trafficante that the Tampa mob boss was not kidding when he said that the president was to be killed. "Rather, he did in fact know that such a crime was being planned… " "Aleman also stated that Trafficante had given him the distinct impression that Hoffa was to be principally

---

[11] Ibid.

involved in planning the president's murder."

Just prior to his appearance in front of the HSCA however, Aleman told the committee members that he now feared for his life in light of his previous testimony regarding his meeting with Trafficante. When he did testify before the committee, Aleman now said he stood by his previous statement from Trafficante that Kennedy was going to be "hit," but countered by saying that Trafficante referred to the hit of lots of Republican votes against JFK in the next election.

On September 28, 1976, Santo Trafficante testified before the committee and flatly denied ever talking with anyone about assassinating President Kennedy, and further said that he played NO role in the event. He also said that he did remember talking with Aleman but denied that a "hit" against JFK was ever discussed.

In its final report, the HSCA wrote the following regarding the Trafficante-Aleman story, "The committee found it difficult to understand how Aleman could have misunderstood Trafficante during such a conversation, or why he would have fabricated such an account."

Regarding Trafficante's account, the HSCA said, "further, the committee found it difficult to comprehend why Trafficante, if he was planning or had personal knowledge of an assassination plot, would have revealed or hinted at such a sensitive matter to Aleman."

In the end, the committee wrote that it had substantial problems with Aleman's version of the story concerning a mob "hit" against the president.

The HSCA did however say this concerning the relationship between Santo Trafficante and the assassination of the president. "The committee found that Trafficante, like Marcello (Carlos Marcello, the mob boss of Chicago), had the motive, means and opportunity to assassinate President Kennedy."

Students of the CIA-Mafia plots have been very suspicious regarding whether or not Trafficante was a double agent for Castro, or had some ties to his government. Johnny Rosselli, who worked with Trafficante in the early plots had this to say regarding his former colleague. "This whole thing has been a scam. Santos never did anything but bullshit everybody. All these fucking wild schemes the CIA dreamed up never got further than Santos. He just sat on it, conned everybody into thinking that guys were risking their lives sneaking into Cuba, having boats shot out from under them-all bullshit."

Santo Trafficante, like Johnny Rosselli, might have been using the CIA in its plots to kill Castro as leverage against the Kennedy administration's activities regarding their long mob history. It seems obvious that Trafficante played a more cryptic role than the story we have been told.

With the demise of the Orta channel, "Joe the Courier" gave the CIA the name of one of his contacts on the island, Dr. Anthony "Tony" Varona, who was an important leader in the Cuban exile junta, and who was disappointed on how feeble the efforts to kill Castro were going. Varona offered his services to the CIA and for all intents and purposes, he took over from the disgraced Orta.

If he was going to take on the assignment, Varona had some perquisites he needed before going any further. He requested that he be given \$10,000 for "organizational expenses" and also, \$1,000 for "communications equipment."

The CIA used Rosselli as the cut out with Varona and he passed along a certain amount of cash (the amounts range from \$25,000 to \$50,000) for the necessary expenses. Authorization for the Varona channel was given by Robert Bannerman who was Sheffield Edward's deputy. Also involved in the Varona plan was Jake Esterline, who was high up in the Cuba Project pecking order. Esterline gave the go ahead for payment, and he recalled it being only \$10,000 plus expenses.

According to the IG Report, when Esterline learned that Varona was part of the plan, he called for its cancellation. This was because Varona, as head of the Revolutionary Front was heavily involved in the plans for the Bay of Pigs invasion and he feared for the safety of the operation. But Varona stayed in the loop, despite Esterline's attempts to end it.

Phase One of the Castro plots came to an end in April 1961 and the CIA had no involvement in any other plans until April 1962, when Phase Two began. It was alleged that Phase Two started with the placing of an asset in a restaurant that Castro frequently attended but whomever that person was, he never got the opportunity to do his dirty work. A three man team was subsequently sent into Cuba to assassinate Castro in September, but that too came to naught. No one knows what happened to that team and the written record is vague on that subject. Whomever was on this assignment was not linked with the actions taken by Tony Varona. Also, the written record says that the CIA had no operational relationship with any of these potential assassins.

A government document titled "Syndicate Plot Against Castro" is succinct in this matter. "Castro claims that a number of people were sent to assassinate him. Presumably a lot of Cubans wanted to kill him and some may have undertaken to do so. CIA has been credited with responsibility for these various people even though it had no connection with them. It is symptomatic of the times, with the tensions between the Kennedy administration and the Castro government. While the CIA has received credit for everything that happened during that time, the Army and Navy had active anti-Castro programs (it seems that those have not been the subject of Congressional inquiry").

After the failure off the Bay of Pigs invasion in April 1961, the CIA plots to kill Castro came to a temporary end. Sheffield Edwards sent word to Rosselli via Jim O"Connell to stop all further attempts on Castro and cut off the funding. There were just too many complications in the wake of the disaster at the Bay of Pigs to continue another, far-reaching covert operation run by the CIA. However, after the abortive invasion, the record becomes distorted about what exactly was the status of the plans to kill Castro. Edwards states that the operation was completely shut down after the Bay of Pigs and was not reactivated until the spring of 1962. O'Connell also states that the operation was shut down after April 1961 but he says that it was only on a temporary basis. He said that there was some sort of activity going on in the intervening year, but he wasn't sure what.

Another CIA officer who had direct responsibility as far as the Castro plots were concerned was William Harvey. Harvey was a bone in the side of Robert Kennedy who did not care for Harvey's brash, abrasive style. Harvey was a former FBI agent who changed allegiances to the CIA, years before. Harvey often times was seen at his desk at CIA headquarters, or in the field, wearing a pistol on his belt. He was a hard drinking, non-nonsense man, who disliked anyone treading on his turf. When RFK made his frequent trips to the CIA base in Florida, dubbed JMWAVE, he always had run-ins with Harvey, who disliked the Attorney General's presence at the base. Often times, both men were seen in shouting matches over how the secret war against Castro was being run, and one time, fists were almost thrown.

More importantly to the story of the Castro plots, Harvey was put in charge of a secret unit called "ZR/RIFLE' which was a CIA run assassination plot that was to be used against certain foreign leaders whom the United states did not like (among them were Castro and Patrice Lumumba of the Congo-this assassination unit was never put into use).

But Harvey stated that when he took over the Castro plots, he was working on an ongoing operation. Harvey was given the job as the chief operating officer in a briefing by Richard Helms in late 1961, early 1962. He met with Edwards in February 1962 and was briefed on the full aspects of the Castro operation. The Assassination Report has this to say concerning Harvey's taking over the Castro function:

> *"After Harvey took over the Castro operation he ran it as one aspect of ZR/RIFLE; however, he personally handled the Castro operation and did not use any of the assets being developed in ZR/RIFLE. He says that he first came to think of the Castro operation and ZR/RIFLE as being synonymous. The overall Executive Action program came to be treated in his mind as being synonymous with QJ/WIN, the agent working on the overall program. He says that when he wrote of ZR/RIFLE, QJ/WIN the reference was to Executive Action capability; when he used the cryptonym ZR/RIFLE alone, he was referring to Castro."*[12]

In April 1962, Harvey contacted Edwards in order to set up a meeting with Rosselli. Edwards then contacted Richard Helms (later to become director of the CIA), who gave his approval. Before and after his covert meetings with Rosselli, Harvey

---

[12] *CIA Targets Fidel: The Secret Assassination Report,* Ocean Press, 1996, Page 50.

informed Helms on their discussions and plans.

"Edwards statement that he "verified Helms" approval is the earliest indication we have that Mr. Helms had been made witting of the gambling syndicate operation against Castro. Harvey added that, "when he briefed Helms on Rosselli, he obtained Helms' approval not to brief the Director."

While there is no dispute as to the turnover to Harvey of the Castro plots, there is some disagreement as to the circumstances concerning how it was done. The Inspector General's narrative goes as follows:

> *"A) Edwards believes that the operation was called off completely after the Bay of Pigs and that there was no further operational activity in connection with it until Harvey met Rosselli and reactivated the operation in April 1962. O'Connell introduced Harvey to Rosselli and Edwards had noting to do with the operation-with the exception of a meeting with Attorney General Robert Kennedy in connection the Phyllis McGuire wiretapping incident. Edwards' records show that on 14 May 1962, Harvey called Edwards and 'indicated that he was dropping any plans for the use of Rosselli in the future.*
>
> *B) Harvey's recollection of the turnover to support Edwards' summary, but he claims that the took over 'a going operation'. Some support for this claim is found in his description of just how it was planned to get the poison into Castro's food by employing someone with access to a restaurant frequented by Castro. The mechanics were identical with those described by Edwards and as reported in our account of phase one of the operation.*
>
> *C) O"Connell 's account of his own role in the operation in the early weeks following Harvey's supposed takeover makes it evident that there was not a clean break between the Office of Security's responsibility and that of Harvey. Further, O'Connell now believes that there must have been 'something going on', between April 1961 (after the Bay of Pigs) and April 1962, but he claims to be unable to remember any of the particulars."*

What is of particular interest in the entire area was the fact that the CIA, in the persons of Edwards and Lawrence Houston, met with Robert Kennedy on May 7, 1962 and informed him of the wiretapping case that involved the mob, the CIA, and the initial plans to kill Castro. According to the IG's report, Edwards, "briefed (Kennedy) him all the way." This is the first incident that we know of that Robert Kennedy learned of the CIA-mob plans to kill Castro. It is inconceivable that Robert Kennedy failed to tell his brother, the president, of this astonishing news. The men were so close, in all respects, both personally, and on such an important policy decision, that he could have kept such a secret from him.

Besides the CIA-Mafia plots, the U.S. government itself, (the CIA), hatched various ridiculous schemes to kill Castro. Among them were, 1) a plan to spay Castro's recording studio in Havana with a mood-altering chemical that would make it look like Fidel had lost his mind while broadcasting to the Cuban people, 2) putting thallium salts on his shoes which was supposed to have his beard fall out, 3) the planting of an explosive sea shell in a cove or beach where Castro liked to swim, and 4), a plot that was so far out that whomever thought it up should have been nominated for some sort of Hollywood award. The plan, which was dubbed "elimination by illumination, "called for a submarine (presumably US), to surface off the coast of Cuba and set off star shells which would prompt the mass of the Cuban people to rise up and overthrow Castro. Before the sub made its appearance, a propaganda campaign would be spread throughout Cuba from the US, telling the people that the Second Coming of Christ was in the offing and the star shells from the U.S. submarine would be the signal that he had arrived. This plot was conceived by General Edward Landsale, who was picked by Robert Kennedy to be the coordinator of the Kennedy administration's secret war against Castro.

Just why Edward Lansdale, a bright, World War 2 combat veteran who worked for the OSS and later in his career, a talented counterinsurgency specialist, would have believed such a scheme could actually work, is beyond belief.

One aspect of the plots to kill Castro was that they were more deadly that the ones outlined above. They involved the use of sniper teams that would be sent into Cuba to kill Castro before, or during a prospective American led invasion of the island. Castro's agents were able to capture at least one of these sniper teams before they could put Fidel into their cross hairs. There was even a blockbuster report by the noted American columnist, Jack Anderson, that one of these teams might have been "turned" and sent to kill JFK in retaliation for the attempts on Castro's life. When the Anderson reports hit the newspapers in the 1970s, they rekindled the fire of interest in the Kennedy assassination that lay dormant for the preceding decade, and added a new twist to the saga of the Kennedy assassination; the use of the Mafia to aid the CIA in their plans to kill Castro.

Operation Mongoose

The failure of the CIA's not so secret invasion of Cuba at the Bay of Pigs in April of 1961 was a turning point in the Kennedy administration's attitude toward Cuba and the Castro regime. Cuba had become the number one priority of the new administration and the defeat of the CIA backed rebels only hardened the policy makers in Washington as to what future steps would be taken to rid the hemisphere of Castro.

What followed was Phase Two of the secret war against Castro called "Operation Mongoose," run entirely by the CIA, eventually becoming the largest war in the agency's history. Phase One of the war against Castro, according to the newly released documents coming out of the National Archives via the "JFK Records Act," began with the Eisenhower administration's early efforts to kill Castro and ended with the Bay of Pigs invasion. The newly released JFK Assassination files that have been made public over the past twenty-five years, paint an entirely new canvas on which we view Operation Mongoose, and the Kennedy administration's secret war against Castro.

The files show a wide spread, all points press by almost every department in the Kennedy administration to get rid of Castro, including State, Defense, Justice, Army, CIA, Voice of America, among others. Most of Kennedy's top level advisors, including some who did not initially favor the Bay of Pigs invasion like Arthur Schlesinger Jr, now, backed the president on more "appropriate" measures to be taken against Castro.

Robert McNamara, the Secretary of Defense, argued that

Castro be removed even if it meant killing him. The man put in overall charge of Operation Mongoose was Robert Kennedy. RFK ran rough shod over the CIA, pelting them with daily calls about what they were doing that particular day to get the "beard." While Bobby was in command of Operation Mongoose, there were other members of the government who formed a secret group that monitored the CIA's activities.

The members of the group who met on an almost daily basis to oversee Mongoose were Kennedy, General Edward Lansdale, who would become Mongoose's unofficial general in charge, General Maxwell Taylor, presidential advisor McGeorge Bundy, Roswell Gilpartick, Arthur Schlesinger, Jr., Richard Goodwin (husband of historian, Doris Kearns Goodwin), and military men such as Defense Secretary McNamara, and General Lyman Lemitzer of the Joint Chiefs of Staff.

On January 19, 1962, the "Special Group," as they were called, met in Robert Kennedy's Department of Justice office to discuss Operation Mongoose. Bobby urged its members to "spare no time, effort or manpower, toward the overthrow of Castro's regime." Another prominent member of the Special Group was the new CIA Director, John McCone, who took over for the fired Allan Dulles.

On August 23, 1962, JFK advisor McGeorge Bundy, issued NSAM 181, ordered by the president, to implement a full course covert operation and propaganda war to topple the Castro regime. The CIA now set up its covert operations headquarters in Miami, Florida, and called it JMWAVE. Soon, JMWAVE would include the most elaborate para-military operation since the creation of the CIA in 1947. Working out of an abandoned site on the University of Miami campus, JMWAVE took on a life of its own. Some 400 CIA agents, their surrogates, and others, began plotting the demise of Castro.

Heading JMWAVE was an ex-FBI agent named William Harvey, one of the CIA's top guns, a man who was disliked by the Kennedy brothers, but who saw in him, the one man capable of getting rid of Castro. JMWAVE soon had its own air force, navy, foot soldiers, radio communications apparatus, banking operation, etc. Soon, Harvey was sending in teams of agents into Cuba to sabotage sugar Cain fields, attack Russian and Cuban ships in port and create as much mayhem as possible. The flip side of

JMWAVE, was the secret CIA-Mafia alliance.

When the CIA-Mafia marriage first started, the three principal Mafia dons helping the CIA were Santo Trafficante, Sam Giancana, and Johnny Rosselli. Soon. Giancana was let loose and the CIA now counted only Rosselli and Trafficante as their principal agents. It is believed that in fact, Santos Trafficante, the mob boss of Tampa, was possibly working as a double agent for Castro. While no positive proof of this allegation is certain, what is known is that as soon as the CIA passed along information to Trafficante that certain hit teams were going to be in Cuba to kill Castro, these assassins were quickly rounded up and killed.

What is still uncertain, and the matter of much heated debate, is to what extent did JFK know about Operation Mongoose, and in particular, the CIA-mob links to kill Castro. It seems logical that if Bobby Kennedy, the president's most trusted advisor and confidant, was put in charge of the Castro plots, than his brother, the president, must surely have known what was gong on.

A newly released document on Operation Mongoose dated November 5, 1962, sums up the Kennedy administration's attitude toward Castro. "Looking back to the origins of Mongoose, one finds the AG (Attorney General) and Mr. McNamara seeking primarily to remove the political stain left on the President by the Bay of Pigs failure. Both the AG and the Secretary of Defense felt it necessary for political reasons that some action with respect to Cuba to ensure the president's future. In a nutshell, they were out to dump Castro or make him cooperate."

* * *

By the fall of 1963, the Kennedy administration decided to adopt a different less bellicose policy toward Castro. While exile raids continued to be run against Cuba, the administration unleashed the Department of Justice to reign in the attacks, especially when they originated from U.S. soil. This so-called "Separate Track" in its relations with Castro, did not go down well with certain parts of the government, especially some in the CIA who still wanted to pursue the miliary option.

One of the Kennedy administration's first secret contacts with the Soviet Union (as a back channel towards Cuba), took place on

September 30, 1963, when JFK sent his Press secretary Pierre Salinger, to meet privately with a Russian named Col. G. V. Karpovich, who was a KGB (Soviet intelligence agent) who was attached to the Soviet Embassy in Washington. Khrushchev himself had approved this secret contact, hoping to by pass the normal diplomatic channels that might stifle important contacts between the two nations. While it was hoped that this back channel negotiations would lead to increasing contact, it did not significantly materialize.

In another diplomatic move, to lessen Soviet-American tensions, JFK sent U.S. Ambassador Averell Harriman to Moscow on April 23, 1963, where he had several meetings with Prime Minister Nikita Khrushchev. Among the topics covered were Cuba and other important items.

On June 6, 1963, a meeting took place in the White House to discuss new overtures to Castro. The participants were CIA Director John McCone, Vice President Johnson and Lyman Kilpatrick. A note of the meeting sounded the new tone of the administration, "On June 6, 1963, the SGA discussed "various possibilities of establishing channels of communication with CASTRO. All members of the group agree that this is a useful endeavor. Mr. Bundy cautioned that of course CASTRO should not be made privy to any U.S. positions, while Mr. McCone empathized the necessity of keeping any such approach entirely secret."

In that light, on November 6, 1963, "higher authority (President Kennedy) disapproved all Cuban operations scheduled to be run before November 12. Two operations dated November 8 and 10 are therefore disapproved."

In September 1963, the administration received tentative feelers from Castro wanting to know if the Kennedy administration would be willing to enter into secret talks. Both JFK and RFK were interested, and privately asked William Atwood, a former editor of *Life* magazine to act on their behalf. At this time, Atwood was part of the U.S. delegation to the United Nations, having formally been U.S. Ambassador to Guinea for two years. Atwood told the State Department that in his opinion, it would be wrong to permanently isolate Cuba, and that might lead Castro further into the Soviet orbit. Atwood asked JFK if he could put out feelers to the Cuban Ambassador to the UN, Carlos Lechuga. He also asked JFK if he could persuade Lechuga to gain an invitation for him to go to Cuba, could he do it? The president gave his permission and soon, a chance encounter was arranged. Journalist Lisa Howard, who had interviewed Castro in the spring, hosted a dinner party at her home. Among those attending the party were William Atwood and Carlos Lechuga.

The day after the party, Atwood reported to the White House where he met with both JFK and RFK. While nothing of real substance took place, the Attorney General thought Atwood's contracts with Castro were "worth pursing."

Lisa Howard's covert contacts with top ranking Cubans continued, and she had a good discussion with Dr. Rene Vallejo, Castro's friend and private doctor. On October 31, Vallejo told Howard that Castro was ready for a meeting with a high-ranking American diplomat. JFK was informed and told Atwood to go to Cuba.

But the Atwood-Vallejo channel was not the only game in town. Another man to be used as in intermediary between the U.S. and Cuba was French journalist Jean Daniel of *L'Express.* The president learned from Daniel that he was about to go to Cuba to meet with Fidel Castro. One day before his departure, October 24, 1963, Daniel found himself talking with JFK about Cuba. Kennedy asked Daniel if he would pass along a message from him to Castro. The gist of the note was that the U.S. could live with a Socialist Cuba if certain conditions were met, among them, the ending of Cuban revolutionary activity in Latin America. Kennedy told Daniel to tell Castro that he had nothing against the Cuban people, and that he would await Castro's reply.

Daniel waited in Havana for three, long weeks, until he was finally granted an interview with Castro, on November 20, 1963. For hours, Castro and Daniel discussed the world scene, including remarks made by JFK to the Cuban leader. After learning that Kennedy had denounced the former Cuban dictator Batista whom Castro had overthrown, Castro called Kennedy "a capitalist whom we can talk." Castro further said of the American president, "I believe Kennedy is sincere... He still has the possibility of being, in the eyes of history, the greatest President of the United States." Castro told Daniel that he was in no rush to start negotiations with the U.S. but saw positive steps in their meetings. They would meet again in two days for further discussions; November 22, 1963.

Castro was with Daniel when they learned the news of Kennedy's assassination. "This is bad news," lamented Castro. "There is the end of your mission for peace." Castro asked Daniel what the knew about the new president, Lyndon Johnson, and what control he had over the CIA.

While the Kennedy-Atwood-Daniel back channel negotiations were going on, Castro lashed out at the United States. On September 7, Castro had a meeting with reporter Daniel Hacker of the *Associated Press* at the Brazilian embassy during at three-hour interview. In that meeting, Castro issued the following warning to the United States. "We are prepared to fight them and answer in kind. United States leaders should think that if they are aiding terrorist plans to eliminate Cuban leaders, they themselves will not be safe."

Conspiracy theorists involving the Cuban connection to the Kennedy assassination, point to this statement as Castro's rational for being behind the president's death. This statement has other, important implications as well. Did Castro know of the CIA-Mafia plans to kill him? Was he privy to the Kennedy administrations "Operation Mongoose" and the ZR/RIFLE program? Did Castro have a double agent in the Cuban exile community, feeding him sensitive information? And could that double agent have been Santos Trafficante? It seems reasonable from all the facts that the answer is yes. Except for the most critical point. Did Castro order the assassination of President Kennedy? The answer to that query, based on the historical record is NO. If it was proved beyond a reasonable doubt that Castro was behind the assassination, Cuba would have been invaded by the U.S. and the Castro government toppled. I believe that Castro truly wanted a political accommodation with the U.S. in November 1963, and was working to that end.

The use of both the New York Mafia in the war years, and the CIA-Mafia plots of the early 1960s, to kill Castro, had its roots just after World War 2 when the newly formed CIA began to branch out, using a series of covert actions to stop the spread of communism that had broken out at the beginning of the cold war. Most of these covert operations were not publicized to the

American public, and it would take historians years to unravel the complete story. One of the groups whom the CIA, in the late 1940,s and early 1950s, began to cultivate for the first time, were certain members of the Corsican Mafia based in the port city of Marseille, France. This was the start of the so-called "French Connection," whose ramifications would, over time, entangle the United States in the drug business that would spread like the tentacles of an eagle, across the globe, culminating in the heroin trade based in Southeast Asia.

Chapter 3:

The CIA Goes Worldwide & the Beginning of the Heroin Connection

President Harry Truman signed the legislation that created the CIA via the National Security Act of 1947. The task of the CIA under Truman's tutelage was much different than the CIA of the 21st century. In 1947, Truman envisioned that the CIA would be a collection and evaluation agency that would provide the president information on foreign countries in order for the United States to formulate its foreign policy. Over the past five decades, however, as times changed, future presidents decided to use the CIA as more of a covert, para-military arm in order to fight the cold war.

On December 22, 1963, long after Harry Truman left the White House, and was in permanent retirement, he wrote an article in the *Washington Post,* spelling out his discomfort over how the agency he created, had changed, all for the wrong reasons.

As with modern day president's, Harry Truman wrote that the president needed to have all the best information available to them from a variety of sources. He said that information reaching the president's desk often times reflected the views of the writer or the government department who was supplying the data. He further stated that it was vital that the intelligence given to the president was being used to influence or lead a chief executive to make the wrong political decision.

The former president, in his usual crusty, no-nonsense way, chastised the CIA on how it was being run, and where he believed it had deviated from its original mandate. "For some time, I have been disturbed by the way the CIA had been diverted from its original assignment. It has become an operational and at times a policy-making arm of government. This has led to trouble and may have compounded our difficulty in several explosive areas. I never had any thought that when I set up the CIA that it would be injected into peacetime cloak and dagger operations. Some of the complications and embarrassment I think we have experienced are in part attributable to the fact that it is being interpreted as a symbol of sinister and mysterious foreign intrigue-and a subject for cold war enemy propaganda."

"...But there are now some searching questions that need to be answered. I therefore, would like to see the CIA be restored to its original assignment as the intelligence arm of the President, and that whatever else it can properly perform in that special field-and that its operational duties be terminated or properly used elsewhere.

"We have grown up as a nation, respected for our institutions and for our ability to maintain a free and open society. There is something about the way the CIA has been functioning that is causing a shadow over our historic position and I feel that we need to correct it."

Harry got it right. Other presidents, as time went on, felt differently.

The origins of America's cold war struggle against the Soviet Union, came not on the battle field, but in the press. In 1946, a little known diplomat serving in the American embassy in Moscow, George Kennan, made history, in a detailed, yet controversial narrative regarding America's role toward the Soviet Union. His policy of "containment," proved to be the catalyst that drove American foreign policy toward the Russians for the next forty years.

In 1946, when both the State and Treasury Department's sent instructions to Moscow calling for an "interpretive analysis of recent Soviet statements about international financial institutions for the purpose of fashioning American policy," the job of fulfilling the request went to George Kennan, who was the deputy to U.S. Ambassador to Moscow, W. Averell Harriman.

Kennan's reply to Washington arrived on February 22, 1947. His narrative consisted of an 8,000-word document, divided into five parts. In short, Kennan's cable #511, or the "Long Telegram," as it was called, "signaled the death knell of the war-time alliance between the Soviet Union and the United States.

Kennan's "Long Telegram" sent shock waves throughout he

State Department, which was known mostly for its "diplomatese" when it came to the writing of official reports. Kennan soon found himself back home in the United States where he took a leave of absence from his Moscow duties. He began teaching at the National War College, and was soon a popular man among the top policy makers in D.C.

He was contacted by James Forrestal, the Secretary of the Navy, to write a report on how the Long Telegram would affect the United States' lengthily foreign policy strategy vis-a-vi the Soviet Union. Upon completion, Kennan handed the report to Forrestal who read it with much interest. Forrestal sent the article to the influential magazine, *Foreign Affairs,* which immediately accepted the piece. Signed under the pseudonym "X," the article caused a major stir in diplomatic circles. The "X" piece said that, "The main element of any U.S. policy toward the Soviet Union must be that of a long-term, patient but firm and vigilant containment of Russian expansive tendencies." Soviet pressure against the free institutions of the Western world is something that can be contained by the adroit and vigilant application of counter-force at a series of constantly shifting geographical and political points."

In the end, the "X" article called for a new American policy of "containment" against the Soviet Union, using all available means, including both overt and covert operations. Soon, Kennan would be responsible for the running of many clandestine missions, headed by the CIA in the late 1940s, and early 1950s, against the Soviet Union. Many of these missions were operational failures, but the seeds set forth in both the Long Telegram, and the X article, written by Kennan, were the nucleus of American foreign policy during the cold war. The first country to feel the CIA's new secret hand was Italy.

By 1947, the cold war between the U.S. and the Soviet Union was in full swing. The former wartime alliance that pitted both nations against Hitler's Germany was now a matter of history, as both sides vied for domination of Europe. The first non-military engagement between the once war time allies took place over the upcoming 1948 elections in Italy between the pro-American Christian Democrats and the Communist inspired PCI party.

In Washington, the Truman administration was deeply worried that the Italian elections would bring into power the communists, thus, adding another country to Moscow's list of client states in the heart of Europe.

As part of the shake up in U.S. intelligence, the newly created National Security Council directed that a program of covert action be implemented to counter a communist victory at the poles in Italy. In a December 9, 1947 meeting of the National Security Council, the top members suggested to the president that he sign off on a policy directive called "Coordination of Foreign Intelligence Information Measures," a.k.a, NSC-4. NSC-4 empowered the Secretary of State to co-ordinate overseas information activities designed to counter communism. A topsecret annex to NSC-4-NSC4A—instructed the director of the CIA to undertake covert psychological activities in pursuit of the aims set forth in NSC-4. It simply directed the CIA to undertake covet actions, and to ensure, through liaison with State and Defense, that the resulting operations were consistent with American policy.

The consequences of NSC-4 was the beginning of the policy of covert action on behalf of the CIA which would stay in place to the present day.

As planning for the Italian election campaign at CIA got underway, the new director of the CIA, Roscoe Hillenkotter, made his disapproval of such actions known to his colleagues. Hillenkotter was apprehensive that any "blown" operations would only diminish the future ability of the agency to perform such tasks. However, President Truman overruled him, and the covert action plan was a go. Two of the instruments used by the CIA to undermine the Italian elections were "black propaganda," providing false information to the communists, and "psychological operations," making them doubt their own thoughts and beliefs.

As electionday neared, CIA agents infiltrated the PCI camp, learning their secrets and reporting back to Washington. CIA men gave 'walking around" money to Christian Democratic candidates to get out the vote, paid off election officials to alter voting rolls, published bogus pamphlets that smeared the opposition candidates, described a number of the communist candidates as anti-Church, and planted false stories concerning their personal lives.

As an operational rule, the CIA could not officially pay off their assets through regular monetary channels. Instead, they funneled the money through a source called the "Economic

Stabilization Fund," a holdover organization that dated back to World War 2. The use of the ESF was the brainchild of John Synder, the secretary of the treasury. Using the doctrine of "plausible deniability," the CIA could refuse to take the blame if the operation was discovered or any untoward event made their secret deal public. A total of $10 million was withdrawn from ESF accounts and then "laundered" through other banking institutions which were then "donated" to front organizations in Italy.

As the program took shape, it was learned from sources inside the Soviet camp that the Soviet leadership did not take seriously the information provided to them by their own agents in Italy that the U.S. was providing millions of dollars directly to the non-communists. Instead, they believed that the money was coming from Vatican sources.

Another long-standing precedent for future CIA operations began in the Italian election campaign. The CIA station chief in Rome, not the U.S. ambassador, ran the entire operation. The local State Department members, working out of the Rome embassy, took no part in the campaign.

When the election was finally over on April 18, 1948, the pro-American Christian Democrats won 307 out of a total of 574 seats in parliament. The CIA's first covert program was a complete success, denying the communists a victory they so baldy coveted.

The next covert step the CIA took in its undeclared war against the Soviet Union, was dubbed "Operation Valuable," a mission to overthrow the communist government of Albania. The mission was doomed from the start, with the infiltration of a top, undercover Soviet mole, Kim Philby, passing the plans for the operation directly to Moscow.

In 1947, the first, limited effort to topple the Albanian government was taken by the British without any luck. A small number of men were covertly sent into Albania but nothing significant came out of it. In the wake of this failure, the British contacted the Americans and proposed a far greater, joint effort. To their relief, the Truman administration agreed to their covert campaign.

Joint planning for "Operation Valuable" began in earnest in 1949. The American side of the operation was run by the Office of Policy Coordination which was the covert arm of the newly created

CIA. Being a joint operation, the British were representated in planning the mission by George Jellico, recently of the elite Special Air Services. The other member of the British delegation was Adrian "Kim' Philby. Unknown to the men on the panel was that Philby was working for the Russians as a spy, and had been doing so since World War 2 began. It was Philby who ultimately betrayed the operation, leading to the deaths of many allied agents.

The American delegation was comprised of Robert Joyce, who had foreign policy experience, and Franklin Lindsay, a veteran of the OSS. Along with Jellico, neither Lindsay or Joyce knew of Philby's treachery. The technical name of this allied group was called the Anglo-American Policy Committee.

Recruits for the operation were picked from the Albanian refuge camps in Italy, Egypt and other places in Europe where men who were loyal to King Zog, the previous ruler of Albania, could be found. The CIA and the British SIS (Secret Intelligence Service), ran the operation behind the scenes, paying the men and giving them training in the covert arts. Their instruction in para-miliary activities took them to such places as Cyprus and Malta. The CIA officer assigned to oversee American interests in the Albanian operation was Michael Burke. Burke served in the wartime OSS and would, many years later, become president of the New York Yankees.

Landings of allied agents into Albania took place in the spring of 1950. Subsequent drops of agents followed in the months to come. While the unsuspecting allied solders were being dropped into Albania, Kim Philby was keeping Moscow abreast of every detail of the operation. Upon landing, these unlucky men were immediately captured and underwent tireless interrogation. In time, a few of these men were able to make their way back to allied lines, and reported the blown operations.

During the next two years, further drops of agents into Albania continued, but with the same lack of success. It was now obvious in allied intelligence circles that something or someone was betraying the airdrops. Due to lack of any progress in wrecking havoc inside Albania, the operation was ended in 1952.

In his book on the history of the CIA, *The Agency: The Rise and Decline of the CIA,* author John Ranleigh writes about the Albanian operation. "The enterprise was doomed because of the campaign against Albania, sitting in Washington on the Anglo-American Special Policy Committee, was Kim Philby. They always knew we were coming."

* * *

When DA Thomas Dewey released Lucky Luciano from prison after World War 2 for services rendered, he had no idea that his decision that fateful day, would have, years later, on the trade of illegal drugs, mostly heroin based, from Southeast Asia across the world. With the release of Luciano, the Mafia delved into a new, lucrative base of operations, one, that it had previously shunned.

Luciano began his decades long foray into the illegal narcotics industry when he was able to use a supply of legally obtained heroin from a pharmaceutical company in Italy called Schiaparelli. Over a period of four years, Luciano was able to divert about 700 kilos of heroin for mob use from covert laboratories based in Sicily and Marseille, France. With his new outlet, he now had no need for the use of the Schiaparelli company.

With Luciano now firmly established in the heroin trade out of Marseille and Sicily, he began to branch out and made new, worldwide contacts with people in the trade who were willing to provide the raw opium that he needed. He traveled to Beirut, Lebanon and made contract with a man named Sami El Khoury. El Khoury was one of the Middle East's major exporters of morphine base and they both made a secret pact that would make both of them very rich men. Using his considerable influence in Lebanon, El Khoury was able, through bribes to people at the Beirut airport, Lebanese customs, the nations narcotics police, and the anti-subversive section of the Lebanese police department, allowed the import of raw opium from Turkey to Lebanon, unimpeded. The raw opium was then transhipped to processing plants in both Marseille and Sicily.

Luciano also made arrangements with local fishermen who came into his orbit, to allow processed opium to be transported from their boats which were then smuggled into Italy along the nations rugged, unprotected coast. From there, the drugs were shipped inland to their final destination.

Once in his hands, the base was transformed into raw heroin at labs owned by Luciano and his family. One of these was located in Palermo, beginning in 1949. This particular lab went unnoticed until 1954 when a newspaper in Rome printed a picture of the lab. The headline under the captain read, "Textiles and Sweets on the Drug Route." The factory was quickly closed and its chemists were smuggled out of the country.

Like any good businessman, Lucky used good logistics to ship his heroin across the globe. Using his shipping contacts, he was able to send the dope to various places, such as Germany, Italy, Paris, the Untied States, before winding up at his labs in Marseille. One of the final destinations for the drugs was Cuba, only 90 miles from the coast of Florida. Over time, Cuba would become one of the principal centers for drug distribution, and a home base for the mob in its clandestine drug dealings.

The one man whom Luciano turned to in order to run his worldwide drug empire, was his old friend, Meyer Lansky. The association they first made during their work for the Navy in World War 2, would now branch out to other, more lucrative endeavors. Over time, Lansky was to become the top money manager for the mob and its worldwide interests. During the decades of the 1940s and 1950s, Lansky was given more responsibility vis-a-vi the drug market by Luciano. He was the one who negotiated the secret deals with both the major narcotics smugglers and buyers in Marseille and Cuba. He was also instrumental in forging links with Santos Trafficante of Florida who was a major narcotics smuggler during this time. Most of the drugs that came to the Untied States arrived from Cuba, and Trafficante was the man to see in order to get the drugs safely to market in American cities. Santo Trafficante's name would come up in the events surrounding the Kennedy assassination, and a government panel that investigated the crime said that he had the "means, motive and opportunity" to kill the president.

Cuba in the 1950s, was run by a brutal dictator named Flugencio Batista, who was in cahoots with the mob. Batista took bribes from the mob in order for them to safely operate their lucrative casinos on that bustling island. Lansky was the prime mover in organizing the opening of the casinos in Havana and managed the take for Luciano before, and after he was released from jail. Luciano was supposed to have deposited a grand sum of

$ 3 million for Batista in his own, personal Swiss bank account, and also provided both Batista and his main cohorts in Havana, a tidy profit of 50% percent of the casino profits.[13]

While Luciano was setting up his new heroin connection, he was able, in October 1946, to quietly slip into Cuba. He wanted to see how his drug business was going, and like any good CEO, took a hands on approach to his domain. During that time, Luciano hosted one of the biggest crime meetings in decades, the co called "Havana Connection," to discuss various business, including the narcotics trade. Luciano asked Lansky to bring in all his fellow mobsters and a who's who of the top mobsters flocked to the warm sun and rolling palm trees to discuss business. Among those in attendance were old acquaintances of Luciano, including, Frank Costello, Vito Genovese, Santo Trafficante, Carlos Marcello (another prominent name to surface in the Kennedy assassination aftermath), Joe Bonanno, Joe Profaci, Moe Dalitz, among others.

One man who made an appearance at the time of the Havana Conference was an up and coming singer of Italian origin, Frank Sinatra. Sinatra was there to sing for the mobsters, but there were reports that Sinatra had been seen carrying a case carrying $2,000,000 for Luciano. Another item that Frank brought with him was a gold cigarette case for Luciano.[14]

One of the unwritten aspects of the Havana Conference was for Luciano to re-enforce his dominant position as the man in charge of the Mafia in the United States. During his time in prison, Luciano gave the job of running the mob to Frank Costello. He now wanted to reassert his position as the number one capo before anyone else could claim that title. For his part, Vito Genovese wanted Luciano to resign and passed the word around to the other attendees. Luciano heard about Vito's push and nipped the incipient revolt in the bud.

As far as the narcotics business was concerned, it was here that Luciano suffered a vote of no confidence. Luciano, for whatever reason, wanted to disengage the mob from the narcotics trade. He faced fierce opposition from the other bosses who did not want to divest itself of a huge source of steady cash. It was decided that

---

13 Sifakis,Carl. *The Mafia Encyclopedia.* Page 179.

14 Ibid. Page 149.

each of the Mafia families would make their own decision as to what action they'd take as far as the drug trade was concerned.

What really prompted Luciano to try to abandon the drug trade was his fierce determination to get back into the United States. He had business there, and he did not want to squander that opportunity. He'd do anything to get back in the good graces of Uncle Sam. After all, hadn't he done them a great favor when they needed him?

Another decision that was made at the meeting was the fate of Benjamin "Bugsy" Siegel. Siegel was a one time partner and friend of both Lansky and Luciano but Siegel had by now, skimmed off huge profits from a casino called the Flamingo that was being built in Las Vegas. Bugsy was becoming too much of an embarrassment and a "hit" was ordered to silence him. Bugsy was killed by an assassin as he sat in the home of his girlfriend, Virginia Hill, in Beverly Hills in 1947.

While Luciano was conducting his business in Havana, the United States government was keeping a watchful eye on the dapper Luciano. The Justice Department had long been watching Luciano's dealings, especially went it came to his new, profitable drug business. Justice had given the responsibility of investigating Luciano to the Federal Bureau of Narcotics, headed by Harry Anslinger. Anslinger had informants keeping a watchful eye on Luciano from their perch at the Hotel Nacional and even tapped his home phone. The FBN agent who was in charge of keeping tabs on Luciano's Cuban sojourn was J. Ray Olivera. Olivera had informants in the Cuban National Police who provided him with detailed information on what Lucky was up to. One piece of information that was passed along to Agent Olivera was plot on Luciano's life.

The murder attempt took place on either December 27 or 28, 1946 when Luciano and his guests were having dinner at the Gran Casino Nacional in a Havana suburb. The gunmen tried unsuccessfully to kill Luciano, but Luciano left the hotel through a back entrance and was unharmed. The gunmen quickly fled the hotel, and into a waiting car. Cuban police gave chase but they escaped.

The next night, Luciano was having dinner at the restaurant when an incident took place that made him stand up and take notice of the precarious position he was in. One of his dinner companions was Chester Simms who was the floor manger at the Gran Casino Nacional. Two officers of the National Police came up to their table, and after a few words, told both Luciano and Simms that they were under arrest. The other people at the table, all high powered Cuban officials, brought the cops aside and gave them payoff money. After the conversation was over, all charges were suddenly dropped. Before departing, the cops told both Luciano and Simms to "Be careful. Those killers from last night are still out there, and they may try again."[15]

In the wake of the attempt on his life, Luciano was assigned two bodyguards who were his constant companions.

In Washington, the heat was getting so intense that it was necessary to have something done about Luciano and after much haggling, the State Department put in a formal request to the Cuban government to have Lucian deported. The Cuban regime balked at first, with Cuban President Grau saying at one point that the Luciano matter "was of no importance." The request was denied, but the U.S. government put more, intense pressure on the Cuban's to do something about Luciano. Harry Anslinger of the FBN, contacted President Truman and brought him up to speed on the Luciano case. The president agreed and in a forceful step, ordered the State Department to stop the sale of all medicine to Cuba until Luciano was deported.

Truman's order made frontpage news in the *New York Times,* and an editorial accompanying the story read as follows:

"There are hundreds of old Mob just waiting for the day their master can return. It is an interesting coincidence that in the three months since Luciano has been in Cuba, we received in this country, the first large shipment of European heroin—$250,000 worth—We believe the best place for him is that place most distant from this nation. He should not be permitted to reside where he can exercise his dangerous influence over the American underworld."[16]

Lucky hired a Cuban attorney to fight the charges but nothing

---

15 English, T.J. *Havana Nocturne: How the Mob Owned Cuba... And Then Lost It to the Revolution.* William Morrow & Co., New York, 2008, Page 45.

16 Ibid. Page 47.

came of the venture. He told both Meyer Lansky and Frank Costello that "Things don't look good."

On February 23, while he was having lunch, he was approached by six police officers who put him under arrest. He was put in holding prison called Triscorina Immigration Camp while paper work was being prepared for his deportation.

In an interesting aside, Santo Trafficante, the mob boss who was implicated in the Kennedy assassination, and who worked with the CIA to kill Castro, was himself held prisoner in the Triscorina Immigration Camp. While waiting deportation from Cuba, Trafficante was supposed to have been visited by an American by the name of Jack Ruby in 1959. On November 28, 1963, six days after the assassination of the president, the CIA sent a memo to President Johnson's aide, McGeorge Bundy, confirming Ruby's meeting with Trafficante in Cuba.

Another person who said he saw Ruby visit Trafficante in Triscorina, was an Englishman by the name of John Wilson Hudson, who was also serving time in the jail.

Meyer Lansky tried to intervene with ex-President Batista who, by now, was living in exile in Dayton Beach, Florida. Batista had no more influence with President Ramon Grau and Luciano's fate was sealed. He quietly left Cuba on March 29, on board a Turkish ship, the *SS Bakir.*

Luciano's departure from Cuba, made Meyer Lansky the undisputed kingpin on the island and he returned to Italy in disgrace. However, the narcotics industry that he and the rest of the mob decided to get into, would now go world-wide, bringing the CIA and the United States government squarely in its tentacles.

In the 1950s, the Sicilian Mafia began ridding themselves of the heroin trade and turned it over to their brethren, the Marseille Corsican syndicate network that would eventually take over the entire operation. The turnover to the Marseille syndicate had the blessing of Lucky Luciano who was now living in Italy. Over time, the once, trusted Schiaparelli heroin link began to dwindle and Luciano now had to decide how to proceed with his clandestine business. The Sicilian gangsters were not very good businessmen and their hold on the drug trade was beginning to take a beating. Luciano himself, if the current state of affairs continued, would be liable for arrest, something he did not relish. In Italy, a number of the heroin labs were being raided and the precious heroin supplies were confiscated by the government.

In a bold decision, Luciano decided to shift his source of supply to the bustling port city of Marseille, France. The Corsican mob dominated the waterfront and its members had a hand, along with the CIA, in breaking up a number of strikes that took place, disrupting the loading, and off-loading of much needed goods and supplies, (including drugs), by the longshoreman. For his part, Meyer Lansky came to Rome where he paid a visit to Luciano to discuss the drug business. He then went to Zurich, Switzerland where he had a meeting with a number of Swiss bankers with the assistance of John Pullman, and old friend. Pullman, who ran Lansky's money matters in Europe (including the deposit of profits from the dope business), used a number of Swiss banks to lauder the funds through untraceable accounts, a practice that is still in use today. As time went on, Lansky and his group were able to buy the Exchange and Investment Bank of Geneva, Switzerland to launder their money.

As his European trip continued, Lansky arrived in France and made his way to Marseille where he met with a number of highranking Corsican gangsters whom he put on his payroll. During these talks, Lansky and the Corsicans made a secret deal whereby they would serve as a conduit for Lansky-Luciano to bring and ship heroin to labs in Marseille for processing and re-shipment aborad.

The new Corsican connection did not go unnoticed by local authorities, and on May 23, 1951, French police raided a narcotics lab, the first of many that they would eventually seize. Over the next five plus months, French police discovered two other labs and confiscated the contents.

The genesis of Marseille as the home of the so-called Corsican connection and the drug trade that would flourish years later, had its roots in he 1920s with the rise of two major gangsters, Francois Spirito and Paul Bonnaventure Carbone. The first joint venture was the establishment of a house of prostitution in Cairo, Egypt in the late 1920s. During the decade of the 1920s, both men returned to Marseille where they opened a series of brothels and made certain arraignments with the local politicians who eagerly agreed to their financial terms, in return for letting them run their illegal business unmolested.

In 1931, Carbone and Spirito made a secret deal with Simon Sabiani, the Fascist deputy mayor of Marseille, who agreed to appoint Carbone's brother as the director of a city stadium, as well as letting local city workers to be employed by the two men. For their part, Carbone and Spirito organized a group of Fascist hoodlums who spearheaded violent street demonstrations in the city. All this played out amid the ever-growing rise of Fascism in Europe, especially in Hitler's Germany, along with other French Fascist groups who were trying to overthrow the government of France. Throughout the decade of the 1930s, there were a series of violent demonstrations between the Fascists and Communists and Socialists groups who were on the side of the French Republic.

In February, 1934, Marseille itself saw bloody clashes between Fascist and anti-Fascist demonstrations stirred up by Carbone and Spirito that led to a series of huge street fights between leftist dock workers and union men. As the rioting took place, Carbone and Spirito ordered their loyal men into the streets who fired on the crowds. As the rioting grew, the French national police had to intervene in order to stop the ever-growing chaos.

In the late 1930s, an election was held in Marseille that voted in a Socialist candidate opposed to Sabiani and a temporary truce went into effect.

However, as the late 1930s and 1940s approached, both men broke into new, fertile grounds in the city. By the late 1930s, they started their first heroin lab in the city and when the Spanish Civil War erupted, they began supplying arms to either side.

With the fall of France to Germany in 1940, a new, large French resistance movement began to take shape. Marseille grew as one of the prime resistance movements against Nazi rule and the Germans began cracking down hard on anyone who got in their way.

Being the opportunists they were, and more importantly, seeing where the bread was buttered, both Spirito and Carbone made a secret deal with the Germans to aid them in the destruction of the resistance movement. On July 14, 1942, the resistance brazenly attacked the headquarters of a German political organization in Marseille called the PPF. Following the attack, Carbone and Spirito gave the names of the gunmen to the Germans.

As the war continued and the Resistance grew stronger, the power of both Spirito and Carbone began to wane. In 1943, Carbone was killed as he traveled to Marseille when his train was attacked by a heavily-armed Resistance group.

After the allies landed on French soil on June 6, 1944 (the day of the Normandy landings), Spirito hurriedly left for Spain with Sabiani.

Spirito emigrated to the United States and for years thereafter, took part in the heroin trade between New York and Marseille. However, three years later, his luck ran out as he was arrested on a heroin smuggling charge and served two years in an Atlanta Federal Prison. After his release, he returned to France where he was tried for being a Nazi collaborator. He served a minium eight months in jail and over time, his role as a major kingpin in the drug trade in Marseille waned.

During the 1950s, the CIA used its considerable power and prestige to influence its worldwide fight against communism, especially in Europe which was the center point for the drugs that were smuggled from other parts to the world for refinement and transshipment. According to various historical records, the CIA began a drug smuggling operation shortly after the end of World War 2 using the resources of the powerful labor organization, the AFL-CIO, and most particularly, its main operative, Irving Brown. Irving Brown's name has been linked in the famous "French Connection" heroin smuggling operation that took place in the mid-1960s, and was made famous by Hollywood in a huge move of the same name staring Gene Hackman. During that operation, a link between Brown and a Corsican labor leader by the name of Maurice Castellani was established.[17]

Narcotics Agent Tom Tripodi, referred to this newly formed CIA network as the "Brown-Angleton" connection. He was speaking of the legendary CIA Counter-intelligence agent, James Jesus Angleton, a fixture at the CIA since the agency was first formed. Tripodi said that both Angleton and Brown ran the operation in cooperation with certain members of the FBN.

---

[17] Douglas Valentine, *The Strength of the Pack: The Personalities, Politics and Espionage Intrigues that Shaped the DEA*, Trine Day Publishers, Walterville, OR, 2008, Page 13.

Another person who allegedly worked with both men was Mario Broad, a high placed attorney who had definitely been linked to the CIA during this time period.

In his groundbreaking book on the history of the FBN, author Douglas Valentine says that Angleton, Broad, and FBN Agent Charles Siragusa, worked together in Italy during World War 2. Charles Siragusa served as the head of the FBN in Rome and also served as the FBN's liaison with the CIA for many years. It is believed that Angleton recruited Siragusa to recruit certain Corsican and mob-connected people to work for the CIA.

Brown's initial foray for the CIA in the heroin connection business began, when he used CIA money to organize certain leftist groups and unions in Marseille and hired both Italian and Corsican's for his own purposes, one of which was to disrupt a strike by communist longshoremen in Marseille.

A French author by the name of Alain Jaubert wrote that in the French city of Bordeaux in 1952, that a noted Corsican gangster of the period named Antonine Guerini had a meeting with Irving Brown, a chemist who worked for Guerini, and two other drug smugglers. Jaubert further reported that Guerini brought Brown into contact with certain high placed Mafia leaders in Italy.

Antoine Guerini's name would play a huge role in the investigation of the assassination of JFK by writer and researcher Steve Rivele. According to several sources gleamed by Rivele, the plot to kill JFK was offered to Guerini who passed it along to other members of the Corsican mob in Marseille (more, detailed information on Antoine Guerini is descried later in this book).

Irving Brown had been the AFL-CIO's chief overseas representative from 1945 to 1962, but his claim to fame (or infamy), would be connected to a Corsican drug smuggler named Etienne Tarditi. In the 1950s Tarditi worked as a middleman for Lebanese drug smugglers and was able to bring their drugs into France. The morphine that he helped transport was then converted to heroin. For his part, Tarditi recruited certain diplomats who were in his favor to smuggle the heroin out of the country, mostly to the United States.

Over time, Tarditi's operation began to fall apart. This all happened when a rival smuggler bragged to an FBN agent who was stationed in Beirut that a certain diplomat who went by the name of "Maurice," was in the process of carrying heroin to the United States. The real name of the man was Maurice Rosal Bron, the Guatemalan Ambassador to the Netherlands. Tarditi blackmailed Rosal Bron, who had a penchant for having sex with young boys to use him for his nefarious purposes. Often times, both Tarditi and Rosal Bron traveled together, and on one occasion, the end came swiftly for both men. In October 1960, when they landed in New York City, FBN agents busted them.

For the FBN, the heroin bust proved to be substantial, with over 100 kilograms being taken off the streets. An unexpected fallout from the bust came when Tarditi told investigators that one of his sources was none other than Irving Brown.

For the next decade, FBN agents had a field day combing through the intelligence provided to them by Tarditi, and one piece of information would prove to be one of the most important cases they ever worked on; the so-called French Connection. In 1962, a task force of made up of both NYPD officers and FBN agents arrested a mobster named Patsy Fuca, and his father Joe, a noted French heroin smuggler named Francois Scaglia (who was also one of the leaders of the Trio Canards Gang that operated out of Paris), and a courier of Scaglia's named Jacques Anglevin, who was a popular TV host in France. Another person who was part of the French Connection operation but was never caught, was Jean Jehan.

A second arrest from the case came in March 1961, when a pretty, Air France stewardess named Simone Christman was arrested by U.S. Customs agents when she was caught smuggling heroin in her bra. When she was being interrogated by police she said that she believed that the powder she was carrying was perfume base, and that it had been given to her by a man she knew only as "Mr. Mueller" whom she met in Paris. Miss Christman was sentenced in March 1962, to four years in jail, but she was released before her time was up by persons unknown.

A source familiar with the Christman case said that she was a spy for the Secret Army Organization (OAS), the group of French soldiers who were battling the forces of French President Charles de Gaulle over the fate of Algeria, a long time French colony. It was an open secret during those days that the OAS got a large portion of its funds via the drug trade.

FBN agents who handled the case said that they were not allowed to investigate why Miss Christman was released from jail and were told that U.S. Customs Agents were handling the case. The CIA, it is believed, by many sources, were the responsible party for blocking the investigation, and they did so in order to hide their role in the OAS drug-smuggling scheme.

In one of the unscripted moments from the French Connection investigation, the real identify of "Mr. Mueller' was finally revealed. In April 1962, Etienne Tarditi, in a plea deal with the feds, named Irving Brown in the Christman-Rosal caper.

Through dogged investigative work, FBN agent Andrew Tartaglino, in May 1962, began an investigation of Irving Brown and came up with some tantalizing information. It seems that Brown was a regular customer in a Paris restaurant owned by George Bayon. Bayon and Brown were friends, and Tartaglino found out that Bayon used the alias "Mueller," and, more importantly, that his place of business was frequently used by drugrunners to "recruit" diplomats, like Ambassador Rosal.

In his investigation regarding Brown, Agent Tartaglino found out from other intelligence sources that Irving Brown had, over the years, been given "port privileges" in the port of New York. That meant that his baggage was never checked by customs agents when he arrived in the United States. As an aside, it was learned that Irving Brown's wife, Lilly, had once worked as a secretary for a noted CIA operative named Carmel Offie, who owned an import-export business in New York.

From here, the story gets a little more convoluted. At the time of the arrest of Ambassador Rosal, authorities found in his pocket the address of Stig Wennerstrom, the former Swedish military attache' to the Unites States. One of Stig Wennerstrom' colleagues was Philippe de Vosjoli who was the French intelligence service's liaison with the CIA, namely James Angleton's Counterintelligence Division. The story goes that Wennerstrom was connected with various French intelligence officers who were stationed in the Washington, D.C. area, and that the SDECE (French intelligence) had been penetrated by the Soviet KGB. Angleton had been an associate of Irving Brown over the years when Brown was setting his up his contacts with the French underworld, including many of the Marseille drug smugglers.

Angleton then proceeded to penetrate the French drug-smuggling network in order to monitor any involvement by the SDECE and the French underworld.

Irving Brown was well connected with the CIA and the OSS, dating back to the late 1940s. At one point in his career, Brown worked as the AFL's representative to the War Production Board during World War 2, and had a clandestine role with the infant CIA when it was founded in 1947.

Brown set up shop in Marseille where he founded a number of leftist labor unions in that port city with Pierre Ferri-Pisani who was a drug smuggler in Marseille. Over time, Brown's CIA case officer, Paul Sakwa, introduced Brown to Antoine Guerini. Ferri also was supposed to have introduced Brown to Maurice "Le Petit" Castellani. Castellani took part in the French Resistance in World War 2 and headed the Trios Canards Gang.

According to all the available evidence, Brown was associated with a number of well-placed French narcotics smugglers in Marseille during the late 1940s and early 1950s, and had established himself with the CIA, not as an agent per se, but as a wellplaced intelligence asset for some time.

The noted French writer Alain Jaubert said that the Trois Canards Gang was established by one of the most important and later corrupt French policeman of the day, Robert Blemant. Blemant had a rather checkered past, having associations with both the French police and the Corsican syndicate based in Marseille.

What is significant about Robert Blemant is that his name has come up in the aftermath of the Kennedy assassination as possibly being the CIA's prime assassin, QJ/WIN. (The following chapters will have a much more detailed description of Robert Blemant and his possible role in the Kennedy assassination, as well as the events leading up to the murder of Patrice Lumumba in the Congo in 1960).

There is circumstantial evidence linking both Robert Blemant and Irving Brown in the secret machinations of the heroin smuggling business in Marseille during those hectic times. CIA Agent Paul Sakwa has hinted that Brown had made contact with certain elements of the Sicilian Mafia at the same time that Robert Blemant, the founder of the Trios Canards Gang established their covert relationship with the U.S. Mafia.[18]

As mentioned before, one of the most influential Corsican gangsters in Marseille at the time was Antoine Guerini, whose links to Irving Brown brought him in contact with the CIA. The Guerini family dominated the heroin trade for many years and it consisted of Antoine, his brothers Barthelemy, who also went by the name "Meme," Lucien, Francois, Pascal, and Pierre. From the 1930s to the 1960s, through violence and intimidation, the Guerini clan rose to the top as far as the people to see when it came to running drugs in Marseille. Throughout their bloody rule, Antoine headed the clan, and made all the major decisions when it came to their illicit business dealings. In time, the Guerini's would become the premier Corsican heroin dealers and ran the Corsican mob in France.

The Guerini's operated a number of heroin labs in Marseille and successfully facilitated the smuggling of opium base from Turkey and other countries in the Middle East. The Guerini's cut deals with other, lesser drug dealers in France and they had to ante up part of their gross profits to them. They used the services of Jo Cesari who was of the best chemists to work out of Marseille during that time. Cesari ran most of the heroin labs in the city until 1972.

In order to successfully operate their drug business, the Guerini brothers made secret alliances with the local Socialist politicians who dominated Marseille politics at the time. One of their principal cohorts was Gaston Deferee, who was the Mayor of Marseille, beginning in 1953. In 1969, Defree was the Socialist party candidate for president of France. They also made secret contact with the CIA through Irving Brown.

Another man who dominated the heroin trade during the 1950s, and was to play an important role in the assassination of JFK, was Tampa, Florida mob boss, Santo Trafficante. Trafficante's real power came after Meyer Lansky was deported from Cuba and fled to Italy. During that time period, Santo Trafficante ruled his mob empire from Florida to the Caribbean. In the 1940s, he participated with both Lansky and Lucky Luciano in heroin smuggling and

---

18 "The CIA, Irving Brown, and Drug Smuggling as Political Warfare." Douglas Valentine. World-wide web.

took over the family business in 1954 upon the death of the father. Santo Junior now had control over all mob operations in Florida and no one did business in the state without his blessing. Trafficante was one of the main narcotics facilitators in Cuba until the revolution in 1959 that brought Fidel Castro to power. At one point, Castro had Trafficante incarcerated in a Cuban jail until his release under mysterious circumstances.

While he was safely encased in Cuba, Trafficante was able to move into other, more lucrative, illegal business ventures, besides heroin. Using his underworld connections in Florida, Trafficante expanded into the bolitia lottery, which was a Cuban numbers game. Over time, Trafficante hired a number of men who would become heroin couriers between Cuba and Miami. Trafficante would soon be able to have enough influence in the illegal narcotics trade to allow him to bring heroin from Europe into Miami through dealers in Latin America.

Trafficante is now dead, but author Alfred McCoy, who wrote a seminal book on the worldwide drug trade some years ago, wrote this about Trafficante, "At fifty-seven, Trafficante is one of the most effective organized crime leaders still operating in the United States. Avoiding the ostentatious life style of Cadillacs and diamonds that is so attractive to many mafiosi, Trafficante cultivates the austerity of the old Sicilian Dons. But unlike the old Sicilians he manages the organization with reason rather than force, and is one of the few major Mafia leaders whose "family" has not been torn apart by internal power struggles or vendetta with other families. Despite his high prestige within the organization, Trafficante's good sense has prevented him from campaigning for a leading position on the Mafia's National Commission. This self-effacing attitude no doubt accounts for his personal safety and considerable influence. Through his studious avoidance of publicity, he is one of the least-known and most underestimated leaders of organized crime."[19]

That description of Trafficante would later be proven wrong, as his worldwide influence in the drug trade expanded to make him one of the most influential people in organized crime, and a

---

[19] Alfred McCoy. *The Politics of Heroin in Southeast Asia*. Harper Publishers, New York, 1973.

principal suspect in the death of John F. Kennedy, many years later.

Another person who was both associated with the assassination of JFK, as well as being a highly placed participant in the heroin trade, was New Orleans crime boss, Carlos Marcello. Carlos Marcello as well as Johnny Rosselli and Santo Trafficante were the three main players whom the CIA hired in 1960 to kill Castro. After the president's assassination, the HSCA stated that Marcello was one of the people who had the "means, motive, and opportunity` to assassinate President Kennedy."

At the time of the president's assassination, Marcello was the main Mafia figure in the New Orleans area. His area of influence also included Dallas, where the mob ran sway. One of the bit players in the upcoming assassination of the president was a little known nightclub owner in Dallas named Jack Ruby. Ruby had low-level mob connections for years in Dallas and was well known to both the police, as well as the mob, including Marcello.

Carlos Marcello was one of the prime mobsters whom Attorney General Robert Kennedy put on his hit list, dating back to his time as general counsel for the Rackets Committee headed by Senator John McClellan. Marcello was one of many mobsters whom Robert Kennedy called to testify before his committee, which was watched by a nation-wide audience.

Like the other prime mobsters of the time, including Santo Trafficante and Jimmy Hoffa, Carlos Marcello had a deep hatred for the Kennedy brothers, with Bobby in particular taking the brunt of his wrath. In April 1961, Robert Kennedy had Carlos Marcello deported to Guatemala with just a moments notice. He was left with only the clothes on his back in a remote area of the country and had to fend for himself. As Marcello made his way back to the United States, he had plenty of time to plan his revenge against the Kennedy's for the nasty treatment he received on their behalf. It is believed that Marcello was flow back to the United States by his friend, David Ferrie whose name would come up in the aftermath of Dallas. It is alleged that at one point Marcello said of the Kennedy's that he wanted to "take the stone out of my shoe."

In the time period of November 1963, David Ferrie was working for Marcello's lawyer, a man named G. Wray Gill. Marcello was in court on November 22, 1963, facing charges of immigration fraud.

The FBI had a longstanding interest in the illegal activities of Marcello and between February 1979 and February 1980, they recorded 1,350 tapes of conversations made by Marcello as part of the FBI's sting operation called BRILAB. The tapes were recorded by two agents, Mike Wacks and Larry Montague. A third man named Joe Hauser, a con man, was also reportedly involved in the operation. The tapes were sealed on the orders of Judge Morey Sear at the beginning of Marcello's trial on bribery and conspiracy in 1981.

HSCA Chief Counsel Robert Blakey would later say that, "Marcello implicated himself in the assassination on three of those tapes... On one tape, Marcello asked the other person to leave the room and resume the conversation in the secrecy of his car when the assassination came up. Marcello said that, "We don't talk about that in here."[20]

The BRILAB tapes are still sealed, and the public still has not been given access to what would probably be a "smoking gun" admission by Marcello in the Kennedy assassination.

Another source who implicated Marcello in the assassination is a man named Ed Becker. He relates the story that in September 1962, he had a conversation with Marcello in which the Mafia don told him of a plot to kill the president. Becker said that Marcello said that a "nut" would be used to take the blame for the assassination. Becker told the FBI about the meeting with Marcello but noting was done to follow up the lead. When the HSCA was in operation, they interviewed Becker in 1978 and found his testimony credible.

A third person implicated Marcello in the plot to kill Kennedy, but when the story came out, it was met with a large dose of skepticism.

The man who implicated Marcello was mob lawyer Frank Ragano who was also the lawyer for Santo Trafficante, as well as Jimmy Hoffa. Ragano told the *New York Post,* the following story. In its January 14, 1992 edition, Ragano said that he was told of a plot to kill JFK that involved Santo Trafficante, Jimmy Hoffa and

---

[20] Michael Benson, *Who's Who in the JFK Assassination: An A-Z Encyclopedia.* Carlo Publishing Co., New York, 1993, Page 277.

Carlos Marcello. Ragano told *Post* reporter Jack Newfield that he was an "unwitting intermediary" in the assassination plot when he met with Jimmy Hoffa at his Teamsters Headquarters in Washington, D.C., in January or February, 1963. Following the meeting with Hoffa, Ragano was to head to New Orleans where he was to meet with both Trafficante and Marcello. According to Ragano's account, Hoffa told him,"Tell Marcello and Trafficante they have to kill the president."

Ragano further stated that Hoffa told him, "This has to be done. Jimmy was ranting and raving for a long time. I didn't take it seriously because I knew Jimmy was a hot head with a short attention span. Marcello and Trafficante never met Hoffa. I had lawyer-client privilege with Hoffa and Trafficante, so I was the designated intermediary. Marcello and Trafficante were extremely cautious. They always wanted to be able to truthfully tell a grand jury they never met Hoffa.[21]

Ragano said that he later met with both Trafficante and Marcello in New Orleans and told them that, "Jimmy wants you to kill the president. They didn't laugh. They were dead serious. They looked at each other in a way that made me uncomfortable. Their looks scared me. It made me think they already had such a thought in mind."

The lawyer said that on the day Kennedy was killed, Hoffa called him a number of times and said, "Have you heard the good news. They killed the SOB. This means Bobby is out as Attorney General."

All of the principal players in the drama are dead, and as the years passed, it is hard to determine the credibility of the scenario that Ragano laid out.

However, if there was no direct link to the Ragano story, there is documented evidence of Marcello's direct connection to the importation of heroin into the Untied States.

The source that linked Carlos Marcello to the smuggling of heroin into the United States was a man named Carl Irving Noll. Noll had an meeting with a member of the Immigration and Naturalization Service in a January 19, 1960 and he told the following story. In the interview, Noll gave detailed information

[21] Ibid. Page 278.

on Carlos Marcello's role in illegal activities in New Orleans, as well as the more important importation of drugs into the United States.

Noll was interviewed by George Corcoran, Jr., a U.S. agent of the Bureau of Narcotics, as well as another agent by the name of Rough. He said that on or about July 1956, he had a meeting that was attended by Sam Mannarino and Carlos Marcello, alias Carlagore Minacore, at the Town and Country Motel, Airline Drive Highway in New Orleans. The original intent of the meeting was to discuss gambling operations and slot machines. However, during the discussion, Mannarino and Marcello asked Noll if his friend, Edward Rodriges Genis could provide them with heroin.

Noll told them that a friend of his wife, named June Bohler was married to a man named Julio Merida who was an assistant counsel for Guatemala in New Orleans. Noll said that he had befriended an army officer from Guatemala. He further said that both he and his wife had become friendly with Antonio Valaderiz, an attorney for the government of Guatemala. Another person whom Noll met was Edwardo Rodriges Genis, a government minister of the Interior Department in Guatemala. Noll said that both "Genis and Valaderiz would do anything for money and felt that because of their official positions with the Guatemala government, they could not get into any trouble."

Noll said that a week after their meeting with Mannarino and Marcello, he flew to Guatemala from New Orleans and that he talked with both Antonio Valaderitz and Edwardo Rodriges Genis about getting heroin. "Genius told Noll he could furnish the heroin and that Valaderitz could handle the transactions. Approximately three weeks later Noll and Valaderitz returned to New Orleans. "[22]

Noll told the agents that he and Valaderitz "met Carlos Marcello and Sam Mannarino at Marcello's home in Gretna, Louisiana. In their talks, Marcello and Mannarino discussed with Valaderitz prices of the heroin, when and where it would be picked up and delivered. Valaderitz stated he could furnish the heroin at $2,500.00 a kilo. Valaderitz stated the heroin would be picked up at Puerto Barrios, Guatemala, and delivered to Guatemala City in a

---

[22] RIF No. 124-10214-10022. This document can be found at the National Archives.

Guatemalan government car which Valaderiz would furnish. Noll stated that Carlos Marcello handed him $25,000,00 for the first trial shipment of ten kilos of heroin. [23]

A bank account was set up in the name of Rodriges Genis at the Whitney Main Bank, located at Charles Street in New Orleans. Noll stated that he made the first deposit of $500.00 for expense money. After that, Carlos Marcello's brother, Joe Marcello, handled the deposits."

In the latter part of August or September 1956, Valaderiz and Noll traveled to Guatemala City and then went to Puerto Barrios. "The heroin was supposed to be obtained from a ship in Puerto Barrios. Noll stated that he did not know who the man was that Valaderiz obtained the heroin from."

Noll and Valaderiz returned to Guatemala City with ten kilos of heroin. They then shipped five kilos of heroin by A.S.A. Airlines to Norman Rothman, a well-connected mobster of the time, to the Sans Souci Night Club in Havana, Cuba. The rest of the heroin was delivered to Willy Sam who was a partner of Sam Mannarino.

Noll told the government that he met with a man named Joe La Piccalo in Guatemala City, and that he and Genis and Valaderiz discussed with La Piccalo arrangements to buy fifteen or twenty kilos of heroin. Later, Valaderiz brought 17 kilos of heroin to Joe La Piccalo and that La Piccalo paid Valaderiz.

Noll then made arrangements for the heroin to be smuggled into the United States by unwitting people who worked for Taca Airlines. Noll gave one of the packets of heroin to a pilot named Scott who delivered it to Joe Marcello in New Orleans.

Noll and Valaderiz then went to Tegucigalpa, Honduras, on or about March 1957. There, they met with the Minister of the Interior and discussed the purchase of heroin on numerous occasions. Noll called his wife in the United States who contacted Carlos Marcello and Marcello would come to their home when Noll called to discuss the price of the drugs over the phone.

The heroin was subsequently smuggled into the United States by Valaderitz using his diplomatic status. Noll related that Marcello paid him about seven or eight thousand dollars for his

---

[23] Ibid.

time and effort in the drug episode.

For his time and effort, Noll related that Marcello gave him money so he could buy the Pelican Bar in Jefferson Parish, Louisiana. He said that "a numbers book" operated in the back of the bar on behalf of Marcello. Crap games were also a staple at the Pelican and "Carlos received the money from the gambling operations through Nick Nuccio, who runs Marcello's gambling operations."

By the spring of 1957, said Noll, the FBI was looking into his shady dealings and Marcello told him that he was too "hot" and that he, Noll, should get out of the narcotics business. Noll said that Marcello promised to pay him further monies for his work but that he never anted up.

In April 1956, Noll said that he provided a fake birth certificate from Guatemala for Carlos Marcello. He said that both he and Antonio Valaderiz went to a small town in Guatemala and that a local official found a place in the old birth records, and that this man entered a false birth date for Carlos Marcello. The false record was then taken to the U.S. Consulate in Guatemala where it was officially given U.S. approval.[24]

Noll also told the Narcotics Agents that Mannarino, Marcello, and La Piccalo also discussed the shipment of small arms to Cuba and that these guns were to be bought from a contact in Ohio. He said that he had no further information if the guns were sent to Cuba.

The testimony of Noll gave U.S. authorities first hand information on Carlos Marcello's entry into the heroin trade. This was just one more piece of evidence that the feds would compile on Marcello. As time went on, more was to come.

Besides the Lansky-Luciano-Navy connection, and the operation headed by Antoine Guerini, the CIA used its considerable contacts across the border in Canada to establish a new heroin smuggling ring that was operated out of Montreal. Like the one set up by Irving Brown in the French Connection case, the CIA turned once again to the American Federation of Labor's Executive Council. The AFL took steps to have its Canadian affiliate expel the pro-communist Canadian Seamen's Union in

---

24 Ibid.

favor of the mob connected Seamen's International Union which was lead by Hal Banks. Over time, this mob connected union lead to the establishment of a new heroin connection between Europe-Montreal and the United States.

Hal Banks led a rather checkered past, to say the least. He spent three and a half years in prison in San Quentin and then spent fifteen years living the good life in Canada. Banks had connections to the CIA which used him for different jobs. It wasn't until the 1960s, that the Canadian government used its power to reorganize the dockworkers away from their mob related pals.

Banks left Canada and returned to the United States. The Canadian government tried in vain to have him extradited back to Canada on perjury charges but U.S. Secretary of State Dean Rusk interceded in his behalf. [25]

* * *

While the Corsican heroin connection based out of Marseille was thriving in the decade of the 1950s, the leaders of the mob decided it was time to branch out and seek newer, more lucrative business opportunities elsewhere. The Guerini-Lansky-Luciano trio decided it was time to expand their worldwide heroin business and decided that the rugged land of Southeast Asia was prime picking. The so-called Golden Triangle that was made up of Burma-Thailand and Vietnam was ripe for lining their pockets and they moved their lucrative headquarters into that vast, lawless region.

For years, the Corsican syndicate that was based in Saigon and Vientiane, Laos, had been supplying the eager European drug markets with raw morphine base that was grown in the lush soil of the region. The drugs were shipped through clandestine routes into Marseille, France and then re-shipped to their buyers.

During the first Indo-China war of 1946-54, before the presence of United States troops over-ran the region beginning in the early 1960s, the Marseille based Corsican gangsters had already established themselves as the main suppliers of heroin

---

25 "Rockefeller's Deadly Needle Trade: How the Heroin Network Was Set Up." Executive Intelligence Review. January 16, 1975.

coming from Southeast Asia. While the war was going on, the Corsicans had a lucrative trade in smuggling all sorts of merchandise, including gold, money and narcotics between Saigon and Vientiane. One of the prime movers of narcotics was Paul Louis Levet, a Bangkok based mob leader, was supplying heroin labs with morphine base from Thailand.

In his book, "The Politics of Heroin in Southeast Asia," author McCoy writes that a number of Corsican charter airlines were responsible for ferrying opium from Southeast Asia from 1955 to 1965. This hugely profitable business was in operation until it was taken over in 1965, (at the height of the Vietnam war), by a number of renegade Laotian generals who took power in that country.

As the Corsicans became the men to see in the region, they decided to make peace with two important Americans who were associated with both the military and the CIA; General Edward Lansdale and CIA officer Lucien Conein. Lansdale would become part of Operation Mongoose, the Kennedy administrations's effort to kill Fidel Castro. For his part, Lucien Conein would become one of the CIA's most influential men in Southeast Asia during the decades of the 1950s and 1960s.

Edward Lansdale was one of the most important counterinsurgency specialists during the cold war period, playing an active and important role in the Kennedy administrations's efforts to kill Castro.

Lansdale was one of the men who served in the wartime OSS, rising to the post of intelligence chief for the U.S. Army. He joined the CIA in 1947, winding up in the Far Eastern division. At the time of the insurrection in the Philippines in the early 1950s, he became one of the most important proponents of psychological warfare against the Huck tribesmen.

After ending his job in the Philippines, Lansdale was transferred to Vietnam where he worked to bolster the western leaning government. His flamboyant style attracted certain journalists, among them Graham Green, a British writer who modeled his main character from his novel called *The Quiet American,* after him. Landsale worked closely with South Vietnamese President Ngo Dinh Diem, bolstering up the South Vietnamese army, and carried out intelligence missions against

Diem's enemies. Such was Lansdale's importance to Diem, that when Lansdale asked Diem to publically state that his country was an independent state (as opposed to a political union with the North), the President broke the contents of the Geneva Conventions and declared the South an independent country.

By now, Lansdale's star had been rising in the Pentagon and he was now given the job of Deputy Director of the Pentagon's New Office of Special Operations, a post that would put him right in the middle of the new counter-warfare strategy that the Kennedy administration was pursing. By the time JFK took over, he had learned a lot about Landsale and even thought about giving him the job of U.S. Ambassador to South Vietnam. It was not offered. But if Lansdale was not to get the Saigon job, he was about to be thrust into the Kennedy administrations efforts to kill Castro, called Operation Mongoose.

Lansdale was not in favor of the ill fated Bay of Pigs invasion and right after the fiasco, Kennedy wanted near him men who would tell him the truth as far as military operations were concerned, not yes men who had caused the debacle. To that effect, Lansdale was offered the post of head of the Cuba Project.

Lansdale soon teamed up with Bill Harvey and the two men soon began to get all phases of Operation Mongoose under way. Soon though, the two men were at loggerheads about what policy to adopt vis-a-vi Castro. Harvey wanted to use traditional CIA methods to oust Castro, while Lansdale insisted on the use any methods necessary to carry out the task; the "boom and bang" that Robert Kennedy insisted on using.

The newly declassified reports on Operation Mongoose reveal Lansdale's efforts to rid Castro from office. Minutes from the Special Group Meeting on January 25, 1962, reveal that he wrote a paper on the Cuba Project that was discussed by General Maxwell Taylor, General Lyman Lemintzer, CIA Director McCone, and Richard Bissell, among others. Among the recommendations presented by Lansdale in his report was the possibility that operations inside of Cuba might lead to an internal revolt that would allow a call for U.S. intervention: "He also said that he had met with the JSC (Joint Chiefs of Staff) and that the latter had responded strongly to the idea of preparing for external actions. Additionally, he had met with the intelligence estimators and it had been noted there will be some delay in the NIE (National Intelligence Estimate) because of the need to acquire more intelligence and to digest a sizeable input from the State Department."

Author Gus Russo writes in his book "*Live By the Sword: The Secret War Against Castro and the Death of JFK,*" about an interview given by Lansdale in 1975 regarding the Kennedy's plans for Castro's assassination. Lansdale told a television interviewer that he was given orders by someone high up in the Kennedy administration to develop plans for assassinating Castro. When asked if this intermediary was McGeorge Bundy, JFK's National Security Advisor, Lansdale said, "No, it was some one much more intimate." When he testified before the Rockefeller Commission, Lansdale said that the person more "intimate" was Robert Kennedy.

If Lucien Conein hadn't been a bona fide spook, stalking the jungles of Vietnam during the early 1960s, he would have made a great Hollywood bad boy. He was called "Black Luigi" and "Lulu" by his contemporaries—a veteran of both the OSS and the French Foreign Legion. He served in Vietnam during the build up of American troops under the Kennedy administration, and played an essential role in the overthrow of the Diem regime in South Vietnam in November 1963.

He was born in Paris and as a youngster, his widowed mother sent him to Kansas City, Missouri where he lived with relatives. His family was of French heritage and he spoke the language perfectly. Even while living in America, he kept his French citizenship. It was said that he joined the French Foreign Legion but his name was never officially on any Legion roster. During World War 2, he left the Legion and transferred to the American army. He joined Donovan's OSS and was assigned to the OSS Special Operations Branch. The main job of that unit was to carry out covert actions against enemy targets and support local resistance groups. Conein was part of the Jedburg Operation, a three-man team comprised of allied agents who parachuted into Nazi occupied Europe (mostly Germany) to carry out sabotage and guerilla operations against enemy positions. In 1944, he left continental Europe and made his way to Asia where the OSS had a large intelligence base. In Indo-China, Conein linked up with

French troops who were waging their own war against Japanese forces who were threatening to overrun the region. It was during his stay in Indo-China that Conein met a number of local resistance fighters like Ho Chi Min, and Nguyen Giap, two men who would later be the leaders of the North Vietnamese government.

In 1954, by now a member of the CIA, he went back to his old haunting grounds in Southeast Asia under the command of Col. Edward Lansdale who headed a CIA support team which was aiding the French in their war against the Communist forces.

Conein remained in Vietnam throughout much of the 1950s and 60s, and would make friends with many of the up and coming South Vietnamese generals who would later play an important role in the American led war in Vietnam.

Newly released documents from the time period in which Conein served in Vietnam, tells the story of a man who was instrumental in aiding the CIA in the overthrow of the government of President Diem of South Vietnam.

By the summer of 1963, it was obvious to the United States that their ally in the South, President Diem, was a running a corrupt and leaderless nation. Decay ran rampant inside the administration, and more important, the war against the North Vietnamese and their Viet Cong allies was going badly. The situation got even worse when President Diem openly waged war against the minority Buddhist population in the country. Things got so bad that a number of Buddhist monks openly killed themselves in public by dousing their bodies with fire. These horrific scenes went around the world via TV, and the Kennedy administration had no choice but to back a coup that was planned by the dissident generals opposed to Diem's dictatorial rule.

US Ambassador to Vietnam, Henry Cabot Lodge, asked Conein to serve as his secret messenger between the insurgent generals led by Gen. Duong Van "Big" Minh. Conein knew both "Big" Minh and the other generals who were behind the coup for many years, and considered many of them his personal friends. He also kept Ambassador Lodge up to speed on how the coup plans were going. "Black Luigi" even outstripped the authority of the CIA Station Chief in Saigon, John Richardson.

In a book called *Triangle of Death,* authors Brad O'Leary and L. E. Seymour, give a detailed picture of Conein's influence in the

Diem coup. Among the facts they bring to light are the following:

*Right before the coup began, Conein met with General Minh and gave the Vietnamese general a direct line to the CIA Station in Saigon.

*Conein was in direct correspondence with certain members of the Kennedy administrations National Security team, including McGeorge Bundy, the president's National Advisor.

*Conein assured the generals that the U.S. would not participate in the coup and would continue military aide once Diem was gone.

*Ambassador Lodge provided the generals with sufficient amounts of cash in the unlikely event that the coup failed and they needed to get out of the country fast. "Lodge made it clear that last-minute funds could be delivered to the generals if necessary. I believe we should furnish them. So when Conein was invited by Minh to staff headquarters just before the coup commenced, he brought a bag full of cash as a last minute emergency fund and as escape money for the generals in the event that the coup failed."

*When General Minh asked Conein to provide a plane that would take Diem and his family out of the country, he refused, on orders from higher U.S. authorities.[26]

Author Neil Sheehan wrote about Conein in his best selling book called *A Bright Shining Lie,* "Few secret agents are ever given an opportunity to scale the professional summit by arranging the overthrow of a government. Conein was transmitting the power of the United States to influence these generals to do his bidding."

Conein left the CIA in 1968, and then joined the Drug Enforcement Agency (DEA). While at the DEA, he organized an elaborate intelligence gathering organization concentrating on drug lords (the same ones whom he met while working in Southeast Asia). He left DEA in 1984 and went into private business.

In the 1970s, Conein's name came up in a U.S. Senate investigation of alleged assassination plots conducted by the DEA. He denied these accusations and no criminal charges were ever filed. He died on June 3, 1998, age 79.

---

[26] Brad O'Leary and L.E. Seymour. *Triangle of Death: The Shocking Truth About the Role of South Vietnam and the French Mafia in the Assassination of JFK.* WND Books, Nashville, Tn. 2003, Page 29-30.

By the start of the 1960s, the CIA had entrenched itself in the drug business on a worldwide scale, playing both sides against the other. The CIA that President Truman had envisioned in 1947 was now a thing of the past, and no genie could get it back into its slender bottle.

They would now turn their attention to events then going on in the continent of Africa where the independence movements following the end of World War 2 were gathering steam. They decided to send one of their prime assassins to the Congo to try and assassinate the ruler of that nation: Patrice Lumumba.

Chapter 4: The CIA, QJ/WIN and the Death of Patrice Lumumba

Before we delve into the events surrounding the murder of the Congolese leader, Patrice Lumumba, and the possible role of the CIA in his death, the reader must be given a course in assassination 101, or as the CIA referred to it at the time, the Executive Action-ZR/RIFLE program whose sole purpose was to assassinate foreign leaders whom the United States did not like. The assassin whom the CIA chose was called QJ/WIN, a man whose identity is still classified today. Numerous researchers have tried to put a name to this man, but until the CIA releases all its files on him, the guessing game is all we have. QJ/WIN may have been one of the men who was on the famous 'grassy knoll" at the time of the president's murder, and may have been the figure people dubbed "badge man," due to the distinctive police type markings on the figures clothing.

One of the many important disclosures coming out of the 1975 Senate Intelligence Committee's investigation on the CIA's top-secret project to assassinate foreign leaders was Project ZR/RIFLE. This program, originally established to get rid of Fidel Castro, turned into a nightmare, finally involving plots to assassinate Patrice Lumumba of the Congo, as well as other foreign heads of state whose policies ran counter to U.S. views.

Project ZR/RIFLE also has its domestic ramifications as well, involving militant anti-Castro Cuban's whose only goal was to re-establish their old business interests on the island. Besides the Cuban's, this top-secret project may have tenuous links to the assassination of JFK in Dallas on November 22, 1963.

In its inception, Project ZR/RIFLE was operated by the CIA to facilitate the removal of Fidel Castro from Cuba. Castro was originally an ally of the U.S. until he surprised the Eisenhower administration in 1960 by declaring he was a communist and turned to Moscow for help. ZR/RIFLE had another name, Executive Action, which was run out of the Technical Services Division of the CIA.

The Executive Action capability included "the development of a general, standby assassination capability." This program included research into the long-term possibilities and capabilities of killing foreign leaders. Despite all the intensive planning for Executive Action, in reality, the program never actually carried out its mandate. But that was history.

The man put in over all charge of Executive Action-ZR/RIFLE was William Harvey. Harvey was well equipped to deal with this new type of operation, having been one of the key players in the CIA's secret war against Castro, later called 'Operation Mongoose."

What was not known by the public at large at that time was the fact that the CIA had hired certain members of organized crimes (the mob) to kill Fidel Castro. Men such as Johnny Rosselli, Sam Giancana, and Santos Trafficante, Jr., were brought in on the action and served as the go between in the Castro assassination plots. Bill Harvey was furious when he learned of the mob connection and he refused to have anything to do with them.

Bill Harvey was head of the super-secret group at the CIA called "Staff D" which was responsible for communications intercepts. All of the CIA's covert activities were given cover ID's with letters for designation. Staff A was foreign intelligence; Staff B was Operations; Staff C was counterintelligence. But Staff D was different, its doors guarded round-the-clock by armed Marines. To insure maximum security, Harvey brought in his own safe to supplement the other three already in the office.

At one point, Harvey called ZR/RIFLE "the magic button" and "the last resort beyond the last resort and a confession of weakness." In the notes he left behind, Harvey never used the word "assassination," instead, when dealing with ZR/RIFLE, his favorite expression was "maximum security" and "nonattributability."

In the world of lights and shadows of the CIA, the agency, when referring to ZR/RIFLE used the cryptonym KUBARK for its internal use. Nothing was to be written down, only "word of mouth" and "strictly person to person, singleton ops," no projects on paper."

Those people involved would "require most professional, proven operationally competent, ruthless, stable, counter-espionage experienced ops officers."

As ZR/RIFLE-Executive Action began to take shape, Bill Harvey began an intensive investigation to find a person or persons to carry out their assassination plots. He used CIA Staff D, code named KUTUBE/D to recruit such individuals.

In *Wilderness of Mirrors,* author David Martin writes, "no chain of connection permitting blackmail." The Executive Action file directed, "…no American citizen or residents or people who ever obtained U.S. visas could serve as assassins. Corsicans recommended, but not Sicilians. Sicilians could lead to the Mafia."[27]

QJ/WIN, it is believed, may have been of Corsican decent and may even have had a connection with the Guerini family of Marseille.

Martin further writes, "As an added precaution, planning should include provisions for blaming Sovs or Czechs in case of blow. Should have phony 201 in RG (Central Registry) to back stop this, all documents therein should be forged and backdated."

But this directive by Harvey seems not to be the case. Under documents obtained under FOIA, a different tack was taken.

A six page memo written to Robert Blakey by S.D. Breckinridge dated September 27, 1978, reveals the following information:

"The ZR/RIFLE file, and the QJ/WIN file, should speak for themselves. It was clear that Mr. Harvey and an associate, initially contemplated trying to establish false files. It is equally clear to anyone willing to purse the question beyond its asking, that they did not do so. Why he did not cannot be recaptured factually as today Mr. Harvey is dead, but that he did not is clear. Perhaps he tried and simply could not. In any event, it was not necessary to do so anyway, if limited records were desired to enhance the security of the operation."[28]

---

27 David Martin. *Wilderness of Mirrors.* Harper & Row Publishers, New York, 1980, Page 123.

28 Exhibit CIA-6114 (found in National Archives).

But did the Kennedy administration know of the ZR/RIFLE program? In a CIA document dealing with the plots to kill Castro, it now seems cleat that President Kennedy did in fact know of the plan as early as February 1961.

William Harvey was briefed in February 1961 (by authority of Richard Bissell) on phase one of the gambling syndicate operation. That briefing was in connection with a sensitive operation that Bissell had assigned to Harvey. Harvey described it thus:

"Early in the Kennedy administration, Bissell called him in to discuss what Harvey refers to as an Executive Action capability, i.e., a general stand-by capability to carry out assassinations when required. Harvey's notes quote Bissell as saying, The White House has twice urged me to create such a capability. Bissell recalls discussing the question of developing a general capability with Harvey. He mentioned the Edwards/gambling syndicate operation against Castro in that context, but he now thinks that the operation was over by then and that reference to it was in terms of a past operation as a case in point. It was on this basis that Harvey arranged to be briefed by Edwards. Harvey's fixing of the date as February was only after a review of events both preceding the briefing and following it. He says now that it might have been as early as late January or as late as March 1961."[29]

These documents provide a further dimension to the Executive Action Program. Further stated in the Inspector General's reports is the following paragraph:

"Project ZR/RIFLE was covered as an operation (ostensibly to develop a capability for entering safes and for kidnaping couriers). It continued on a course separate from the Edwards/gambling syndicate operation against Castro until 15 November 1961. Harvey has a note on that date he discussed with Bissell the application of the ZR/RIFLE program to Cuba. Harvey says that Bissell instructed him to take over Edward's contact with the criminal syndicate and thereafter to run operations against

---

29 *CIA Targets Fidel.* Page 48.

Castro."[30]

Events began to move more quickly as Bill Harvey hired his first "principal agent," code named "QJ/WIN" and such other principal agents and sub-agents as may be required." QJ/WIN was to be paid $7,200 per year ending on December 31, 1962. A further allocation of up to $16,200 was approved if necessary.

QJ/WIN, according to the now, declassified documents, 'is under contract as a principle agent, with the primary task of spotting agent candidates." It is now known that QJ/WIN worked for both the CIA and the Bureau of Narcotics.

While it is not known who QJ/WIN is, much can be told about him. WIN is probably a European soldier-of-fortune, man "capable of anything." According to the late CIA Director Richard Helms, QJ/WIN was a man who could carry out a murder at a moments notice. QJ/WIN's fist assignment was to kill Patrice Lumumba of the Congo. However, WIN arrived on scene too late and Lumumba had already been killed by his enemies.

While in the Congo, WIN teamed up with another man, code-named WI/ROGUE and brought him into the ZR/RIFLE program. It is speculated that WI/ROGUE had ties to the French Corsican mob based in Marseilles.

As we shall see in the later part of this work, both QJ/WIN and QI/ROGUE may have had ties to the Kennedy assassination, as well as possibly having a connection to the Corsican mob that ran the French Connection heroin ring. The writer and researcher, Steve Rivele, wrote extensively on the possible identities of both men and we will delve into that area later in the book.

If this is not complicated enough, there is a possible WIN/ROUGE connection to the JFK assassination. When Jack Ruby, the man who killed Lee Harvey Oswald went on trial, he was asked by his attorney, Tom Howard, if there was anyone whom the state of Texas could produce who could do him serious harm. Ruby mentioned the name of Thomas Eli Davis.

Tom Davis was a convicted bank robber, gunrunner, and friend of Jack Ruby's who frequently came to Ruby's nightclub. When JFK was killed, Davis was in North Africa, probably setting up a

---

30 Ibid. Page 49.

deal to provide arms to the OAS, the same militant group that was responsible for trying to assassinate French President Charles de Gaulle. He was subsequently placed under arrest in a Tangier, Morocco jail. The Moroccan police found a letter on Davis' person mentioning Oswald and the president's death. Author Seth Kantor, in his book "*Who Was Jack Ruby?* (Everest House, 1978) writes that Davis was released from his cell by QJ/WIN.

Davis had a checkered past, having been arrested in 1958 on charges of attempting to rob a bank in Detroit. He was given a 5-year probation and then found himself in New Orleans in January 1963 where he applied for a passport. He then went to California in an attempt to recruit mercenaries in order to invade Haiti and oust the government of President Duvalier. The FBI found out about his Haitian adventure and when he was questioned, Davis said he was a freelance writer doing an article on soldier-of-fortune types.

Later in 1963, Davis was arrested in Tangiers for attempting to sell weapons. His wife told members of the U.S. State Department that her husband had worked previously as a soldier-of fortune in such places as Indochina, Algeria, and Indonesia.

According to author Henry Hurt in his book *Reasonable Doubt,* Thomas Davis had a strong resemblance to Lee Oswald. Hurt also says that Davis oftentimes used the name of Oswald in his travels.

After his arrest for killing Lee Oswald, Jack Ruby told his lawyers that he and Thoms Davis were in the gun running business together and that he hoped some day to return to that profitable trade with him. Davis was also associated with the anti-Castro cause, and had trained these men in camps in Florida and other places in South America.

The HSCA looked into the Thomas Davis-Jack Ruby relationship but time constraints stopped them from pursuing the matter any further. If they did, who knows what tidbits of information they might have come up with.

Due to the flurry of the release of hundreds of previously classified files from the CIA via the "JFK Records Act," and those coming from the National Archives, a clearer picture of just how the CIA used both QJ/WIN and WI/ROUGE is now available (even if we still don't know who they really are).

The files on the ZR/RIFLE program say that QJ/WIN was responsible for spotting and assessing individuals whom the CIA could use as safecrackers and to obtain foreign codes and ciphers. He was supposed to have been part of ZR/RIFLE but was never put in the program. The documents on QJ/WIN say in one sentence that, "There are a few references in the files that might be constructed as a connection with this activity, but they are so cryptic that, without additional information it would be difficult to tie them together." What reference we have on him deal with cable traffic, dispatches, administrative, financial records, and name/personality traces.

The files do say that besides the CIA, another secret agency of the government at the time had an operational interest in QJ/WIN- the National Security Agency.

While ZR/RIFLE was supposed to be used to "spot, develop", and use agent assets for Division D operations, part of the objective was to procure codes and cipher materials for the clandestine service of the CIA, primarily by the National Security Agency. "QJ/WIN is under written contract as a principal agent, with the primary task of spotting agents candidates..." Just why QJ/WIN was being shared by both the CIA and the NSA is still in doubt.

African nationalism was one of the spreading themes on that continent shortly after the end of World War 2. The old colonial empires, i.e, England, France, and Portugal, were dead in the geopolitical waters, only to be replaced by the two superpowers, the United States and the Soviet Union.

One of the countries on the continent of Africa who had its own violent revolution was the Congo, which was previously ruled by Belgium. When the Belgians granted independence to the Congo, various political factions in the country began to battle each other, separately seeking to become the dominant faction in the nation. As the situation got worse, United Nations forces were airlifted into the Congo to try and keep the peace. The civil war in the Congo was made up of three separate groups, all vying for the share of power; the Kasavubu-Mobutu-government in Leopoldville, the Antoine Gizenga-Patrice Lumumba government in Stanleyville, and the group headed by Mosie Tshombe in Elisabethville.

But the flash point as far as the Congo was concerned was the threat of Joseph Mobutu in the Katanga Province to succeed from the Congo. The Province of Katanga was rich in diamonds, copper and cobalt, all vital materials needed for weapons and commercial use. It was the threat of the Katanga succession that lead to the arrival of U.N. peacekeepers.

The Congo was granted independence in the summer of 1960, leaving a void that its former benefactor, Belgium, failed to plug. The Belgian's let the nation fend for itself and soon, a civil war broke out. It was decided that the government in Brussels would keep a token force of troops in the Congo to try and keep some semblance of order. The Belgians backed Joseph Kasavubu to lead the newly created country. The Congolese picked Patrice Lumumba as their Premier. As tensions mounted, Lumumba threatened to ask Moscow for military help in kicking out the Belgian forces. The rift between Lumumba and Kasavubu threatened the peace of the Africa, and in the cold war atmosphere of the time, any time bomb, no matter how small, could erupt into a new battle between East and West.

Soon though, civil war began in earnest in the Congo and those events were not missed by the Eisenhower administration, then, in its final days in office.

In the winter of 1960, a secret meeting of the "5412 Group," of the National Security Council met to discuss the ever-growing worsening situation in the Congo. In further meetings with President Eisenhower, along with CIA Director Allan Dulles, it was decided that "something had to be done" about putting an end to the Congolese crisis and in particular, getting rid of Patrice Lumumba who was by now, beginning to become America's new bogy man in Africa. The job was given to the CIA, although it is not absolutely certain that President Eisenhower knew of, or gave the order that Lumumba was to be killed.

A July 21, 1960 meeting of the NSC between Allen Dulles and others to discuss the Congo crisis, the note takers in the room made the following remarks:

"Mr. Dulles said that in Lumumba we were faced with a person who was Castro or worse... Mr. Dulles went on to describe Mr. Lumumba's background which he described as "harrowing." It is safe to go on the assumption that Lumumba has been bought by the Communists; this also, however, fits with his own orientation."

By late 1960, a cable was sent to Lawrence Devlin, the CIA

Station Chief in Leopoldville, under the signature of DCI, Allan Dulles, to plan an assassination attempt on the life of Patrice Lumumba. Devlin was told to try and have some individuals try and poison Lumumba. When that attempt failed, Devlin asked the CIA for a shipment of a "high powered rifle with a telescopic sight and silencer… "

Lawrence Devlin served in World War 2 in North Africa and Europe, then went to Harvard to pursue a Ph.D. One day, he got a call from his professor, William Elliot, a noted historian at the college. Waiting in Professor Elliot's office was McGeorge Bundy (who would later become the National Security Aid to JFK). After a few minutes of small talk, Bundy asked Devlin if he wanted to join the newly created CIA. Devlin accepted the challenge, beginning his long career in the CIA.

He began his work for the Agency as a "noc" for non-official cover. He said he was writer of travel guides and at age 38, landed his first job for the CIA in the Congo.

His alias in the Congo was "Victor Hedgeman," and in September 1960, he got a call from Washington telling him that he would be getting an important message from "Joe from Paris." The mysterious "Joe from Paris" was Sidney Gottlieb, the CIA's foremost expert in the development of poisons. When Gottlieb arrived in the Congo the told Devlin that the assassination order of Lumumba had been given by Ike, but that he, personally had not seen the order. The poison, said Gottlieb, when administered to Lumumba, would look to the world as someone who had died from natural causes.

"Morally I thought it was the wrong thing to do," said Devlin many years later. "And I thought it was a very dangerous thing to do. If I screwed up and brought in the wrong person and it got out that the United States had done this, I had visions of even Africans who didn't like Lumumba wiping out every white man they could find. It might have cost hundreds of lives."[31]

Devlin took an active role in administrating the covert work the CIA Station needed to do in order to drive Lumumba from power. Years later he told a reporter that if he refused to carry out

---

31 "Memories of a CIA Officer Resonate in New Era." Scott Shane, *New York Times*, February 24, 2008.

headquarters orders then someone else would just come in and take his place. Once Gottlieb gave him the poison, he put it in his office safe where it would be hidden from view. Devlin did the dirty work for the Leopoldville station, feeding anti-Lumumba stories to the newspapers and bugging the offices of the opposition parties. He often times met with Colonel Mobutu, one of the leaders of the anti-Lumumba clique. Mobutu told Devlin that the army was ready to overthrow Lumumba at the proper moment and, after checking with Washington, he gave Mobutu the go ahead with the plan.

The path that leads to the death of Patrice Lumumba is a tangled one that needs to be told. On February 20, 1960, Joseph Mobutu, the Commander of the Congolese National Army (ANC), gave the order for the arrest of Lumumba if he tried to leave the country. On October 10, 1960, 300 ANC soldiers surrounded Lumumba's home and prevented him from fleeing the country. The Foreign Minister of the Congo, Bomboko, began talks for Lumumba's arrest. Ghanian UN troops sent by the Security Council were protecting Lumumba's residence, and later on October 10, Mobutu arrived and threatened to attack the UN troops if they continued to protect Lumumba.

On November 28, the U.S. embassy was told by its UN sources that Lumumba had left the residence the day before by car. The sources said that Lumumba left with a secretary and a chauffeur. After confirming that Lumumba had fled, the UN troops withdrew from their defensive positions. For the rest of the month, Lumumba was under house arrest some where in the city. While Lumumba was in hiding, QJ/WIN secretly arrived in Leopoldville, as the CIA asked him to do.

On November 30, UN sources said that they saw Lumumba somewhere in the northern part of the Congo and he was arrested a few days later. He was placed under arrest near the city of Kinshasa (at the Thysville Military Camp). Lumumba and two others were then transferred to Elizabethville on January 17, 1961, three days before John F. Kennedy was sworn in as president. Sources reported that Lumumba was severely beaten during his transfer. According to several witnesses who were present at the time, Lumumba was killed before arriving in Lumbumbashi. Mosie Tshombe said that when he saw Lumumba, he was almost dead.

The CIA wrote of the circumstances surrounding the death of

Lumumba thus:

"The exact circumstances of Lumumba's death remain a mystery, although it is clear he expired his least breath in or around Elizabethville in early 1961. His burial place is unknown, It is also clear that from 9 November, and possibly even from 10 October, this Agency was either unable to determine the whereabouts of Lumumba or was aware that he was under detention by units of the Congolese and UN forces. It seems highly unlikely that anyone within the Agency would have given serious consideration to the assassination of Lumumba when he was, in fact, either virtually incarcerated or his whereabouts were unknown."[32]

As we shall see from the CIA's own investigation of the assassination of Lumumba, and the testimony of Lawrence Devlin and others, that was not the case.

The written record is replete with documentation by the CIA dating back to the 1970s, of Agency involvement in the circumstances surrounding the death of Lumumba, as well as their secret agent sent to the Congo to aid in his demise, QJ/WIN.

A CIA document dated March 10, 1975 called "Alleged Agency Involvement in the Death of Patrice Lumumba," is one of many such documents that reveal the backstory of the CIA's involvement in the event. The material comes from the CIA's Africa Division and it refers to QJ/WIN in this regard, "There is traffic originated from FT/D involving the travel to Leopoldville of an asset made available to CIA by a friendly European liaison service (possibly French secret service). This traffic could lead one to the conclusion that there was a connection between the travel of this asset and Lumumba's death… The conclusion reached is that it is highly doubtful that this individual was connected with any agency planning regarding Lumumba."

Talking about QJ/WIN, the report goes on in detail as to how he was recruited by the CIA. "The European asset in question came to Agency attention for the first time in 1958 as a known smuggler with contacts among illegal traders and petty criminals. His name was surfaced to CIA in response to a request for an individual who could be used in a dangle operation against KGB

---

[32] RIF No. 104-10310-10201 "Memorandum: Alleged Agency Involvement in the Death of Patrice Lumumba" 3/10/75.

activities and, particularly, against a known KGB officer. He next came to Agency attention in the spring of 1959 in connection with a reported Chinese Communist attempt to smuggle opium into the U.S. He offered his services on 14 October 1960. FI/D asked the appropriate Chief of Station to see whether "the asset can be available the week of 14 October 1960." The reply was affirmative. On October 27, a communication from Europe indicated "Some required shots not available and subject must get Paris. Will not complete series until November 1960. On 2 November 1960, Headquarters was informed that the asset was met on 2 November. He accepted offer Leopoldville. Precise mission not conveyed to him. He only informed mission might involve element of personal risk. The cable also indicates that the FI/D case officer who met the asset in Europe was planning to travel to Leopoldville to study the local situation and subsequently to cable European station the details of cover and time of travel, presumably of the asset. On 5 November 1960, the Leopoldville Station asked that the asset should be told to proceed to Leopoldville as soon as his shots were completed. Presumably this would be shortly subject to 11 November… A 6 December cable requested a salary advance be deposited in a European bank for the asset's wife who was ill. This places the asset in Leopoldville on 6 December. On 8 December 1960, a cable from Leopoldville indicates that the asset had developed close relationship with Yugoslav who had agreed to smuggle industrial diamonds for him to Italy. The Station proposed an operation to entrap the Yugoslav pilot for intelligence purposes."[33]

By the tone of the memo, it is safe to say that the CIA's asset, known as QJ/WIN, was sent to Leopoldville, the Congo, at the same time that the plot to oust Lumumba by the CIA, as well as his domestic enemies were under way. By the tone of the memo, it is unclear just why QJ/WIN was sent to the Congo, but it was not for the purpose of sightseeing. He was there for some CIA operation, not revealed in the abovementioned memo.

This revealing memo continues to describe the events as they unfolded.

"Simply on the face of the events, we suggest there is

---

33 Ibid.

considerable room for doubt that the asset in question was ever involved in any operation involving Lumumba. Had he been so involved, it is highly unlikely that he would have been allowed to circulate in Leopoldville making contact with persons involved with smuggling or that he would have been suggested for use in an entrapment operation. The writer recalls that in late 1960,s there was much concern in Congo about King Kalonji who had just, or was shortly to, declare himself the king of an independent Kasi Province. Kalonji, in early December 1960, had shown a station asset $20,000,000 worth of diamonds that the asset wished smuggled out of the Congo. It is conceivable that the asset in question was used, because of his smuggling background, in an attempt to thwart Kalonji and to collect intelligence on his activities in the smuggling field."

According to the CIA memo, QJ/WIN was in the business of diamond smuggling, and if the scenario just described is right, then there is a plausible reason for his appearance in the Congo at the time of the plots against Lumumba, not as an assassin, but in another capacity.

But, as we shall soon see, QJ/WIN had numerous covert contacts with nefarious people in the short time he was in Leopoldville that tends to debunk that theory.

The memo ends by saying, "It should also be noted that a cable dated 2 June 1961 from FI/D to the appropriate European station asked that the asset should be contacted and paid his May salary. This might mean that he was in Leopoldville and in contact with a case officer through April of 1961. *Had he been dispatched to Leopoldville for the purpose of assassinating Lumumba, whose death was public knowledge in February, it would not seem logical to keep him in Leopoldville two extra months. The FI/D cable also indicates that FI/D intended to keep the asset in Europe for at least six months longer. Presumably, therefore, he was in touch with the Agency for purposes other than the specific allegation referred to above* (italics by author).

We have seen that the CIA had sent QJ/WIN to Leopoldville at the same time that plots were underway to assassinate Patrice Lumumba. However, the documents released by the CIA report that the Agency had plans to send him back to the Congo in the spring of 1961.

The document in question comes from the CIA's Luxembourg Station to CIA headquarters and refers to the ZR/RIFLE program. In a dispatch dated 17 April 1961, the writer says that QJ/WIN's return to Leopoldville was to be delayed because they needed him for some unidentified job in Europe. The Agency decided to keep him in Europe for an additional six months for a "spotter" assignment. "The reasons for this decision are simply that the pressures for certain types of KUTUBE/D operations are increasing and that QJ/WIN is one of our very few assets who can deal with the kinds of persons we are seeking."

The CIA agreed to pay him $7,200 per year, and he was to be given $600.00 at the end of each month. He was to be paid expenses but not for the purchase of information.

The Luxemburg station had a long conversation regarding QJ/WIN on May 2, 1961 in which many items were discussed. They took his family into consideration when it came time to move him by saying, "When it is decided to move him, we would appreciate our timing the move if possible, to enable his children to complete their then current school term in Luxembourg and to register for the next following term in Leopoldville. Please inform him that this desire will be given the fullest possible consideration."

It seems that QJ/WIN was a family man, had a wife, and children, and that he had spent a considerable amount of time in Luxembourg working in some capacity for the CIA.

However, the CIA had reservations about sending him to another nation in Europe, Belgium. "He cannot, of course, move to Belgium with a sentence hanging over his head there. We are reluctant to move him to France since he was once convicted there, and application for a residence permit would result in a police file check with possible resultant and understandable police attention to him. Furthermore, since a good deal of his search activity has taken place and will take place in France, we far prefer to have him reside elsewhere. Switzerland might be a possibility. If QJ/WIN does move to Leopoldville, at the end of this year, he can probably survive the period in Luxembourg. If the move is to be postponed beyond the end of the year-and we shall let you know as soon as this is decided-he should be relocated. In the meantime, please discuss the above possibilities with him and let us know his ideas on residence other than Luxembourg and on possible cover for his residence elsewhere."[34]

This is a revealing document that tells us a lot about QJ/WIN. It seems that he had committed some crime in France and was a wanted man by the authorities. This fact alone did not stop the CIA from hiring him in the first place. This was during the cold war and the CIA, in its long history, never shied away from hiring people of ill repute if they believed they could be some intelligence help to them.

The CIA hired the mob to kill Fidel Castro, using Santos Trafficante, Johnny Rosselli, and Sam Giancana.

He could not go to Belgium because of an outstanding warrant on his head. Again, the document does not say exactly what he was wanted for in those two nations but it was probably something substantial if the CIA was reluctant to send him back to two of our cold war allies.

The document does, however, shed some light on just what he was doing in France.

"During April 1961, QJ/WIN spotted some candidates in France. Two or three of these will have to be revisited by him for a second look at them, and to obtain data which he was not able to obtain during the first contact without arousing suspicion on their part. We shall inform you and send pertinent details when we desire that this be done. In the meantime, please inform QJ/WIN that the need for his recontacting these people without undue delay is recognized and is on the front burner."

Further documentation released via the "JFK Records Act," sheds new light on what kind of trouble he was in in Belgium.

A cable dated April 26, 1962 from the Luxembourg Station to the Director of the CIA, reads as follows:

> Per QJ/WIN Luke customs prosecuting nickel smuggling charge since 1954. He and two Belgians involved. Trial over and verdict due week of 29 April. He

[34] RIF No. 104-10185-10047 "Dispatch-Lauricle" ZRFIFLE/QJWIN. 6-7-61.

expects fine but confident can negotiate reasonable figure on basis ability to pay and can arrange small monthly payments. Customs has no authority investigate source his income.

QJWIN doubts jail sentence will be included in verdict as customs interest is possession of merchandise which verdict will authorize. If jail sentence included, he can contest within 12 days of verdict on basis not present past proceedings. New trial could not begin prior Sept. Subsequent verdict could be appealed. Trial and appeal would of course mean substantial cost for QJ/WIN.

Will advise content verdict. Do not recommend our intervention even if jail sentence included. Offense not extraditable.

While we do not know present long term plans for QJWIN, he had no lead to other candidates. His potential appears restricted" [35]

At the time that he worked for the CIA, QJ/WIN was 45 years old, 6 ft. 1 inch, thin build with dark-brown hair. He spoke German and French and it was said that he could pass as a native of France. His English was good but that he had to speak slowly and distinctly, "choosing his words which leave no doubt as to what is meant."

A CIA dispatch from the Chief of Station in Luxembourg gives a description of an assignment that the CIA had planned for QJ/WIN.

"In view of the extreme sensitivity of the objective for which we want him to perform his task, he was not told precisely what we want him to do. Instead, he was told that we have evidence of Soviet operations among nationality groups on Africa, specifically, Corsicans, and that we would like to have him spot, assess, and recommend some dependable, quick-witted persons for our use. (Comment; It was thought best to withhold our true, specific requirements pending the final decision to use him). He agreed to go on the trip for us."[36]

---

35 RIF No. 104-10185-10345. Dated 26 April 1962.

36 RIF No. 104-10185-10015.

This entry is cryptic enough to make one wonder what the CIA was holding back from him. They wanted him to go to Africa for some cover purpose, but they decided it was not in their interest to tell him what it was. Could his assignment have anything to do with the plots to kill Lumumba that were already under way?

The document tells more about the covert nature of QJ/WIN's assignment to Africa and how it was to be carried out.

"Regarding cover for the trip, he suggested that he travel as a salesman for a German firm producing coin-operated soft-drink, coffee, etc, machines. He already had a brochure from this company and stated the he could easily obtain an authenticating to-whom-it-may-concern letter from the owner."

"He stated that in dealing with Corsicans, it is sometimes advisable to give Corsicans as a reference."

"Since he is known to the Surete (French police) in Paris because of his assistance to U.S. Bureau of Narcotics, he was told to obtain visas for his trip in Germany. His passport was reviewed, and there appeared to be no objective to his using it for his upcoming trip."

"He was told that contact with an American would be available at his destination in case he needed it. He was not told that the person meeting him would be from the American Embassy, nor should he be told of this."

Why?

"He was told to spend some time actually trying to sell his coin-operated machine. "

It goes on to say that, "If he is not able to find the types we want and arrange future contact within two weeks, approximately, it is unlikely find the type we need in Dakar (Africa), we will look elsewhere. (The operation we have in mind is too sensitive to risk blowing it in this phase, and the search for assets must be conducted with truly minium risk.)"

Once again, we see the paradox the CIA had in regard to their asset, QJWIN. It seems they didn't trust him enough to give him the complete picture of just what they wanted him to do. We don't know why, and only can only postulate as to their mind set. Is it because the operation they had in mind was so sensitive that only a few people in the higher echelons of the CIA had a need to know? Was it because of his criminal background that they didn't trust him completely?

What is obvious is that the CIA had some sort of assignment for him in Dakar (Africa), including, or excluding his mission to Leopoldville at the time of the Lumumba assassination.

Once he reached Dakar, the CIA was to pay him $400.00 for living expenses, and $300.00 for operational expenses.

There isn't that much of an official paper trail on QJ/WIN that the CIA released (a good deal is still classified), but there is an interesting document that sheds some light on his trip to Leopoldville. A cable dated Dec. 8, 1960 to "Director" from the Leopoldville Station, fills in some of the story of what he was doing there.

"QJWIN has cultivated close personal relationship with iden who agreed to smuggle industrial diamonds for him to Italy. QJWIN has promised him remuneration.

"Station's proposed plan. If approved by Hgs, is to purchase 25 dollars of worthless diamonds whose value iden am unable to appraise. Conceal them in object of which iden a witting and have him hand diamonds to Kubark (CIA) arranged contact in Rome who would represent himself as QJWIN associate. After turnover diamonds completed, (turnover should be photographed), and assessment by KUBARK (CIA) officer, decision could be made whether try recruit iden A without expressly stating so.

"If his new plans in Rome would Hqs (headquarters) desire QJWIN make recruitment pitch ostensibly, but not expressly."[37]

It seems that QJWIN had a background and knowledge of industrial diamond smuggling that would pass him off to any potential buyer as a professional. One does not go to school to take classes in industrial diamond smuggling, so it is safe to assume that he was in the trade for some time and had a working knowledge of how to handle himself in such delicate situations. In doing their background checks on him, the Agency surely knew about his expertise and probably hired him for that specific reason, (among others). This would seem to be a good cover story for QJWIN to use in Leopoldville (or any wherever the CIA sent him), and it is a good bet that he passed himself off in that capacity in his travels for the Agency.

---

[37] RIF No. 104-10185-10060.

It is obvious that the CIA had its own reasons for using QJWIN in the manner they did. He was a somewhat trusted agent, (but not that far), a man of ingenuity, recklessness, a smuggler of diamonds, and a man who was capable of doing anything the CIA asked him to do. He was tasked to take part in the Agency's ZR/RIFLE assassination project, but, as the records says, he never actually took part in the program. He was to be sent to Leopoldville in the Congo at the precise time that the Congolese themselves were in revolt, and as we have seen, events took on a life of their own, ending in the assassination of Lumumba by his enemies. He was also asked to make a trip to Dakar, Africa on CIA related business.

The documents relating to QJ/WIN and the Lumumba assassination say that the Agency did not use QJWIN for any assassination attempt on Lumumba's life. This may be true or not. The records are still ambagious, and there are still a lot of missing pieces to the puzzle.

The next chapter will tell the story, written by the Congress of the United States in 1975 when they investigated the tale of assassination plots against foreign leaders, including Fidel Castro, Patrice Lumumba, Rafael Trujillo, and President Diem of South Vietnam. The story of the CIA's role in the death of Lumumba is told in detail, including the involvement their principal agent, QJ/WIN.

Above: Patrice Lumumba: Leader of one of the factions in the Congo in 1960 and the target of numerous assassination plots, possibly involving CIA assets QJWIN and WIROGUE. *Right*: William Harvey: The CIA officer who ran the ZR/RIFLE project. Harvey's prime assassin was the elusive QJ/WIN.

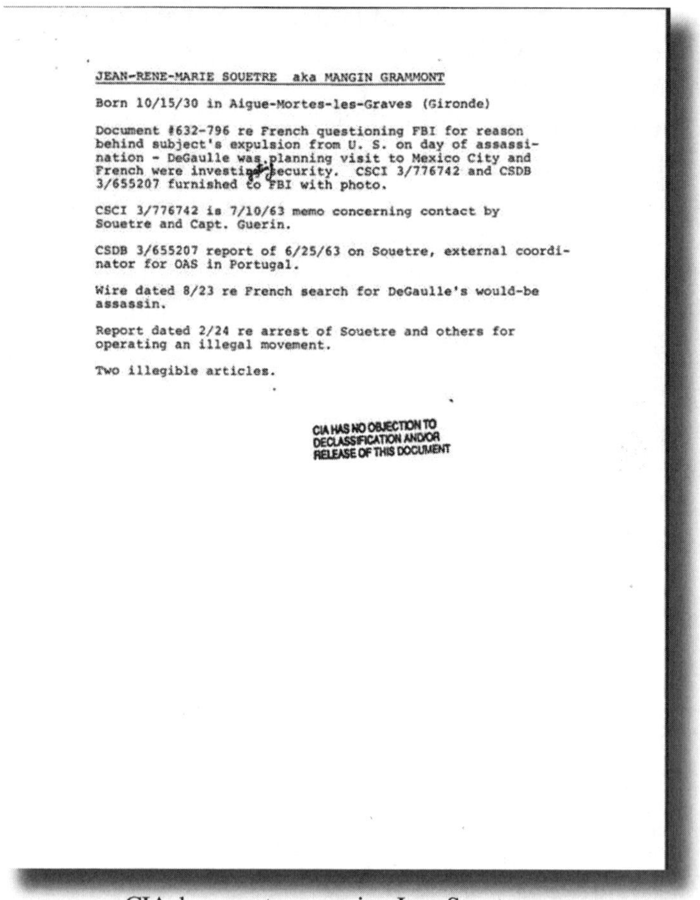

JEAN-RENE-MARIE SOUETRE aka MANGIN GRAMMONT

Born 10/15/30 in Aigue-Mortes-les-Graves (Gironde)

Document #632-796 re French questioning FBI for reason behind subject's expulsion from U. S. on day of assassination - DeGaulle was planning visit to Mexico City and French were investigating security. CSCI 3/776742 and CSDB 3/655207 furnished to FBI with photo.

CSCI 3/776742 is 7/10/63 memo concerning contact by Souetre and Capt. Guerin.

CSDB 3/655207 report of 6/25/63 on Souetre, external coordinator for OAS in Portugal.

Wire dated 8/23 re French search for DeGaulle's would-be assassin.

Report dated 2/24 re arrest of Souetre and others for operating an illegal movement.

Two illegible articles.

CIA HAS NO OBJECTION TO DECLASSIFICATION AND/OR RELEASE OF THIS DOCUMENT

CIA document concerning Jean Souetre.

Chapter 5:

The U.S. Senate Select Committee on Intelligence "Assassination Reports"—The CIA and Lumumba

> *Congo: Introduction:*
>
> *"The Committee has received evidence of a CIA plot to assassinate Patrice Lumumba. The plot proceeded to the point where lethal substances and instruments specifically intended for use in an assassination were placed in the hands of the CIA (blank) Station in Leopoldville by an Agency scientist.*
>
> *Although these instruments of assassination were never used, a number of questions are presented by the Lumumba case which reflect general issues that run throughout the Committee's assassination inquiry. First, did CIA officers and operatives in the Congo take steps to attempt the assassination of Lumumba.*
>
> *Second, how high up in the United States government was the source of authorization for the CIA assassination plot? Finally, was the CIA connected in any way to the events that actually led to the death of Lumumba while in Congolese custody?"* (Senate Select Committee on Intelligence Draft, 1975)

That is the pertinent question that the Senate Committee asked when it began its investigation into the Lumumba assassination, and the inquiry goes a long way in providing us with the answer. It is a detailed and comprehensive report that answers most of the appropriate questions in the Lumumba assassination case. I will try to synthesize the important points, as it relates to CIA involvement and the role of QJWIN in the tale. I used the Committee's report in detail to answer many of the questions and quote from the report as it is written to fill in the blanks where necessary. It is sometimes dry reading, as most government documents are, but it is necessary so that the reader will come away with the entire picture.

By 1960, the CIA was getting reports from its embassy and

spies on the ground that the Congo was ripe for revolt. In June 1960, the CIA assigned an agent to travel to Leopoldville, (most likely Lawrence Devlin) to assess the situation and report back to headquarters his observations. One such cable to Washington reads as follows:

> *Embassy and Station believe Congo experiencing classic communist effort takeover government. Many forces at work here. Soviets, Communist Party, etc. Although difficult determine major influencing factors to predict outcome struggle for power, decisive period not far off. Whether or not Lumumba actually Commie or just playing Commie game to assist his solidifying power. Anti-west forces rapidly increasing power Congo and there may be little time left in which take action to avoid another Cuba.*

The cable also stated that it was the CIA's Station's operations "Objective of replacing Lumumba with a pro western group." Bronson Tweedy, then Chief of the Africa Division of the CIA's clandestine service, replied to the State Department's approval for the operation based on "Our belief Lumumba Must Be Replaced if Possible."

On August 19, 1960, Richard Bissell, Director of the CIA's covert operations branch, signed the following cable to Leopoldville, "You are authorized Proceed with Operation."

The CIA station wrote Washington several days later saying that some anti-Lumumba forces asked President Kasavubu if he and his allies were willing to plan the assassination of Lumumba. Kasavubu said no.

On August 25, 1960, Allen Dulles, the Director of the CIA, attended a meeting of the National Security Council that was responsible for planning covert operations. They discussed the plans to oust Lumumba and the Special Assistant to President Eisenhower said that the president:

"Had expressed extremely strong feelings on the necessity for very strong straightforward action in this situation, and he wondered whether the plans as outlined were sufficient to accomplish this."

The Special Group then decided that it "finally agreed that

planning for the Congo would not necessarily rule out "consideration" of any particular kind of activity which might contribute to getting rid of Lumumba."

Days later, Dulles sent the following cable to Leopoldville:

> *In High quarters, here it is the clear-cut conclusion that if Lumumba continues to hold high office, the inevitable result will at least be chaos and at worst pave the way to Communist takeover of the Congo with disastrous consequences for the prestige of the UN and for the interests of the free world generally. Consequently we conclude that his removal must be an urgent and prime objective that under existing conditions this should be a high priority of our covert action.*

Dulles authorized the expenditure of up to $100,000 for use by the Leopoldville station and even gave them instructions to inform the US ambassador of what they were up to but not to work with him if he so desired.

On September 5, President Kasavubu dismissed Premier Lumumba and he subsequently sought protection from U.N. troops. Even while he was in UN custody, the U.S. still believed that he posed a threat and believed that the parliament might bring him back to power. The Eisenhower administration believed that the Soviet Union might intervene in the Congo and try and bring Lumumba back to power.

Despite the fact that Lumumba was in U.N. protective custody, the CIA began an all out effort to have him killed. In the fall of 1960, a scientist from the CIA delivered a batch of poisons to the station in Leopoldville. The scientist told the chief of station that he was to carry out his instructions in regard to administering the poisons.

The poison was never used, "but despite the fact that Lumumba had placed himself in the protective custody of the UN peace-keeping force shortly before the poisons were delivered to the station, there is no clear evidence that the assassination operation was terminated before Lumumba's death. There is, however, no direct evidence of a connection between the CIA assassination plot and the events which led to Lumumba's death." [38]

In the middle of September 1960, Sidney Gottlieb arrived in Leopoldville for talks with Lawrence Devlin(who goes by this code name of "Hedgman throughout the Senate report). The Senate report says that Gottlieb, whom they do not name, arrived later that month on a "highly sensitive assignment" Hedgman, the report says, recalled that, "...it is my recollection that he (Gottlieb) advised me, or my instructions were, to eliminate Lumumba."

When asked by the committee members if that mean assassination, Hedgman replied, "Yes. I would say that was... my understanding of the primary means. I don't think it was probably limited to that, if there was some other way of doing it."

Hedgman said that when told of the plot to kill Lumumba, he had an "emotional reaction of great surprise when it first became clear that (Gottlieb) was there to discuss an assassination plan."

Hedgeman testified that both he and Gottlieb discussed President Eisenhower's orders when it came to the plans to kill Lumumba. Hedgman said unequivocally that is was his impression from his discussions with Gottlieb that the president knew of the plans to kill Lumumba. Hedgman said, "It is my recollection that he identified the President, and I cannot—the President of the United States—and I cannot recall whether he said "the President" or whether he identified him by name."[39]

Question: "You are not the least unclear whether or not you became aware with a very clear impression that the President's name had been invoked in some fashion?"

Hedgman: "Yes. I came—certainly that is my recollection."

Question: "You have no doubt about that?"

Hedgman: "At the time, I certainly felt that I was under instructions from the President, yes."

He later clarified his statement by saying, "Gentlemen, after fifteen years, I cannot be 100 percent certain, but I have always, since that date, had the impression in my mind that these orders had come from the President."

The Senate report now begins to discuss the sending of a

---

38 Senate Select Committee Report on Assassinations (Draft), 1975. Page 14.

39 Ibid. Page 23.

clandestine agent to the Congo for their pending operation against Lumumba. Without actually mentioning QJWIN, there is no doubt of whom the report was referring to.

"On the basis of his talks with (blank) Hedgman listed a number of "possibilities" for covert action against Lumumba. At the top of the list was the suggestion that a particular agent be used in the following manner:

"Have him take refugee with Big Brother (most likely CIA). Would thus act as inside man to brush up details to razor edge."

Hedgman said that the CIA should then begin by recalling the agent to Leopoldville. On September 30, the Leopoldville Station cabled headquarters to ask that "exploratory conversations" with the agent should begin as a top priority:

> *No really airtight op (operation) possible with assets now available. Must choose between cancelling op or accepting calculated risks of varying degrees.*
>
> *"In view necessity act immediately. If at all, urge exploratory conversations to determine if agent willing take role as active agent or cut-out ths op. (Would approach on hypothetical basis and not reveal plans). If he appears willing accept role, we believe it necessary reveal objective to him.*[40]

The Senate Report details the conversations between the Leopoldville Station and Hedgman regarding the operational details of the upcoming poison plan when discussing their agent.

"Although too early see specific details (agent's) part in Op, believe risk minimized if he leaves the area before effects op are apparent."

In a cable dated September 30, 1960, Hedgman received the go-ahead from Langley for the operation to proceed:

"You are authorized have exploratory talks with (blank) to assess his attitude toward possible agent or cutout to problem."

On October 7, 1960, a cable to Washington reads as follows:

"Conducted exploratory conversations with (agent). After exploring all possibilities (agent) suggested solution recommended

---

[40] Ibid. Page 25.

by Hqs. Although did not pick up ball, believe he prepared take any role necessary within limits security accomplished objective."

Hedgeman testified before the Senate Panel years later and answered when questioned about the steps what were to be taken by saying,

"Certainly I looked on it as a pretty wild scheme professionally. I did not think that it was practical professionally. Certainly to keep the U.S. out of it. I explored it, but I doubt I ever really expected to carry it out."

Hedgman was always keeping his options open in regard to the pending poison plot and he said so in his testimony before the committee:

"In Hqs believe (agent's circumstances) bar his participation, with stress necessity provide station with qualified third country national."

While the CIA was progressing with its own plan to use an agent (QJWIN) in its anti-Lumumba plan, they still had fallback position in case they decided to change their minds. The back up plan was to use local Congolese to kill Lumumba if necessary:

"Only direct action we can now stand behind is to support immobilizing or arresting Lumumba. Desirable as more definitive action might be, any action taken would have to be entirely Congolese."

If the U.S. changed its mind in taking care of Lumumba themselves, they had other options available to them:

"Possibility use commando type group for abduction (Lumumba). Either via assault on house up cliff from river or, more probably, if (Lumumba) attempts another breakout into town."

The CIA's involvement in the plots to kill Lumumba took on a new urgency by October 1960 with the dispatch of an individual of the CIA's clandestine operations division to the Congo. This unidentified man testified before the Senate committee and told the following story.

He said that he was approached by Deputy Director of Plans, Richard Bissell, to got to the Congo to carry out the assassination of Lumumba. This man said that, "he refused to participate in an assassination operation, but proceeded to the Congo to attempt to draw Lumumba away from the protective custody of the UN guard and place him in the hands of the Congolese authorities."

The report now refers to QJWIN and his part in the operation:

> *Shortly after (blank) arrival in the Congo he was joined by a CIA agent with a criminal background who was used the following year by the CIA as part of a program to develop a stand-by assassination capability (the ZR/RIFLE program). Late in 1960, one of the operatives of the (blank) Station in Leopoldville approached this agent of (blank) with a proposition to join in an "execution squad."*
>
> *"Despite the fact that (blank) was initially approached to be part of the plot to assassinate Patrice Lumumba, it is unlikely that (blank) was actually involved in the implementation of that plot by (blank) Station. Whether there is any connection between the assassination plot and either of the two operatives QJ/WIN and WI/ROUGE–is less clear.*[41]

From what this section says, one can assume that the CIA sent *another* person-possibly an unnamed assassin-to the Congo to aid in the assassination schemes against Lumumba. Could there have been 3 men chosen to kill the Congolese leader?

The Senate report goes further in explaining the sending of the CIA officer to the Congo for the Lumumba operation. On October 7, 1960, CIA officer Bronson Tweedy told Hedgman that he "would expect dispatch TDY (temporary duty) senior case officer run this op by supervising a third country national operative..."

Richard Bissell, according to the Senate report, talked to the subject with an unidentified CIA officer. This man said that in October 1960, he was asked by Bissell to undertake the mission of assassinating Patrice Lumumba. This unidentified man testified before the Senate Committee and told the following story.

He said Bissell asked him to go to the Belgian Congo and "eliminate Lumumba."

The senators asked him if he understood the meaning of the word "eliminate" and he said yes. "It was not neutralization. Clearly the context of our talk was to kill him."

---

41 Ibid Page 52.

When he was asked what his reaction to being told to kill Lumumba was, he said, "I told him I would absolutely not have any part of killing Lumumba."

Bissell told the man that once he got to the Congo he should talk a CIA scientist (Gottlieb): "...(blank) said it was inconceivable that Bissell would direct such a mission without the personal permission of Allen Dulles."

While this unknown man told Bissell unequivocally that he would take no part in a plot to kill Lumumba, he did proceed to the Congo as requested by the CIA.

"I said I would go down and I would have no compunction about operating to draw Lumumba out (of UN custody), to run an operation to neutralize his operations which were against Western interests, against, I thought American interests."

Both Richard Helms and William Harvey (the CIA operative who ran the ZR/RIFLE assassination program), testified that they had discussions with the unidentified man and that he told them the same story—he declined to participate in the Lumumba assassination project.

Bissell later testified before the Senate Panel and said that he did indeed have talks with this agent about killing Lumumba in the fall of 1960 and that he "reacted negatively."

Bissell testified that despite the fact that the assassination plot was now stopped, he still believed that the poison plots was still something to be considered.

> *"...But I seem to recollect that after this conversation with him, I wanted this put on the back burner and inactivated for quite some time. Now that doesn't rule out the possibility that some action through completely different channels might have gone forward. But the best of my recollection is, I viewed this not only as terminating the assignment for him, but also as reason for at least postponing anything further along that line."*[42]

The CIA Leopoldville Station was so overwhelmed with their own regular duties, as well as the plans to kill Lumumba that often

---

[42] Ibid Page 60.

times no one really knew what the other was thinking. As we have seen, there were multiple options for the demise of Lumumba including either shooting him or poising him. At one point, Victor Hedgman sent the following cable to Washington about shooting Lumumba: "If case officer sent, recommend Hqs pouch soonest high powered foreign make rifle with telescopic scope and silencer. Hunting good here when lights right. However as hunting rifles now forbidden, would keep rifle in office pending opening of hunting season."

What Hedgman was referring to was trying to kill Lumumba "at the first opportunity to find Lumumba outside the residence where he remained in UN protective custody."

Before Hedgman left his Congolese assignment, "he destroyed all cable traffic relating to the assassination mission. Hedgman's best recollection was that he had received instructions to destroy those cables. Hedgman said he had never before in his tenure as (blank) Station in the Congo destroyed cable traffic because of its sensitivity. But he stated that the cables relating to assassination were destroyed because of their extremely sensitive nature."

In October 1960, the Congo station received on what was called the PROP channel, a message that a senior agent was being sent to the Congo to take part in the Lumumba assassination. This man went by the name of "Michael Mulroney, but his real name was Justin O'Donnell. In his later testimony, Hedgeman said that he believed the arrival of O'Donnell/Mulroney to the Congo was a bad reflection on his handling of affairs at the CIA Station. Hedgeman believed that the arrival of O'DONNELL/Mulroney was "similar to mine, that is, the removal or neutralization of Lumumba. I have no clear recollection of his discussing the assassination."

O'Donnell said that he had no compunction about doing whatever it took to helping anyone else in getting rid of Lumumba but that he, himself, wanted no part of the operation. O'Donnell said that he would aid others in luring Lumumba into the hands of his enemies so that they could do the dirty work in killing him. O'Donnell later testified that he would try to use any trick at his disposal to lure Lumumba away from his UN force captors. He said that he was not opposed to capital punishment, and if the local forces got hold of Lumumba, that would be fine with him.

Later, Victor Hedgman testified before the Senate Panel and gave his recollections about what role O'Donnell played during that period of time. Hedgman told Mr. Baron, his questioner that O'Donnell did not seem to be very active as others in the CIA station while he was there. He said that O'Donnell was sent on a "special mission, although just what it was, he had no idea.

Another person who should have known a lot more about what Justin O'Donnell was doing (or not doing) in the Congo was Richard Helms, later to become Director of the CIA. During his testimony, Helms dissembled and really did all he could not to answer the panel members questions. Helms had a lot to hide, and he wasn't going to let a bunch of senators push him around. Helms, for instance, knew about the plots to kill Castro, and, like Allan Dulles, hid that fact from the Warren Commission. A later biographer of Helm's would call him the "Man Who Kept the Secrets," and Helms lived up to that reputation.

He was asked by two questioners, Mr. Baron and Mr. Schwarz, to recollect about what he knew regarding O'Donnell's time in the Congo. Helms toyed with the panel by asking Mr. Baron if there was a code name for the operation O'Donnell was on. Mr. Baron said no, and Mr. Schwarz responded by mentioning the ZR/RIFLE program:

> Mr. Schwarz: Do you mean ZR/RIFLE?
>
> Mr. Helms: Is it this?
>
> Mr. Schwarz: I don't believe so, Mr. Ambassador.
>
> Mr. Helms: It was not ZR/RIFLE. I don't remember what Justin O'Donnell was doing out there.

Helms was lying. He knew all about the ZR/RIFLE-Execution Action that was run by William Harvey out of the CIA's Staff D and had known so for a long time.

Mr. Baron then asked Helms if he had any follow up in any way on his talks with O'Donnell regarding the subject of assassinating Lumumba between O'Donnell and Richard Bissell:

> Mr. Helms: I don't recall ever saying anything to anybody else about it. I just advised with him. I assume that what I did was advise him and drop it.

Mr. Baron: Is there any reason why you would have thought the subject as assassination if it had come up in that way?

Mr. Helms: Well, I think we're still working on my assumption of what would have been most likely to take place. He probably would have taken the attitude well, look, let's not make a big fuss about it. I don't want to get into difficulty with the boss. I mean all I want to do is get out of this assignment.

Mr. Baron: So far as you were concerned, it would have been a matter between O'Donnell and Bissell?

Mr. Helms: I think so, yes.

A third member of the CIA to testify before the Senate Panel regarding this time period was CIA officer Bronson Tweedy. Tweedy was questioned by Mr. Baron—and he had some interesting things to say regarding the dispatch to the Congo of two of the CIA's prime assassins of the day, QJWIN and WIROGUE.

Mr. Baron asked Tweedy if O'Donnell was the new case officer who was sent to the Congo on the Lumumba assassination mission by Bissell. He responded in the affirmative.

Mr. Baron then began questioning Mr. Tweedy regarding QJWIN-WIROGUE:

Mr. Baron: The third country national referred to in this cable and in other cables as someone you are considering dispatching to the Congo to help with the operation, would that be QJWIN or WIROGUE?

Mr. Tweedy: As I told you before, definitely not WIROGUE Presumably this other fellow, whose identity and what he was is very, very unclear to me.

Mr. Baron: The agent was run by (blank).

Mr. Tweedy: Yes. This would have been the man that would have worked with Justin O'Donnell if it had all happened.

Mr. Baron: That was QJWIN. I will represent you to that QJWIN was the agent who was supervised by Justin O'Donnell.

Mr. Tweedy: We read that that time, which is my only

recollection of it. That is the person I am sure.[43]

The testimony by Bronson Tweedy confirms one of the mysteries surrounding the trip to the Congo by QJWIN. His operational officer was Justin O'Donnell, a.k.a, Michael Mulroney.

In mid-November 1960, the Leopoldville Station sent two cables to CIA headquarters asking them to send QJWIN to Leopoldville as soon as it was feasible. QJWIN was described as "a foreign national with a criminal background" who was recruited in Europe. He was given his travel orders by the CIA and dispatched to the Congo "to undertake a mission that might involve a large element of personal risk."

A report from CIA headquarters about his trip to Africa gives the reader a close look at just what he was to expect when he arrived on the ground:

> *In view of the extreme sensitivity of the objective for which we want him to perform his task, he was not told precisely what we want him to do. Instead, he was told that we would like to have him spot, assess, and recommend some dependable, quick-witted persons for our use. It was thought best to withhold our true, specific requirements pending the final decision to use him.*[44]

QJWIN stayed in the Congo for a month, until December 1960, before the death of Lumumba and the Senate records reveal that he took no part in the events that led up to Lumumba's death. The case officer, Justin O'Donnell, knew that his prime agent was not to be used in this matter.

Documents relating to the use of QJWIN in the Congo operation were released via the "1992 JFK Records Act," and it gives the reader a much clearer understanding of how the CIA's prime asset was used, and his background.

QJWIN met with two unidentified CIA officers in Luxembourg in October 1960 and the notes of that meeting list the names of

---

43 RIF No. 157-10014-10067. Testimony of Bronson Tweedy, Sept 9, 1975.

44 Ibid. Page 67.

police officers and members of the criminal underworld and alluded to the possibilities of finding some safe-crackers and document suppliers.

He was met in Luxembourg on October 19 and 20th 1960 by two CIA officers who asked him if he would make a trip for the CIA to Africa, most likely, Dakar. He was not given the exact nature of the trip due to it sensitivity and was told that the final decision was up to him. He was told a cover story that the Soviet's were operating in Africa among different nationality groups, specifically Corsicans, and he was asked to "spot, assess, and recommend some dependable, quick-witted persons for our use."

Since he was told that the CIA was interested in Corsicans, it is safe to assume that QJWIN knew, or was known by certain Corsican criminal elements operating in the Congo at that time. If he didn't have some concrete knowledge of these people, it is safe to assume that the CIA would not have sent him in that regard.

During the meeting, he agreed to make the Congo trip and, on November 2, he was met in Frankfurt by a CIA officer and instructions went out for his arrival in the Congo.

Once he arrived in the Congo, events moved fast. On December 8, QJWIN was in Leopoldville where he cultivated a close relationship with a Yugoslav pilot. CIA headquarters sent him messages on what approach he should take in order to try and recruit him. However, it was decided by Washington that the pilot was of no intelligence use and he was told to stop any action on his part if he had already made a pitch. A CIA cable relating to his trying to recruit the pilot says, "We would like restrict QJWIN to activity directly pertinent his mission Leopoldville or forthcoming mission Dakar and possibly elsewhere, (e.g., Milan). He our only asset of this type and we wish keep him clear of any operational involvement other than that originally planned for him."

The document that this refers to says," This cable would tend to rule out involvement in an assassination plot, since it is highly unlikely that an individual picked for such a sensitive and dangerous assignment would be burdened with other chores or assignments immediately thereafter."[45]

Let's back up a little now. Lumumba was still alive, although

[45]RIF No. 104-10059-10223 Document Re QJWIN No date.

under house arrest when QJWIN was in the Congo. However, when he was first recruited in Luxembourg and told he was going to the Congo, the CIA decided not tell him of the exact nature of his job, due to its sensitivity. Did the CIA have a change of mind about using him in the Lumumba hit while he was in country?

He left the Congo in December 1960, (after the death of Lumumba), and returned to Luxembourg on December 21 where he was paid $1,000,00 by the CIA station there.

This document says that:

> Subsequently, it appears that QJWIN operated in Europe trying to spot and assess individuals whom the Agency could use in safe-cracking operations, in line with one of the principal missions of FI/D. A 24 May cable to Luxembourg mentions that a decision was made to keep him in Europe and that the Leopoldville assignment had been cancelled. A transfer to Baden-Baden (Germany) is deemed a good choice. Also, a 24 April 1964 dispatch from Luxembourg, which mentions the termination of QJWIN's contract, refers to the fact that his only assignment since January 1962 has been to establish cover.

The CIA knew what kind of man they had recruited when they took on QJWIN and they were blunt in their assessment of him. A CIA cable dated November 29, 1960 to the Leopoldville station reads as follows:

> Mulroney: I would say that he would not be a man of many scruples.
>
> Question: So he was a man capable of doing anything?
>
> Mulroney: I would think so, yes.
>
> Question: And that would include assassination?
>
> Mulroney: I would think so.

As we mentioned before, QJWIN was run by O'Donnell/Mulroney while he was in the Congo. Mulroney told the Senate Panel that as far as he knew, QJWIN was never used for the Lumumba assassination mission. He said that as far as he knew (Mulroney) was the only agent responsible for running QJWIN.

When he was asked if it was possible if QJWIN had another mission that he did not know about he said, "Yes, that is possible- or it could have been that somebody contacted him after he got down there, that they wanted him to do something along the lines of assassination. I don't know."

Additional information about what QJ/WIN's job in the Congo was is given in more detail in the Senate report. Victor Hedgman knew what QJWIN was up to, at least up to a point. A CIA cable sent to the Leopoldville Station and read by Hedgman, said that QJWIN had begun to start a plan to "Pierce both Congolese and UN guards and enter Lumumba's residence," and that QJWIN was supposed to "make the acquaintanceship of the member of the UN Force whose help he sought for the plan to snatch Lumumba from UN custody." But Lumumba had left UN custody at this point to travel toward his stronghold in Stanleyville. This did not deter QJWIN:

"View change in location target. QJWIN anxious to go Stanleyville and expressed desire execute plan by himself without using any apparat."

By the tone of this cable, one can assume that QJWIN was interested in carrying out whatever task the CIA was to give him vis-a-vi Lumumba, whether it concerned an assassination attempt or a kidnap attempt.

In any event, the CIA sent another cable to the Congo regarding QJ/WIN'S next step.

"Concur QJWIN go Stanleyville. We are prepared consider direct action by QJWIN but would like you reading on security factors. How close would this place (United States) to the action? "

After QJWIN left the Congo following the end of his mission, William Harvey, the man who ran the Executive Action-ZR/RIFLE program, wrote a note for the record regarding his assessment of QJWIN's time in the Congo:

> QJWIN was sent on this trip for a specific, highly sensitive operational purpose which has been completed. I was kept informed of the arrangements for QJWIN's trip to the Congo and, subsequently, of his presence in the Congo. I do not know specifically what QJWIN did in the Congo. I do not think that I ever had such knowledge. If QJWIN

were to be used on an assassination mission, it would have been cleared with me. I was never informed that he was to be used for such a mission.

In the "Interim Report: Alleged Assassination Plots Involving Foreign Leaders," the final language on QJ/WIN's most interesting trip to the Congo in the fall of 1960 reads as follows:

> *Despite the suggestive language of the cables at the end of November about the prospect of "direct action' by QJWIN and an indication in the Inspector General's Report that QJWIN may have been recruited initially for an assassination mission, there is no clear evidence that QJ/WIN was actually involved in any assassination plan or attempt. The Inspector General's Report may have accurately reported a plan for the use of QJWIN which predated Mulroney's refusal to accept the assassination assignment from Bissell. But there is no evidence from which to conclude that QJWIN was actually used for such an operation.*

As mentioned before, the CIA knew all about QJWIN's criminal back ground before they recruited him, and despite that knowledge, they decided to at least put that part of his past behind him. A cable dated 1962 from the CIA succinctly noted the risks they knew about their primer agent had when they put him on the payroll. In it they noted that QJWIN was about to go on trial in Europe on smuggling charges and they said, "If information true, we may wish attempt quash charges or arrange somehow salvage QJ/WIN for our purposes."

QJWIN and the Plots to kill Castro

There has always been a debate that QJWIN might have had some role in the CIA's plans, beginning in 1960, in coordination with the mob (Trafficante, Rosselli, Giancana), to assassinate Fidel Castro of Cuba. The documents released via the "1992 JFK Records Act" shed more light on that highly charged subject.

The agents who were handling QJWIN while he was in Europe, according to the records, "were almost certainly unaware of the fact that he was being considered as an asset by the senior Agency official who had begun to become active in February 1962 in the assassination plot against Castro (William Harvey)."

A February 19, 1962 memo from the Deputy Director (Plans) authorized the retention of QJWIN "in activities which we have identified as coincidental with the assassination plot against Castro."[46]

While QJWIN was being talked about at CIA HQ regarding the ZR/RIFLE program, there was no real proof that he ever took part in any attempt to kill Castro. However, the story does not end there. William Harvey had a real interest in recruiting QJ/WIN for ZR/RIFLE, despite the fact that he was never used. Harvey wanted QJ/WIN to be used to "spot" figures of the European criminal element who could be used by the CIA at a later date if necessary. Harvey said that before the implementation of ZR/RIFLE that "not previously used QJWIN as an assassination capability or even viewed him as such."

"The first mention of the ZR/RIFLE code name came in a May 24, 1961 memo from the Chief, FI/D to the Cable Secretariat and states that two copies of all traffic bearing the ZR/RIFLE indicator are to be delivered in a sealed envelope to Chief, FI/D." No other person in the CIA was to be notified about the ZR/RIFLE project.

"The purpose of Project ZR/RIFLE was to spot, develop, and use agent assets for Division D operations. The objective of the project is the procurement of code and cipher materials, and information concerning such materials in accordance with requirements levied on the Clandestine Services, primarily by the National Security Agency. QJ/WIN is under written contract as a principal agent, with the primary task of spotting agent candidates."

The documents reveal that the terms of the ZR/RIFLE project were so secret at the CIA that the FI/D "decided to conceal the executive action capability under the ZR/RIFLE cryptonym when he was assigned responsibility for developing this activity." One prerequisite was not to keep any written records on the project in order to keep its secrets secure.

The National Security Agency's connection to ZR/RIFLE is in

---

[46]RIF No. 104-10059-10223 "Document Re QJWIN."

of itself, noteworthy of further review. The NSA had been in the news during the Bush years due to it use (or misuse) by the administration in its use of the NSA for illegal, domestic surveillance on American citizens in the war on terror. In order to monitor communications between citizens living outside of the United States who were making calls to this country, the Bush administration issued orders that circumvented the laws regarding the use of wiretap communications. No judicial review was asked for in order to tap communications between parties across the world and those American citizens who received such communications.

The task of the modern day NSA is to monitor all electronic communications from across the world, looking for any signals that might mean an attack on the United States or its interests around the globe. The NSA of the Kennedy years was not the monolithic enterprise it is today. At the time of the ZR/RIFLE program, what interested the NSA the most was acquiring code books and other communications intelligence that would help in breaking an enemies code. That was the specific rational for Staff D which was headed by William Harvey. What the men of Staff D really did was break into safes, and were called affectionately, "Second Story Men."

The modern day safe crackers were led by Earl Harter of the CIA. Their main objective, according to the CIA's IG report which was written in 1967, was to break into safes and kidnap couriers, just the description of what QJ/WIN was doing. If one puts all the clues together, it is obvious that QJ/WIN was probably working for Earl Harter at Staff D.

In his 2006 book called *Flawed Patriot: The Rise and Fall of CIA Legend William Harvey,* author Bayard Stockton gives a further description of just what the "Second Story Men" of Staff D did. Their headquarters was located in a warehouse in Alexandria, Virginia, inside a US army compound. The men were locksmiths, photo experts, building tradesmen who formed a cohesive unit. They only worked outside the United States and received help from the CIA Sation Chiefs of the countries they operated in. They conducted dozens of missions and were never caught in their elusive trade.

By what we know today of the ZR/RIFLE program and its

penchant for total secrecy, it is not unusual for Harvey to put that operation-the assassination of Castro-inside the most secure CIA facility at the time.

A very interesting sidelight regarding the activities of QJ/WIN has to do with the activities of Johnny Rosselli and his ties with CIA activities against Castro. William Harvey wrote in his notes regarding the QJ/WIN file that Rosselli's expenses were paid out of the QJ/WIN program. Now, this just might be a housekeeping matter in order to allocate funds for the operation or it may have a more sinister meaning; that the CIA's mob star, Johnny Rosselli, was some how working hand in glove with the QJ/WIN assassination program.

In their book, *Ultimate Sacrifice,* authors Lamar Waldron and Thom Hartman write that the French intelligence service was in touch with the U.S. in a possible attempt on Castro's life. They also write that Phillipe de Vojoli, who headed the French intelligence service in 1963, offered his country's help in assassinating Castro.

Even to this day there is not much in the public record dealing with either QJ/WIN or another CIA asset who was sent to the Congo at the same time that QJ/WIN was there, a man dubbed "WI/ROUGE (see next section on him). In the case of QJ/WIN, what little the record reveals over the years gives us a rather limited story of who he really was. What we do know is that the CIA, in order to keep the true identity of QJ/WIN a secret, backdated and forged a number of their records on him. We also know that in August 1963, he met with his European case officer in Luxembourg and that he was paid by the CIA's Paris station.

The only people who had any idea of who QJ/WIN really was, were limited to a few men in Staff D. William Harvey, it is assumed, knew the true identity of their prime asset. It seems the CIA Director John McCone was not fully briefed when it came to the activities of QJ/WIN. Six months after the assassin was officially dropped from the CIA payroll, Director McCone sent a cable to the CIA's Luxembourg station asking for "a brief roundup of QJ/WIN Project and activities up to the time of termination last February, and any knowledge you have of him since that time." In a change of heart, McCone sent another letter to the Luxembourg station asking that his previous letter be destroyed immediately.

Just why McCone sent this second cable has never been determined.

John McCone, it seems, was kept out of the loop regarding many aspects of the Cuba plots in order to insulate him from any wrong doing in case the operation was ever exposed. But why was he kept in the dark regarding the CIA's number one assassin at the time? One would think that McCone should have been privy to such an important operation. Maybe Bill Harvey decided on his own not to inform McCone for his own, personal reasons.

QJ/WIN's Criminal Background

When QJ/WIN was recruited for the Executive Action Program, he was to be paid $7,200 per year, ending on December 31, 1962. A further allocation of up to $16,000 was approved if needed. QJ/WIN "is under contract as a principal agent, with the primary task of spotting agent candidates." It is known that he worked for both the CIA and the Bureau of Narcotics (now ATF).

The newly released files paint a much more important picture of QJ/WIN's shady background and the role he played for the CIA during the early 1960s. He was first recruited by the CIA in Frankfurt, Germany on November 1, 1960 to take part in an undisclosed operation in the former Belgian Congo (the Lumumba plot). Because of the dangerous conditions that he was expected to work under, the CIA paid him $1,000 per month plus expenses. His term of contract was for a period of one to two months maximum:

> Prior to departing for the Congo, QJ/WIN was obliged to travel to several European countries in order to make cover arrangements. The entire period of his employment from the beginning of his mission until his return from the Congo covered the months of November and December 1960. For this period he was paid completely in various sums by the Luxembourg and Leopoldville stations.

According to CIA documents, QJ/WIN was hired by the agency as an "agent provocateur" and/or double agent against Soviet's. QJ/WIN also goes by the name "Pierre," was a well known smuggler with extensive ties to the underworld in Europe."

The documents paint a picture of a man who was an informer on the activities of smugglers in Luxembourg, a man who was financially in debt to those same smugglers who gave him money to start a legitimate business:

> Subject (QJWIN) has many and varied contacts among illegal traders and petty criminals as well as among influential legitimate businessmen. He is described by the (deleted) as a quick thinker and one who can "think on his feet." When the question arose as to who a suitable candidate for *provocateur* might be, (deleted), suggested subject.

The documents show that whatever future role the CIA had in store for QJ/WIN, his initial assignment was to be Europe:

> According to the (deleted) assessment of Subject, he is the type of person who would appeal to (deleted) and since we have been searching for a means for probing into KGB activities in Luxembourg, Subject may well be the man for the job.

The 201 file (201-236504)—a CIA file on an individual who is of any operational interest to the CIA-paints a varied criminal past on Bill Harvey's newest recruit. A February, 1965 CIA report says that QJWIN was arrested in Luxembourg for East/West nickel smuggling. The report also says that it was at this time that WIN began to renounce his criminal past and was about to turn legitimate. But the CIA report goes on to say that, "Once a smuggler, always a smuggler, but if you think (deleted) can control him, it's worth a try to interest the Soviet's in him."

Despite the fact that WIN had a somewhat checkered past, the CIA made him an agent, and set up a secret bank account in his name where he would-be able to collect his pay. The savings was established in U.S. dollars at the Banque International de Luxembourg. Whatever the reason the CIA had in keeping track of the illicit diamond smuggling operations in Europe are not mentioned in the documents, but they arranged for WIN to penetrate the various groups. A priority cable to the Director of the

CIA dated December 8, 1960, shows just how important this operation had become. The cable says that WIN has cultivated "a close personal relationship" with an unidentified smuggler of industrial diamonds who has agreed to smuggle some merchandise for him to Italy. The CIA station Luxembourg proposed a plan to buy $25,000 worth of diamonds from this man and hand them over to an undercover CIA agent who passed himself off as a colleague of WIN. After the turnover was completed, the agent in charge of the operation would then make an appraisal of the situation to ascertain if the smuggler might be "pitched" by the CIA into working for them. In the end, the CIA refused to follow up on the operation but a cable dated December 9, 1960 makes the following reference. "Have no ops (operational) interest pursuing lead but request pursuing intel (intelligence) coverage important developments in diamond sales picture."

With the CIA no longer interested in the diamond smuggling business in Luxembourg, they now set their sights on a much more important illegal business; the importation of heroin from Europe into the Untied States. And whom did they send to check out the landscape? QJ/WIN.

The records reveal that the CIA was monitoring a rather large "Chi Com," Chinese Communist heroin operation centered in Europe. This operation had its historical roots, as described in previous chapters, dating back to the old OSS operations after World War 2, the French connection in Marseille, France, and the CIA's and OSS's role with the Guerini family in the late 1940s and early 1950s.

QJ/WIN contacted these dealers, became a part of their operation, and soon was sending back valuable intelligence to the CIA. At one point, the Chinese Communists were receiving "gratis," large amounts of heroin from an unidentified French National organization for importation to the United States. They asked if WIN would be interested in joining their operation. WIN, the documents say, was "willing to under guidance Americans." At this point, WIN was under the control of both the CIA and the Bureau of Narcotics, and a BN officer was dispatched to Luxembourg to brief him. The documents point out that the CIA had an ongoing operational interest in the heroin smuggling business. A cable to the Director of the CIA says of a related incident, “FYI this may tie in case symp double agent in similar ring which run by Chicom Emb Bern” (most likely Bern, Switzerland).

QJWIN was now getting in way over his head. While still in Luxembourg, he was approached by an unidentified person who stated that two Sicilians who were living in Paris who were heavily involved in the trade were able to get 50 kilos of heroin into the United States. WIN’s contact, according to the record, was 47 years old, brown hair, brown eyes, with a crooked nose, and a heavy cigarette smoker. He also smuggled narcotics before and after the war from North Africa.

By the summer of 1961, QJWIN was safely settled in Luxembourg for the CIA, while they decided what to do with him. An event took place that turned out to be an embarrassing situation for both the CIA and QJWIN. It seemed that when the CIA was making arrangements to deposit a check for QJWIN in his regular bank, things began to go suddenly wrong. A deposit slip in QJWIN’s code name of “Pierre Copel” was taken by a messenger to the bank for deposit. The slip not only had his fictitious name, but a fake address as well. The messenger was known at the bank, while QJ WIN was not, and it seemed safe for the deposit to be handled that way. The officials at the bank turned the messenger away because they believed the deposit slip and identification by the messenger was not right. He returned to the CIA station, more than a little embarrassed.

In their discussions with QJWIN, the CIA asked him if he would agree to stay in Europe for at least 6 more months. WIN agreed, and he made arrangements to enroll his son in a European school in Luxembourg for the time period September 1961-July 1962.

The Agency told WIN to contact a candidate whom he knew (otherwise unidentified), in France for an undisclosed mission. WIN met a person named Roland Gallord who arrived in Luxembourg City on June 25, 1961. Gallord asked WIN if the deal with his candidate was still on and he answered in the affirmative. WIN told Gallord that, “they (his sponsors) took their time and he suggested that Gallord request the candidate to be patient.” WIN was told not to try and contact the candidate until further notice. WIN told his CIA handlers that he believed he would not be successful in finding out the identities of either candidate by any further meetings on his part. WIN did say that he would try and meet with these people in a hotel outside of France in the near future in order to obtain their true identities.[47]

This document mentions that QJWIN had discussions with the CIA regarding a man named Camille Seavals. This man was a Belgian who owned a café in Stockern, Belgium, near Arion. Seavals and another man met with QJWIN on June 30 "for the purpose of asking him to find someone to purchase some stolen stocks." WIN said he had could not help him. However, Seavals told WIN that he knew two professional safe men. When the CIA queried QJWIN about his conversations with Seavals, he told them that he told Seavals "it was foolish to take such easily traceable things as stocks if he ever got into a safe, and then asked Seavals if he knew any safe-men. After mentioning that he knew two men, Seavals asked him if he had a job for them. QJWIN replied that he did not, but one could never tell." WIN was told that the agency had no interest in his new friend and that he should be wary of contacting him again.

In their talks with WIN, the CIA asked him about the possibilities of relocating somewhere in Europe. He said he would not like to move to Germany, but would go if he was asked. He had no suggestions about getting work outside of Luxembourg but said that he might be able to get employment in a job as a commission salesman for a large Italian flourmill. If he got the job, he wouldn't have to live in Italy and might even move to Switzerland to do the work.

WIN had a cover to protect, and the CIA asked him if his friends and acquaintances had any idea of the work he did. He told them that his friends assumed he had some "successful deals." He said that in order to protect his legitimate employment, he could use his past experience in working for a holding company and that they could probably obtain an office for that purpose. The CIA agreed to his terms and the record says that, "We (CIA) believe the above idea is a natural for resolving QJWIN's cover (and eventually morale) in Luxembourg and also furnishing him with a

---

47 RIF No. 104-10185-10356. "Dispatch: ZRRIFLE/QJWIN: The Security Breach." 7-7-61.

legitimate background if and when he is moved from Luxembourg. If you agree in principle, we will go into more detail with QJWIN on the subject."

By July 1962, the CIA was discussing sending WIN to a new assignment; Baden-Baden, Germany, but no decision was made at that time.

The CIA though, had additional information on the two "candidates" who QJWIN was talking about with Gallord, some months before. It seems that WIN was in Italy to see these men but the documents are vague on what went on. The Agency said that they might use them if needed, but only by a member of the CIA's Trieste (Italy) base. The CIA, via WIN, had the real names of these two French candidates, but that no action on them had been taken.

As we can see by the historical record, QJWIN was one of the most successful, yet enigmatic men the CIA had ever handled. They wanted him to go to the Congo in 1960 just prior to the murder of Patrice Lumumba on a mission that he wasn't fully briefed on. The CIA took him on as a "spotter of candidates" despite his criminal background which was well known in Washington. He worked for the CIA in Europe doing whatever they asked him to do. However, by June of 1963, the CIA, it seems, no longer had reason to keep him on as an active agent.

A June 27, 1963 memo for the "Chief, Foreign Intelligence" on WIN is worth reading in full:

> *1. Confirming our conversation of 26 June 1963, I make the following recommendations concerning the future handling and possible disposition of QJWIN;*
>
> *A. I Believe the original purpose for which QJWIN was continued and sent to his present undercover assignment is no longer sufficient validity to justify the continuation of QJWIN beyond the termination of his present contract for this purpose alone.*
>
> *B. QJWIN, in my opinion, is a competent, usable agent who is capable of operating in certain circles in Europe where we have very few assets. Whether this is of sufficient worth to continue his services depends on the determination of how he can be used either by the German Station or by the Austrian Station or by any other KUBARK*

(CIA) informant as a long term unofficial cover agent. He is not being used at the present time. He is being paid but he is on ice as far as any operational assignment are concerned.

C. It is recommended that the present Chief of Station Luxembourg and RABNEY (code name for someone at CIA) be consulted by Headquarters for their best recommendations as to the continued use of QJWIN. After these recommendations are received, I suggest that the German and Austrian stations be consulted for their possible interest in using him. If after these discussions a sensible framework for the operational use of QJWIN can be established. I would recommend we continue him. If not, I would recommend that he be terminated at the time his present contract expires.

2. *As far as the ZR/RIFLE aspects of this operation which have been covered under the QJWIN authorization for security reasons and with which Fletcher Knight is fully familiar as I orally advised you on 26 June 1963, except for one precautionary "life line," aspects of this case have been terminated and need a longer, except perhaps for minor accountings be considered as a part of this project."*[48]

This memo was signed by the head of the ZR/RIFLE program, William Harvey.

The memos on the ZR/RIFLE program that were run by William Harvey give tidbits of information that historians will find more than interesting when researching the case.

The CIA files on the ZR/RIFLE case give the names of two people who were in some way linked with QJWIN. They are Harold Meltzer and Hanna Yazbeck. There is not much biographical information on both of these people, so we will have to read behind the lines to gain any information on just who they were.

"Harold Meltzer with aliases was involved in the rackets with upper echelon 'hoodlums' throughout the U.S. In 1959 he

[48] RIF No. 104-10185-10403.

furnished information to our QJ/WIN California office but has not since cooperated with us. N.B. he has the background and talent for the matter we discussed but it is not known whether he would be receptive."

So, what do we have here? A man named Harold Meltzer was somehow involved with "hoodlums" in the United States and may have been a candidate for some sort of role in the ZR/RIFLE program. We also learn that there was a QJ/WIN California office that probably refers to a CIA office somewhere in the Golden State. Just why would a domestic CIA station have reason to be interested in a foreign assassin, QJ/WIN? Was this base "running" him at some point in time?[49]

The other person mentioned in the report is Hanna Yazbeck. "Yazbeck lived in Beirut and worked for QJ/WIN's office intermittently the past 10 years (dates not given-possibly 1951-61). Yazbeck's chief bodyguard from 50-58 (not named) was a convicted murderer. The bodyguard was murdered. States that YAZBECK has an available pool of assassins."

We don't know if "Hanna Yazbeck" is a man or a woman, or was some other entity entirely, but due to the first name, one can assume that he was a man, due to the nature of the work involved (assassination). The fact that he lived in Beirut is interesting in of itself, as that was one of the places in the world where freelance assassins congregated and were hired by various organizations, both governmental and private. The fact that Yazbeck's bodyguard was murdered, puts both of them in a very dangerous line of work. Also interesting is the fact that Yazbeck was one of a pool of assassins that could be used for various clandestine missions around the world.

But, all this was in the future. Now, with his adventure on behalf of the CIA in the nickel/diamond/heroin smuggling operations in Europe at an end, he now made his way to the Congo where he was to meet up with another agent whom the Agency sent there, another mysterious man, code named WI/ROGUE.

QJWIN and WIROGUE in Africa

In its investigations into the assassination plots against foreign

---

49RIF No. 104-10308-10287. "Review of ZRRIFLE File."

leaders, the Senate Select Committee, divulged the name of a second, CIA asset who was sent to the Congo at the time of the plots to kill Patrice Lumumba. Like, QJ/WIN, this mysterious person's real identity is still one of the most highly guarded secrets of the CIA. However, there is enough information in the released files to fill in some of the missing blanks in this convoluted story. The code name given to the man was WI/ROGUE. Like QJ/WIN, WI/ROGUE, was a soldier of fortune, a man of action, someone whom the CIA would have no trouble hiring for a covert mission like the one in the Congo.

WI/ROGUE was handled by a team of CIA officers in Washington beginning in 1960. His original assignment was for action in the Congo and in that regard, he was trained in "small arms, demolition and inoculation." The "Interim Report: Alleged Assassination Plots Involving Foreign Leaders" reveals a much deeper background of who this man was.

WI/ROGUE was an "essentially stateless" soldier of fortune, a forger and former bank robber. He was sent to the Congo after giving him plastic surgery and a toupee so that any of the other members of the European soldier of fortune community in the Congo at that time whom he might know, would not recognize him. The CIA called him as a man who "learns quickly and carries out any assignment without regard for danger." When writing about him, the CIA's Africa Division described him in the following terms:

He is indeed aware of the precepts of right and wrong, but if he is given an assignment which may be morally wrong in the eyes of the world, but necessary because his case officer ordered him to carry it out, then it is right, and he will dutifully undertake appropriate action for its execution without pangs of conscience. In a word, he can rationalize all actions.

Victor Hedgman, the same agent who controlled QJWIN, also knew WIROGUE and said that he was "a man with a rather unsavory reputation, who would try anything once, at least." Hedgman used him as a "general utility agent" because "I felt we needed surveillance capability, developing new contacts, various things."

The Inspector General's Report had this to say regarding WIROGUE:

> In October 1960, a cable to Leopoldville stated that Headquarters had intent to use him as utility agent in order to a) organize and conduct a surveillance team, b) intercept packages, c) blow up bridges, and d) execute other assignments requiring positive action. His utilization is not to be restricted to Leopoldville.

When WI/ROGUE arrived in the Congo, he attempted to hire another person to be a member of an "execution squad." That person, believe it or not, was QJ/WIN.

After learning that WI/ROGUE had tried to enlist QJ/WIN to become a member of an "execution squad, "Victor Hedgeman cabled CIA Headquarters with this most startling news:

QJ/WIN who resides same hotel as WIROGUE, reported that WI/ROGUE smelled as though he in Intel business. Station denied any info on WI/ROGUE. 14 Dec. QJ/WIN reported WI/ROGUE had offered him three hundred dollars per month to participate in Intel net and be member of an "Execution Squad." When QJ/WIN said he not interested, WI/ROGUE added there would be bonuses for Special jobs. Under QJ/WIN questioning, WI/ROGUE later said he working for (American) service. In discussing local contacts, WI/ROGUE mentioned QJ/WIN but did not admit having tried to recruit him. When Station Officer tried learn whether WI/ROGUE had made approach latter claimed had taken no steps. Station Officer was unable contradict, as did not wish reveal QJ/WIN connections (with CIA).[50]

As CIA headquarters began reading Hedgeman's cables regarding WI/ROGUE, alarm bells must have begun to ring in earnest. Now, they had two possibly out-of-control agents—QJ/WIN and WI/ROGUE—about to conduct god knows what mayhem in the Congo at the same time that plots to kill Lumumba

---

50 Interim Report: "Alleged Assassination Plots Involving Foreign Leaders." Page 46-47.

were under way.

Hedgeman sent another cable to Washington, not masking his feelings in the slightest terms:

"Leop (Leopoldville) concerned by WI/ROGUE free wheeling and lack security. Station has enough headaches without worrying about agent who not able handle finances and who not willing follow instructions. But if continue have difficulties, believe WI/ROGUE recall best solution."

Hedgman told his superiors in Washington of WI/ROGUE's attempt to recruit QJ/WIN for the "execution squad as an unauthorized contact. He said that under no circumstances had he given him any such order. He later testified that:

"I would like to stress that I don't know what WI/ROGUE was talking about as an"execution squad," and I am sure he was never asked to go out and execute anyone."

He testified that WI/ROGUE probably made the pitch to QJ/WIN himself, without any official CIA authorization.

"His idea of what an intelligence operative should do, I think, had been gathered by reading a few novels or something of the sort."

Other members of the CIA who had some knowledge of the activities of both QJ/WIN and WI/ROGUE, Bronson Tweedy and Richard Bissell, also testified as to what they knew about each man's mission to the Congo.

Bissell reported that he had no recollection about anything related to WI/ROGUE's approach to QJ/WIN. Bronson Tweedy recalled that WI/ROGUE was "dispatched on a general purpose mission" to the Congo. Tweedy also testified that WI/ROGUE would "absolutely not" have been used on an assassination mission against Lumumba because "he was basically dispatched, assessed and dealt with by the balance of the Division, rather than by the two people in the Africa Division, Tweedy and his Deputy, who would have known that the assassination of Lumumba was being considered."

Hedgeman, further spelled out his assessment of WI/ROGUE, by saying, "I had difficulty controlling him in that he was not a professional intelligence officer as such. He seemed to act on his own without seeking guidance or authority. I found he was rather an unguided missile, the kind of man that could get you in trouble before you knew you were in trouble."

However, Hedgeman did stick up for WI/ROGUE by saying, "If you give a man an order and he carries it out and causes a problem for the Station, then you accept responsibility."

When the "Report on the Alleged Assassination Plots" was written, the committee members had a hard time reconciling what they had learned. They wrote:

"In sum, the testimony of the CIA officers involved in the PROP operation and the concern about WI/ROGUE's "freewheeling" in Hedgeman's cable suggests that agent WI/ROGUE's attempt to form an "execution squad" was an unauthorized, maverick action, unconnected to any CIA operation. However, the fact that WI/ROGUE was to be trained in "medical immunization" precludes a definitive conclusion to that effect."

So, who is this elusive figure whom the CIA sent to the Congo at the time of the Lumumba plots?

"WIROGUE1 was an ethnic Georgian recruited and trained for the old (blank) program. Although born in the Soviet Union, he moved to Western Europe when two years old. He fought in (deleted) and as of 1960, was essentially stateless. Involved peripherally with the French Resistance, he was sentenced to death by the Germans but liberated by the U.S. Army in 1945 and returned to (blank). By 1950 he had managed to rob a (blank) bank of a sizeable sum of money, receive a prison sentence and be released five years later for good behavior. He was brought to the United States originally for use as one of two agents for Project SENTINEL. He spoke (blank) French and fluent Georgian, German and English."[51]

It seems that WI/ROGUE "was a World War 2 veteran, of Georgian ancestry, and was born in the Soviet Union. He was a criminal by trade, a member of the French Resistance in World War 2 and was of sufficient interest to the Germans as they put a death sentence on him. From his World War 2 adventures, it is not making too much of a stretch to believe that he was probably a member of some intelligence service, and was associated with the French who were battling the Germans to rid them from their

---

[51]RIF No. 104-10059-10238 "WIROGUE/1 Mission to Kinshasa," December 1960.

homeland. After the war, he turned to armed robbery and was arrested in those pursuits. In other words, he fit the overall bill of a person whom the CIA would recruit into their ranks.

In 1960, according to CIA documents, the agency tried to resettle him to Mexico. The mission that the CIA had for him was cancelled, but what sort of mission, is not revealed. On September 19, 1960, WI/ROGUE was met by two members of the CIA's Africa Division to "discuss an operational assignment in Africa Division. In connection with this assignment, WI/ROGUE/1 was to be trained in demolition, small arms and medical immunization." He was then given a code name and immunization shots prior to his leaving for his assignment. In October 1960, CIA headquarters sent a cable to their Leopoldville station saying that their new agent was "being prepared for a deep cover assignment to arrive Leopoldville late November." His job, once he arrived in Africa was to use him as "a utility agent in order to a) organize and conduct a surveillance team, b) intercept packages, c) blow up bridges and d) execute other assignments requiring positive action."

He was ordered to work with other CIA Africa Stations besides Leopoldville if needed. The documents on him reveal an interesting side to his character. He is described as "an inventor, photographer, architect, forger and former bank robber. He was judged to be ingenious, observant, shrewd, glib and one who relished intrigue and daring." His personality chart says that he was able to "learn quickly and carry out any assignment without regard to danger." It seems that WI/ROGUE/1 was in the United States under CIA supervision and did not enter the country in a legal way. "As he was in the United States black (untraceable, undocumented), the plan was for him to depart black, documented as an (blank) to surface in West Germany and from there to proceed on his own to Leopoldville."

Like QJ/WIN, WI/ROGUE/1 had a checkered past which was known, and accepted by the CIA for the work they had planned for him. It seems that the CIA went to great lengths to hide his real identify before shunting him off to Africa.

"In November 1960, to prevent his identification with the U.S. Government or BKHERALD (a code name for a CIA operation), and to preclude any unexpected recovery of his past which would associate him with his pre-BKHERALD life, WI/ROGUE/1 underwent plastic surgery to change the shape of his nose. He was provided with a toupee for constant wear and documented as an (blank) who had never been to the United States. Cover for his presence in Leopoldville was to be as (blank). A rather lengthy assessment of his character can be summed up by saying that he was able to rationalize any action if he had strong case officer direction."[52]

He arrived in Leopoldville on December 2, 1960 and was given the following instructions from his CIA case officer, "to a) build cover possibly by opening a (deleted) and b) to try to spot persons for a surveillance team, intel assets." Very shortly after arriving in Leopoldville, WI/ROGUE/1 met QJ/WIN.

Both men were staying at the same hotel but did not know that the other was working for the CIA. Apparently, WI/ROGUE/1 had been observing WIN for some time and decided that he looked like a good intelligence contact. Without CIA direction, ROGUE tried to recruit WIN into an "execution squad." CIA files relating to this attempted engagement of WIN by ROGUE stated that, "WIROGUE/1 exceeded his authority." WIN refused ROGUE's offer and he quickly reported the attempted recruitment to his handlers.

Here is where things get more interesting. As both men were then residing in the same hotel in Leopoldville, they had a chance to get to know each other over drinks and small talk. QJWIN told his CIA handlers that WI/ROGUE/1told him that he had lived previously in Alaska, Japan, South America, Germany and other areas of Europe. "QJWIN said WI/ROGUE smelled as though he in intel business." WIN also reported that his new friend offered him $300.00 per month to take part in a "intel net and be member of an execution squad." When WIN refused the offer, WIROGUE told him that if he accepted the job, there would be bonuses for special jobs in the future. After many hours of discussions, and probably to make him look better in QJWIN's eyes, ROGUE told him that he worked for the United States government.

In his cables to CIA HQ regarding his run in with ROGUE, WIN said that his new pal was spending money like he had just

[52] Ibid.

won the lottery. He said that WIROGUE bought 3 automobiles since his arrive in Leopoldville; a Chrysler for 8500 Francs, a Citroen for 2500 Francs and a Triumph for 11000 francs. He later said he sold the Citroen for 15000 francs but still parked it near his hotel.[53]

This intriguing document does not say where WIROGUE got the money to buy these three cars, but even in 1960 they had to cost a lot. Maybe he used his CIA salary or, maybe he got the money elsewhere.

The document says that WIROGUE mentioned QJWIN, but did not admit to having tired to recruit him. At this critical point in the pitch, QJWIN did not want to reveal that he too was working for the CIA and did not want to reveal that secret.

After being told of ROGUE's wild spending, headquarters had a fit when it came to their new recruit. This cable gives their reaction to the news of the car purchases"

"Leop concerned by WIROGUE free wheeling and lack security. Station has enough headaches without worrying about agent who not able to handle finances and who not willing to follow instructions. If HQS desires, willing keep him on probation, but if continue have difficulties, believe WIROGUE recall best solution."

WIROGUE fired back, saying that he bought the cars in order to set up his new cover. The CIA, in an internal memo, said that if they were going to keep him in the field, they would have pay him an additional one thousand dollars, because he said he was short of funds.

At one point during their stay in Leopoldville, QJ/WIN borrowed WI/ROGUE's car and he noticed that the key ring contained his postal box key. QJ/WIN was going to make an impression of the ring in order to find out what was in the postal box. He never got the chance because he left the country a day earlier than he expected.

In January 1961, the CIA Leopoldville station decided to give him flying lessons so that the station could conduct some clandestine missions.

---

[53]RIF No. 104-10185-10057. "RYBAT WIROGUE." December 17, 1960.

By April 1961, it was decided to use him in a mission to obtain arms and instructors in Western Europe. It seems that the CIA sent WI/ROGUE/1 to some sort of school where he was reading undisclosed manuals at night "to stay ahead of his class."

In July 1961, WI/ROGUE/1 left Leopoldville because he was unable to keep his residence permit (it seems that spies too need permission to stay in place). He was let go by the CIA in September 1961. The documents relating to his time in their employ say that, "In a summary of his activity in August 1961, Leopoldville Station said WI/ROGUE/1 knew very little about station activities."

The CIA summarized their operational use of their assassin by saying:

> *It is the writer's opinion that WI/ROGUE1/ was recruited for his Congo assignment because of his third country national background in order to establish a support mechanism in Leopoldville. At the time the Congo was in chaos, BKHERALD had few assets and there was some likelihood that the political situation would degenerate quickly. The Station possibly also wanted to have a latent para-military capability and WI/ROGUE/1's background and previous training for the (word partially spelled, REDSO-) program made him a suitable candidate. This is, of course, conjecture.*

By October 1964, WI/ROGUE/1 had been turned over to another CIA station (not known) and was resettled in another area of the world. According to the documents on this time period, "Resettling him had turned out to be an enormous problem. (He) had an intense desire for intelligence service and enjoyed the role of lower echelon action agent. Although he threatened to go to work for the French IBS, it was not believed that he thought he would be accepted. The assessment indicated there was little flap potential with WI/ROGUE/1 since he knew little about Agency. In particular, in the Congo he was aware only of the COS's contact with contact. WI/ROGUE/1 spent most of this time trying to develop contacts and was not directly involved in any particular operation."

It seems that both QJ/WIN and WI/ROGUE/1, were sent to Leopoldville, at the behest of the CIA for some sort of intelligence operation that may, or may not, have been associated with the plots to kill Patrice Lumumba. Both men, as we have seen, had criminal backgrounds (QJ/WIN more so than WI/ROGUE/1). They both had extensive intelligence training by the CIA and were well prepared to take on whatever assignment was requested of them. WI/ROGUE/1 had a penchant for spending money, given the fact that he purchased three cars, was a freewheeler whose actions were watched closely by the local CIA Station, tried to recruit QJ/WIN without authorization into taking part in an "execution squad," and even went so far as to bribe him with money for extra missions. He was part of the French Resistance and was liberated by the US Army after World War 2. He was given plastic surgery in order for him not to be recognized by others in the same line of work. He was essentially a "stateless person" who had no ties to his mother country.

QJWIN, on the other hand, was originally associated with the CIA's assassination operation, code named ZR/RIFLE, headed by William Harvey. He had a rather large criminal past, was both a nickle and diamond smuggler, and his talents were to be spread around to other CIA stations across Europe after his assignment in the Congo was over. He was to be sent to the Congo on an important mission whose purpose was purposely not given to him prior to his arrival on site. He was thought so highly of, that the Company gave him a secret bank account that only he could access.

He spent a considerable amount of time in Luxembourg and was run by that station. While in Luxembourg, the CIA tried to set him up in a real job, and make his cover as iron clad as possible. As part of his assignment, he met two Sicilians who were involved in the heroin trade and worked for both the CIA and the Bureau of Narcotics. While he was in the Congo, the CIA asked him to spot Corsicans (people of French background). Is it possible that QJ/WIN himself was Corsican, or was he known to them from his previous criminal activity? He was to be used by the CIA as an "agent provocateur" or as a double agent against the Soviet's in Europe. His job in the Congo was to pierce Lumumba's UN guards and try to enter his residence.

The CIA grave QJ/WIN a lie detector test on March 31, 1961 to see if he "was presently working for another intelligence service." He was not. Besides working for the CIA in the Congo assignment, he had previously worked for other allied intelligence agencies such as the French, the Belgians, and the West Germans. The paper trail for his payments went through Paris, not CIA headquarters or other areas such as the Luxembourg CIA station of which he had a solid relationship with. QJ/WIN's wife, according to CIA files, was called "extremely discreet" and was certainly aware of her husband's covert activities.

One payment to her husband went through her own, private bank account. The CIA knew that QJ/WIN was supposed to stand trial in 1962 in Europe on smuggling charges but the CIA intervened and the trial was never held. QJ/WIN's CIA employment was ended in April 1964, after the Agency decided he was of no further use to them. As will be described in the next chapter, a man named Jean Souetre was expelled from Dallas one day after the assassination of JFK. Jean Souetre also went by the alias "Michael Mertz" (a real person).

Michael Mertz was in Fort Worth, Texas the day before the assassination, and was also in Dallas on November 22, 1963. Some researchers who have studied the French Connection to the Kennedy assassination, believe that QJ/WIN might have been one of the shooters in Dealey Plaza that terrible day. Might the CIA have put two and two together and realized that their prime, European assassin, QJ/WIN, might have played a part in the president's murder? If that in fact were the case, and the U.S. government had somehow linked both Michael Mertz and Jean Souetre, possibly QJ/WIN, to the death of the president, then they had no choice but to sever all links with him and terminate his contract as soon as possible.

Richard Helms, on February 19, 1962, who knew all about the ZR/RIFLE program, (along with Bill Harvey), told Harvey to keep QJ/WIN on its payroll through the end of 1962. This might possibly coincide with the CIA's use of California ZR/RIFLE office in that state. Did QJ/WIN, while he was in the United States, have anything to do with that station? No one knows for sure.

The Senate Select Committee's Assassination Report sums up their reporting on WI/ROGUE/1's mission to the Congo and the plots to kill Lumumba by saying:

> In sum, the (blank) Station testified that despite the fact that the CIA was interested in the assassination of Lumumba during this period, agent WI/ROGUE's attempt to form an "execution squad" was an unauthorized, maverick action, unconnected to the CIA assassination plan.
>
> Nonetheless, the fact that WIROGUE was to be trained in medical immunization raises the possibility that he was connected to the plot to assassinate Lumumba by means of lethal biological substance. The 1975 report on WI/ROGUE's case by the Inspector General's office leaves this question open.

The House Select Committee on Assassinations delved deeply into the ZR/RIFLE program and, unlike those referring to both QJ/WIN, and WI/ROGUE/1, there is a considerable amount of information in the files to make a complete picture of just what the program was used for. The writers of a document on the ZR/RIFLE program said they "were compelled to look into the Central Intelligence Agency's executive action project, ZRRIFLE, because of the known antagonism between the head of that project, William Harvey, and the Kennedy's. Even though the Church Committee Interim Report concluded that the ZRRIFLE program was never implemented, this Committee believed that Harvey, due to his contacts with the La Cosa Nostra (American mob) and the anti-Castro Cubans, and his known hatred of the Kennedy's coupled with his position as the head of the CIA's executive action project made him a suspect in the Kennedy assassination."[54]

This is damming stuff indeed. There was no love lost between the Kennedy brothers and William Harvey and after Harvey's freewheeling activities during the height of the Cuban Missile Crisis, the administration gave him the boot.

A further connection between William Harvey and QJWIN comes from Peter Wright, a onetime top British intelligence official who had close ties with both Harvey and James Angleton,

---

[54]RIF No. 180-10142-10336. "ZRRIFLE." (Date left out).

the CIA's legendary head of counter-intelligence. Wright wrote in his memoir of a discussion he had between both men in which the topic of killing Castro came up. Harvey told Wright that"We're (the CIA) developing a new capability to handle these kinds of problems, and we're in the market for the requisite expertise."

Wright said that Harvey told him he was looking for untraceable people to carry out such assignments (the ZRRIFLE program), preferably foreign, people who could not be traced back to the United States. Wright proposed the French, saying, "It's more their type of thing, you know, Algiers and so on."

The use of foreign assassins, people who could not be traced back to the United States, fits both QJWIN and QI/ROGUE/1 to a tee.

Another high-ranking CIA agent who had revealing comments to make regarding William Harvey was John Whitten, who for years, went by the alias, "John Scelso." Right after the assassination, the CIA asked Whitten/Scelso to write a report on what the CIA knew about the assassination. He did so, using only the data given to him by the CIA, leaving out such important information such as the CIA-Mafia plots to kill Castro.

Scelso/Whitten testified before the congressional committee in the 1970s regarding the Kennedy assassination and he made these comments regarding Harvey and his prime assassin, QJ/WIN:

> Mr. Goldsmith: What was Mr. Harvey like?
>
> Mr. Scelso: Well, he is dead now. Harvey was real hard boiled, unstable, ruthless guy who was, in my opinion, a very dangerous man. I had run-ins with him several times. I also had to investigate one of his big cases and although I was on friendly terms with him-we never slugged it out with each other-he never liked me and I never liked him.
>
> Mr. Goldsmith: Did you know if Mr. Harvey had any negative feelings toward the Kennedys?
>
> Mr. Scelso: I only heard he was sore at Bobby Kennedy. Bobby Kennedy fired him because Harvey was a three martini-lunch man—not because of the expense involved.
>
> Mr. Goldsmith: Did you know if Mr. Harvey was running any operations outside the ordinary course of his

business?

Mr. Scelso: I did not know at that time. I just heard about this assassin he had on his payroll and so on. To me, knowing nothing except that the man was a criminal, the assassin he had on the payroll, and Harvey's nature, the thought of our engaging in assassinations as distinguished by guerilla warfare or coup d'etat, and so on, setting out by stealth or surprise to kill an important foreign person was abhorrent to the standards of the clandestine service and the fact that the way-you know, what the response was in the Lumumba case. They refused to carry out the order, but they were guilty of conspiracy to commit homicide.[55]

In his testimony, Scelso/Whitten also had some rather harsh words regarding the possibility that Harvey was involved in the murder of Chicago mob boss, Sam Giancana:

Mr. Scelso: Harvey was not the kind of personality who appeals to me and I certainly was not the kind of personality that appeals to him. I have wondered-wonder if the government has ever looked into the possibility that Harvey did not knock off Giancana. He lived in the same area, when he was retired. He was a great one with guns. I was overseas and I said to myself, I wondered if they looked into Bill Harvey.

The Church Committee, in its conclusion regarding its investigation of the ZR/RIFLE program had this to say about the CIA's most guarded secret of the 1960s:

In general, project ZR/RIFLE involved assessing the general and requirements of assassination and developing a stand-by assassination capability; more specifically, it involved "spotting" potential agents and "researching" assassination techniques that might be used. The 1967

---

55 Peter Kross, *Oswald, The CIA and the Warren Commission: The Unanswered Questions*. Bridger House Books, Hayden, ID, 2011, Page 77-78.

Inspector General's Report found "no indication in the file that the Executive Action capability was ever used," but said that "after Harvey took over the Castro operation, he ran it as one aspect of ZR/RIFLE.[56]

The use of agents for "spotting potential agents and researching assassination techniques," as reported in the Senate Committee report, make both agents QJWIN and QI/ROGUE/1 ideal candidates for that purpose. Even though they were not used in the Executive Action project, they were trained in all aspects of assassination techniques, given extensive training in all aspects of espionage methods by the CIA and were on hand if needed by Washington.

The Senate Report said that "No information in the ZR/RIFLE file would directly connect William Harvey to the assassination of John Kennedy."

However, they were still not quite ready to entirely vindicate William Harvey when it came to the assassination of the president. What they wrote involved speculation, as well as fact and it included a mention of the actions of QJ/WIN. They wrote:

> *It is possible to draw some speculative comparisons between Harvey's blue-print for assassination and the killing of John Kennedy, but the Committee has no indication that the similarities are anything more than coincidence.*

They mentioned the fact that a Dallas reporter named Seth Kantor alleged that QJ/WIN bailed out Thomas Eli Davis, a gunrunner with ties to the CIA, as well as being a fiend of Jack Ruby's, from a Moroccan jail. In December 1963, Thomas Eli Davis "was being held by the Moroccan National Security Police because of a letter in his handwriting which referred in passing to "Oswald" and to the Kennedy assassination."

The incident involving Thomas Eli Davis got the attention of FBI Director J. Edgar Hoover, one month after the assassination of the president. On December 20, 1963, Director Hoover sent a

---

56RIF No. 180-10142-10336 "ZRRIFLE" No date.

telegram to the Deputy Assistant Secretary for Security at the Department of State regarding Davis' arrest. This memo referred to the FBI's learning from State about the arrest of Davis because of the letter in his possession regarding Oswald. The cable also mentioned a man named Howard Loeb Schulman who was arrested by the Moroccan police after he said that he was wanted by the United States government in connection with the assassination of JFK. In the note, Hoover said that the FBI received information that Davis was possibly recruiting people for an invasion of Haiti. The report went on to say that Davis wanted to meet with certain soldier-of-fortune types so that he could get material for a newspaper article he planned to write. The cable also noted that Howard Loeb Shulman was pro-Castro in his political leanings, and that there were reports of his "suicidal tendencies." Hoover went on to request from the State Department, any and all information they had on Davis that was in the hands of the Moroccan police.

The Senate Panel did not have time to look into the Davis-QJWIN story and it is one of the flaws of its time limited investigation.

They ended their exchange of views of the possible role played by William Harvey in the events of November 22, 1963 by saying:

"Even though Mr. Harvey personally had a motive and had access to the means and the opportunity to kill Kennedy, the above discussion represents the sum of the investigation conducted by this Committee into any possible connections between ZRRIFLE and the assassination."

Chapter 6:

Who Where QJ/WIN and WI/ROGUE/1?

In the classic espionage movie *Casablanca,* Claude Rains, playing the part of Captain Renault, makes the following statement in one of the most dramatic parts of the movie, “Round up the usual suspects.” The same comment can be said in relation to the true identities of the CIA’s two most talented, and secretive assassins of the cold war era; QJ/WIN and QI/ROGUE/1. Since most of the files on these two men are still kept locked up in government vaults, waiting for the right time to release them, writers and historians can only speculate on just who these two men really are. There are a number of “suspects” being bandied about for the past 40 years, and each name is just as plausible than the others. This chapter will present the case for three men who just might fit the bill, all of whom had connections to both the United States CIA, the French Secret Service, as well as being part of the Corsican heroin network that was run by Auguste Ricord; Christian David, Lucien Sarti, and Robert Blemant. Both Christian David and Lucien Sarti were implicated by Christian David in the assassination of JFK and their story will be told later in the book.

One of the first writers to speculate that Christian David was WI/ROGUE/1 was JFK researcher and writer, J. Gary Shaw. Shaw first approached the possibility that Christian David was the elusive WI/ROGUE, in an article he wrote for the now defunct magazine, *The Continuing Inquiry.* Shaw wrote that QI/ROGUE was part of the ZR/RIFLE program run by the CIA in the 1960s as part of its effort to kill Fidel Castro of Cuba. Christian David was once employed by the French Secret Service and went to work for them as a counter-terrorist against the O.A.S, the anti-De Gaulle organization which were against de Gaulle’s instance that Algeria be given its independence from France. Shaw wrote that "David was considered the most uncontrollable member of a Corsican group which itself had been labeled as wild and undisciplined. Arrested at one time traveling as a vacationing diplomat—he was found to be carrying Browning and Beretta pistols with silencers, a S.W. pistol loaded with dum-dum bullets and stamps for forging passports. At times he was said to travel to various African countries on small missions. He was a professional killer and there are reports that he assassinated a number of African officials. Christian David was a petty hoodlum who had escaped at one time from a French prison."[57]

In the same article, Shaw wrote that an ex-Army intelligence officer, William Spector, told the *Fort Worth Star-Telegram*'s reporter, Jim Marrs, that Christian David was WI/ROGUE. Marrs, who later wrote a book on the Kennedy assassination called *Crossfire: The Plot that Killed Kennedy,* said that Spector told him he got the information that David was ROGUE from his former wife's smuggling work for Paul Weiller who was once a former chief executive officer for Air France. It seems that the former Mrs. Spector at one point stuffed toy animals with heroin and smuggled them into the United States.

Christian David also had a connection with a noted heroin smuggler named Michael Victor Mertz. As we will see later in the book, Michael Victor Mertz went by the alias Jean Souetre and Michael Roux, both real men. Jean Souetre was expelled from the United States two days after the assassination of JFK and there is speculation that he might have been one of the shooters in Dealey Plaza on November 22, 1963, (more about Jean Souetre in the next chapter).

Over the years, speculation was ripe that Christian David might have played a part in the assassination of Mehdi Ben Barka in 1965. Ben Barka was a Moroccan opposition leader who worked against the Moroccan ruler, General Oufkir, an enemy of the French.

In November 1972, right after Richard Nixon had been re-elected president of the United States, a number of articles

---

[57] Shaw, Gary, "The Continuing Inquiry". Volume 111 Number 10, May 22, 1979 "QJ/WIN Identified?"

appeared in the nation's newspapers regarding the arrest of a number of men in one of the largest heroin smuggling cases ever to be seen in United States history. One of the men arrested was 41 year old Christian David, along with his accomplices, Paul Navarro, 39, Domingo Padron, 61, Michel Nicoli, 42, whom the newspapers said was one of the people whose character was portrayed in the hit movie *The French Connection* starring Gene Hackman.

The men were taken from Brazil, kicking and screaming, to a Federal Courthouse in Brooklyn, New York where they were charged with allegedly smuggling 500 kilograms of heroin worth $250 million into the United States. Federal authorities said that the men processed Turkish opium in Marseille, France and smuggled the heroin via South America to Miami and then to New York City. Both Christian David and Michel Nicoli were held in lieu of $2.5 million bail. At the time of his arrest in New York, David had a long history as being one of the most dangerous men in the world, and faced the death sentence in France for the murder of a police commissioner in 1966. He was alleged to have been the right hand man in the worldwide heroin smuggling network of Auguste Ricord. After his sentencing, David was transferred to Levaneworth Penitentiary where he served his sentence.

Both Nicoli and David left Rio de Janeiro via plane, accompanied to the airport by Brazilian police. David, who was known as "*Le beau serg*," or handsome sergeant, was 5 feet 7, was wearing tan slacks and a green sports shirt and swede jacket.

The U.S. Department of State received a telegram from its embassy in Brasilia to the Secretary of State in Washington regarding the arrival of David to the United States. The telegram said that the Federal Police in Brazil had issued a note "denying that Christian David had been tortured while under arrest in Brazil or that his belongings had been confiscated. The note pointed out a series of artifices employed by David to effect escape."

The plane on which David was on, had to turn back when David began shouting that he needed medical help. "David tried to flee from the hospital to which he had been sent for examination. On a second flight, he yelled that he was being kidnaped."

Before the plane left Brasilia, David claimed that he had swallowed a nail and a spoon handle. However, when he was xrayed by doctors, no foreign objects were found in his system. David exhibited more erratic behavior prior to his flight from Brazil. In Rio, David banged his head on the floor and was treated in-flight. After his antics, David was given a sedative during the flight to New York in order to keep him under control.

The end of the telegram says, "The Federal police note revealed that David had established in Brazil a pattern of alleging torture or self-abuse to accomplish his own ends."

The U.S. Attorney who handed the case at the time, Robert Morse, said that the men smuggled $217 million worth of heroin into the United States between January 1969 and May 1971. The heroin, according to U.S. officials, was hidden in cans of imported fish, luxury European cars and in both private and commercial airliners.

The man whom Christian David worked for was a ruthless, Corsican drug smuggler named Auguste Ricord who, at one point, ran a vast drug trafficking network out of Buenos Aires, Argentina. He began his smuggling career in the 1930s, and during World War 2, was wanted by the free French government for being a Nazi collaborator. In 1947, Ricord fled to Argentina where he established a number of prostitution rings throughout the continent.

Ricord's role as the number one drug kingpin in Argentina did not go unnoticed by the federal police and through a series of generous bribes to the top Argentine police authorities, he was able to use a number of his old Corsican thugs who had ties to the French Secret Service during the height of the Algerian crisis to be part of his network.

The Bureau of Narcotics in the United States knew all about Ricord's drug business and they monitored his every move using undercover operatives, as well as the services of allied intelligence groups in South America. At one point, US authorities believed that Ricord was responsible for bringing 50 to 75% of all heroin shipments into the United States.

The US Bureau of Narcotics traced Ricord to his new home in Paraguay in 1968 where he made a deal of protection with that nation's corrupt president, Alfredo Stroessner. While living in Paraguay, Ricord used a secure drug network that brought heroin from Marseille, France, to Madrid, Spain and then via Chile and Paraguay, for final distribution in Miami, and other cities in the

U.S.

The US BNDD got their first break in tracking down Ricord's narcotics shipments when they got a tip on October 18, 1970. The tip concerned the registrations letters of a plane making a drug flight from Paraguay. The tip came via a letter from Eddie Cantrell, who, at one time, was a CIA asset and drug smuggler. Cantrell had his own motive for helping the US. It seems that his son was killed in a plane crash that was taking drugs into the United States. Cantrell decided to work for the BNDD and gave up the name of his former partner, Cesar Bianchi, who flew the downed plane.[58]

In a joint effort by both U.S. customs and the BNDD, the feds watched as Bianchi's drug loaded planed landed in a small airstrip near Miami. He was arrested and the feds took into possession, 42.5 kilograms of heroin. Under arrest, Bianchi decided to cooperate and he gave the feds just what they were looking for. Bianchi provided the feds the name of a contact in Miami, Felix Becker, a native of Paraguay. Becker gave up the name of Enio Varela who served as Ricord's main logistics man. Becker provided the feds the names of his main customers who lived in New York, Jose La Torriente and Pierre Gahou. Gahou sang, and turned over the name of a mafia figure, Nick Giannattasio who was supposed to be the end man in the drug shipment. Giannattasio revealed that the ultimate owner of the drugs was Ricord.

Due to the sting operation that the feds undertook, Auguste Ricord and seven other men were indicted in the Eastern District Court in New York. Ricord was arrested on March 25,1971 in Paraguay and U.S. authorities began the extradition process.

It was not easy to get Ricord back to the United States. Ricord was so well connected with the most powerful political and military leaders in the country, including President Stroessner, that every time the Nixon administration put pressure on President Stroessner, he pushed right back. One of the impediments to the release of Ricord was Pastor Coronel, the chief of the secret police in Paraguay. He spied on BNDD informers in the nation and gave that vital information to other drug traffickers in Paraguay.

The Paraguayan court system got into the act and after lesser

---

[58]Valentine, Douglas, *The Strength of the Pack,* Page 87.

officials tried to circumvent Pastor Coronel's efforts, a judge refused to allow the extradition of Ricord to proceed. It would take until September 1972 for Ricord to finally be extradited back to the United States for trial.

After he killed police lieutenant Galibert in 1966, Christian David was one of the most wanted men in France. If he was caught, he realistically stood little chance of getting a fair trial and he went underground, using his vast Corsican mafia connections to hide him from the manhunt that was hot on his trail. Using his contacts, David headed for the Fetich Club of Nueville-Sur-Ain, near Lyon, France. The club was also a bordello that was frequented by the Guerini brothers who knew Christian David quite well (the Guerini family, as well as Christian David were both linked together in the events leading up to the Kennedy assassination as will be described in later chapters of the book). After some time, David decided it was getting too hot with the Guerini's, and in March 1966 he fled to a new hiding place in Marseilles.

David knew that to stay in one place for any length of time was not conducive for his health, and he made contact with his girl friend, Simone Mauduit. She arrived at his place of safety in Marseille with a load of cash. He decided it was to his advantage to leave France, and arrangements were made to take him by car to Genoa, Italy, where he booked passage on a ship for Latin America. When he arrived in Latin America, he carried with him a letter of introduction to Auguste Ricord who was by then, gearing up to make him the largest heroin dealer in South America. Christian David needed no introduction to Ricord. His shady past was well known to Ricord and he welcomed David into his family like a long lost relative.

The Ricord organization that David moved into was divided up into four different areas. Ricord ran the main unit from Asuncion, Paraguay under the protection of President Stroessner and his henchmen. Francios Chiappe, a gangster who was wanted in France for two murders, as well as Michel Nicoli (another name that was linked to the president's assassination), ran a second team. Dominique Orsini and Luis Bonsignour, ran their own group, while Andre Condemine and Lucien Sarti, the last one (Sarti was also linked to the investigation of the JFK murder by journalist

Steve Rivele).

Besides having a major role in Ricord's drug smuggling operation, David branched out into the gunrunning market and sold his arms to whomever gave him the best price.

Using his underground connections, David got a false Argentine passport via Francois Chiappe in the name of Carlos Eduardo Devreux-Bergeret. In his book, *The Great Heroin Coup,* author Henrik Kruger wrote that David went on various secret missions for French intelligence. His first job was to infiltrate Douglas Bravo's Venezuelan urban revolutionaries. This mission was a bust.

David was then given another assignment in Mexico where he met with two African agents. He was given the job of killing a number African politicians and he traveled to Africa for several months. It is not clear if David succeeded in his assignment but after spending some time in the Dark Continent, he returned to Argentina. If Christian Davis was in Africa, could he have been assigned the job of killing Patrice Lumumba? If he did, was he the CIA's secret assassin, WI/ROGUE/1?

In 1967, David took on another job, using his alias of Eduardo Devreux-Bergeret. He infiltrated a group called Forcas Argentines de Liberacion (FAL), a notorious guerilla group then operating in Argentina at the time. One of FAL's most dramatic adventures was the capture of Waldemar Sanchez who was Paraguay's consul in Argentina, as well as being a friend of Ricord. Over time, David became FAL's number one arms instructor and became quite close to its high command. However, David decided to betray his new friends and stole $250,000, as well as documents from them. While making his escape, David killed a FAL member. Once he returned to his Ricord headquarters, he made arrangements with the French intelligence service, the SDECE and the Argentine government to take control of the papers. The files stolen by David led to the arrest of several guerillas by the Argentine government.

By 1968, David was becoming a highly paid, freelance agent for hire. He took on jobs for the corrupt regimes in Argentina, Uruguay, and Brazil. His one time mistress, a woman named Theresa, was then working for the Tupamaros guerilla organization that was waging a deadly war against the government in Uruguay. David agreed to work with President Pacheo Areco of Uruguay in the government's battle against the Tupamaros, and during this time period he came into contact with many CIA agents on the ground who kept an eye on what he was doing. The Tupamaros had no idea that they had a traitor in their midst, as David reported on what he learned to the government. They trusted him so much that after their band robbed a bank, they gave him $400,000 in order to purchase weapons for them. David had other plans and he double-crossed the guerillas by making his way to Gabon in Africa, for new pickings.

However, David returned to Uruguay and learned from his sources that the Tupamaros had set a trap for him. David headed straight for the safety of the national police and they informed his friend and patron President Areco of what he learned. In a sting operation, the national police arrested 150 guerillas, thanks to the work of Christian David.

For his trouble, the Uruguayan government gave him the generous sum of $400,000 and a new, diplomatic passport in the name of Edouard Davrieux. In his book, *The Great Heroin Coup,* author Henrik Kruger relates a most incredible story involving both Christian David and his one time lover, Theresa. As David was leaving Uruguay from the airport in Montevideo, a stewardess came up to him with a package. Not knowing what to do, but suspecting trouble, David asked the girl to open the package. Inside the package was the severed head of Theresa, courtesy of the Tupamaros's.

By 1971, things had changed dramatically for Christian David, all for the better. His old mentor and rival, Auguste Ricord, was now in jail in Paraguay, and one year later, he would find himself in a courtroom in New York on drug smuggling charges. For all intents and purposes, David was now in charge of the worldwide Ricord network and he took on the job with gusto. David, and his new partner in crime, Lucien Sarti, (another name that was linked to Steve Rivele's investigation into the Kennedy assassination), moved their new headquarters to an island called Ilha Bella, in Brazil, about two hours from Sao Paulo. The island proved to be a great hiding place, and included an airstrip for drug planes to land and depart. David was now in charge of what U.S. Narcotics police would call "The Brazilian Connection." The leaders of the group included Christian David, as the number one honcho, a French-

Corsican heroin smuggler and killer named Lucian Sarti, Michel Nicoli, and others that included such associates of David such as Andre Condemine, Francois Canazzi, Jean Lunardi, and other men who had previously worked with Auguste Ricord and his organization.

Michele Nicoli went by the alias "Miguel dos Santos, and was a leading member of the Ricord network. He arrived in the United States in 1968 using the Miguel dos Santos name but was arrested for drug smuggling. The court system gave him bail of only $50,000 and he immediately fled the States in pursuit of greener passages. For his trouble, both the United States and Interpol—the International Police Unit—issued a warrant for his arrest.

As time went on, "Beau Serge" as David was called, began to manage the lucrative heroin trade from Marseille to Ilha Bella, and then on to New York and other locations in the United States.

While David's profits soared, the news of his rise to the top of the Ricord network did not go unnoticed in Italy, the home of the Guerini's and the other Italian Mafia families who ran the trade for years. They did not take kindly to Christian David taking over their honey pot and they put a plan in motion to nip him in the bud. In 1970, they sent one of their top killers, Tomasso Buscetta, a Sicilian who killed twelve people, including seven cops, to take over the narcotics trade in Brazil. Using a legitimate cover as owner of large taxi fleet consisting of 250 cabs, food bars and an aluminum plant, Buscetta took on Christian David.

David knew that his hold in the Brazilian connection was in peril and arrangements were made for a mini-summit of all concerned to air their differences. In 1971, a top Mafia don named Carlo Zippo arrived from New York for a meeting with David, Lucien Sarti and their trusted friends at Rio de Janeiro's magnificent Copacabana Palace Hotel. The meeting resulted in a number of changes as far as heroin routes and buyers for the drugs were concerned. In time, David's mistress, Simone Delamare arrived to join him in Rio. Her arrival was not unnoticed by the police and national authorities who kept a discreet watch on both of the activities.

David's presence in Brazil was proving to be an embarrassment to the government who were just waiting for the right moment to pounce on him and end his illegal heroin operation. The Brazilians's notified the CIA and the BNDD—the American Narcotics Agency, that they had David in their sights and were ready to go after him at the first, opportune moment. That time came in October 1972 when Brazilian authorities found sixty kilos of heroin in the harbor of Rio de Janeiro, ready for shipment. The drugs were going to be put on a ship called the *Mormac Altair,* bound for Miami. After further tips, the police arrested Michel Nicoli in Sao Paulo and other members of the David gang in the coming days. On October 17, police raided the home where Simone Delamare was living, believing that David would be with her. David fled shortly before their arrival.

The police got a lucky break when, on October 21, two policemen followed an attractive woman behaving oddly on the streets of the Brazilian state of Bahia. They followed her to one of the more seedy hotels in the city and brought her in for questioning. Under interrogation, they found out that the lady in custody was none other than David's mistress, Simone Delamare.

Days later, Brazilian police cornered Christian David in his room and tried to arrest him. What followed was a brutal fight between David and six, heavily armed policemen. In the ensuing struggle, one cop later said that, "He (David) threw us around like balls. If there had only been four of us, I don't see how we could have handled him." The police finally managed to get him under restraint by using foot chains and handcuffs. While he was being forcibly taken away, David tried to bribe the guards, offering them as much as $100,000 each and safe passage anywhere in the world. When that did not work, he managed to slice his wrist with a glass. He was immediately taken to a local hospital where his wounds were quickly bandaged. Without wasting any more precious time, the police whisked him away before he could try to escape. When the police went through his belongings, they found a mini arsenal, consisting of one 9 mm Browning, one silenced Beretta, one short-barreled Smith and Wesson revolver, three cartridges of a poison, ninety bullet cartridges, a Uruguayan diplomatic passport in the phony name of Edouard Davrieux, with his real photo attached.

While many police and government officials in France deeply wanted David brought back for his previous crimes, others just wanted to see the whole episode go away as quickly as possible. To their astonishment, the Brazilian government decided it would extradite him not to France, but to the United States.

David had no idea that he was going to be sent to the United States instead of France and as mentioned before, he tried to do himself harm en-route to his new destination. He claimed that he was drugged by U.S. agents, and said that he was broke (despite having access to millions of dollars in illegal drug profits stashed away). David, along with Michel Nicoli and Claude-Andre Pastou appeared in federal court where they all faced charges of illegal drug possession and narcotics smuggling.

U.S. justice was swift, more so than David and his cohorts expected. Auguste Ricord got twenty-seven years in jail, David and Michel Nicoli received twenty years, while Pastou got the lightest sentence, seven years behind bars. Other members of David's external gang, including Tomasso Buscetta, who was captured on November 5, 1972, and three other men, were deported back to Italy to face charges. During the trial, Claude Pastou revealed that David told him to go to New York in 1971 in order to take possession of a load of heroin. In order to get the operation underway, David introduced Pastou to Francois Orsini. Orsini told Pastou that another man, Roger Delouette was going to deliver 50 kilos of heroin in a Volkswagen Camper. Unknown to all of them, one of the members of the operation was an undercover narc.

After being convicted, David was sent to the maximum-security prison in Marion, Illinois. With David now behind bars, his once grand network began to fragment into conflicting pieces, with a number of mobsters vying to take over. The new leaders were members of the Francisci-Venturi mob. Marcel Francisi and Dominic Venturi, along with Antoine Guerini, and Joseph Orsini, were believed by both the French and the US BNDD to be the new leaders of the drug business in Marseille, France. Marcel Francisi had a rather checkered past, to say the least and his exploits in the drug trade were legendary. He ran a bank in Beirut, Lebanon, called the Casino du Liban, which was owned by a Palestinian national named Yousef Beidas. The *New York Times,* called Francisi, "One of the richest and most influential members of the Union Corse." In what can be called nothing but a case of cutsuph, Francisi sued the *Times* for libel.

By the mid 1970s, a number of men who were associated, one

way or another with Christian David's heroin ring, began to meet violent deaths.

On July 28, 1973, the body of Andre Condemine, who was David's minister of transportation, was found dead in a trunk drifting in the Seine River. He was shot in both the heart and neck.

Roger Dadoun, a noted gunrunner whom David had known for years, was killed in a Paris suburb on March 13, 1973.

Louis Nesmoz, a partner with Joseph Orsini in the drug smuggling trade, was killed, gangland style, while he dined in a Paris restaurant on May 19, 1973.

Based on the facts provided, is Christian David WI/ROGUE/1? Lets examine what we know. He was a Corsican hoodlum who was the right hand man of Auguste Ricord, the head of the Brazilian heroin network that operated, worldwide. He had connections not only with most of the top heroin smugglers of the day, but also the French Secret Service, and to a lesser extent, the CIA. He had no compunction when it came to murder; he had killed a number of French policemen and was wanted for that grizzly crime. He also eliminated his rivals in the mob, without the blink of an eye. He was a member of the anti-OAS faction that tried to kill de Gaulle and his exploits in that effort surely did not go unnoticed by the top men in French intelligence.

He used his mafia connections to hide him after he killed Lt. Galibert in 1966, and with the help of the Guerini brothers, made his way to Marseille, and then, to South America. Once in South America, David became Ricord's number one lieutenant in his vast heroin network and was given assignments commensurate with his new standing. He traveled to Africa to kill certain African politicians, although we don't know if he ever carried out that assignment. While he was in Africa, it could have been possible, due to his intelligence connections with both the French and the CIA, that he was tasked with the job of killing Patrice Lumumba. However, with the CIA still keeping most of its files on the true identity of WI/ROGUE1/ secret, that will remain a mystery.

He worked under the protection of the corrupt regime of President Stroessner in Paraguay, was a gunrunner in South America, had a fake passport under the name of Carlos Devreux-Bergeret (which could only have come from people high up in the government), he infiltrated the FAL guerilla group, something he could not have done without help from high government officials, freelanced for such repressive regimes in Brazil, Uruguay and Argentina. He took control over the so-called "Brazilian network" after Ricord was put on ice, and would have continued on his merry way if it weren't for the fact that he was arrested in Brazil and extradited to the United States to stand trial. He also came in contact with other people during his heroin smuggling days who would play an role in the later investigation of JFK's death; the Guerini family, his close friend, Lucien Sarti, and Michel Nicoli. Most importantly, Christian David was a master sniper, a craft which would serve him well if he, indeed, was one of the shooters on the Grassy Knoll in Dallas on the day the president was shot.

Investigative reporter, Steve Rivele, whose years long work trying to track down the killers of President Kennedy, led him to France in the late 1980s to conduct his investigation. He met with numerous people who tried to nudge him in the right direction, including policemen, judges, mercenaries of all stripes who worked in various parts of the world in the decades of the 1960s and 1970s, attorneys, newspaper reporters, retired CIA agents, and even, Christian David's attorney at the time, Sophie Bottai. In one conversation he had with her, Ms. Bottai said that the presiding judge in the case told her that new testimony was in the works, and that she believed that her client would be tried for murder.

She told Rivele that she had been hired by a former gangster who was then living in Paris, who she would not name. She said the person who was threatening David was Le Mouel, a friend of Lt. Galibert (the policeman whom David killed). Le Mouel, was at that time, the chief of police in Paris. Ms. Bottai said that Le Mouel was doing everything in his power to see that David was convicted.[59]

One of the people whom Steve Rivele spoke to on his trip in June 1985, was a former CIA agent named Paul Sakwa. In his notes on his interview with Sakwa, Rivele reported that, "Sakwa was in charge of funneling money to the French unions after

---

[59] Files by Steve Rivele on his investigation of the French Connection. Located at the Assassination Archives and Records Center, Washington, D.C. "From Steve Rivele Re: European Trip, June, 1985." Referred later as "Rivele Files."

WW2. He was aware of the longstanding relationship of the OSS-CIA with the Guerini brothers. He said, "There's no telling what they (CIA) could have gotten the Guerini's to do for them."

In his research, Rivele tried to find out the name of the "mystery man" whom the CIA thought was Lee Harvey Oswald who was impersonating him in Mexico City in September 1963. There is still some debate, all these years later, if the real Lee Harvey Oswald was in Mexico City between September 26 and October 3, 1963. While he (or someone else) was in Mexico at the time, the Warren Commission said that Oswald visited both the Cuban and Soviet embassies, trying to get credentials that would enable him to return to Cuba and then back to the USSR. He made quite an impression in both embassies, arguing with the employees, telling them of his ties to Cuba and the Soviet Union, and generally making a nuisance of himself.

The CIA routinely conducted photo surveillance of all people coming and going into both embassies, and the man whom the CIA said was Oswald, a rather large built man, older than Oswald, not fitting his description whatsoever, was definitely not him. So, if the "mystery man" in Mexico City was not the real Lee Oswald, who was he?

During his many research trips to Europe seeking the "Men Who Killed Kennedy," Steve Rivele met with various people and in the end he came away with the name of a man whom he believed was the real "Mystery Man" in Mexico City. He said the man went by the name of "Edmond Meunier."

Rivele asked Paul Sakwa if he recognized the name of "Meunier" and he said no. However, "he did say that he was the kind of person the CIA was looking for—brutal, criminal background, do anything for money. I asked how they would recruit someone like Meunier in Katanga. He shrugged, said there were many ways, then suggested that QJ/WIN might have recruited him."[60]

Another source whom Rivele spoke with on his trip was an unidentified, retired DEA intelligence analyst. He spoke with this person regarding both Christian David and his partner, Lucien Sarti, and got back some rather, interesting comments about both

---

60 Ibid.

of them.

He said that Christian David was in the Congo but did not work for the CIA. He said that he was probably there on some sort of mission for the French Secret Service in one of their plots to kill Lumumba. He said he did not know whether Sarti was there, but other French gangsters were there, including a man named Andre Labaye. He expressed the idea that the French Secret Service, the SDECE, recruited many criminals in Marseille.

Rivele also had a conversation with author Richard Mahoney who wrote a book called, *JFK: Ordeal in Africa,* (Oxford University Press, 1983) about both QJ/WIN and WI/ROGUE. Mahoney said that he knew the true identities of both men but would not reveal their names to him. He did, however say that they were both Belgians, one lived in Antwerp and the other in Brussels. He said that both WIN and ROGUE were contacted for recruitment by the CIA by the same person who worked full time on the staff of the Leopoldville station at the same time of the plots to kill Lumumba. "Says categorically that David was neither WIN nor ROGUE. Not so categorically about Sarti."

Mahoney said he did not know (1986) if either WIN or ROGUE was still alive, and said he knows of "no connection between the Lumumba plot and the Castro plots, nor between Lumumba plot and Kennedy killing." He said that he never saw a picture of either man. "He said this is a dangerous area of inquiry since the people involved in the Lumumba plot now hold very powerful positions and would not hesitate to destabilize anyone who got in too close. Says danger comes both from those powerful people involved as well as from the programmed killers of that era who are still alive. Says they have never been de-programed and will still kill to protect the operation."[61]

Christian David's life of international crime had now come to an end. However, his name was to surface, once again, when investigative reporter, Steve Rivele, began an international probe into the death of President John F. Kennedy, over a decade later.

* * *

---

61 Rivele Files: From Steve Rivele: Re "Conversation with Richard Mahoney," June 1, 1986.

While there are a number of documents that referenced the covert career of the CIA's agent dubbed "QJ/WIN," as have been described in this book, there is still no verification as to his true identity. Names have popped up in the ensuing years as to who he might be, but until the U.S. government finally decides to release his name, conjecture is all we have.

Nevertheless, there are a number of documents that have been released that give the historian a tidbit of information as to his identity. A contract that the CIA prepared for QJ/WIN before he was hired, references the type of conditions that the government expected him to do while he was in their employ. This undated document refers in the opening line to a name that possibly is the real QJ/WIN. It is addressed to "Mr. Jose Marie Andre Mankel." It is a standard employment form that begins:

> Dear Mr. Mankel;
>
> Effective 28 February 1961, all contacts, oral or written, by and between you and the United States Government, as represented by the under-signed Contracting Officer are hereby terminated by mutual consent of the parties thereto, and in lieu of the following agreement is substituted.
>
> The United States Government, as represented by the Contracting Officer, hereby contracts with you as an independent contractor for the submission of certain information and related services of a confidential nature under the following terms and conditions.

The rest of the document is standard employee agreement that outlines just what the U.S. government would pay him and what they expected of him. He was to get $7,200.00 in annual salary, would be reimbursed for travel expenses and transportation for himself and his dependants, to and from his permanent post, would be given operational expenses for such standard items as entertainment, etc. They expected him to reimburse the government, and if he did not, then that money would be deducted from his pay. Part of his contact called for him not to reveal the contents of his work to any unauthorized person or persons and, "It is agreed that any revelation whatsoever of the above information will constitute and be an immediate and final breach of this agreement and will result in forfeiture by you of any and all benefits which may then have accrued to you by reason of this agreement."[62]

From this official agreement, one would assume that QJ/WIN's real name was Jose Marie Andre Mankel, and that all further speculation was now over.

Not so fast. A CIA background sheet dated 8 October 1997 regarding QJWIN, only seems to muddy up the waters.

The document gives his name as Jose Marie Andre Mankel, born 1 October 1917. If Mankel was the real QJ/WIN, that would make him 43 years old in 1960. If he was the same man whom the CIA sent to the Congo in 1960 to assassinate Patrice Lumumba, he would be a little over the age limit for a man who was on such a sensitive assignment. That is not to say that he could not have carried out the job, but if the CIA wanted a man for such an important mission, they might have asked for someone a little younger. His contract was set up for at least until March, 1961, and his current residence at the time was unknown.

Under the heading "Sensitive Assignment/Activities, the CIA wrote:

> Mankel was recruited as a ZRRIFLE agent in late 1960. The objective of the ZRRIFLE project was to procure foreign code and cipher materials and information concerning such matters. Except for a two month (Nov-Dec 1960) TDY to Africa, Mankel apparently operated in Europe establishing his cover while trying to spot and assess individuals that the CIA could use in safe cracking operations, in line with one of the principal missions of FI/D. Agency contract terminated in Feb. 1964.

In a sub-section called "Other Notes," it says:

> First Agency contact with Mankel in 1958 (blank) in connection with illegal narcotics operation into the US. For

[62]RIF No. 104-10185-10409. "QJWIN Contract." No date.

18 months, he was contacted sporadically on behalf of the Bureau of Narcotics. (The Bureau's files reflect an excellent performance by contact. Virtually all data on Mankel—*except his true name—have been released. (Italics by author)*

This is a most interesting document, to say the least. First off, they say that QJ/WIN was referred to in his contact by the CIA as "Jose Marie Andre Mankel." At the end of this document, however, it ends by saying, "virtually all data on Mankel—except his true name—have been released."

That, seems to be the rub. If he was Jose Marie Andre Mankel, then why say that all the data on him was released except his real name? Is Mankel another alias? If so, then the CIA's own documentation reveals subterfuge on their part. It looks like Jose Marie Mankel was just another cover name for him used by the CIA for whatever job they wanted him to perform.

The other part of the document that catches the eye is the part that reads, "For 18 months, he was contacted on behalf of the Bureau of Narcotics."

As we have seen before, both Christian David and Lucien Sarti were both heavily involved in the narcotics business, as well as having ties with the French Intelligence Service (in David's case more so than Lucien Sarti). They both were of French heritage and frequented the same anti-de Gaulle politics that lead them to make contact with the anti-de Gaulle, OAS. They both could easily have been a perfect fit for an intelligence operation in the Congo (or any place else). If they were in the Congo as part of the CIA's operation against Lumumba, their presence in the nation would not have raised any eyebrows by the same people who frequented that life style.

* * *

Lucien Sarti

Lucien Sarti was a top lieutenant of Auguste Ricord, along with Christian David and Michel Nicoli in the lucrative, Brazilian heroin network that flourished in South America in the 1960s and 1970s and, according to investigative reporter Steve Rivele, was one of the men who participated in the assassination of President John F. Kennedy in Dallas, Texas on November 22, 1963. In his dogged research into the French Connection to the president's assassination, Rivele also believes that Lucien Sarti was none other than the CIA's elusive assassin, QI/ROGUE/1.

Lucien Sarti was born in Marseille, France, to a Corsican mother. He grew up in Nimes and as a young man, he lost an eye and was thought by many people in the Corsican network, as well as those mercenaries who knew him, that he was a better shot with one eye than with two. During his years as a member of the drug smuggling network, he managed to get an Italian passport under the name of Roberto Sconamiglio. From everything we know about the life of Lucien Sarti, is that he was a hired killer, a man whom others would keep at a distance if they wanted to live.

For two decades, the South American heroin connection was run by two of the most powerful people then operating freely; Auguste Ricord and his partner in crime, Lucien Sarti. Sarti was wanted for the murder of a Belgian policeman, and he arrived in South America in 1966 at the tender age of 29. Michel Nicoli was Sarti's most trusted ally and together, they ran their operation like the profitable business it was, killing off the competition when it fit their purposes.

Another member of the heroin smuggling connection at the time was Armando Nicolai, who, in 1975, was a 46-year old native of Argentina who had been under indictment on narcotics charges in New York since 1971. Once Ricord was finally extradited back to the United States, the field was left open to Mr. Nicolai to pick up the pieces.

It was during this hectic time that both Lucien Sarti and Armando Nicolai met when both men cemented their relationship with the South American drug smugglers who operated so freely in the region.

Mr. Nicolai was a physically imposing man, was 6 foot 3, and weighed about 230 pounds. When he was arrested in 1962, he broke away from the arresting police officers by breaking the handcuffs that was placed on him and beat up seven cops while doing so. While both men worked together for their mutual benefit, Lucien Sarti was more of a tough guy than his partner, Armando Nicolai. Sarti and his French Connection henchmen, also known as the "Pietra Forte" (hard rock), "a Mafia like organization that specialized in extortion and bank robbery in addition to heroin dealing." Among this group, Lucien Sarti was known as "Iron Head," due to his tough character. Over time, Sarti's partner, Armando Nicolai, was able to bring into his criminal organization a large number of people in both government and elsewhere that allowed him to safely get his vast amount of heroin across most borders in South American without any problem. As his illegal profits grew, Nicolai was able to buy the cooperation of police and judicial officials throughout South America, leaving him free to purse his illegal activities without government interference.

As his influence and power grew, Nicolai moved his headquarters from Buenos Aires to Montevideo, Uruguay. It was said that his contacts with various governments was so iron clad that he was able to pick up his heroin shipments himself and carry them through customs without having his bags inspected.

However, things began to get more heated for Mr. Nicolai, in an incident that took place on July 8, 1971 at John F. Kennedy International Airport in New York. A man named Rafael Richard, a native of Panama, was arrested at Kennedy when customs officials found 70 kilograms of heroin in his suitcase. He told customs inspectors that his father was Panama's Ambassador to Taiwan and refused to open his suitcase. The suitcase was opened anyway and he was subsequently arrested. While being questioned, Rafael Richard agreed to cooperate with federal officials. It turned out that this was not the first time that Mr. Richard had smuggled heroin into the United States. He told U.S. authorities that he made five other smuggling trips to the U.S., as well as to both Brazil and Argentina. Along with him on these trips were his uncle, Guillermo Gonzalez and his aunt, Nelva Juardo de Gonzalez. In one of their trips to Buenos Aires, his aunt gave one of the packages to heroin to a man named Armando who gave her cash in return.[63]

It was subsequently learned that Uncle Juardo de Gonzalez was a close confidante of Armando Nicolai dating back ten years, and that Mr. Gonzalez at one time worked as an air traffic controller in

---

63"Gage, Nicholas, "Argentine Filled Key Role in Latin's Drug Network." *New York Times*, April 23, 1975.

Panama and allowed Armando's drug planes to enter the country without any scrutiny.

In their federal investigation of the Kennedy airport incident, Armando Nicolai was indicted in New York for conspiracy in connection with Rafael Richard's arrest. In time, both Mr. Richard and Mr. Gonzalez were convicted at trial and went to jail.

With the arrest and conviction of both Mr. Gonzalez and Mr. Richard, U.S. officials began a full-fledged investigation of both Lucien Sarti and Armando Nicolai. They pressured Uruguayan government officials to allow them to put a tap on Mr. Nicolai's phone.

In the beginning of 1972, Lucien Sarti, along with his lady friend, and two other men whom Sarti wanted to bring into his nest, went to La Paz, Bolivia. It was believed that the purpose of their visit was to purchase a 6,000-acre ranch where they could grow their coca leaves that would then be turned into cocaine.

They were all traveling under assumed names and phoney passports, and when Sarti checked into his hotel, he was spotted by a clever hotel employee who knew him from a previous trip in which he used a different name and passport. Police were called and they were all arrested. (Police found in their possession, $380,000).

It seems that Armando Nicoli's lawyer tried to get them bailed out but failed to obtain their release. Coming to the rescue was Sarti's live-in girl friend, a Miss Ferreira. She told Bolivian officials that she was his sister and somehow persuaded them to release Sarti and three of his companions. When they departed Uruguay, they did not have with them the $380,000 that they had when they arrived, days before.

They first went to Peru and then were flown down to Mexico where Sarti immediately called Armando Nicolai to tell him what happened. Sarti told Nicolai that he wanted him to come down to Mexico in order to meet with two French Corsican heroin dealers, as well as a member of one of the New York Mafia families in order to cement a new deal. What neither Sarti nor Nicolai realized was that the Americans drug enforcement agency was tapping Nicolai's phone and heard the entire conversation. For whatever reason, Nicolai failed to come to Mexico and the feds did not have a chance to nab them in the act of making their dirty deal.

It seems that both Nicolai and Sarti were using false identities while living in Mexico, making it difficult for the feds to find them. They got a break due to their taps on Nicolai's phone. During one of their talks, Sarti told him the name of his daughter, Veronica. A member of the Drug Enforcement Unit did a little research and found out that Lucien Sarti's had a daughter named Veronica.

Still, Nicolai did not come to meet with the two French drug representatives in Mexico. However, it was decided that it was worth the risk, and Sarti set up a meeting with them.

The local police were informed of the meeting and they went into action. On April 27, 1972, Mexican police, who had staked out the area where the meeting was to take place, 107 Temistocles Street, approached Mr. Sarti as he was about to get into his car. With him was his wife, Liliane Rous Vaillet, and their young daughter. Sarti, seeing the approaching police had an immediate choice to make. Either shoot it out with the police, thus endangering his family, or risk being taken captive. Mexican police knew of the warrant for his arrest for killing a Belgian policeman and approach him caustically. Sarti took out his Colt Cobra pistol and began firing at the police. In the ensuing gunfight, Sarti was mortally wounded. In a subsequent raid, police nabbed his partner, a man named Angeletti, who was in bed with his mistress.

In his investigation of the French Connection to JFK's death, reporter Steve Rivele spoke with many people who had some knowledge of Lucien Sarti. One source was Pierre Domenech, the Editor of *Le Meridional,* a French periodical. When Rivele asked him what he knew about the death of Sarti, he replied that he believed it was a set up, really an assassination attempt by persons unknown.

Another retired DEA intelligence source whom Steve Rivele spoke to said that while in his official capacity he monitored the cable traffic between Mexico and Washington and he helped coordinate the take down of Sarti from his headquarters. This source said that the CIA had nothing to do with Sarti's capture. This source told Rivele that in his opinion, "Sarti was impulsive. Said he frequently got his colleagues into trouble by his rashness, which made him unpopular. Said he was very clever at disguise, and could change his appearance easily and effectively. Said no two pictures of his look alike."

In the aftermath of the murder of Lucien Sarti, most of his lucrative South American heroin connection dried up. A number of his associates were arrested or killed.

No one knows just who was responsible for the murder of Lucien Sarti. Needless to say, he had quite a number of people who wanted to see him dead; both his rivals in the heroin trade, as well as police and narcotics agents who had been seeking him for years. For whatever reason, his wife decided not to claim the body and he was buried in a cemetery in Mexico.

A few months after the death of Sarti, Armando Nicolai returned to Argentina where a nation-wide manhunt for him was initiated. He was arrested, but not for long. It seems that Nicolai had such good friends in the government that his lawyer managed to obtain a writ of habeas corpus from the Supreme Court of Argentina. Authorities had no choice but to release him from custody. Argentine authorities tried to get the United States to make a deal with them in order to get him back to the United States, but the Americans decided not to go along with the deal.

Was Lucien Sarti, WI/ROGUE1? According to reporter Steve Rivele, the two men were the same.

Let's back up a little and re-examine what the Church Committee had to say about WI/ROGUE/1. He, along with QJ/WIN, were sent to the Congo in 1960 in preparation for the plots against Lumumba. He was a lesser quality agent than QJ/WIN, and was described as being "essentially stateless." If he was "essentially stateless" one can assume that he traveled the world under various aliases. We know that Lucien Sarti went by the name of "Lucien Sabatier," was a known Marseille gangster, and was the number two man in the South American connection headed by Auguste Ricord, as well as Armando Nicolai.

His CIA controller, Victor Hedgeman, said that:

> I had difficulty controlling him in that he was not a professional intelligence officer as such. He seemed to act on his own without seeking guidance or authority. I found he was rather an unguided missile, the kind of man that could get you in trouble before you knew you were in

trouble.

He tried to enlist QJ/WIN in an execution squad which QJWIN wisely turned down. WI/ROGUE/1was an ethnic Georgian recruited and trained for the old (blank) program. Although born in the Soviet Union, he moved to Western Europe when two years old. He fought in (deleted) and as of 1960, was essentially stateless. Involved peripherally with the French Resistance, he was sentenced to death by the Germans but liberated by the U.S. Army in 1945 and returned to (blank). By 1950, he had managed to rob a (blank) bank of a sizeable sum of money, receive a prison sentence and be released five years later for good behavior. He was brought to the United States originally for use as one of two agents for Project SENTINEL. He spoke (blank) French and fluent Georgian, German and English.

In 1960, the CIA tried to resettle him in Mexico (Sarti would, in the 1970s, travel frequently to Mexico on his drug dealing operations). The mission that the CIA had for him was cancelled, but what sort of mission, was not revealed. On September 9, 1960, he was met by two members of the CIA's Africa Division to "discuss an operational assignment in Africa Division. In connection with this assignment, WI/ROGUE was to be trained in demolition, small arms, and medical immunization."

He was then given a code name and immunization shots prior to his leaving for his assignment. In October 1960, CIA headquarters sent a cable to their Leopoldville station saying that their new agent was "being prepared for a deep cover assignment to arrive Leopoldville late November."

His job, once he arrived in Africa was to use him as a "utility agent in order to a) organize and conduct a surveillance team, b) intercept packages, c) blow up bridges and d) execute other assignments requiring positive action."

He is described as an "inventor, photographer, architect, forger, and former bank robber. He was judged to be ingenious, observant, shrewd, glib and one who relished intrigue and daring." His personality chart says that he was able to "learn quickly and carry out any assignment without regard to danger."

What we now know of Lucien Sarti, that kind of operation

would fit him perfectly.

Like QJWIN, WI/ROGUE/1 had a checkered past which was known, and accepted by the CIA for the work they had planned for him. It seems that the CIA went to great lengths to hide his real identity before shunting him off to Africa.

"In November 1960, to prevent his identification with the U.S. Government or BKHERALD (a code name for a CIA operation), and to preclude any unexpected recovery of his past which would associate him with his pre-BKHERALD life, WI/ROGUE/1 underwent plastic surgery to change the shape of his nose. He was provided with a toupee for constant wear and documented as a (blank) who had never been to the United States. Cover for his presence in Leopoldville was to be as (blank). A rather lengthily assessment of his character can be summed up by saying that he was able to rationalize any action if he had a strong case officer direction."

What we see here is that QI/ROGUE/, was a much less talented agent than his counterpart, QJ/WIN. He was not, what the CIA would consider a prime operative, but someone whom they could use in a pinch, or when no other qualified agent was available. His job in the Congo was as a surveillance operative, a person who was supposed to blow up bridges, and intercept packages. From the record, it is clear that he did nothing of the sort. If so, then why did the CIA go to such lengths as to give him a topee, give him plastic surgery, train him in medical immunizations, skills that a trusted, trained asset would be given. They had to have some other motive to take the steps they did in ROUGE'S case.

What is undisputed is that WI/ROGUE was in the Congo at the time of the plots to kill Lumumba and that he was to have some sort of operational role in the event, i.e, infiltrating Lumumba's headquarters and possibly killing him by injecting some sort of poison into his food, thus, his training in medical immunization.

The Church Committee did not give details as to how WI/ROGUE/1 left the Congo, or if he had any help in that effort. Lawrence Devlin, who handled ROGUE while he was in the Congo was aided in his Lumumba assassination plot by the chief of the Congolese Intelligence Service. This man says that Devlin asked him for his help in the actions against Lumumba. The Congolese officer refused to help and it was said that he deported

ROGUE from the Congo. This intelligence chief sent ROGUE across the Congo River to Brazzaville, in the French Congo, where he was turned over to members of the French Intelligence Service. Is it possible that ROGUE himself was French?[64]

In his article on Lucien Sarti and his possible role as being WI/ROGUE, Steve Rivele writes that there may have been a second plot to kill him using ROGUE. He cites Belgian court documents that refer to Devlin, posing as an American financier named Davidson, hired a French criminal by the name of Francis Bodenan, to kidnap the exiled leader of Katanga Province, Moshe Tshombe. At this time, Tshombe was the only credible alternative to Joseph Mobutu who was then the number one man in the Congo. Devlin established a clandestine company in Liechtenstein, opened a Swiss bank account, and created an airline that had one plane in its feet.

The mysterious Bodenan, had been released from a French jail where he had served a ten year term for taking part in the murder of two French heroin dealers. He was then appointed president of Devlin's bogus company (all linked to the CIA), based in Brussels, Belgium. Bodenan then managed to get Tshombe into a bogus real estate deal, and then he injected him with a tranquilizer when he was having lunch. Note that QI/ROGUE/1 was trained by the CIA in medical immunization prior to his journey to the Congo in the Lumumba plot.

Bodenan then put Tshombe into a CIA loaned plane and took him to Algiers. Upon arrival, Tshombe was arrested and subsequently died in jail.

Rivele, in his article ("*The Plot to Kill Lumumba: The Corsican Connection*"), notes that Bodenam was a French criminal who also had underworld dealings in Brussels. (Sarti was also of French heritage). Devlin, at one time, served as the CIA station chief in Brussels. With his knowledge of the criminal underworld in Belgium, might he have known of the criminal past of ROUGE, who might, at one point, have operated a criminal enterprise in Belgium?

Rivele writes of the possible connection between ROGUE and

---

64 Rivele, Steven. "The Plot to Kill Lumumba: The Corsican Connection." The National Reporter, Fall 1987.

Bodenan:

> Since he seems to have been Devlin's personal asset, it is possible that Devlin found him during his tenure in Belgium. If this is true, then ROGUE's two centers of operation, France and Belgium, might explain his "essentially stateless" condition. As both a French and a Belgian criminal, he would have had at least two passports and two identities, and, being an adventurer, would have used those countries as a base for operations around the world.

Rivele gives the following facts regarding WI/ROGUE's career as a CIA asset, as well as a French-Belgian criminal. ROGUE was a European based criminal, most likely French, and may have done some "jobs" in Belgium. He was possibly recruited by Lawrence Devlin when Devlin served as CIA station chief in Brussels from 1957 to July, 1960. (It should be noted that both QJWIN and WI/ROUGE/1, were recruited by the CIA for operations in the Congo in 1960). ROGUE was not an active intelligence agent, but a man who was more of an adventurer, who spent lavishly (his buying of 3 cars), someone whom the CIA could not control. At the time of his assignment to the Congo, his appearance was altered, but for what purpose?

But, one can speculate. If he was a known commodity in the criminal world in Europe, might he be recognized by his compatriots in the trade in the Congo? Was he given surgery to hide his old identity from these men? He knew QJ/WIN when he saw him at the same hotel in the Congo. Did WIN possibly recognize ROGUE without his new facelift? However, he did not know that WIN was working for the CIA, but still, asked him to join an "execution squad" that he was going to head. ROGUE was supposed to have killed Lumumba with a poison substance but he didn't have the chance to carry out his assignment. Devlin asked the head of the Congolese intelligence service to aid him in the plot and he refused. The Congolese intelligence chief then had ROGUE deported to the French Congo.

It seems that while WIN and ROGUE were in the Congo at the time of the Lumumba plots, there was another plan to ferment mayhem that never got off the ground. The unidentified Congolese intelligence officer who possibly got ROGUE out of the Congo, told writer Steve Rivele of an attempt by certain members of French intelligence, the SDECE, whereby a number of French criminals, led by the notorious French gangster Andre Labay, were up to no good in the Congo during this tumultuous time.

In his book, *The Strength of the Pack,* author Douglas Valentine writes that Andre Labay was associated with the SDECE, and since, April 1970, was responsible for the delivery of heroin into the United States. Labay's heroin smuggling activities had gotten the attention of both the French police, as well as the Bureau of Narcotics in the U.S. through an informer, since September 1970. Through the informer, the French police were informed that Labay met on September 28, 1971, with a wealthy Russian moneyman. Labay had a secret compartment built into an expensive Bentley automobile in a garage that was owned by a French narcotics dealer.

In an unexpected move, Labay, on October 5, 1971, went to the BNDD office in Paris and offered to betray Roger Preiss, a noted check forger, who was working with Labay. Labay and Preiss were then attempting to import a large amount of heroin into New York on behalf of members of the gang lead by members of the Picpus gang. For some reason, Labay had a change of heart. Labay said he wanted $200,000, his share of the money after he delivered the Bentley. The police agreed and a sting operation was set up. On October 6, Labay was arrested by the police in a trap in which he carried 106 kilos of heroin on his body. Soon thereafter, many members of the Picpus gang were arrested.

Whatever the Labay operation was never materialized, but it was just another occurrence that linked QJ/WIN and WI/ROUGE to the strange events then going on in the Congo. In 1960, Lucien Sarti was 23 years old, and had a criminal record for such crimes as bank robbery, assault and the use of forged identify cards. His colleagues in the Corsican underworld would call him "The Al Capone of Belgium" and by the late 1960s and early 1970s, he was a leading figure in the heroin ring operated by Armando Nicolai. He was hired by the CIA to perform some sort of operation in the Congo and was also acquainted with the top brass of the French SDECE who possibly spirited him out of the Congo at the time of the Lumumba assassination. He was a perfect candidate for both security services, if and when they needed such a person. He also had lost his left eye, but in a picture of him, his face and eyes looked right. Did the CIA perform plastic surgery on him, as noted in the documents, because of his prior condition?

The mystery of whether Lucien Sarti was the notorious WI/ROGUE, takes another interesting twist that involves a man who only went by the name of "Duncan." Steve Rivele writes that, "A law enforcement official who followed Sarti's career closely has said that his agency was aware that, in the late fifties and early sixties, Sarti had a crucial and mysterious relationship with a man named Duncan. Duncan, so far as could be learned, was based in Africa, and his relations with Sarti were known only to a few of Sarti's closest friends. Even Sarti's family did not know about Duncan, a fact that was confirmed recently by Sarti's widow."

This same law enforcement official who told Rivele about "Duncan," said that every time he tried to learn more about who he was, he was never allowed in the door.[65]

Rivele postulates that the mysterious "Mr. Duncan" was Lawrence Devlin, a.k.a. "Victor Hedgeman," who worked in the CIA's Leopoldville station in the Congo. Rivele writes that his law enforcement friend told him that "the use of the name Duncan was a signal that one had direct access to Sarti."

Additional information on the mysterious Duncan comes from a DEA source of Rivele's whom he had numerous conversations with during his investigative work. The DEA source said that Sarti met Duncan in the late 1950s and they became close friends. The source said that if a person mentioned the name of Duncan it meant he was in touch with Sarti or knew how to find him. Duncan was most likely a South African, although he didn't know if Duncan was born in South Africa. The DEA agent did not know how both men met nor what kind of relationship they had. He said that only the people whom Sarti trusted the most—knew of their relationship. "Said he could not tell me more because there are people alive today whose lives would be in danger if more was known."

Another person whom Rivele spoke to in relation to the

---

65 Ibid.

identities of both WIN and ROGUE was David Atlee Phillip, a name that is well known in the Kennedy assassination case. Briefly, David Phillips was a former CIA Station Chief in Mexico, and was one of the main CIA agents in Mexico City whose job it was to run propaganda operations during that time. It has been alleged that David Phillips went by the name "Maurice Bishop," and that he knew Oswald in 1963. Phillips and Rivele had two discussions, and when Rivele brought up the names of WIN and ROGUE, Phillips said he'd try and make inquiries about them. Phillips subsequently told Rivele that the people with whom he talked to refused to name either man but did say they were Europeans, and that both men were alive during the Church Committee era, i.e., 1975-77. It should be noted that both Christian David and Lucien Sarti were both European (French).

To his brethren in Marseille, France, Sarti was known to excel with a rifle, his one eye, making no difference in his ability to take on contract assignments. Police officers in Marseille said that Sarti was one of the top-of-the line killers in Marseille in the 1960s a man who would take on even the toughest jobs. Despite his Corsican roots, Sarti, who went by the name "Sabatier" spent more of his time in Belgium and as the years went by, he and his gang were able to dominate the under ground in Brussels.

As mentioned before, Lucien Sarti was wanted by Belgian police for the murder of a policeman. How did it happen? One night in February 1966, a Brussels police officer was keeping an eye on a stolen car. As he surveyed the scene, he saw a car with three men stop near the abandoned auto. When nothing happened, the cop approached the car, wanting to see what was going on. As he neared the car, one person bolted out and fired many shots, instantly killing the officer. The men in the car dumped the cop's body into the trunk of the stolen car and took off.

The body of the dead officer turned up many months later on the Belgian coast. Over time, in one of the largest criminal investigations in its history, two of the three culprits were arrested. The man who fired the fatal shot was Lucien Sarti. He eluded the police and managed, with help of the Guerini family, made his way to South America.

As told earlier in the book, Lucien Sarti joined the heroin smuggling empire of Auguste Ricord and together, they built the so-called Latin Connection into one of the most profitable enterprises that sent untold tons of heroin from Southeast Asia into the United States.

The CIA, as well as other western intelligence agencies, had infiltrated a number of these networks over the years and kept a watchful eye on the business dealings of both Ricord and Sarti. Sarti was Ricord's number one man, and he oversaw the shipment of drugs from Marseille to Mexico City and into the States.

He also had dealings with both the Canadian and American Mafia families who took extensive profits from the drugs sold in the United States. Sarti's drug business was so profitable and transparent that he even set up his own office in the Empire State building in New York. It is estimated that Sarti's share of one shipment of drugs in 1970 dollars came to $400,000. When Ricord was finally arrested and extradited back to New York, Sarti's star fell, along with the other unlucky members of the organization who were subsequently arrested.

The United States government file on Lucien Sarti, according to a source cultivated by Steve Rivele, was over ten inches thick, and taking up three volumes. After Sarti's death, this U.S. government source asked to see Sarti's file. When he was given the file, it only contained one volume, only one inch thick.

Steve Rivele asks the following question: Did the death of Lucien Sarti and the disappearance of his large file have anything to do with the fact that he was possibly WI/ROGUE/1, his possible clandestine association with the mysterious "Mr. Duncan," or the plans of the Nixon White House to target the most dangerous drug dealers in the world?

Rivele writes that, "What is clear is that Lucien Sarti was much more than a heroin smuggler, and that his career embraced mysteries which went far beyond the shadowed dealings of the drug trade. For by the time he was gunned down on a Mexico City street, his life had traced a twisted trajectory which may have caused more than the brief embarrassment of a bar room brag. Through this brilliant but unstable opportunist, the CIA may have become implicated in the world's most massive heroin network. And, as they had learned in Leopoldville, his CIA handlers may have found that Sarti was once again dangerously out of control."

* * *

The Plumbers, Drugs, and the Torrijos Assassination Plot

When Lucien Sarti was gunned down on April 27, 1970 in a Mexico City street, his murder might not have been just a routine take down by local police, doing their job. There had been speculation during this time that the Nixon White House, which had declared a "war on drugs," was "taking out" the leading drug dealers by the use of assassination. Was the murder of Lucien Sarti part of that operation?

While going over the newly released files on the Kennedy assassination at Archives 11 in College Park, Maryland, the author came across a lengthy report detailing a possible assassination attempt on the life of the late President of Panama, Omar Torrijos in the early 1970s. What made this reported incident most interesting is the fact that the hit did not involve the CIA (as in the Castro assassination plots), but may have been instigated by Richard Nixon's infamous "Plumbers," headed by Howard Hunt and Frank Sturgis (both of whom are now deceased). While there is no solid proof that an assassination attempt was actually carried out by Nixon's men, the circumstances and other evidence makes the case that a Torrijos hit was actively being planned.

In their investigation of the Kennedy assassination, members of the Church Committee came across information that led it to believe that at the time of Richard Nixon's involvement in the unraveling Watergate scandal, the late president's undercover team called the "Plumbers" might have been involved in another foreign murder attempt.

The focus of the Nixon administration's interest was the President of Panama, Omar Torrijos. During this period of time (early 1970s), the United States and Panama were beginning discussions for the eventual return to Panama of the Panama Canal Zone which remained under Untied States sovereignly.

But more importantly to our story were reports by the Untied States Drug Enforcement Agency (BNDD) that President Torrijos and certain members of his administration were heavily involved in the heroin trade coming out of Latin America. President Nixon made the war on drugs one of the main topics of his administration. There were even reports that a covert action team made up of ex-spook, and former CIA clandestine warrior, Lucien Conein, were under orders from the Nixon camp to begin preparations for the murders of the top drug lords then operating in South America. Conein, along with Howard Hunt, (who would later play an important role in the Torrijos plot), would be involved in a scheme to fabricate cable traffic that would have the Kennedy administration deeply involved in the murder of South Vietnamese President Ngo Dinh Diem in early November, 1963.

The Church Committee's investigation first got wind of the Torrijos plot in a March 14, 1972 newspaper column by nationally known investigative reporter, Jack Anderson. Anderson heard of the story from Rep. John Murphy's House Panama Canal Subcommittee that was then referred to the House Merchant Marine Committee. The report said that, "high ranking Panamanian officials were deeply involved in the world heroin trade. American narcotics agents have implicated the foreign minister of Panama and the brother of Panamanian dictator Omar Torrijos in a scheme to smuggle hundreds of pounds of heroin into the United States." Anderson wrote that Panamanian Foreign Minister Juan Track and Mises Torrijos, the President's brother, were the principal ringleaders of these drug shipments.[66]

Anderson's article was picked up by other news organizations including the *New York Times* which told its readers on March 16, 1972, that both the U.S. Customs Service and the Federal Drug Agency had told Rep. Murphy's Committee that the government of Omar Torrijos was deeply involved in the Latin American drug trade.

In the wake of the Anderson and the *New York Times* article, Panama expelled two U.S. narcotics officers who were employed in the American embassy in Panama City. It seemed to both countries that the alleged drug involvement of the top leaders of Panama were about to derail the delicate negotiations over the future of the Canal Zone.

The man whom President Nixon turned to in order to stem the flow of drugs coming into the United States was a legendary ex-spook, former OSS agent, and all around bad boy, Lucien Conein.

66Kross, Peter, "The Plumbers and the Torrijos Assassination Plot". Back Channels Magazine, Volume 4, Number 1, Page 12-15.

Conein was not a person to be taken lightly and he intimidated as many people as he charmed. The story goes that as a young man of 17, he left his home in Kansas and joined the legendary French Foreign Legion at the start of World War 2. He then entered the wartime intelligence agency, the OSS, Office of Strategic Service headed by William Donovan. He was supposed to have joined the dreaded Corsican brotherhood and fought with them as part of their Resistance movement against the Germans. Due to his military prowess, the Corsicans made him an honorary member. The Corsican Brotherhood, in the war and after, was largely involved in both the illegal arms and drug trade that would take shape after the war.

After the war ended, Conein parachuted into Vietnam, where the French were battling the Communists. During the 1950s's, Conein was part of the American CIA team headed by Col. Edward Lansdale whose CIA backed team was helping to shore up the corrupt regime of President Ngo Dinh Diem who was battling the Viet Cong, lead by Ho Chi Min and his followers. He also had a small role in the events that lead up to the assassination of Diem in November 1963, only a few months before the Kennedy assassination.

He was later re-assigned to Washington, but was soon back in Vietnam where he was part of a ten-man counterinsurgency team under the leadership of General Lansdale. One member of the team was Daniel Ellsberg who, at that time, was in favor of U.S. policies in Vietnam (later, Ellsberg, would be known as the person who leaked the Pentagon Papers, a voluminous study of American involvement in the Vietnam War to the *New York Times* and incurred the wrath of the Nixon administration in the process).

Conein's reputation for his patriotism and gung ho attitude got the attention of the Nixon administration in the person of Howard Hunt, a former CIA agent and mystery writer. In 1971, Hunt was working for Charles Colson whose job at the White House at the time was to ruin the reputation of the late President Kennedy by any means possible. His other job was to discredit the character of Conein's one time friend, Daniel Ellsberg, who by then was a frequent critic of the Nixon White House.

By the time he was recruited by Hunt, Conein's life had begun to spiral out of control. He left the CIA in 1968, and went from one failed business venture to another, leaving his inventors in hock, and his once stellar reputation in ruins. Hut came to the rescue, and gave Conein a new life.

Now, Conein's fortunes began to change for the better. He was appointed to the post of chief of the DEA's Special Operations Branch. When questioned by a reporter on what he was doing as chief of the DEA's Special Operations Branch, he said, "I'll tell you anything you want to hear but it's probably not the truth."

When asked what kind of operations he'd run against the drug dealers he said rather starkly that he'd never "dream of mounting operations against one of the chief sources of narcotics traffic-the Corsicans. You can get killed that way. I will not talk about the Corsicans period. I happen to be a member of the Corsican Brotherhood."

"Let me tell you something. When the Sicilians put out a contract, it's usually limited to the continental United States or maybe Canada or Mexico, but with the Corsicans it's international. They'll go anywhere. There's an old Corsican proverb: If you want revenge and you act within 20 years, you're acting in haste. It wouldn't just be me. They'd take it out on my children and maybe even some grandchildren. This is the code."[67]

Conein said that he would be hesitant about running operations against the CIA's old Cuban agents who lived in Miami. Many of these people were both anti-Castro and anti-Kennedy in the early 1960s, due to the failure of the Bay of Pigs invasion of Cuba in 1961. A lot of the anti-Castro Cubans who lived in Miami during that time, and who took part in the abortive invasion, blamed the Kennedy administration for the invasions failure, and faulted the president personally for his betrayal of Brigade 2506 who languished on the beaches of Cuba.

A number of these same Miami agents went into the drug trade, making life miserable for succeeding American administration's who tried desperately to crack down on the ever expanding importation of heroin into the United States. "The Cubans have received all the trade craft from the Agency (CIA)," said Conein. "If they could get into Cuba to raise hell, they can sure as hell get

---

[67] Crile, George, 3rd. "The Colonel's Secret Drug War." *The Washington Post*, Sunday, June 13, 1976.

into the U.S. with drugs."

The man who was in overall charge of the Special Operations Branch was George Belk. Belk joined the BNDD in 1948, was the district supervisor in the Chicago office (1959-63), and later in New York (1963-68). Belk hired Conein to run a new arm of the agency, a team of men whose intelligence prowess would identify the major drug traffickers in the world. Belk and Conein hired a number of men from the CIA who had the requisite intelligence background. Initially, twelve men were hired but they immediately got bogged down in the political wars. The old, established DEA agents did not trust the new men from the CIA and visa versa. Conein, at one time, even placed his new agents in a safe house, away from the other DEA agents. In time, however, a truce was established, and the two groups finally got down to the work at hand.

In June 1986, reporter Steve Rivele tracked down Lucien Conein, in what turned out to be meaningful two-and-a-half hour, no holes barred conversation. They met in a Chinese restaurant in McLean, Virginia. A great deal of the initial conversation concentrated on the Corsican Mafia, how they were run, etc. Conein described the Corsicans as being ruthless, not very talkative, "effective and professional in their killing."

Conein said that both sides did not trust each other, but that they did share some of the same values and cultures. "Said Corsicans preferred to deal with Sicilians in the U.S. for that reason. Said they would do a contract for Sicilians only if it were a very important one, handled at the very top of the respective organizations. Said they would not ask for money, but would do it so that the Sicilians would owe them a favor. Said if killers were hired they would use knives if it were to even a score, but would use rifle if it were to teach a lesson or set an example. Then it would be done publically instead of in private. Said it would all be carefully worked out in advance and that the killers would get away with it. Said someone like the Guerini's would never offer an important contract to anyone they suspected would turn it down. Said if they did turn it down, they would be killed on the spot."[68]

What Conein said, fits the pattern of the Kennedy

[68]Steve Rivele Files, Re "My Lunch with Lou," June 29, 1986.

assassination. The terrible event was in the open, in the middle of the day, in Dealey Plaza, Dallas, Texas. Both David and Sarti were of Corsican background. Both men were expert shots (Sarti had one good eye), and if one were to believe that a conspiracy was behind the Kennedy assassination, then the shooters got away scott-free.

Rivele then asked Conein if he knew either Lucien Sarti or Christian David. He said that he did not, but had read their files. He said that Sarti was not killed on the orders of the U.S. government and said, "They could not have found anyone with enough guts to do it."

Rivele picked Conein's brain regarding the actions of the CIA during the era of the 60s and 70s, and told him of his investigation into the Kennedy assassination and all it entailed. He discussed his views on the Mexico City Mystery Man (the person whom the CIA said was Oswald but wasn't), "said this was a very interesting angle, and asked me if I was sure I wanted to get the truth about all this. Said he didn't envy me my job, that it was very dangerous."

Conein then walked an astonished Steve Rivele out of the restaurant and into the broad daylight. He gave Rivele a quarter to call a cab. "Said he keep in touch."

In 1974, two sources gave information to the United States government that Lucien Conein might have been involved in a plot to tap the phone of United States Senator Howard Baker (Tenn).

On July 15, 1974 the FBI's Atlanta office was informed of the alleged plot by Conein by a man named Howard Gibson, a resident of Powder Springs, Georgia. Gibson said he was a former Deputy Sheriff in Cobb County, Georgia, and was forced to resign his position after he was alleged to have fired a gun into the house of a narcotics informant with whom he had a fight. Prior to his position as a Deputy Sheriff, Gibson worked in a private investigative agency called the Central Investigative Agency, located at 6650 Powers Perry Road NW in Atlanta.

In his interview with FBI agents, Gibson that the Central Investigative Agency had a branch office called Security Consultants International (SCI) that was located at 1028 Connecticut Avenue in Washington, DC. Part of the office space of SCI had been sub-leased by Lucien Conein, whom Gibson knew was a DEA agent. Gibson also told the FBI that one of his business partners in Central Investigative Agency was Mitchell Werbell, 3rd, a man who a checkered past, a gun dealer who was well known to the FBI.

Gibson said that he believed that Conein "was actually a covert CIA agent and further suspects CIA has been operating a wiretap out of the space leased from SCI. Gibson bases these suspicions on statements made by Werbell alleging that he has worked for CIA in the past, that he is friends with CIA agents and officials, that he believes Conein to be an ex-CIA agent and knows that John Muldoon is a former CIA agent." [69]

Gibson told the agents that he observed two or three men enter and leave the office during the day but he thought that no work was being done during that time. One of Gibson's friends told him that he overheard people in the office that was allegedly leased by the DEA, discussing "tapes." The FBI memo on the Gibson interview says, "Based on the above information and based on Gibson's experience with wiretapping while employed with the Cobb County, Georgia Sheriff's Office, Gibson believes a wiretapping operation was being conducted in the space allegedly sub-leased by DEA from SCI."

The FBI said that since they believed that an on-going CIA operation was "being compromised and that the CIA should be aware, our Atlanta Office contacted (blank) CIA, Atlanta and informed him of the above on 7/11/74."

Gibson expanded on what was going on in the office. He told the FBI that the suite above his, which was located on the 12th floor was an efficiency apartment. It was connected to his own suite (1109) on the floor below by a stairway. Gibson said that the 12th floor apartment was the one that was rented by Conein.

Gibson said that he was told of the attempted taping by Conein of Sen. Howard Baker by Steve Van Cleave, a friend of his, and a private investigator from Atlanta. One day when Van Cleave showed up for work, he was told by Werbell that he could not stay in the room because Werbell was having a discussion with a client. Van Cleave later told Gibson that he went to the 12th floor entryway to the SCI offices, which was leased by Conein. He

---

69 RIF No. 124-90060-10006 "Alleged Tapping of Telephone of U.S. Senator Howard Baker." 7/16/74.

overheard a conversation through the door in which the words "tapes" could be heard.

Van Cleave told Gibson that he had a conversation with Lucien Conein in Washington, DC one month prior at Conein's office at DEA headquarters. During that meeting, "at which time he had told Conein that he suspected Conein had some sort of a CIA clandestine operation going on at 1025 Connecticut Ave, Washington, DC and Conein did not deny this. Van Cleave further commented to Conein that Sen. Howard Baker would be very interested in exposing such a CIA operation and might use it to assist President Nixon. According to Van Cleave, it is 'common knowledge' in WDC, that Baker would like to assist in exposing CIA taps and also in blaming the Watergate situation on CIA." [70]

The FBI memo on the Gibson interview gets more interesting, as it involved the on-going Watergate affair that was consuming the Nixon presidency at the time:

> According to Gibson's "grapevine," CIA was interested in Senator Baker because allegedly President Nixon's ultimate defense in the Watergate matter would be an allegation that the CIA had infiltrated his re-election campaign organization for the purpose of carrying out certain covert operations without the knowledge of President Nixon. Allegedly, the allegation would then be made by President Nixon that the CIA was therefore responsible for the Watergate matter. According to Gibson's "grapevine," Senator Baker is a staunch supporter of President Nixon and is cooperating with the President to blame the CIA for the Watergate matter.
>
> Gibson further advised he now believes he was to be the "fall guy" for the above described covert CIA operation since he is knowledgeable in the matter of wiretap operations and feels that if anything had gone wrong with the alleged CIA operation, the CIA would have placed the blame for the entire operation on Gibson. Gibson felt that, considering this expertise in wiretapping operations and the fact that the space allegedly sub-leased by DEA to Conein

[70] RIF No. 124-90060-10021. July 16, 1974.

was on a month-to-month basis without a written lease, he could have undoubtedly been made to appear at fault in any wiretapping operation that may have been occurring.[71]

The Atlanta office of the FBI asked Gibson to find out any further information on the alleged taping case so they could conduct further inquiries. However, the memo continues, "It is noted that the CIA has not been informed of the allegations that the leased space is being used by the CIA to tap the telephone of Senator Baker."

One of the theories behind the Watergate affairs is that the CIA, for whatever reason, might have been behind the break-in at the Democratic National Committee headquarters in the Watergate complex in June 1972. Two of the members of the Watergate team who were arrested after the affair were former members of the CIA. Rolando Martinez, a Cuban who took part in various anti-Castro operations for the CIA in the early 1960s, was still on the payroll of the CIA at the time of his arrest. Bernard Barker was a close, personal friend of another of the members of the Watergate team, E. Howard Hunt who was a long time CIA officer. Hunt worked with the members of the anti-Castro leadership who were slated to take over, if and when Castro was overthrown. He was the first CIA officer to consider that the CIA use assassination in an effort to remove Castro from power in Havana. Hunt was also a noted writer of spy novels and the CIA let him use their officers to write his pulp novels.

The same memo relating to the allegations regarding the taping of Sen. Baker, also mentions FBI interest in Gibson's partner, Mitchell Werbell, 111. The FBI had an open file on Werbell entitled, "Mitchell Livingston Werbell III, IS-Abaco; Neutrality Matters-Abaco." Werbell was a manufacturer of machine guns and other automatic weapons, based out of his home in Marietta, GA. He operated a company by the name of Security Defense Systems. Werbell boasted a handle bar mustache, wore a monocle on one eye, dubbed himself "Prince Eric Steraf," and in later years, "Mitch the Fifth" which came from all the times he decided not to incriminate himself before various courts of law.

71 RIF No. 124-90060-10006. July 16, 1974.

He also made a name for himself during this time as an arms dealer who sold his advanced weapons to anti-Communist groups, including the CIA, and most importantly, the various anti-Castro organizations in the United States. One of his companies was called the Military Ordnance Corporation, along with its parent Washington based entity, Quantum Ordnance Bankers. These companies sold items like the Ingram M-11, hand held machine guns to revolutionary groups around the globe.

When the House Select Committee first encountered Mitchell Werbell, he was living high on the hog on his farm in Power Springs, Georgia. It was from here that Werbell trained many of the soldiers of fortune who came to pay their respects, made his silent kill devices, and discussed his efforts to fight Castro, among other Latin American dictators of the 1960s and 1970s. Werbell was often seen in such places of revolutionary ferment as the Dominican Republic, Guatemala, in Miami when the anti-Castro crusade was in full swing, Venezuela, and other hot spots.

The declassified CIA files on Mitchell Werbell are extensive and paint a picture of a man whose killing skills were not unnoticed by the boys in Langley. The files deny any official CIA contact with Werbell but the CIA knew exactly where he was during this period (the 1960's), and what he was doing. The CIA first learned of Werbell in July 1959, when he contacted General Charles Cabell indicating knowledge of Cuban and Dominican Republic affairs. Werbell met with an agent of the CIA's Los Angeles Division but by October 1959, "it was apparent that he did not have the access to information as hoped and he apparently looked upon his association with CIA as a means of furthering his various business schemes. All contact was severed."

An August 7, 1974 CIA memo sent to the CIA Director concerning Werbell states that there were three Agency employees then working for him in various capacities. These men expressed their concerns to the Agency regarding Werbell's illegal activities and asked if anything could be done. The CIA wrote back that it was out of their charter to give any help but that the matter would be turned over to the FBI.

In 1966, Werbell told the CIA's Miami Station about his own groups plans to assassinate Fidel Castro. "Our records do not indicate what was done about this information," says the CIA.

In 1965-66, Werbell pressed the CIA for help in his "Organization to Combat Communism." Again, no CIA action was undertaken.

By 1971, the U.S. government, now tired of Webell's nasty covert activities, canceled his security clearance. Werbell in turn, asked the CIA's Domestic Contact Division for help but was told they could do nothing for him. This was done in relation to his flagrant actions in regard to the possible overthrow of the government of Haiti lead by Rolando Masferrer and his breaking of the neutrality laws of the United States.

In the 1970s, Werbell found his way to Thailand where he passed himself off as the Chief of the CIA in Thailand. He also tried to sell arms, including pistols and sniper rifles to groups in that country. In regard to Werbell's Thai mission, a CIA memo reads in part, "he is characterized as unscrupulous, a wheeler-dealer as a promoter of grandiose schemes."

For his part, Mitchell Werbell said that he wanted nothing to do with the CIA.

When the Church Committee began investigating an alleged Panama/Torrijos hit, staff members interviewed Howard Hunt on February 25, 1977. While little documentation exists from that meeting, what can be learned is that when questioned about the Panama plan, Hunt said that there was talk about such an assassination plot but that no firm date, or any other hard plan was put into effect.

But what has fascinated investigators since that time is the timing in which the Torrijos plot was hatched.

It was at this time that the Nixon administration was being rocked by the newly released "Pentagon Papers" affair by a then little known figure by the name of Daniel Ellsberg. Ellsberg was a minor government official who had worked in Vietnam for the CIA's infamous "pacification" program during the 1960s. Early on, Ellsberg considered himself a "hawk," believing in the Johnson/Nixon positions concerning the U.S. role in Vietnam. After his tour of duty in Vietnam, Ellsberg returned to the United States embittered about what he had seen and done in Southeast Asia. His political thinking had reversed itself and he was now opposed to Nixon's Vietnam policy. When he came back home, Ellsberg taught at MIT, and later worked for Henry Kissinger in the White House at the start of the Nixon presidency. He also did a stint as a staffer at the RAND Corporation.

If one is to believe the story, Ellsberg began copying the top-secret "Pentagon Papers," a highly critical report on how the United States got involved in Vietnam, beginning in 1969. To Nixon, the leaking of the Pentagon Papers to the *New York Times,* on June 13, 1971, was nothing but treason. Both Ellsberg and the other papers such as the *Washington Post,* which printed major excerpts, had to be stopped at any cost. To that end, the Nixon team took legal action to seek the *Times* and the other papers from publishing the report. Eventually, the Supreme Court ruled against the administration and the full Pentagon Papers record was made public.

In order to plug the leaks, such as the Pentagon Papers, and other highly secretive documents from leaking out of the Nixon administration, a secret organization, operating out of the White House was started. The genesis of the so-called "Plumbers" was put into effect in a White House meeting on July 2 between the President, John Ehrlichman and Bob Haldeman. Nixon wanted to be able to control the fallout over the Ellsberg/Pentagon Papers affair and the only way to do that without running into any outside interference, i.e., Hoover's FBI or the CIA, was to command the investigation from 1600 Pennsylvania Avenue. Nixon and Ehrlichman decided that David Young, who was then working as an assistant to National Security Advisor Henry Kissinger, would head up part of the new unit.

When the president informed Kissinger that Young was to be taken out of his staff for work on the secret unit, Kissinger objected fiercely. "Haldeman saw it later as an Ehrlichman stroke of genius to involve a Kissinger man."

On July 17, Ehrlichman appointed his own man to head the Plumbers. He chose Egil Krogh, White House aide who was director of the president's domestic council. Krogh was to head the Special Investigations Unit, a.k.a., the "Plumbers" (an apt name, as it was their job to plug leaks), while Young would serve as its staff director. When taking on the job as head of the unit, Ehrlichman told Krogh that he would have direct contact with the president at any time. Another job of the new Special Investigations Unit was to take over the investigation of the Ellsberg matter from the

Justice Department and concentrate it in the White House.

As the Plumbers operation was getting started, Krogh began his search for people of a certain caliber who would be totally loyal to Nixon. One of the first recruits to come on board was a former FBI agent by the name of G. Gordon Liddy. Liddy had served as an assistant district attorney in Poughkeepsie, New York, and was totally opposed to any type of gun control, and harbored harsh right-wing political views (nothing has changed since then). In 1968, he ran against Congressman Hamilton Fish in the Republican primary contest but lost the election in November. When Nixon won the presidency over Vice President Hubert Humphrey in November 1968, Liddy was given a job in the Treasury Department, but he didn't last long. After getting into one too many scrapes with his boss, Liddy was transferred to the White House, working for Attorney General John Mitchell where he specialized in "narcotics," bombing and guns." For Liddy, the Plumbers assignment was manna from heaven.

The other individual who was to play a part in the Watergate/Torrijos affair was a former CIA agent, whose shadowy past would bring him right smack dab into the investigation of the assassination of John F. Kennedy, E. Howard Hunt. A detailed narrative of Hunt's background is not necessary as it would take up an entire book, and most researchers familiar with both the Watergate scandal and the Kennedy assassination are by now most familiar with Hunt's resume. Suffice it to say that Hunt was introduced to the Plumbers by Nixon staffer Charles Colson. Hunt, working out of a separate spot in the Executive Office building opposite the White House, was to gather as much dirt on the president's potential Democratic opponents as he could find.

In this time period, when the Plumbers were beginning to carry out their covert action plans, the Jack Anderson article concerning the Torrijos/heroin connection story hit the newsstands. It should be noted that during this time, Gordon Liddy had proposed an assassination plot against Jack Anderson! As the government report on this phase of the Torrijos affair states:

> *In setting forth this March 1972 period as a likely period in which the alleged Panama assassination plan was initiated by the Nixon men, one should bear in mind that*

other Plumber assignments were later revealed to have been set in motion by a single news report such as Anderson's March 1972 column on Torrijos... Thus, the Plumbers plot against Torrijos (if in fact one did exist), might quite reasonably be traced to these March 1972 disclosures about the heroin trade.[72]

By the spring of 1972, the CIA had hard evidence concerning the use of Panama as a shipping and receiving point for the sale of drugs throughout the Latin American region. In the Anderson article, the columnist reported that the CIA had in hand, a 20-page document detailing the Torrijos connection, and that this report was being circulated to other interested government agencies.

Other news organizations soon got wind of the story and on June 18, 1973, *Newsweek* reported that presidential counselor John Dean had told the Ervin Committee, which was investigating the Watergate affair, of administration plans to kill Torrijos.

With regard to this plot, the government report states:

That some low-level White House officials at one point considered assassinating Panama's head of government. Dean's story is that the administration suspected high Panamanian government officials of being involved in the flow of heroin from Latin America into the U.S. and were also concerned about strongman Omar Torrijos's uncooperative attitude toward renegotiating the Panama Canal Treaty. Thus, in Dean's telling, some officials found a Torrijos hit doubly attractive. The contract, he said, went to E. Howard Hunt, later a ring-leader in the Watergate break-in. Hunt, according to Dean, had his team in Mexico before the mission was aborted.[73]

The first hint that the "Plumbers" were contemplating an assassination attempt on the life of Torrijos came in an article in *Newsweek* which reported that John Dean was about to reveal to

---

72 Kross, Peter, "The Plumbers and the Torrijos Assassination Plot," Back Channels Magazine, Volume 4, Number 1, Pages 12-15.

73 Ibid.

the Senate Watergate Committee that "low level White House aids" were planning such an attack on the president of Panama. It is interesting to note that John Dean, wrapped up as he was in the unfolding Watergate affair, did not make any mention in a public forum on the alleged Panama hit. The story was not confirmed until *four* years later when Hunt testified to it in February 1977. To this day, it is still unclear who *Newsweek's* source was concerning this mater.

As in many other areas of Howard Hunt's professional life, his involvement in the Panama hit remains a mystery (Note: Ervin Committee investigators said that they called in Hunt regarding the Torrijos hit and that he *denied* any involvement in such a scheme. Yet, after Hunt's release from jail for his participation in the Watergate affair, he confirmed his participation (in a February 25, 1977 interview) that a Plumbers plan to kill Torrijos was in the works. Which story is true?

Hunt expanded on his knowledge of the plot to kill Torrijos after he finished his jail term. He told a televison reporter that the Nixon administration had a "concern" over the drug smuggling operations going on in Panama and that, "if Torrijos didn't shape up and cooperate, he was gong to be wasted." Hunt also cryptically told a reporter that the Plumbers had organized a covert foreign mission but he would not go further in describing what it was. When the reporter asked for Hunt's opinion as to whether or not a foreign head of state should be put on an assassination list he said, "I didn't know any of the people asked to participate other than the people in the plumbers unit. They had that as part of their brief."

However, there was one person who could add more to Hunts' story about the role of the plumbers in the Torrijos hit. This was first reported in an article written by Jack Anderson and Les Whiten called "Watergate Plotters Reportedly Marketed Torrijos For Assassination." The source was Martin Dardis, who, in 1973, was the Dade County (Miami, Florida) investigator.

In 1973, Martin Dardis was the chief investigator to Dade County's state attorney Richard Gerstein, and later served under U.S. Attorney General Janet Reno. As anyone knows who saw the film, *All the President's Men,* Carl Bernstein, played by Dustin Hoffman, waited all day to see Mr. Dardis, only to be kept waiting by his intrepid secretary. Hoffman/Bernstein finally burst his way into the office of Martin Dardis, telling him that he was from the *Washington Post* and that he was waiting all day for their scheduled meeting. During the Watergate affair, Dardis connected the Watergate burglars to President Nixon's Committee to Re-elect the President (CREEP),

As reported by Anderson, Dardis wrote a memo on the affair after he had a meeting with Manuel Artime, one of the leading anti-Castro people of the era. Artime was one of the leaders of the Bay of Pigs invasion of Cuba in 1961. During their talk, Artime told Dardis that he had been contacted by Hunt to recruit a number of Artime's Cuban allies to "take care of the situation in Panama." Artime said that Hunt did not use the word "assassination," but used a "key phrase" and said that "something had to be taken care of in Panama."

Artime later told Dardis that whatever plan was scheduled to take place in Panama was called off, but one of Dardis's sources told him that the plumbers "were going to bump off Torrijos at the racetrack" in Panama.

During his testimony before the Church Committee, Hunt was questioned about his possible role in the Torrijos affair. He was asked by a member of the committee staff, Mr. Genzman, if he ever contacted Artime regarding the Torrijos action.

Hunt said that he never contacted Artime but that at one point, Artime mentioned to him his concern as to the ever-growing drug trade in Latin America., and those going on in Panama. Hunt, however, came prepared for such a question. He told the committee that he wanted to quote from the above mentioned article by Jack Anderson from a press release that was given by Attorney Ellis Rubin on December 16, 1977, responding to Anderson's column:

> Anderson's column recites the so-called 1973 secret memo from Richard Gerstein's investigator Martin Dardis, allegedly quoting Manuel Artime, Hunt's close friend and god-father to one of his children. This office represents both Hunt and Sturgis (Frank Sturgis, one of the arrested Watergate burglars) now, and we were the attorney for Dr. Artime over the years. I would have known of any so-called plot because Dr. Artime confided in me, and I

possess the facts concerning both Hunt and Sturgis and all of their activities.

Jack Anderson made no detectable effort to contact Howard Hunt to refute the charges. He knows I represent both Hunt and Sturgis, and he could have contacted Mr. Hunt through this office. I now ask why did Mr. Dardis and Anderson wait until after Dr. Artime's untimely death from cancer to make Artime their sole authority for Hunt's so-called involvement in the conspiracy. Along those lines, I challenge Mr. Dardis or anyone else to procure any written memorandum, signed by Manuel Artime, or a tape recording of his voice substantiating these outrageous lies.[74]

Another interesting sideline to the Panama plot involves another of the Watergate burglars, Bernard Barker. Barker, who was arrested with Sturgis, Hunt, et al, registered at the Watergate hotel posing as businessmen from Miami representing a firm called Ameritas, supposedly a real estate company. Barker even sent a letter to the Watergate hotel registering the men on Ameritas stationary. A subsequent FBI investigation of Ameritas found that the firm did not exist under the state of Florida. The president of Ameritas was a Miami resident named Miguel Suarez who was a lawyer for Barker on previous occasions. When questioned by the Watergate staff, Suarez said that the company had not begun business and that he had no idea why Barker would be using Ameritas stationary for any reason. However, Suarez told investigators that he ran another business called "All State Investment Fund, Inc." which was located in Panama. What this second company did in Panama is not known.

On June 1, 1974, *ABC* news reporter, David Schoumacher, aired a report that—according to his sources—Hunt sent a Torrijos murder team to Mexico in preparation for the attack. The plan was subsequently aborted. Hunt, the report said, had made frequent trips to Mexico using the alias, "Edward J. Hamilton." Interestingly, Watergate evidence also establishes the fact that

---

74 Howard Hunt interview, November 3, 1978.

Frank Sturgis had also apparently traveled to Mexico in 1972, during the same period of time in which he was working on various assignments for the Hunt/Liddy team. Following his arrest in the Watergate break-in, and the extensive news coverage devoted to him, it was reported that Sturgis had applied for, and received a Mexican visa in early 1972.

The House proceedings in which this story is based, reported a secret trip made by Hunt to Nicaragua in the time period covering January to April 1972. What Hunt was doing in Nicaragua is still unknown but it is speculated that he was there on the behest of the Nixon re-election committee. During the time of Hunt's alleged trip to Nicaragua, Howard Hughes, a secret contributor to Nixon's presidential campaign, was living in that country.

If the Howard Hunt story that he was in Mexico to plan the Torrijos hit is true, this opens up a whole new area of investigation; it leads right up to the "smoking gun" tape of June 23, 1972 between President Nixon and his top aides. During that meeting, both the president and Bob Haldeman talk about the White Houses' effort to have the FBI call off their investigation of the "Mexico connection" to Watergate (the money funneled to the burglars was laundered through Mexico by Liddy). After the meeting, the president's men had CIA Director Richard Helms order FBI Director L. Patrick Gray to halt the FBI's investigation into covert activities in Mexico. What is still not known is what was going on in Mexico at that time.

The testimony of two of the principal players in the CIA/Watergate affair spell out an intriguing aspect of this "Mexico connection." When CIA Deputy Director Vernon Walters testified about the June 23 White House meeting, he said, "that Haldeman warned that there is concern that these investigations—this investigation in Mexico—may expose some covert activities of the CIA."

Even more interesting is the statement by ex-CIA Director Richard Helms to the Ervin Committee concerning the same June 23 meeting. Helms stated:

> *At this point the references to Mexico were quite unclear to me. I had to recognize that if the White House, the president, Mr. Haldeman, some-body in high authority,*

had information about something in Mexico which I did not have information about, which is quite possible-the White House constantly has information which others do not have-that it would a prudent thing for me to find out. This possibility always had to exist. Nobody knows everything about everything.

The author of this account states that he spoke with an unnamed Nixon White House official who said that the original *Newsweek* article caused a major stir at the White Hose. The aid said that Chief of Staff Alexander Haig tried to quash any further talk among the staff on the Panama allegation and that he (Haig) had indeed talked with President Nixon about it. The aide also said that he was positive that these conversations (if indeed they were held), would probably be on the taping system Nixon had installed in the Oval Office to record all his conversations.

A side note to this affair is the arrest on May 19, 1972 of a group of men with a large cache of arms off the coast of Panama. Arrested aboard the yacht was a Miami businessman named Edwin Hill.

Hill and his party were kept for questioning for five days and then released. After the arrest took place, the Panamanian authorities contacted the U.S. State Department which promptly issued a statement that said that the Hill party was not conducting gun-running activities.

Hill and the crew pleaded guilty to charges of "carrying excessive weapons on a pleasure craft without a permit" and were fined $3,700.00 and quickly released.

When looking into the Hill affair, government probers found links with Hill to both the 1972 Nixon re-election committee and to local Democratic candidates.

Many questions still remain concerning the possible Torrijos assassination plot, if indeed, there really was one. But this strange episode is just one more riddle from the vast network of illegal activities that dominated the Nixon years.

The Vesco Capers

Another prominent American who was a target of the Drug Enforcement Agency at the time was Robert Vesco, a swindler, criminal with links to the drug trade in Latin America, and an early take-off of Bernard Madoff in our own time.

In June 1995, an unexpected announcement was made over Cuban television. It stated that the American financier/ fugitive and swindler, Robert Vesco, had been placed under arrest by Cuban authorities on charges that he was a "provocateur and agent of foreign special services." The announcement brought the American Justice Department on alert, hoping that finally Mr. Vesco would be brought to justice. For Robert Vesco was the mastermind of a huge financial swindle that amounted to over $200 million, looted the savings of hundreds of fund investors in the 1970s, made a an illegal campaign contribution to President Nixon's 1972 presidential campaign, and last but certainly not least, had allied himself with the number one drug kingpin of the day, Carlos Lehder Rivas of Columbia.

Over the years, Mr. Vesco's flight from the United States would begin an entirely new career, trying to break the thirty-year American economic embargo of Cuba, and tying himself into the politics of the Bahamas. He'd also become involved with various Mafia types, soldiers of fortune and other nefarious hoodlums of all sorts.

Since his flight from American shores in 1971, Robert Vesco's persona would become that of legend, alibied of the worst kind. Pursued by American authorities, he leapt from Caribbean country to country, always keeping one eye on the horizon, looking for his kidnappers or the betrayal of his various hosts.

Robert Vesco grew up in Detroit, the son of a factory worker, suffering the vestiges of his Italian roots among the dozens of other ethnic's who worked in the Motor City. The Vesco's were not rich and at an early age, young Robert knew that he had to leave the fold or be swallowed up by it. At age sixteen, he quit high school and went to work in an auto-body shop. At that early stage of his life, he'd already compiled a police blotter for car theft (no charges were ever filed). At seventeen, he married a young girl named Pat who lived in Bad Ax, Michigan. Soon, a son would be born.

Vesco was nothing but ambitious, telling himself and his wife that he would make something of himself, no matter what route he had to go in order to accomplish that fact. Over the next few years he worked at various jobs, lying about his education and work experience, when, at the age of twenty-four, he doubled his salary and landed a good position with the title "Project Engineer." What his duties as a Project Engineer called for, and what he actually did, were two different things entirely. But what is known of this time is that Vesco made numerous contacts with important people in the banking industry who had heard of his reputation as a can do manager and a go-getter.

By age twenty-five, Vesco had made enough business contacts that he was able to go out on his own and in a very short period of time, proceeded to buy minority holdings in various insolvent businesses by purchasing large blocks of company stock. Acting as a "consultant," Vesco was able to purchase many of these financially troubled firms, making for himself in the process, a rather rich man.

As his reputation grew, the older movers and shakers whom Vesco had ingratiated himself with, actually loaned him money to buy out those companies he originally "parlayed" with. He was now, at the ripe age of thirty, able to form his own company, made up of the ones he taken over, called International Controls Corporation (ICC). Shortly after forming ICC, Vesco took control of a company called Cryogencics, Inc. The acquisition of ICC was most fortuitous as far as Vesco was concerned, as Cryogenics was a publically traded company whose stock was sold over the counter. Vesco now had access to large pools of new cash, mutual funds, investment trusts and other means of capital. He was now on his way to being a rather wealthy man.

Among the companies that Vesco brought under ICC's control were; Century Special, Fairfield Aviation, Intercontinental Industries, Golden West Airlines, and, most importantly, Electronic Specialties Inc. This last firm was ten times larger than ICC itself. In less than three years, Vesco had climbed from being a consultant to a handful of small New Jersey manufacturers that were on the edge of insolvency to become the maximum leader of a $100 million conglomerate employing thousands—a conglomerate almost literally created out of thin air.

But Vesco was not content to stay put with ICC. He'd now venture out into the unknown territory of off shore investment, mutual funds with a company owned by Bernard Cornfeld called Investors Overseas Services (IOS), that would lead Vesco into the world of criminal activity, one that was probably inevitable.

The owner of IOS, one Bernard Cornfeld, was a Brooklyn native who was definitely not the true corporate type. His politics leaned toward the socialist side, looking out for the poor of the world, yet playing around with the moneymen of the time. He had a mansion in Geneva that was originally built by the French emperor Napoleon for his Empress Josephine. IOS was huge in makeup, an international holding company that controlled insurance companies, real estate and mutual funds, all over the world.

Cornfeld founded IOS in the 1950s, when, as a mutual fund salesman, he sold shares in the Dreyfus Fund for members of the American military stationed near Paris. By 1960, Cornfeld's salesmen had covered most of Europe, allowing him to incorporate IOS in Panama, where banking regulations were slim to none.

But Cornfeld found the jungles of Panama not to his liking and he moved IOS's headquarters to Switzerland where the banking laws were even tighter than Panama, and the secrecy of accounts would be assured. Cornfeld's baby, The International Investment Trust (ITT), was incorporated in Luxembourg, the heart of the covert financial capital of Europe. Soon, other of IOS's corporate entities would form in such places as Liechtenstein, Singapore,, Hong Kong, the Netherlands Antilles, and more importantly to this story, the Bahamas.

IOS was Bernie Cornfeld's baby, a privately controlled entity that he, and a few of his most trusted aides fussed over. At the apex of IOS's career, over then thousand of its salesmen roamed the world in search of investors. The more Cornfeld's salesmen sold, the more they would be able to purchase in IOS's stock options, consequently, the richer they'd get. In reality, IOS "served only as a middleman, selling shares in mutual funds owned and maintained by other companies."

But more important to Cornfeld was that being incorporated in Switzerland made IOS immune to the strict banking regulations then in force in the United States. This "offshore" status allowed IOS to charge much higher prices for its services than for American based companies. But more importantly, by selling other groups mutual funds, IOS had a huge cash reserve on hand, at one point totaling $600,000,000.

As the Cornfeld empire grew, he allied himself with such diverse people as Tibor Rosenbaum, a Hungarian Jew who headed the International Credit Bank of Switzerland who helped Bernie funnel "hot" money around the world, the Rothschild banking family, James Roosevelt, the son of the late president, Franklin D. Roosevelt, and of course, Robert Vesco.

From his perspective, Vesco saw Cornfeld's IOS as the ultimate black bag job. Vesco saw his chance to get his hands on IOS when that company's stock went into decline and its cash reserves dipped. Vesco offered to loan Cornfeld five million and subjected a number of harsh conditions upon IOS including the proviso that Cornfeld could not hold any position in the firm without Vesco's permission. Another requirement was that if any of these loan terms were abrogated, then Vesco had the right to liquidate IOS and collect three million in damages. But Vesco's eventual takeover of IOS was a masterful underhanded ploy; in order to cover the five million dollar loan he gave to IOS, IOS had to put up $5.5 million "as collateral for the loan made by ICC Investments." Vesco now had total control over IOS and he quickly brought the company down.

Vesco instructed that all of IOS's loans be called in. Foreclosures followed suit and the rape of IOS was all but a certainty. But Vesco's actions caught the attention of the Securities and Exchange Commission. In order to derail any SEC investigation, Vesco gave a $250,000 campaign contribution to President Richard Nixon's upcoming presidential campaign (this was on April 7, 1972). The two hundred fifty grand was laundered out of his credit account at the Paradise Island casino in the Bahamas. Vesco was associated with James Crosby, a high rolling contributor to Republican politicians, and also, a friend of Richard Nixon's.

Over the years it has been rumored that Nixon was a silent partner in Crosby's Bahama enterprises, even going so far as to allege that Nixon had a secret interest in the revenue generated from the toll bridge linking Nassau to Paradise Island. Another Nixon-Vesco connection was the fact that the late president's nephew, Donald Nixon Jr., and at the time of Vesco's arrest, had been a houseguest of Vesco in Cuba. Vesco's "contribution" was delivered on April 10, 1972.

Vesco's payoff to the Nixon re-election committee was handed over to Maurice Stans, then Commerce Secretary in the Nixon administration, and also the chief fundraiser for the president's re-election drive. Stans was able to rake in $60 million for Nixon's re-election drive, some of which was sent to the Watergate burglars. More of this money went to pay for dirty tricks that were used against the Democrats, including the president's political opponents in the 1972 election year.

When he was later questioned by the Ervin Committee which investigated the Watergate affair, Stans denied any knowledge about what the money was used for. Stans was later to be indicted on charges of conspiracy, obstruction of justice and perjury in connection with his efforts to influence the SEC to protect Robert Vesco. At his trial, Stans was acquitted of all charges filed against him.

Prior to his giving the money to the Nixon re-election fund, Vesco and I.C.C. president Laurence Richardson met with Maurice Stans on March 8, 1972. Stans had previously served as President Eisenhower's budget director. He was now head of CREEP's (Committee to re-elect the president) mammoth financial committee, responsible for raising as much cash as it would take to insure the president's re-election. Vesco told Stans that in 1968, he had given $50,000 to Nixon's election effort and would do even more now.

He looked Stans in the eye and said, "But I have a problem. My company and I are under investigation by the SEC. The investigation has been going on for more than a year now and not produced any charges nor arrived at any settlement. It's completely without merit and amounts to a personal vendetta and harassment. I want to find a way to bring the case to a conference and settlement."

Stans said that he could not help, but offered the name of John Mitchell. Stans then asked Vesco how much he was willing to give. Stans said $1 million would get Vesco a front row seat at Nixon's table. Vesco said he'd give two, $500,000 checks, in installments. Stans nixed the idea, saying that after April 7 all contributions of that amount had to be put in the public record, along with the donors name. Stans said that Vesco should make at least one contribution before April 6.

After Vesco's flight to Costa Rica, some months later, federal prosecutors changed him with making an illegal campaign contribution to the Nixon campaign for the purpose of heading off the expected SEC probe into his looting of IOS.

In April 1972, Vesco resigned any position he had with IOS, He then announced that all financial interest in IOS was in the hands of a Bahamas shell company called Kilmorey Investments, Ltd. What the SEC didn't know was that Kilmorey was controlled by a number of Vesco's business cronies. In fact, Vesco handed off parts of IOS to a number of his friends in the Bahamas who controlled untraceable funds, and in an elaborate shell game, the liquidated IOS funds were funneled back to Vesco through these untraceable groups. In the end, IOS was bankrupt on paper. In reality, Vesco had looted over $200 million from the company.

By November, 1972, with an SEC suit pending against him, Vesco fled the country for the safer havens of Costa Rica.

Once safely encased in Costa Rica, Vesco began an association with Mitchell Werbell, who was Howard Gibson's partner in the Sen. Baker bugging affair.

During the early 1960s, Werbell and his assorted mercenary buddies carried out raids against Castro's Cuba, recalling his days during World War 11 when he served in the OSS. As Webell's fame grew, so did his bank account. He was in charge of at least seven companies specializing in arms manufacturing and clandestine services, acquired some $7 million in loans from people on Wall Street to finance his burgeoning business, owned a bomb testing range, flew his own Lockheed Jetstar, and had plenty of women along for the ride.

And so it was no surprise to anyone that Werbell would show up in Costa Rica at the same time that Robert Vesco just happened to be enjoying his newly won sabbatical from justice.

In Costa Rica, Vesco was welcomed with open arms by that country's president, Jose "Don Pepe" Figueres who saw in Vesco's arrival, the possibility of new riches for himself (if not his country). Vesco also made quick friends with Figueres's son who saw the same possibilities.

When Vesco arrived in Costa Rica, he made a $2.1 million investment in a company that was owned by President Figueres. In exchange for getting Vesco's money, the Costa Rican leader disregarded all U.S. attempts to get Vesco back into U.S. hands. President Figueres's even went so far as to have a law passed that would guarantee that Costa Rica would not extradite Vesco back to Washington. Vesco bought a lavish home on the island, along with a dairy farm. He also had a 137-foot yacht, the *Patricia,* in the Bahamas, and a Boeing 707 in Panama. Vesco made many trips to Panama where he cemented a business relationship with the strongman/dictator of that nation, Manuel Noreiga, a known drug dealer, and all around crook.

When the S.E.C. filed its complaint against Vesco, President Figueres personally called Richard Nixon and asked him if he could intervene with the S.E.C. to drop the charges against his new friend and patron. He told Nixon that, "I am concerned that any adverse publicity emanating from the S.E.C. against Mr. Vesco might jeopardize the development of my country. My son Marti recently met with your brother Edward in New York through Mr. Vesco, and we have extended to him an invitation to visit our country."

Later, as the squeeze began to tighten around Vesco, Figueres called Fidel Castro on Vesco's behalf. In 1978, the successor to President Figueres had the law keeping Vesco in Costa Rica dropped and Vesco had to leave Costa Rica for the Bahamas.

While living in Costa Rica, Vesco was introduced Werbell to President Figueres, a well as his son. The president's son wanted to buy 2,000 silenced Ingram pistols from Werbell. But, in reality, Figueres was really fronting for Vesco who saw in Cost Rica, the prefect place in which to ferment his own revolution across the Caribbean basin. But a checkmate was thrown into the possible deal when the country's new president, Daniel Oduber, failed to see the humor in the Vesco-Werbell connection:

> The deal offered fringe benefits to Werbell. He could manufacture his Ingrams in Costa Rica, free from nettlesome U.S. export license restrictions. There were fringe benefits for Vesco too-an armed to the teeth home base from which in indulge his most megalomaniac plans, which included some sort of super-capitalist nation-state tax haven, not a little dabbling in the lucrative international drug market, a private army, and a gambling empire all his

own.[75]

It also seems obvious that Webell had another, more dangerous gambit to pursue, and in all probability it included Robert Vesco. In 1973, Werbell organized a covert operation called the "New Country Project" which called for the violent takeover of the island of Abaco in the Bahamas. Abaco, which was part of the Bahama chain, according to Werbell, was ripe for succession. Werbell it seems, saw in Abaco a new home for gambling, rackets, and tourism, mostly American. According to Bill Turner in his book *Deadly Secrets,* Werbell contacted "his contacts in the high Arctic of the CIA" who told him that he could go ahead with the invasion so long as there was no killing. Werbell then gathered together a number of his old Vietnam vets who were out of work to mount the attack. D-Day for Abaco was slated for New Years day, 1975. But it was not to be.

A few months before the invasion was to take place, the U.S. Treasury Department indicted Werbell's son, Mitchell Werbell IV, and his company, Defense Services for allegedly trying to sell two thousand silenced Ingrams to an undercover agent. At the trial, the younger Werbell was acquitted of the charges.

The year 1975 was a busy one for Mitch Werbell. In that year, the U.S. State Department began an investigation of an attempted marihuana smuggling conspiracy involving Werbell. In the course of its investigation, a plan to overthrow the government of Grenada was uncovered... In April of that year, Werbell contacted federal agents in Miami saying that he was in financial difficulties and that he requested the agencies help in the smuggling multi-ton quantities of Columbian marihuana into the Untied States. The agents, posing as pilots and smugglers for the Columbian gangs, began clandestine negotiations with Webell in a sing operation.

Along with Werbell in this operation was William Bell, born 6/27/28, a resident of North Carolina. Bell was an ex-Marine Corps pilot and worked for the Marine Reality and Development Corp in Raleigh, North Carolina. Bell had an arrest record for carrying a

---

[75]Hinkle, Warren and Turner, William, *Deadly Secrets: The CIA-Mafia War Against Castro and the Assassination of JFK,* Thunders Mouth Press, New York, 1992, Page 398.

concealed weapon and driving under the influence, and in 1973, for writing a false check.

As described by Werbell to the feds, the plan called for the landing of thirtysix armed men on Grenada during the late evening of a Saturday in mid or late June 1975. The raiders were to be Scottish mercenaries, but in reality, were really Americans. The landing would take place at the same time as the shut down of the island's radio station, and other communication facilities. Bell was supposed to lead an assassination squad that was supposed to kill twentyone political and government officials. If all went well, the raiders were to take control of the island, the next day.

A resident of Grenada, Ken Mill or Mills, was supposed to have provided them with $3 million in expense money. He would then be put in charge of the new government.

All this leaves the interested reader with an enigma. Was Vesco secretly working for the CIA in the Abaco invasion matter? Surely the CIA knew that the two thousand guns were being shipped from Werbell's Powder Springs "farm" to Costa Rica. Why did they not stop it? Vesco had implied to Werbell on numerous occasions that he was indeed working for the CIA. The fact that Vesco was not forcibly extradited from Costa Rica for his looting of IOS and then, the plot on Abaco, makes one wonder how much the Nixon administration really wanted Vesco back home. If he did return to stand trial, what secrets might Vesco have revealed regarding Nixon, the mob, his possible contacts with the Watergate affair, and a whole list of other illegal Nixon adventures?

After Vesco's arrest in Cuba, a source reported that the Castro government never offered Vesco back to the United States. The source said that, "The only thing they asked was if we had any information on him in terms of U.S. law. I asked him whether there was any substance to the espionage charges against Vesco. Was it possible that Vesco, in maverick James Bond fashion, could have been doing favors for his enemy as a double agent? The official had evidently been thinking along the same lines. We contacted the CIA and said, "Is it possible he's an agent?, and the CIA said, No, he's not. But when I worked in Guatemala, I'd routinely ask the CIA for information and they would always tell me that the person was not an agent, and I'd find out later that they were."[76]

Two years after Vesco's covert campaign contribution to the Nixon re-election bid, the SEC indicted him for the looting of IOS. At the same time his welcome in Costa Rica was up and in April 1978, Vesco moved to the more promising political climate of the Bahamas where he would take on another venture; drug smuggling.

Vesco moved into a large mansion with all the amenities one could want; a pool, yacht, helicopter and servants. He also made himself known on the island and began to ally himself with Prime Minister of the Bahamas, Linden Pindling. Pindling's Progressive Liberal Party had taken control over the island chain and Pindling saw in Vesco a new tool for his own greedy adventures. Vesco also made a secret alliance with the baron of the drug smugglers in the Caribbean, Carlos Lehder. One of the first politically powerful people whom Vesco made contact with in the Bahamas was a white auto dealer named K.C. Cartwright from Nassau. Cartwright introduced Vesco to a man who would play an even larger part in his machinations, Gorman Bannister. Bannister in turn, acquainted Vesco with Lehder.

Lehder's headquarters was the island of Norman's Cay, one of the out islands of the Bahama chain. When Lehder arrived on Norman's Cay, he plunked down $100,000 cash at the sprawling home of Charles Beckwith, one of the richest men on the island. Lehder said he "wanted" Beckwith's home and the startled Beckwith took the money and fled. Lehder, trying to look respectable in the eyes of the Pindling administration, incorporated a business in the Bahamas called International Dutch Resources, a cover for his illegal drug smuggling business. Soon, Lehder brought in his goons, his mistress, and set up shop. By October 1978, Vesco too decided to plant himself near to Lehder, and bought a home on nearby Exuma Island, some ten miles from Norman's Cay. It was at this time that the Vesco-Lehder connection was established.

At the time that Lehder arrived on Norman's Cay, he had to deal with another smuggling operation that had set up shop there.

---

[76]Bardach, Ann Louise "Vesco's Last Gamble." Vanity Fair, March 1996.

Edward Ward and Charles Von Eberstein had been using Norman's Cay as their own marijuana smuggling bastion from which they would send the grass by the planeload to Florida. Soon though, Lehder made an "arrangement" with Ward and Von Eberstein whereby they would work for him if they wanted to stay in business (or stay alive).

In January 1979, Ward flew Lehder to Columbia, bringing back to Norman's Cay over 500 kilos of cocaine. From there, the coke was smuggled across the border into the U.S. As time went on, Lehder brought in highspeed boats, helicopters, radar equipment to monitor his drug flights. It was at this time that the U.S. Drug Enforcement Administration finally got wind of what was taking place on Norman's Cay and they mounted a covert operation to keep track of Lehder and Vesco.

Lehder's drug smuggling out of Norman's Cay did not go unnoticed. According to Timothy Minning, a convicted drug runner, turned informant, Bahamian Prime Minister Pindling arrived by helicopter at Lehder's pad in early January 1979. Mining told this story to a 1984 Bahamian Commission's inquiry into the Pindling administration's ties to drug smuggling. In his testimony to the Commission, Pindling denied that he met with Lehder, but that he had gone to Norman's Cay because "his suspicions had been aroused by the sophisticated nature of the radio equipment installed there." The Inquiry board believed Pindling's story.

But the farce was not over. The Bahamian police undertook "Operation Raccoon," a large covert raid on Lehder's home on Norman's Cay. As the mini-invasion took place, Lehder fled on his highspeed boat, *Fire Ball.* He was fired upon by pursing police, managed to drop into the sea some white powder and was arrested. Lehder was booked but the next day was back on his own turf. Not so lucky were Edward Ward and Lehder's mistress. In the raid, the police confiscated a huge supply of arms.

Minning also testified to the Commission of Inquiry that in September 1978, Vesco came to Pindling's office and gave him a $100,000 bribe for the Prime Minister's acquiescence in his, Vesco's drug operation. Mining said that he was the one who personally brought the cash to Pindling. Minning said that he originally met Vesco in Nassau in 1977. Like Vesco, Minning was facing indictment in the U.S., and was trying to purchase the island of Cistern Cay, near the home of Vesco. He also said that Vesco paid Pindling $100,000 per month in order for him to stay in the Bahamas. Pindling again, denied the charges.

By 1979, Vesco had found himself a permanent home in the Bahamas. But the United States government was not yet ready to give up on his return. In that year, the FBI mounted "Operation Kingfish," a plan to forcibly bring the fugitive back for trial. The plan was to use a large pleasure boat docked near Vesco's island sanctuary, man it with FBI agents dressed up in scuba gear, take secret pictures of Vesco's estate with the hope of capturing Vesco and make illegal bribe transactions, and use that leverage with the Bahamian authorities to whisk him off to a U.S. submarine testing base nearby.

But foreign policy considerations interfered before the operation could take place. Only a few months before, Iranian "students" seized the U.S. Embassy in Teheran, holding the employees hostage. The Shah of Iran fled his home and was looking for a place to live. The Bahamas was one of those places the Shah was looking into. The U.S., not wanting to incur the wrath of the Bahamian government by nabbing Vesco at such a delicate time, was hesitant to act. They didn't have to worry. Vesco was tipped off concerning the FBI raid and slipped out into the night before the FBI swooped down.

It seems that the CIA had a good deal of knowledge about Vesco's activities. A CIA memo of Vesco's Cistern Cay period noted "special analysis" of the fugitives's radio broadcasts, as well as coverage of his mail and telephone, and even referred to the accuracy of "NOAA (satellite) material."

By 1981, Vesco had outlived his welcome in the Bahamas. The next year saw him in the Caribbean island of Antigua. However, he didn't stay there for long. Seeking safer havens, he fled to Castro's Cuba in 1983.

Living in the same house of Robert Vesco in sunny Cuba, was Donald Nixon, the nephew of President Richard Nixon. Donald Nixon had been Vesco's business partner and long-time friend, and had spent the previous three years living under his roof. While in Cuba, Vesco lived better than most of the nation's poor residents. He lived in a two-story home, not far from the beach. He had two cars, a vintage Russian Lada and a 1985 silver Honda Civic. He had a twenty-four hour security detail and was followed by Cuban authorities wherever he went. During the two decades he spent in Cuba, Vesco dabbled in various businesses, including pharmaceutical products, educational projects and computers. Vesco brought his wife and young son Patrick to Cuba with him and they soon made the most of their new surroundings. Besides, Fidel, Vesco also made friends with Castro's brother, Raul, who was then head of the Cuban military.

Before he ever stepped foot on Cuban soil, Vesco showed how indispensable he would be to the Castro brothers. In 1977, five years before landing in Havana, Vesco brokered a huge military deal when he attempted to arrange the delivery of a fleet of eight military cargo planes to Libya's then leader, Muammar Qaddafi.

The planes had originally been bought and paid for but had been subsequently held back due to Qaddafi's worldwide links to international terrorism by both the Carter and Ford administrations. Vesco flew from Costa Rica to Havana and then to Tripoli by way of Moscow to make the deal a reality. According to the article by Ann Louise Bardach in *Vanity Fair,* the deal lead to a 1980 U.S. congressional investigation in which it was alleged that Vesco and the Libyans had planned to offer a $15 million dollar bribe to unnamed Carter administration officials, in addition to a $220,000 payment to the brother of President Carter, Billy. Robert Vesco's son Dan, said that his father brokered the deal without any help.

Robert Vesco and Donald Nixon had a business relationship that lasted 25 years. Donald Nixon first met Vesco in 1971 by way of introduction by friends of his father, Donald senior. Vesco hired the younger Nixon and got him a job at IOS. Hiring Donald Nixon could open many doors to Vesco at the time and he took advantage of anything that could make him a buck.

For whatever reason, Donald Nixon went with his new partner when Vesco fled to Costa Rica and followed him to Havana, years later. Both Donald Nixon and Vesco worked to develop a medicine called TX that would be used to eradicate certain infections. They would use the Cuban laboratory called Labiofam, one of Cuba's better-known biotechnology firms. Ramon Castro, Field's brother who was a farmer, backed them in developing TX. They tested the drug on a pig that was owned by Ramon Castro when the animal contacted a foot infection. They gave the drug to the pig which made a full recovery. Donald Nixon began the project, but soon Vesco told everyone who'd listen that he was the man in charge.

As time went on, Vesco's stock with the Cuban authorities began to wain. He underwent intensive questioning sessions by Cuban authorities, despite the fact that he was once on good terms with Fidel and his pals. In December 1994, the Cuban Ministry of Agriculture pulled the plug on Vesco and Nixon's TX project and took it over. When Donald Nixon told the Cuban's that he would not sign the agreement, they told him that if he did not, he wouldn't be allowed to leave the country. He signed immediately.

Prior to his ever-growing troubles in the early 1990s, Vesco was welcomed by Castro with open arms. Castro, it is assumed, knew of Vesco's ties with Carlos Lehder but decided to turn the other cheek. As he established himself in Cuba in 1983, he continued his relationship with Lehder. Shortly after arriving in Havana, an emissary of Mr. Lehder's arrived at Vesco's palatial home with a message from the drug king; would Vesco be able to persuade Fidel Castro to allow the transshipment of drugs from other parts of the Carribean over Cuban territory? According to intelligence sources familiar with the Vesco/Lehder connection, Castro agreed (for a price, of course), and a new, trilateral drug connection was formed.

In the deal with Castro and Lehder, Vesco served as the financial middleman in the funneling of the drug profits. Using the expertise he gleamed from his defrauding of IOS, Vesco got his share of the profits and even went into business himself. It has been reported that Vesco persuaded Castro to begin shaking down drug boats as they passed Cuban waters, charging them a huge port tax, and sending them on their way.

It is not clear how much Castro knew or approved of the Vesco/Lehder connection but one can assume that nothing really got by the ultimate leader of Cuba.

Another charge leveled against Vesco is that he used some of the profits from his drug ventures to shore up Cuba's intelligence network, the D.G.I., in order to become more independent of the Soviet KGB.

In a huge blow to Vesco's new drug business, Carlos Lehder was arrested on drug smuggling charges, taken back to the United

States, and was convicted in Federal court. At the trial, Vesco was identified as a co-conspirator with Lehder. In 1989, Vesco was indicted by a Federal grand jury in Jacksonville, Florida on charges of importing cocaine into the United States.

Why Castro decided to arrest Vesco is not known. Maybe he finally had outlived his usefulness, Maybe one of his own drug ventures got so far out of hand that Castro had to reign him in.

When he was arrested in 1995, Cuban authorities charged him with "fraud and illicit economic activity," and was tried on allegations that he plotted to deceive the Cuban Ministry of Public Health and unnamed investors in the marketing of a "miracle drug" (most likely TX).

All that became a moot point when Robert Vesco died in Cuba in November 2008 of cancer. Cuban authorities did not make a public announcement until five months after he passed away. When they did announce his death, the commentator said that the reason for the late public notification was because Vesco became a "nonissue" for the Cuban people. He was buried in the Colon Cemetery in Havana on November 24, 2008. It was not known how many people attended his funeral.

* * *

Charles Siragusa

Another possibility for QJ/WIN is Charles Siragusa, Siragusa worked for the FBN, Federal Bureau of Narcotics and was its authority on the Mafia, as well as working in conjunction with the CIA. Siragusa made a name for himself when he undertook a ten-year surveillance of one of the top Mafia figures in the United States; Charles "Lucky "Luciano who has been prominently mentioned in this book. Through his investigative efforts, Siragusa was able to have Luciano convicted on prostitution charges in 1944.

It was through Luciano's secret efforts that the U.S. Navy was able to prevent German sabotage on the New York docks during World War 2. Following the war, Luciano was expelled to Italy where he continued his worldwide narcotics distribution. He served in the FBN from 1939 to 1963, and headed the U.S. Bureau of Narcotics office in Rome, Italy from 1948 to 1960.

After his stint in Rome, he returned to the United States where he became the chief investigator of Organized Crime in Interstate Commerce for the U.S. Senate. While in this position, he was able to discover a direct link between drug trafficking between the U.S. and Cuba. Among drug kingpins involved in the Cuban-US connection were Carlos Marcello, Santo Trafficante Jr., Auguste Ricord, among others.

In 1963, Siragusa became the executive director of the Illinois Crime Investigating Commission which looked into wrong doing in state government.

In the early 1950s, Charles Siragusa became involved a joint CIA-FBN operation code named MKULTRA. MKULTRA was one of the CIA's most guarded secrets in the 1950s and its revelation would not come until years later. The man put in charge of MKULTRA was a CIA chemist by the name of Sidney Gottlieb. During a congressional hearing in the 1970s, Sidney Gottlieb testified about his role in the project. The project involved developing sophisticated mind control programs beginning in the early 1950s. The CIA administrated LSD to as many as 40 unwitting subjects, including prisoners in jail and patrons of houses of prostitution to see how they would react. In one tragic case, a person who was given LSD jumped out of a ten-story building and died in the subsequent fall. Others wound up with years long symptoms of depression and psychological damage.

The brainchild of MKULTRA was then Director of the CIA, Allan Dulles who was informed of reports of mind control techniques supposed to have been conducted by Soviet, Chinese, and North Korean agents upon U.S. soldiers who were captured during the Korean War. If this worked for the Chinese, and their allies, Dulles said, why not be of use for the United States in time of war?

The man who discovered the project was John K. Vance, then a member of the CIA's inspector general's staff in the early 1960s. Mr. Vance learned of MKULTRA in the spring of 1963 when the CIA conducted a large scale IG's survey of the agency's technical services division. Their later report on MKULTRA said in part, "The concepts involved in manipulating human behavior are found by many people both within and outside the agency to be distasteful and unethical."

When the Church Committee announced that it was going to hold hearings regarding the Kennedy assassination and other secrets of the CIA, CIA Director Richard Helms learned that one of the areas in which the committee was going to delve in was MKULTRA. He had the agency destroy as many files on MKULTRA as possible. However, over 20,000 pages of MKULTRA documents that contained the CIA's financial records were kept. From these files, the complete story of MKULTRA came to light.

Project MKULTRA was terminated in the late 1960s, but by that time, the damage to the CIA's reputation had been irreversibly damaged.

According to author Douglas Valentine in his book *Strength of the Pack,* the CIA hired FBN agent George White to set up a safe house and test LSD on unsuspecting U.S. citizens in New York in 1955. In 1961, two FBN agents, Charles Siragusa and Andy Tartaglino set up an MKULTRA safe house in the Big Apple. It consisted of two apartments that had a two-way mirror so that the agents could film the people being tested. The safe house was operated until 1966 when it was not longer of use.

Information regarding Charles Siragusa and his possibly being QJWIN, and his alleged ties to the Castro assassination plots is found in a memo dated October 11, 1977 from Robert Young with the title: "Subject: John Mertz and Robert Bannerman-Relations with Charles Siragusa."

The memo says that Charles Siragusa "alleged to Senator Kennedy that he was approached by an Agency employee in 1960 or 1961 who told Siragusa that CIA needed assistance in establishing assassination teams. CIA would pay one million dollars for each hit. Siragusa, who had underworld/mafia connections as a result of his position, says that he refused to cooperate. He believes the CIA employee's name was Vincent Thill. Siragusa also stated that other Agency employees he dealt with were Shef Edwards, Robert Bannerman, Jim Angleton, and John Mertz.: The memo goes on to say that Senator Kennedy gave the information to the Senate Committee on Intelligence (SSCI)."

In his investigation, Robert Young interviewed John Mertz who told him the following story. He said that in 1960 or 1961, the CIA had mounted an undercover audio operation in Havana which was directed at the Chinese news agency, NCNA. The Agency sent three operatives to man the job and they were all arrested. The men's affiliation to the CIA were never revealed but they served ten years in jail at a prison at the Isle of Pines. The leader of the CIA team was Dave Crist.

Mertz was given the job of trying to rescue the men and Jim Angleton told him to talk with Siragusa, who had various underworld ties, many of them still in Cuba. In turn, Siragusa put Mertz in contact with certain people in Cuba, including Batista's chauffeur and wife. The plan never materialized and eventually the three CIA agents were released.

"Bob Bannerman remembers Siragusa as an Office of Security (OS) covert contact/informer. He says that when an OS investigation turned up information related to narcotics, Siragusa might be contacted to see if he could provide assistance... "

It is interesting to note that one of the people involved in this event, John Mertz, has the same name as Michael Mertz, a French assassin linked to the anti-de Gaulle OAS, as well as Jean Souetre, the man who was expelled from Dallas two days after the Kennedy assassination. However, putting all the pieces together in this rather large jig saw, we can assume that they are different people.[77]

In the 1950s, the FBN set up an investigation against Joseph Orsini, a member of the Corsican mob, and a Nazi collaborator during World War 2, for the importation of drugs into the United States. Orsini used willing French sailors to smuggle heroin on their boats coming into the United States, the same avenue that the real Michael Mertz would use in the 1960s while working with Santos Trafficante and Carlos Marcello. This began the FBN's long struggle against what came to be known as the "French Connection."

When Bill Harvey was setting up the ZR/RIFLE program, he met with Charles Siragusa, and asked him for his advice. Harvey said that Siragusa was his source on "Corsican and Sicilians." Harvey was nothing but careful when it came to organizing the Executive Action program and he wrote in his notes regarding Charles Siragusa, "How much does Siragusa know?"

---

[77] RIF No. 1993.07.20.17:46;05:710440.

This was followed up with Vincent Thill's approach to him to become part of an assassination program. Siragusa, to his credit, refused.

A fact that might tie Siragusa to the elusive QJ/WIN (but not conclusively), is the fact that William Harvey wanted to recruit a member of the Corsican network to spy on the Soviet's because the "Soviet's were operating in Africa among nationality groups, specifically Corsicans, and that he was being asked to spot, assess, and recommend some dependable, quick-witted persons for our use." Note-the assassin that Harvey hired was supposed to go to the Congo to assassinate Patrice Lumumba.

So, is there conclusive evidence that Charles Siragusa was the assassin known as QJ/WIN? The fact that he was an expert on the Corsican mob for many years, was schooled in espionage, had assets in all the major heroin producing countries in the world, knew all the players, and was approached to take part in an assassination project, are all good circumstantial evidence that may link him (or any of a number of other candidates) to QJWIN.

The ZR/RIFLE project never succeeded in assassinating Fidel Castro or any other foreign leader. The CIA went to considerable expense to create the program, hire assassins like QJ/WIN and WI/ROGUE, possibly using QJ/WIN in its secret war against Castro, including WIN's possible relationship with Johnny Rosselli at the CIA's secret JMWAVE base in Miami, and at the very least, tolerate the illegal activities of Michael Mertz in his drug smuggling business.

Robert Blemant

Gary Hart was an ambitious man, and everyone who knew him believed he would go far. He was born Gary Hartpence on November 28, 1936 in Ottawa, Kansas. He graduated from Nazarene College in 1958, Yale Divinity School in 1961, and went on to Yale University Law School. After graduation, Hart landed a job as an attorney for the U.S. Justice Department from 1964 to 1965. He went on to become a special assistant to the solicitor of the Department of the Interior from 1965-67. Leaving government, he opened a law practice in Denver, Colorado.

Hart, who always had the political bug, offered his services to George McGovern, who was Democratic nominee for president in

1972. Hart, then a young man, ran the ill-fated campaign against Richard Nixon, the incumbent president. McGovern, the weakest of all the potential Democratic candidates, lost the general election a landslide, winning only Massachusetts, and the District of Columba.

Hart's career did not end with the McGovern debacle, and in 1975, he was elected as the new Democratic Senator from Colorado. Hart would serve from 1975 to 1987, making a national reputation for himself along the way.

Hart had set his sights on 1600 Pennsylvania Ave, the White House, but he had to do the political grind work in order to cement his bid for higher office. That unexpected chance came in 1975, when the Congress, in it's post Watergate search for scapegoats, set up body of elected officials called the Senate Committee to Study Governmental Operations with Respect to Intelligence Activities, otherwise known as the Church Committee. The members of the committed included its chairman, Frank Church, (D. Idaho), Walter Mondale (D. Minnesota—later to become Vice President under Jimmy Carter), Richard Schweiker (R. Pennsylvania), Philip Hart (Michigan), Howard Baker (R. Tennessee), and Barry Goldwater (R. Arizona—he was the 1963 GOP presidential candidate who lost to LBJ).

The committee's mandate was to investigate the alleged abuses of power by the Central Intelligence Agency and the Federal Bureau of Investigation, especially after the lurid revelations of domestic spying that took place under the Nixon administration and its ramifications in the Watergate scandal.

As the committee heard testimony, more shocking and revealing testimony came forth regarding the abuses of power in both the CIA and FBI. Among the series of scandals that were brought forth to an astonished American public were the once secret CIA-Mafia—plots to kill foreign leaders, i.e., Fidel Castro and Patrice Lumumba (QJ/WIN and WI/ROGUE), Operation Shamrock, a vast domestic intelligence operation conducted by the NSA (National Security Agency) that intercepted overseas cable traffic, as well as domestic communications by American citizens, and the Huston plan, a covert operation started by the Nixon administration in order to spy on anti-Vietnam war dissenters in the United States. The committee also brought to light the FBI's undercover mission called CointelPro, a program to infiltrate and disrupt domestic political organizations, abuse by the IRS, and other illegal activities of the secret government.

In time, the Committee began a limited investigation of the Kennedy assassination, looking into how well or poorly the FBI and CIA aided the Warren Commission in its 1964 in investigation of the president's death. Both agencies took the heat for the events of November 22, 1963, and deservedly so. The committee said in relation to the FBI and CIA, the "the committee developed evidence which impeaches the process by which the intelligence agencies arrived at their own conclusion about the assassination, and by which they provided information to the Warren Commission. This evidence, indicates that the investigation of the assassination was deficient."

The Church Committee was one of the larger funded committee's on the Hill, compromising about one hundred staffers, many of them lawyers. To those senators on the panel, they knew a good thing when they saw it and realized that if they could find the hot potato in their investigation, their careers would surely blossom. Both Senator's Hart and Church had presidential ambitions and any publicity, good or bad, would either aid or hurt their respective causes. Sen. Church, who was undergoing a lot of internal pressure from his staff to look into more than what their mandate required, agreed to extend the committee's lifetime to March 5, 1976, which happened to be a presidential election year.

To its critics, the Church Committee had to do a better investigative job that its predecessor, the Warren Commission did in 1964. The Warren Commission was a rush job to begin with, never fully investigating all the myriad events that lead up to the Kennedy assassination. Leads were never followed up, on scene—witnesses in Dealey Plaza were never called, or if they were called, some of their testimony was altered to fit the pattern of the lone gunman—Oswald did it—case closed. They were also dealing with an ever increasingly skeptical public when it came to the assassination of the president. Poll after poll of Americans revealed that they did not believe the findings of the Warren Commission and wanted to see an impartial probe of the president's assassination.

Buckling to the ever-growing pressure from within the

committee and general public, Senator Church made a compromise that would expand the committee's mandate to include the Kennedy assassination. He assigned both Senators Hart and Schweiker to set up a subcommittee that would look into the events surrounding the Kennedy assassination with the proviso that they would wind up their probe at the same March 5, deadline. Agreeing to that condition, they began their investigation.

Years later, Senator Schweiker would say in an interview concerning Lee Oswald, the president's alleged assassin, that he saw "the fingertips of intelligence" all around the ex-Marine. For his part, Gary Hart, on May 1, 1976, said, "I don't think you can see the things I have seen and sit on it."

* * *

In 1975, Gary Hart thought he'd hit the jackpot, as far as the Kennedy investigation was concerned. If things worked out as he hoped they would, his ticket to the presidency was all but assured.

In July of that year, Gary Hart and a number of other U.S. government officials were en-route back to the States from a trip to Europe. They had been visiting Moscow as part of an official delegation and would soon return home. One night, while in Amsterdam, Holland, Gary Hart received an unsigned letter. The message was cryptic, only saying that he'd be informed of the note's content at that time. The note said that Hart was to wait until the rest of the party turned in for the night, then make sure he was not followed, and go to a bar near the hotel he was staying in. Hart had been planning for this moment for a long time, ever since he took on the job as a two-man member of the sub-committee looking into the Kennedy assassination.

Hart delved into the myriad ins and outs of the Kennedy case, finding more flaws than answers. He knew there was more to the story than that revealed by the Warren Commission and he was determined to find out the complete story.

And who was the mysterious person whom Gary Hart wanted to see that night in Amsterdam? None other than QJ/WIN, himself.

Before departing for his European trip, Gary Hart had a meeting with CIA Director William Colby and asked if he could try and arrange a meeting between him and QJ/WIN. Colby was intrigued, and told Hart that the CIA had no idea where QJ/WIN was, since his release by the CIA in 1965. However, Colby told the Senator that he'd send an agent whom he trusted to try and find the elusive assassin.

William Colby was a member of the wartime OSS, and was sent on various clandestine missions over France during the war. After the war, he got a law degree from Colombia University and then joined the CIA where he served in Rome and Stockholm. From 1959 to 1962, Colby was CIA Station Chief in Saigon at the time that American forces were first beginning to pour into that nation. He then headed the Agency's Far Eastern division from 1962 to 1967. From 1968 to 1971, Colby headed the infamous CIA Phoenix program whose harsh actions targeted the communist's battling the U.S. and South Vietnamese government.

During the Watergate scandal, President Nixon appointed Colby as CIA Director in 1973, amid allegations that the CIA was possibly behind the break-in at the Democratic National Committee headquarters. Two of the Watergate burglars, E. Howard Hunt and Eugenio Martinez had previously worked for the Agency and Nixon and his White House aides tried to get then CIA Director Richard Helms to pay hush money to Hunt who was threatening to blow the whistle on the scandal. Helms refused, and in February 1973, was fired. Taking over at CIA was James Schlesinger, who was replaced by Colby's. His tenure at CIA was dominated the congressional investigation of illegal domestic CIA activities that was conducted by the Church Committee. One of the major items to come out of Colby's tenure at CIA was the release of the so-called "Family Jewels," a detailed investigation of past CIA abuses that had been going on for years. Colby took a lot of flack from many longterm veterans of the CIA and they did not take kindly to his cooperation with the congress in looking into past CIA abuses.

The agent whom Colby sent to find QJWIN located him and he was the one who sent the note to Gary Hart in Amsterdam. The note told Hart to be at a particular bar at midnight and to come alone. When Hart arrived at the bar, Colby's agent approached. However, he was alone. The man told Hart that WIN had just arrived from another country and wanted to know Hart's background before he'd meet with him. The agent told WIN that

Hart was a U.S. Senator and that he was looking into the Kennedy assassination. Hearing that bit of news, WIN said that he wanted nothing to do with Hart. Crestfallen, Hart left the bar, never meeting the man whom he'd come so far to see.[78]

Just who was the man whom Gary Hart was supposed to meet that, dark night? Steve Rivele says he was a notorious Marseille policeman, intelligence agent, and later mobster, Robert Blemant, QJ/WIN.

Robert Blemant was born on February 2, 1911 at Valenciennes, France. He joined the police force in 1938 and rose that year to the rank of commissioner. He served in that post until his firing in 1947.

In 1941, Blemant left the Marseille police force and joined the Resistance movement in France whose members were risking their lives to combat Nazi occupation of the country. He joined the DGER, the French counter-espionage service in North Africa and helped prepare for the allied invasion of North Africa called Operation Torch. During the war, Blemant was appointed to a position at staff headquarters of General Giraud in Algiers, which was planning the allied invasion. He was noted for his expertise in counter-intelligence operations and specialized in what was called "D Measures," the assassination of German intelligence agents during the war. During the conflict, Blemant met and befriended many members of the OSS who were working in tandem with the French resistance. He also made contacts with the French Corsican mob under the auspices of the Guerini brothers, a link that would have profound implications for him, after the war. He also was on good terms with certain members of the Moroccan ruling family (if Blemant was QJWIN, then he had the means and opportunity to free Thomas Eli Davis from a Moroccan prison years later).

After the war ended, Blemant returned to Marseille and his old job as a policeman. He was made chief inspector of the DST, the French FBI in Marseille and later in Nice. He had two important jobs to do in his new position; battle crime and make friends with the powerful crime syndicate in Marseille run the Antonine Guerini. His police superiors soon learned of his close ties with the

---

78 Rivele, Stephen, "Death of a Double Man." Rivele files.

Guerini's and he was given an ultimatum-stop associating with them or leave the force. Blemant decided on the latter.

Now, as a powerful ex-inspector of police, Robert Blemant was freed to cement his relationship with the Corsican gangs and he did so with relish. In 1947, the newly created CIA branched out into its first foray in clandestine operations, and Europe was the place to begin. The CIA wanted to stop the tightening control of the French Communist party in the port city of Marseille and Robert Blemant was eager to help. With Blemant's assistance, he introduced the CIA to the Guerini's and a longstanding relationship was born between both parties. Blemant was able to funnel money to the Guerini's in their battle with the communist labor unions in Marseille. The money was used to set up CIA dummy corporations in the city and hire goon squads to battle the communist laborers on the docks. Antoine Guerini used a portion of CIA money for his own, illegal purposes, with the CIA none the wiser.

Over time, Robert Blemant became a full partner in crime with Antoine Guerini and he soon joined them in the smuggling of cigarettes, gold, heroin, and prostitutes. He was able to buy a number of lucrative nightclubs in Paris and Marseille. Blemant was part owner of a casino called the Grand Cercle in Paris. He even started his own gang, called the "Trois Canards" (which was named for a club in Paris).

In 1954, their once strong relationship came crashing down in flames. Blemant had one of Guerini's friends, Joseph Leca, murdered. The hit took place on April 18.

Throughout his career, Robert Blemant had in his possession, files that could blackmail his contemporaries, be they friend or foe. Among those whom he had incriminating information on were Antoine Guerini and his family and he'd use them if put in a corner. In an interesting aside, Blemant's first wife, Nicole, remarried the lawyer for the Guerini's, named Pollack.Using his now considerable mob contacts, Robert Blemant began to operate in other parts of the world, including Tangiers (where Thomas Eli Davis was being held). One of his partners in the heroin smuggling business in Tangiers was a French gangster named Joe Renucci who had links back in the 1950s with Charles "Lucky" Luciano.

Steve Rivele writes in *Death of A Double Man,* that, "When Renucci died in 1958, Blemant became the unchallenged crime boss of Tangiers, running virtually all the prostitution, gambling and narcotics traffic. His wartime contacts served him well, earning him the protection of the police, the secret services and prominent politicians in Morocco and Algeria. By 1960, Blemant's influence had spread to gambling in Beirut and London, gold smuggling in Frankfurt and Antwerp, and narcotics trafficking from Turkey to the United States." Note that the files on QJWIN say that he was a gold smuggler who operated in Europe, sometimes in Frankfurt.

In 1960, Blemant suffered a personal tragedy with the death of his father. It is not all together clear just what happened to the elder Mr. Blemant but here is the gist of the story. In April of that year, the elder Mr. Blemant, who was a prominent French attorney, was accused of badly managing his client's money. He was going to be prosecuted by local authorities and so the story goes, he killed himself in order to hide his shame.

After the autopsy, it is believed that another body was put in its place and that the real Mr. Blemant had faked his own death. After this incident, Robert Blemant suddenly let Marseille in a hurry, sold his three nightclubs in France, and left the country. He was gone for one year and was said to have traveled to England, Germany, and North Africa. During this time, Robert Blemant bought an estate called the Petits Birons in the Pelisane-Lambesc region of France. His lawyer said that Blemant went to the United States during the 1960 time period. During the time of QJ/WIN's training by the CIA, the actual whereabout of Robert Blemant were not known.

After his return to Marseille, Blemant renewed his longstanding relationship with the Guerinis. However, their was so much spilled blood between them that tensions began to run high and there seemed to be no one who could bridge the ever widening gap between the two factions. Blemant was by now gaining the upper hand as the number one mob force in Marseille, and the Guerini brothers did not take their demotion lightly.

Something had to be done and the sooner the better. In January 1965, a conclave of the Guerinis met in Marseille to take up the Blemant matter. After a highly cantankerous debate, it was decided that Blemant had to be eliminated (killed). In April, the Guerini's had put together a hit squad made up of Blemant's killers; Rene

Mondoloni, Etienne Carrara, Pierre-Antonie Colombani, and Armand Sessa. The leader of the team was Jean Pierre Alfonsi. On May 4, 1965, as Blemant, and his wife were driving his Mercedes from Marseille to his home, his car was ambushed by another automobile. Machine gun fire erupted from the chase car and Robert Blemant was killed. When the police found him, he had over a dozen bullet holes in his body.

The death of Robert Blemant did not go unnoticed. In February 1966, Armand Sessa was captured by Blemant's men and tortured him until he gave up the names of the other conspirators. Over the next several months, Sessa, Colombani, Mondoloni were all killed. Etienne Carrara disappeared and was said to have died sometime later in Spain. Steve Rivele writes that the leader of the group of killers who avenged Blemant's murder was Jacques-Jean Imbert. Imbert took over Blemant's organization and was himself severely wounded on February 1, 1977 when he was shot seven times (he lived).

Antonie Guerini met the same fate as that of Robert Blemant. Guerini was shot to death in 1967 in an apparent revenge killing by a man named Gaeton Zampa, who was a confidant of Blemant.

In his research on the French Connection, Steve Rivele met with an unnamed police inspector who was planning to write a book on is memoirs (which was never done). Rivele writes what Christian David was supposed to have known about Robert Blemant and his death. David was cagey in responding but did say that Robert Blemant was a "cerveau," or big brain. "He said that Blemant was the reason that Antonie Guerini was killed. He added that no one has ever understood the importance of the plot to kill Lumumba. He would not confirm or deny that Blemant was in the Congo. He said that no one has ever understood how much pressure was involved in killing Lumumba, or how complicated it was. He said that the people who actually killed Lumumba were dead, but that did not mean the affair was finished. He added that the person behind the plot was a "cerveau."

The question we now have to answer, is Robert Blemant QJWIN? Here are the similarities. He worked for both the CIA and the OSS in an intelligence gathering capacity. He was on both sides of the law, as a police inspector and later, a major heroin dealer and assassin. He knew where to find potential assassins for the CIA due to his years long training in the intelligence bushiness and his heroin-narcotics contacts. "WIN advised his CIA superiors that he was in touch with assassins in Beirut; Blemant was intimately involved with organized crime in that city. WIN was recruited for the Lumumba mission in November 1960 in Frankfurt and was known to have traveled there in late 1960. WIN was arrested in Europe on smuggling charges in 1962; Blemant, at various times, smuggled American cigarettes, gold, and narcotics through Europe. WIN is believed to have been brought to the United States for training for the Lumumba job; Blemant is known to have visited America at about the same time."[79]

In his notes regarding his research into Robert Blemant at the Assassination Archives, Steve Rivele spoke with his ex-police contact who provided him his views on the Blemant/Tommy Davis story. Rivele proceeded to tell his informer about Seth Kantor's research on the freeing of Tomas Eli Davis from a Moroccan jail. Rivele writes that his contact said, "that Blemant had excellent contacts in North Africa, especially Algeria and Morocco, from his wartime counter-espionage days. He said these included contacts in the police, secret services and the entourage of King Hassan of Morocco. Given his close CIA contacts, Blemant would have and could have gotten Tommy Davis out of a jail in North Africa on short notice, simply on the strength of his personal political contacts. He could have been tapped by the CIA in Marseille, flown to Algeria or Morocco, walked into a prison there and walked out with Davis with no problem."

Rivele further wrote that, "I have spoken twice to Kantor about the WIN/Davis story. He vouches for the reliability of his source, and leads me to understand that it came from within the CIA, though he has not said so. He insists the source is sound."

The remaining question is why did the CIA, in the part of Director Colby, agree to try and locate WIN for Sen. Hart? If Robert Blemant was QJ/WIN, then there is a major problem. The real Robert Blemant was killed in 1965. So who was the mystery man whom Sen. Hart was going to meet in Amsterdam? Was QJWIN someone else? If the real QJWIN had showed up in 1975

---

79 Ibid.

in that European café, then the CIA would have made a positive identification on their one time assassin. The CIA parted company with QJWIN, years before and if Colby was right, they had no idea where he was. If Sen. Hart had indeed met with QJ/WIN he'd assuredly report back to Washington on his meeting. The CIA would then have been brought up to date on the man whom they hadn't seen in at least a decade. If it could have been proved that WIN was indeed dead, then the Senate committee would have had on reason to look further into his background. If the CIA had provided the Senate committee with all its documents on QJ/WIN, who knows what interesting tidbits of information it may have provided.

The similarities that Robert Blemant was indeed, QJ/WIN are strong. But, if Robert Blemant was QJ/WIN—that would have left the CIA in a very embarrassing situation, if it were ever revealed to be the truth. First, Robert Blemant was not only an intelligence asset, but a well known drug smuggler with worldwide connections. He was an asset of both the wartime OSS and well as the modern day CIA. If Blemant was WIN, then his actions over the years, allowed tons of drugs into the United States, with the knowledge of the American government that was trying (not very hard, it seems), to stem the flow of drugs into the country. If Blemant was WIN, then he had connections with two of the major drug kingpins of the day; Santos Trafficante and Carlos Marcello, both of whom the CIA hired in their plots to kill Castro. He had close, personal ties with Antonie Guerini, the man whom Christian David told Steve Rivele had asked him in 1963 to kill JFK. Did Robert Blemant know any of this?

William Colby can't answer that question. He disappeared in a canoe on the waters of the Chesapeake Bay in May of 1996, in circumstances that are still cloudy.

Who knows how the story might have been different if Sen. Hart had met the elusive QJ/WIN in that dark, cabaret in Amsterdam in July 1975? Answers, it seems, are still to be found.

Chapter 7:

Who Was Souetre?

The next two chapters will describe the activities of two men, Michael Victor Mertz and Jean Rene Souetre, who played a significant role in the plots to kill French President Charles de Gaulle, as well as possibly being a key participant in the assassination of President John F. Kennedy. Both men had direct ties to the militant French right wing organization, the OAS, Organisation de l'Armee Secrete. One of these men was a double agent working for French intelligence, as well as being one of the premier drug smugglers of the day. The other was a militant anti-de Gaulle, former French military officer who took part in various attempts on de Gaulle's life.

Before describing each man, it is necessary to give the reader a crash course in just what the OAS was, who were its main leaders, and its reason for its existence.

The OAS was a secret army established by French right-wing military men and activists who were vehemently opposed to Algerian independence from France in 1961. The main leader of the group was General Salan and it was formed on December 3, 1960, along with two other retired French army officers, Pierre Lagaillarde and Jean-Jacques Susini. Taking their war directly to the French government, the OAS went on a bombing campaign in France and Algeria, they attacked pro-independence targets across both countries. A pivotal moment came in March 1962, called the Evian Accords that began the process of independence for Algeria from French rule.

The OAS sprung into violent action, by acts of terrorism, assassination, and called for the other French colonies into revolt. The revolt of some of these French generals culminated in an assassination attempt on the life of President De Gaulle at Petit-Clamart, a suburb of Paris (this incident will be described later in the chapter). After the failed attempt on de Gaulle's life, a nation-wide crackdown on the OAS went into effect, looking for the suspects and any of their collaborators. Hundreds of OAS members across France and Algeria were arrested and in June 1962, three of their leaders, Roger Degueldre, Claude Piegts, and Albert Dovecar, were executed. By the end of 1963, the OAS, for all intents and purposes, ceased to exist as an effective organization.

The OAS, in its heyday, was an impressive, nationalistic, militant organization that had offices and interests across Europe. The United States government followed the goings on of the OAS closely and a document trail was established detailing who was in charge, and what they were up to.

One part of the OAS was the Conseil National de la Resistance Exterieur (CNRE). The CNRE was created in May 1962 in Rome, Italy in order to "effectively assure the conduct of the war on the diverse theater of operations in the Metropole, Algeria, and outside France." In November 1962, a meeting was held in Lisbon, Portugal by representatives of the Algerian refugees who were members of the OAS and who were then living in Spain. After the meeting, the OAS joined up with the CNRE with the exception of ex-Colonel Pierre Chateau-Jobert and his men. The leaders of the group brought together their Spanish and Algerian counterparts in one cohesive group.

The leaders of the organization were ex-General Paul Gardy, as Vice President, Georges Bidault as President, ex-Colonel Antoine Argoud, commander of the theater of metropolitan operations, and Jacques Soustell who was responsible for the exterior theater of operations.[80]

This information was supplied to the U.S. government by a "French official with good contacts in the Ministry of Interior" but is not named, and was prepared by the Securite Militaire as a background study for its internal use."

The document says that the members of the Executive Committee of the CNRE were located in various Western European nations-West Germany, Belgium, Austria, and Italy, "not clandestinely but with false identities." (note—QJWIN was active for the CIA in Western Europe, especially in Belgium and Italy).

---

80 "Current Status of Activist Groups," 26 April 1963. Held at National Archives, College Park, Md.

George Bidault and the Ribeaud brothers were in West Germany, along with ex-Colonels Yves Godard, and Roland Vaudrey. Doctor Jean Claude Perez was in Spain (until his arrest), along with "ex-Captain Jean Souetre, among others. A man named Georgeopouls called "Tassau the Greek," Lucien Carrerno, a former member of the police force in Algeria, were also there. "These being considered the principal amimators of CNR subversion. A certain number of commandos composed of deserters and sought-after individuals, members of OAS groups in Algeria, have also used Spain as their headquarters."

On February 23, 1961, Jean Souetre, along with seven other men, were arrested by French police while staying at a house near the region of Bouguirat in the Oranie area of France. There are two accounts of their arrest. The first scenario had the police making a routine patrol when they found a group of irregular, armed, European soldiers, loitering near the town. The police told their superiors and after a stand off, the Europeans surrendered peacefully. The second scenario had a group of maquis (resistance fighters) at the town of Bouguirat. The men spent ten days in the city and "everyone knew about them." They were subsequently arrested.

Also arrested along with Souetre and his men were a number of parachutists from Souetre's own formation, the Commandos de l'Air. After their arrest, the prisoners were transferred to Algiers and put under military custody.

Before his arrest, Souetre had been the commander of a parachute company made up of a 1,000 man elite Air Force parachute formation. He received the Chevalier de la Legion d'Moneur and the Croix de la Valeur Militeaire medals.

There were other subversive groups operating in France who were allied with CNR, like the ORO, Deuxieme Bureau-20, Troisoime Bureau-30, and Quatrieme Bureau-40.

The ORO was in charge of "action and intelligence collection." It was headed by Captain Baille, who went by the alias "Michael 01." French intelligence placed him in Paris at various times beginning in October 1962, but they had no concrete idea what he was doing there. Captain Baille was the liaison with other ORO agents throughout France and his activities were well documented.

The Deuxieme Bureau was a nation-wide intelligence service

whose job it was to "assure the centralization and exploitation of the intelligence gathered by the regional intelligence bureaus." The documents say that on the fifteenth of each month a synopsis of their activities was written up and sent to the other group's in the organization. Their Paris bureau was headed by a man named Georges Buscia, who was arrested in Paris, (date unknown).

The Troisoime Bureau was the action arm of the group whose main job was to take violent action against their enemies and installations, targeting de Gaulle personally. This action arm—which consisted of about 30 men—was headed by Gillies Busscin and it operated throughout France. These men were described as "hard core, secure, and secret to the central echelon". The French government wrote of this group saying, "With the uniting of the OAS group in Spain with the CNR, it is possible that the Bureau Action was reinforced by some elements formerly belonging to the "commandos" of Alicante and Saint Sebastian which had been used for limited missions."

The Quatrieme Bureau 40 was the "logistical branch that was responsible for the security and support of the members of the organization, the lodging, the clandestine crossing of the frontiers and the provision of false identity documents."

Over time, the CNR split with it rival the MCR with both groups being watched closely by French authorities. CNR was created by ex-Colonel Chateau-Jobert and was installed in Spain since the independence of Algeria. They produced a pamphlet called Appel that spelled out its political and social manifesto as described by Chateau-Jobert. The French government wrote of the split between the two groups by saying that:

> Despite many urgent appeals, Chateau-Jobert refused to rally to the CNR and his movement retained its autonomy. Following a particularly violent polemic carried on in pamphlets, the uplift between the two movements became known to the public. The MCR asserts that in the immediate future it will devoted itself solely to political action and getting a valid organization in place in the country for conditioning of the population for the takeover of power by violence.
>
> In effect, although it prescribes neither extortions, nor

plastic explosions, nor hold ups, the MCR urges its followers to grease their weapons and to hide them for future use. It is therefore apparent that under propitious circumstances recourse to violent action to seize power has been condoned, and several deposits of arms, one of which was very large, have recently been discovered. In principal, the doctrine of the MCR and the personality of its founder must limit the audience of the movement to Catholics of the extreme right and the certain military circles.[81]

The French government received a report from a source who had intimate knowledge of the goings on of both groups and he sent a rather ominous note to his superiors.

"On April 18, an usually reliable source who has good contacts in French security services stated that the Government was very much concerned about CNRI. They believe the directors of the CNRI are influential miliary and civilian leaders and that there are CNRI collaborators on the highest police levels. Source speculated that this included the bureau credited specifically to combat the OAS (probably the Bureau de Liaison is meant)."

He also said that, "nevertheless it is advisable not to lose sight of the fact that there still exists a core of bitter officers, Algerian refugees, and irresponsible members living in hiding, waiting for the right moment to perpetrate assassinations and sew disorder."

One of these "bitter officers" was none other than Jean Rene Souetre.

On June 25, 1963, the CIA disseminated a memo about Souetre with information dating back to late May of that year from Lisbon. Portugal. The source was a "competent American observer from a Western-European journalist, in close touch with Captain Jean Souetre, official of the OAS, who expected the information to reach officials of the U.S."

The contact wrote:

1) On 23 May, 1963, Rene Souetre, who claimed to act as external coordinator for the OAS organization based in Portugal, said that after de Gaulle, there would be only two

---

81 Ibid.

choices in France: Communism or the OAS. Therefore, the OAS believed that it was important to allow de Gaulle to remain in power while the OAS strengthened its organization. Souetre pointed out, however, that the OAS must be prepared to counter a Communist plot at any time, as de Gaulle was an old man and also since he could easily meet with an accident. Souetre smiled as he made this last statement, but hastened to add that the Communists might see fit to assassinate de Gaulle in order to precipitate the revolution.

2)Souetre claimed that the OAS had a list of the Communist penetrations of the French Government and expressed the belief of the OAS that the de Gaulle government was aiding the Communist takeover by seeking a rapprochement with the USSR. Souetre particularly mentioned what he termed de Gaulle's "chief advisor," Jacques Foccart, as being a witting collaborator of the Communists. The OAS, according to Souetre, was now trying to penetrate the French army and the Government in order to build a counter force to the Communists within the French Government.

3) Souetre explained that the OAS intended to prevent a Communist takeover at the post-de Gaulle election by the expedient of preventing the election from taking place.[82]

The document ends with a short "Headquarters Comment" on both Souetre and Foccart.

"Information from both press and official French sources indicate that the Souetre is the name of a former French army captain who escaped from a detention camp in 1961. Subsequently to his escape he was alleged to have been involved in an assassination attempt against de Gaulle. Souetre was born 15 October 1930, in the Gironde Department of France."

"Jacques Foccart is the Secretary General to the Presidency for African and Malagasy Affairs. He also has an undetermined role in intelligence matters probably derived from the fact that from 1958

82 "Alleged Plans of Secret Army Organization in Portugal for post-de Gaulle Takeover in France." Report No. DB-3/655,207, 25 June 1963.

to 1959 he was acting as technical advisor on security and intelligence matters to the President. One of his responsibilities is believed to concern political action in Black Africa, and another that of collating and digesting for the President the intelligence reports from the various French Services."

Souetre was one of the core of "bitter officers" who conspired to assassinate Charles de Gaulle in France, on numerous occasions.

1962 was a busy year in the OAS attempts to kill Charles de Gaulle and at one point, they almost succeeded. One of the top leaders in the attempts to kill de Gaulle was Jean-Marie Bastein-Thiry, who organized the effort to kill de Gaulle at Point-sur-Seine. Another effort against the French president took place near the Elysee Palace, de Gaulle's official residence during the visit of a foreign head of state. The gunman was supposed to occupy a building with the address 86-Rue du Faubourg-Saint Honore. Another attempt was to have taken place during a visit by De Gaulle to the Republic of Vesoul in 14 June, 1962, which was the day before the proclamation of Algerian independence on 3 July 1962 was announced. The leaders of these plots were like-minded men who hated de Gaulle and his call for Algerian independence; Col. Antoine Argoud and Captain Pierre Sergent. Bastien Thiry went by the nicknames of "Didler" and "Germain."

Jean Bastien-Thiry was born on October 19, 1927 and served as a French Air Force, was a lieutenant colonel, was an air weaponry engineer, and created the Nord SS10/SS.11 missile. He came from a Catholic family whose father had once known de Gaulle and was a member of the Gaullist RPF party. He attended the Eclole Polytechnique, before joining the Air Force. He broke with de Gaulle's Algeria policy in 1959 when the French leader decided, in a move that shocked France, especially its highest-ranking military officers, to grant independence to Algeria. De Gaulle went to the French people for approval of his new policy and two referendums on self-determination were held—the first in 1961, and the second on April 8, 1962 (which became known as the French Evian Accords). (Only people living in France proper were allowed to vote—not the citizens of Algeria).

One of the most daring assassination attempts on de Gaulle's life took place on August 22, 1962 when Bastien-Thiry and his men set a trap for de Gaulle at Petit-Clamart, which was the seventh assassination attempt on his life with a few weeks time. The other attempts took place in May 1962 at the Avenue de Maine in Paris, in June at the Porte de Chatillon in Paris, then in Meudon, and in July in the Orleans region of France where de Gaulle attended the wedding of a great-niece. Bastien-Thiry learned about these visits by de Gaulle from a source named "Pierre" who worked somewhere in the Elysee Palace. De Gaulle was not worried about his safety and when he traveled, he told Interior Minister Roger Frey that, "You do your job, and I'll do mine."

De Gaulle had a home at Colombey-les-Deux-Englises. When he was there in August 1962, there had been warnings of an attempt on his life by air, called "Turtle-dov." The French police set up a no fly zone for 20 miles in radius, mounted anti-aircraft batteries near the town of La Boisserie, and a jet fighter was on alert from 30 minutes before dawn to 30 minutes after sunset.

On August 8, 1962, de Gaulle left Colombey to have lunch with visiting ex-US. President Dwight Eisenhower at the Elysee Palace. As de Gaulle's convoy neared Avenue De Versailles, 3 cars of the Bastien-Thiry commando unit entered via the Rue de la Convention on the Point Mirabeau. De Gaulle rode in a Citroen DS-21. The plan was for the cars to penetrate the convoy and open fire. However, the chauffeur, Paul Fontenil, took another route on the other bank of the river. As the commandos went after the convoy, a car driven by a civilian in a Renault 4 came between them. At the Trocadero tunnel, the assassination attempt came to an abrupt end. Bastien-Thiry later said of the attempt that day, "It's only our seventh attempt."

Another plot took place on August 22, 1962. De Gaulle left Colombey for Paris to attend a meeting of the Council of Ministers. His wife and son-in-law accompanied him on the trip. The conspirators were waiting at a location called the Palace Saint-Francois-Xavier. As luck would have it, they were stopped in traffic and missed the motorcade by several minutes.

While the Council of Ministers meeting was going on, Interior Minister Roger Frey told de Gaulle that he had learned of an assassination attempt on his life. At 7:30 P.M. de Gaulle and his wife entered their Citroen DS19. They took the route they had taken earlier in the day—Clamart. Bastien-Thiry's mole, "Pierre," was out in front of the palace when the caravan left and he contacted him immediately.

At 8 P.M., the commandos were waiting at the Avenue de La Liberation at Petit-Clamart crossroads. Twelve men armed with automatic weapons, automatic rifles, and explosives, were patiently waiting for their victim to arrive. Bastein-Thiry waited in a Simco 1000 that was parked near the intersection in order for him to get a good view of what went on. He held a copy of the newspaper, *L'Aurore,* which was to be waved when the convoy arrived. Along with him were five men in a van armed with machine guns, a Citroen ID-19 that held three other men with Sterling automatic pistols, a Peugout 403 was kept in reserve. Bastien-Thiry saw the car approach at 8:08 and the firing began.

A fuselage of shots hit de Gaulle's car and the gunmen fanned out in the middle of the road, firing. Glass in the car shattered as the bullets ripped into the auto's body. During the shooting, one police motorcyclist was hit. Miraculously, de Gaulle only suffered a cut on his finger, and a slight neck wound. Luckily, no one as killed.

Later, de Gaulle said, "It was touch and go, this time." Upon arrival at his destination, the French leader said regarding the assassination attempt, "My dear fellow, those men shot like pigs." The president's car was hit fourteen times.

Ten weeks later, a nation-wide manhunt caught six of the shooters. On September 17, Bastien-Thiry was arrested. He told the court that he wanted to capture de Gaulle and bring him before a court for trial for his crimes against France. On March 11, 1963, Bastien-Thiry was shot.

* * *

On November 23, 1963, while the United States and the world were still reeling in shock of the assassination of President John F. Kennedy, a seeming unrelated incident took place in Dallas, Texas, the scene of the crime. United States authorities expelled a known deserter from the French army who also had connections to the outlawed OAS (Organisation del'Armie Secrete) which had been battling the government of French president Charles de Gaulle over the status of Algeria. This mysterious figure was later identified as Jean Souetre who also went by the aliases Michael Roux and Michael Mertz.

Souetre was seen in Fort Worth, Texas on the morning of the President's murder and was placed in Dallas that afternoon. What this French soldier of fortune, ex-heroin smuggler, and gifted assassin was doing in Dallas at the same time that the President of the United States was being struck down, is open to much speculation.

The life of Jean Souetre and his possible link to the President's murder came from the diligent investigative efforts of the late Bernard Fensterwald, the one-time President of the Assassination Archives and Records Center in Washington, D.C. The AARC is now run by attorney and Kennedy assassination expert James Lesar. The Archives was founded in 1984 to allow scholars, as well as anyone interested into the arcane world of the Kennedy assassination.

Mr. Lesar, at one time, served for six years as the attorney for the late accused assassin of Martin Luther King Jr, James Earl Ray. Mr. Lesar has as undergraduate degree from the University of Illinois and a J.D. from the University of Wisconsin. In 1984, he joined the law firm of the late Bernard Fensterwald. During their time together, both men became good friends who shared a mutual interest in the Kennedy case. In time, they decided it was time to pool their resources and the AARC became their stepchild.

In a 1991 interview that the author did with Jim Lesar in preparation for the first issue of my magazine, *Back Channels,* we had a wideranging discussion on the Kennedy case. "Bud was obsessed with the Kennedy killing," remarked Mr. Lesar, talking fondly about his old friend. "He spent $55,000 of his own money per year for 6 years to keep the AARC alive." When I asked him at that time if he and his researchers were looking into any new angles on the President's death, he replied by saying, "that we are continuing to look at all relevant aspects." Speaking of the president's death, Mr. Lesar said, "I am still mystified that afer 30 years we still haven't learned the truth and we may not know."[83]

One of the first documents to be revealed concerning Jean

---

[83] Kross, Peter. "The Assassination Archives," Bach Channels, Volume 1, No. 1, October, 1991. Page 23-24.

Souetre was document number 632-796 (dated April 1, 1964), which dug into the life of this mysterious French assassin and his troubled background. What this document revealed was a tangled web of intrigue concerning the French OAS, international drug smuggling, and assassination.

The top heading of the document says, "Jean Souetre's Expulsion from U.S." The document reads as follows:

> Jean SOUETRE, a.k.a. Michael Roux, a.k.a. Michael Mertz—On March 5, 1964, the FBI advised that the French had (blank) the Legal Attache in Paris and also the (blank) had queried the Bureau in New York City concerning subject, stating that he had been expelled from the U.S. at Fort Worth or Dallas 18 hours after the assassination. He was in Fort Worth on the morning of 22 November and in Dallas in the afternoon. The French believe that he was expelled to either Mexico or Canada. In January he received mail from a dentist named Alderson... Subject is believed to be identical with a Captain who is a deserter from the French Army and an activist in the OAS (a right-wing French militant group). The French are concerned because of De Gaulle's planned visit to Mexico. They would like to know the reason for his expulsion from the U.S. and his destination. Bureau files are negative and they are checking in Texas and with the INS (Immigration and Naturalization Service).

The dentist mentioned in the document was a one-time friend of Captain Souetre, Lawrence Alderson. The FBI had a considerable file on Dr. Alderson in which they complied various tid-bits of information on both him and Souetre. A March 5, 1964, FBI document on Dr. Alderson, begins to shed life on their relationship. The document concerns a phone call from FBI Supervisor Richard Cotter of the Dallas Bureau. It says that, "Dr. Lawrence Alderson advised me he knew Jean Souetre in 1953 when both were stationed in Petit Malion, small town near Rheims, France. Alderson at that time, First Lieutenant U.S. Army, and Souetre with Security in French Fourth Air Force. Since leaving France, Alderson has occasionally corresponded with Souetre, usually in the form of Christmas cards. Did not receive card from him for over a year. States in about 1955, Souetre went to Algiers and was there for approximately four years."

"Knows no background other than fact Souetre married girl from well to do family in Bordeaux, France. Never knew him to be in the United States."

"Alderson denies ever telephoning or cabling Souetre."

The document then goes to state a rather interesting fact about two of Souetre's aliases, "Roux," and "Mertz" (both real people).

"Inquiry at Pan Am World Airlines, Houston, for flights to Mexico City during period November 23rd through 25, 63, disclosed no information re Souetre under name or known aliases. However, Pan American records indicate Dominique P. Roux and Viviane Roux departed Houston for Mexico City on November 22 last and John Mertz."[84]

Another FBI document on Dr. Alderson, gave more information on Souetre. Dr. Alderson said that after he left his base at Rheims, he was replaced by an officer whose first name he did not recall, last name Letouneau (phonetic), and "it is his understanding that Captain Letourneau became well acquainted with Souetre. He stated that Letourneau was from Texas, but he does not know his address."

On March 5, 1964, Horace Harris of the INS in Houston, Texas, made a search of his records but could not find anyone by the name of Souetre or his known aliases in his files. The Houston Police Dept and the Harris County Sheriff's Office also made a search but also found no records relating to Souetre.

The FBI also did a check on airline flights in Houston and found out that there was no direct air service between Houston and Canada (Souetre was supposed to have been either expelled to Canada or Mexico). People who were flying to Canada at the time had to go to New York or other cities for their connections.[85]

The FBI did, however, generate a memo on one of Jean Souetre's alias, "Michael Mertz" (see next chapter) regarding his

---

84RIF No. 124-10224-10059 "Souetre, Jean, Assoc, Mil Ser." TRA 11/22-24/63.

85RIF No. 124-10224-10061. "US Dept of Justice-Jean Souetre a.k.a. as Michael Roux, Michael Mertz."

arrival in the United States. Michael Mertz, born 8-31-40, at Soyaux, Charente, France, arrived in the U.S. on November 19, 1963 destined for Houston, Texas, aboard Air France Flight 007. He left France at Orly, Paris and gave his address as 46 R. De Mauberge, Paris. He departed the U.S. at Laredo, Texas for Mexico on 12-6-63. The FBI contacted the Visa Office and a search of their records and that of the Office of Security, Department of State, found no records on Mertz.[86]

After the president's death, Dr. Alderson said that he was being followed "by unknown persons." "The unknown persons" turned out to be FBI agents, keeping tabs on him. Dr. Alderson later said that, "they (the FBI) were trying to find Jean under any circumstances, under any conditions... They felt that Jean knew who, or he himself, had assassinated Kennedy. And what they wanted to know was who in Washington had had him flown out of Dallas. And to my knowledge, nobody ever found out or nobody ever knew."

This entire incident involving Dr. Alderson is ripe with questions. Dr. Alderson said that the FBI came to interview him about Jean Souetre "shortly" after the assassination. The FBI first went to see Dr. Alderson because the FBI found a four to five year old Christmas card in the dead letter area of the post office that he had mailed to Souetre. However, the documentation says that in January 1964, Souetre received mail from Dr. Alderson. If they found the out dated letter in the post office five months after the assassination, they why did the FBI say they interviewed the Doctor "shortly" after the assassination? It does not make sense.

The U.S. government's interest in the activities of Jean Souetre took on another dimension with a routine letter from Sam Papich of the FBI regarding the elusive Frenchman. The memo, dated March 9, 1964 went to a man named D.J. Brennan and it mentioned a CIA analyst named Jane Roman. It read, "With regard to information in CIA files concerning the subject, Mrs. Jane Roman, CIA, advised the Liaison Agent on March 6, 1964, that her agency furnished information to the Bureau (FBI) by letter dated July 12, 1963, to the State Department captioned "OAS Attempt to Enlist the Cooperation of the United States for its anti-de Gaulle

[86] RIF No. 124-10224-10070. "Souetre, Jean, AKA Bkg, Tra, Res, Rck."

Activities," a copy of which was designated to the Bureau. In addition, Mrs. Roman furnished the following: a) a photograph of Souetre, b) A copy of a CIA report dated June 25, 1963, captioned "Alleged Plans of Secret Army Organization in Portugal for post de-Gaulle Takeover in France."[87]

The name of Jane Roman is well known to many JFK researchers but for those who don't know who she is, here is just a small background of her activities with the CIA. Jane Roman was the senior staff liaison officer on the Counter-intelligence staff at CIA headquarters in Washington. After the assassination, the CIA did an internal investigation into the assassination and asked John Whitten to head it up. (John Whitten went by the alias "John Scelso for many years). At the time of the assassination, John Whitten was the chief of the covert operations branch for Mexico City and Central America at the CIA.

As Whitten began his investigation, it soon became apparent that he was being stymied in his search for answers by none other than Richard Helms who stopped him from looking into Oswald's Cuba related activities in New Orleans in the summer of 1963, information that the FBI had on hand for months. In the end, Helms' decision to withhold vital information from John Whitten forced him to end his investigation and stop an avenue of intelligence that may have altered what the public knew about the activities of Lee Oswald, and which have clouded the investigation of the JFK case for decades to come.

It seems that Jane Roman's name had been listed on routing slips attached to certain CIA documents about Lee Oswald before November 22, 1963. Jane Roman was interviewed by Dr. John Newman who wrote about her in his book (*Oswald and the CIA),* and writer, Jefferson Morley who wrote book on the CIA called "*Our Man in Mexico—Winston Scott and the Hidden History of the CIA.*"

The Oswald file was handled by James Angleton's Counter-intelligence Staff, one of the most secretive parts of the agency. The Counterintelligence Staff was the mole-hunting group at CIA headquarters and when Oswald returned home, the agency did not

---

87RIF No. 124-10224-10065. March 9, 1964, "Souetre, Jean, Anti-De Gaulle Act." Secret Army Organization, Post-DeGaulle Act.

know if he was an agent of the Soviet Union or just a disgruntled American who had seen the light. Another secret group at CIA HQ who had possession of the Oswald file was the SIG-Special Investigations Unit-whose mandate was to hunt potential moles inside the CIA. At this point, no one inside the CIA knew who Oswald was and they needed to find out as soon as possible. Jane Roman read the early files that passed her desk, signed them, and passed them on to her supervisors.

The fact that Jane Roman, an analyst in the Counter-intelligence branch at CIA at the time of the Oswald investigation, was looking into the allegations against Jean Souetre is interesting in itself. The CIA had a valid interest in finding out as much information about any possible assassination attempt against De Gaulle and pass that information along to the French. After all, France was an important ally of the United States, even if both countries had different geo-political views on certain important matters. It also should be noted that President de Gaulle attended JFK's funeral and walked in the funeral procession.

If the CIA and FBI thought their investigation of Jean Souetre was over in the early 1960s, other people, especially certain journalists who learned about the elusive Frenchman, did not.

On April 14, 1977, the SAC (Special Agent in Charge) of the Dallas FBI office sent a memo to the Director of the FBI on the Souetre case. The memo was in reference to a reporter by the name of David Duffy who worked for the *National Enquirer."* It seems that Duffy, who was a British citizen and foreign correspondent for the "National Enquirer," wanted to know about any investigation the FBI was conducting on Jean Souetre.

In his letter, Duffy said that, "Souetre, aka was supposedly a former French Army Captain who deserted and who was a militant member of the OAS and who was deported to Mexico or Canada after the assassination of President Kennedy." Duffy enclosed a copy of the government document regarding U.S. interest on Souetre (which is presented earlier in this chapter) for the FBI to read. Duffy said that the "Enquirer" wanted him to find out as much background material on Souetre as he could find and to find out "why such a dangerous man was in Dallas, Texas on 11/22/63. Duffy is pursuing the possibility that Souetre was an assassin in Dallas, Texas on 11/22/63, and might have been responsible for the assassination of President Kennedy."

In their memo, the FBI wrote that:

> *Duffy further advised that he is also working on a news story and is attempting to develop facts on the following:*
>
> *1. That Lee Oswald was an FBI or CIA informant.*
>
> *2. That Lee Oswald and Jack Ruby personally knew each other.*

Duffy made an oral request to determine if he could obtain any information on Souetre, via FOIA (Freedom of Information Request).

The memo ended by saying, "The above is being furnished for the information of the Bureau in the event the Bureau should receive any other inquiries from DUFFY or become aware of any newspaper articles on JEAN SOUETRE."[88]

The inquiry by David Duffy must have woken up the FBI Dallas office who believed that they had heard the end of the Kennedy case, and anything to do with the so-called French assassin, Jean Souetre, aka, Michael Mertz or Michael Roux. They could not have been more wrong. It was during this time that the U.S. Congress was re-opening both the Martin Luther King and JFK assassination cases to an eager American public who wasn't buying the 1964 Warren Commission's conclusion that Lee Harvey Oswald was the lone assassin of JFK… One of the areas of investigation that got much national attention was the CIA-mob plots to kill Fidel Castro and the abuses of power by the CIA over many decades. However, like many areas of investigation that the WC did not look into was the so-called "French Connection" to the Kennedy killing and the role, if any, by Jean Souetre.

As mentioned before, the late Bernard Fensterwald was very much interested not only in the Kennedy case but in the French Connection as well. In November 1982, he went on a trip to Europe to try and find out as much information on Souetre and any confederates he might have had. When he returned home, he left a number of reports on his trip at the AARC.

---

88 RIF No. 124-10224-10072. "Souetre, Jean, AKA, JFK 11/22/63," Dated 4/14/77.

One report is listed on the letterhead of his law firm, Fensterwald & Associates and is called "Summary of Paris Trip—November 13-22, 1982." He went on the trip with another man whose name is not mentioned in the file. They met with a number of contacts, both in the French police establishment, and others of ill repute. One of the contacts gave Fensterwald a summary of police files on Souetre-Mertz-Roux, (the latter are the two aliases that Souetre used).

Fensterwald writes that his investigation began in February 1964, when a French journalist named Louis Assemat-Tessandier, wrote an article in a little-known French newspaper which told the story of his meeting with Michael Roux in Montreal, Canada, from January 20-21, 1964. Louis Assemat-Tessandier said that Roux was in Fort Worth, Texas and also in Dallas on November 22, 1963 "and that he had tried to recruit Louis to participate in an attempt on the life of de Gaulle when he was to visit Mexico in March." Fensterwald wrote that there were a number of contradictions in Roux's story, especially as to how Souetre and Mertz were concerned.

Fensterwald met with Bertrand Le Gendre of the newspaper *Le Monde.* Gendre told him that the newspaper was going to conduct its own investigation of the affair and would publish its findings.

Through his contacts, they met with a French police captain (name not known) who explained the political situation in France with them, especially as it related to French Socialist party. The policeman said that Fensterwald would be ill advised to seek out Souetre because any trip "would be 1) dangerous, 2) unproductive (he won't talk) and 3) probably counterproductive. We did not visit Souetre."

The notes he took on Mertz were very telling. "According to both (blank) and Le Cavelier, Mertz was pro-OAS, was caught by the government in a minor OAS operation, and was 'turned' into a double agent and sent to Beaujon, where he informed as to Petit Clamart (the assassination attempt on de Gaulle), and ultimately sent to Canada. (Blank) also said that Souetre visited the United States and Canada in 1963."

On Saturday, November 20, the Americans had a meeting with Jean Claude Perez, M.D. the ex-chief of O.R.O, the OAS intelligence organization. Dr. Perez told them the following story.

“I) The OAS did dispatch a three-man team to assassinate de Gaulle in Mexico City in March, 1964.”

“2) He did meet with Guy Banister in Madrid.”

“3) The OAS had contact in New Orleans with an anti-Castro group which he called the Rosa Blanca.” (More about this later in the chapter).

“4) As to Souetre, saw him for the first time in Spain in 1962.”

“5) The OAS made a real effort to help via right wing U.S. Ambassador to Portugal, Amb. Anderson. They thought Anderson would understand de Gaulle’s true nature, i.e., pro-communism, even Anderson could not swallow this and,

“6) Importantly, Perez said that, post 1962, Souetre was part of an ultra-right wing, ultra-Catholic splinter group which included four men named Pichon, Lefevre, Bourget, and Grossouvre. Group called Intergraliste.”

“Perez believes that JFK was killed by anti-communists; he also believes that they “got the wrong man”; believes, despite veneer, that JFK was anti-communist, and equally, despite veneer, de Gaulle was pro-communist.”[89]

In the Fensterwald narrative, there is a detailed and revealing Appendix that outlines more information on the article by Louis Assemat-Tessandier, and a long biographical sketch of Michael Roux.

The article written by Louis Assemat-Tessandier, was published in the paper, *Cote-Basque Soir* of Bayonne. In the article, Louis states that he was in Montreal in January 1964 and met another Frenchman who had recently been to Texas, gone to Mexico, and then came to Montreal. The Frenchman, according to Louis, “was a young officer from Algeria who wandered back and forth between the three OAS centers in the Western Hemisphere, i.e., Montreal, Mexico City and Rio.”

Louis would not reveal the Frenchman’s name, but he introduced himself as a “former paratroop officer in Algeria (like Souetre) and said that he had arrived that morning by plane from Mexico City. He said that he had been in Dallas at the time of Kennedy’s murder but had been expelled by the American police

---

89Summary of Paris Trip-November 13-22, 1982. Fensterwald files AARC.

18 hours later."(All this fits the known events as described in U.S. documents on either Souetre or Mertz).

"Here's what I know about Dallas," said the Frenchman. "It was a plot of the extreme right. I was at Fort Worth for breakfast and heard JFK deliver his last speech. I knew that in Dallas it would be over for him. I jumped in a plane for Dallas. In Dallas, there was a cross fire with several men shooting. But I won't tell you anything more. Louis implies that he knows more."

"When asked about Oswald, his answer was devastating; an idiot and an innocent in this matter."

"Moreover, now, we (or they). are setting up for Mexico City. De Gaulle is coming in March. Hidden in a crowd of Indians and in all of the confusion, you may be sure that an excellent marksman will do the job. This time it will be like Dallas and not like Petit Clamart."

In the Fensterwald report, there is a headline called "Document 4 entitled "Intelligence report concerning an individual suspected of preparing an assassination against the President of the French Republic in Mexico."

The notes refer to Michael Roux and are described as follows:

"Page 3 seems to be referring to Roux, although this is not entirely clear. He whoever he is, claims to have been expelled from Texas within 48 hours of Kennedy's murder. He bragged about flirting with a secretary in the Houston consulate in order to get a visa (to where?), "because he did not want to be recorded as having been in a French consulate in North America. He claimed to have traveled a lot in Latin America and had gone to Montreal to arrange an attempt on de Gaulle. He gave everyone the impression that he was very dangerous, capable of robbing the arsenal, etc."

An arsenal at Montreal was burgled by a group of unidentified Frenchman in which rifles, machine guns, were taken.

The document has a heading, "Possible identification of Michael Roux" which says:

> At the direction of Military Security (blank), Michael Roux has been discovered in one very important set of photographs. He is supposed to have been identified as ex-Captain Jean Souetre, sentenced to three years in prison,

and incarcerated in (blank).

Nevertheless, Roux seems more corpulent than the photos of Souetre that were shown. The lips of Roux are apparently thicker than those of Souetre.

Note that Souetre has a relationship with a dentist in Houston.

Souetre is an important member of secret French activist organization (OAS and CNR). He is perfectly capable of organizing assassination attempts or thefts of weapons. His possible presence in North America is particularly disturbing at the time of a visit of General de Gaulle to Mexico.

The CIA wasn't the only U.S. government agency who was interested in Jean Souetre. On March 13, 1964, an FBI memo to Director Hoover was sent from the New York office regarding "Jean Souetre, aka Michael Roux, Michael Mertz. IS-France."

They noted that a person named Michael Roux (a real person whose alias Souetre often times used), born 8-31-40 in Soyaux, Charente, France, arrived in the U.S. on 11-19-63, final destination being Houston, Texas. Roux arrived in the U.S. via Air France flight #007, having left from Orly airport in Paris. Roux left the U.S. at Laredo for Mexico on 12-6-63. "No information was located in INS records under the names SOUETRE OR MERTZ."

On March 5, 1964, a few days before the FBI's memo on Mertz was issued, Special Agency Kenneth Haser reported that there was no information in their files or the visa office or that of the Office of Security, Department of State, regarding Mertz.

What the documents reveal is a keen interest on behalf of both the CIA and FBI on the activities of Jean Souetre, alias Michael Roux, and Michael Mertz. In March of 1964, the FBI received information from two brothers who, while traveling in France on business, met with the real Michael Roux. Leon Gachman, the President of Gachman Metals of Fort Worth, Texas, and his brother Dan, arrived in Paris in October 1963 and checked into the Hotel Proust. The room clerk at the hotel was Michael Roux. Roux served as their guide during their stay in Paris, spoke good English, and the three men became friends. Roux told them that he had served in the French army as a Lieutenant and served in Algeria.

He said that he was attending a school in order to learn the restaurant and hotel business, and wanted to come to the United States in order to open his own French restaurant. Before the Gachman's left France, they told Roux that if he was ever in the United States he should call on them, and said that the city of Houston was a good place to start as business.

Michael Roux arrived in the United States on November 20, 1963 and went to Houston, Texas. He called Leon Gachman and asked if they could meet. Roux left for Fort Worth and arrived in that city on November 21. Leon Gachman met Roux at the bus station and they went back to his home for the evening. Gachman then took Roux to a hotel in Fort Worth. The next day, November 22, 1963, Leon's son Arnold took Roux to a class at Texas Christian University from ten to twelve noon. Both men were in a local restaurant when they heard the news of the president's assassination. After the assassination, both Gachman's told the FBI that "he (Roux) was not involved in any matter with the local police or federal authorities and was almost constantly in their company."

After a brief trip back to Houston, Roux arrived in Mexico City and worked briefly in a hotel. In February 1964, Leon Gachman got a letter from Roux stating that he had returned to France and was living in Paris.

In the Fensterwald files, there is an affidavit signed by Michael Roux which was taken in Paris on March 7, 1964, that makes interesting reading. He stated that his full name was Michel Pierre Gabriel Louis Roux, born August 31, 1940 at Soyaux (Charente). He gave the name of his wife, and had one child. He served in the French army in Algeria in 1961-62 and was let go from service in Paris on October 7, 1962 with the rank of Sergent. He said that he had heard of the article written by Louis Assemat-Tessandier and said, "I contest all of the facts reported there. I will tell you the conditions under which I undertook my trip to North America where I went to try to find work."

He told the story of meeting the Gachman's in Houston in November 1963, and said that he went to the Bamer Hotel in Mexico City but could not find work. He left Mexico on January 8, 1964 due to the lack of funds. He arrived in the U.S. at Laredo on January 10 and crossed the border into Canada on January 13,

1964, at Windsor. He stayed in Montreal from the 12th to the 30th of January. At the end of January he got sick and returned to France.

Roux writes that while he was in Montreal, he met two young ladies by the names of Jean and Eva and asked them out for a drink. The girls told him that they knew of a Frenchman who was in Montreal and that they should all meet. They went to one of the girl's apartments and Jean called her French friend. Roux talked with the Frenchman by the name of "Louis" on the phone and he wrote of the conversation the two men had:

> I took the phone and told him that I had just arrived from Mexico after a stay in Fort Worth, where I was the day of President Kennedy's murder. Louis asked me what I thought of that affair. I responded that, in my view, Oswald could not have acted alone. I had read the local papers which had given contradictory details. We then spoke of the trip that General de Gaulle was to take to Mexico in March, and I said something to the effect, "They should reinforce security, because in Mexico people kill at the drop of a hat. They even pay Indians to kill people."
>
> I wish to make clear that my only contact with Louis was limited to this one phone conversation. I never saw the man, and I never knew his name until you gave me his article to read. Therefore, I deny the interpretation that Louis gave to my statements. I request to be confronted by him. And I reserve the right to initiate against him any and all legal actions which I judge useful. I have nothing to add. I remain at your disposal in case you have further need of me.[90]

The Fensterwald files reveal an interesting tidbit on one of the girls whom Michael Roux met in Montreal, Eva Gerold. It seems that two members of the Swiss intelligence service, a M. Raspail, the intelligence chief at Annemassee and a Major Roques of Military Security, had contacted or had been in contact with Louis Assemat-Tessandier regarding a visit to Switzerland by Eva

---

90 Affidavit of Michael Roux, March 7, 1964. Fensterwald Files, AARC.

Gerold.

Eva Gerold learned that the Swiss intelligence agents wanted to speak with her about Michael Roux but she refused to meet with them.

On March 5, after intervention by members of the French government, Louis Assemat-Tessandier met with M. Raspail at the Contrin Airport. After their talk, the writer agreed to return to Geneva on March 6.

"It was then agreed that between the French and Swiss that Louis would return to Geneva on March 6 but that a Swiss police officer would put the following questions to Eva:

> *1. What was the name of the Frenchman who paid several visits to your office in Montreal between 1 Jan. and 15 Feb?*
>
> *2. What was the address of this man?*
>
> *3. Would she recognize his photo in a group of photos?*
>
> *The Canadian girl answered the three questions:*
>
> *1. Michael Roux.*
>
> *2. She had his address at her office in Montreal and that she would supply it, but she knew that in France it was Angouleme.*
>
> *3. Among the photographs which were presented to her, notably that of Souetre, she was not able to recognize the man in question.*

In conclusion, the Swiss asked her if she wished to meet Louis. She replied, "No… "

There is nothing in the records that reveal why Swiss intelligence was interested in speaking with Michael Roux. Did they have their own file on him, and if they did, how did they get it? One would assume that the CIA (or the French) provided the Swiss (an ally in the cold war era) with information on Michael Roux, but if they did, why? Was Michael Roux on the Swiss radar for something he had done in Europe, or Switzerland that might have caught their attention?

A man with a similar name as that of Michael Roux needs mentioning in this narrative. While looking into its files on Jean Souetre and Michael Roux, the FBI came across a name of a man named Dominique Roux. Like Souetre and Michael Roux, Dominique Roux, of whom there is little documentation, caught their radar. On March 5, 1964, an employee of Pan American World Airways in Houston, Texas, a Mr. A. Crixell, made a search of flights to Mexico City during the time period of November 22 to November 30, 1963 and found nothing relating to Jean Souetre or any other person using his aliases. However, they did find out that a person named Dominique Roux and Viviane Roux left Houston, Texas for Mexico City on November 22, 1963, the day of the Kennedy assassination. Also leaving for Mexico City from Houston one day after the assassination were John P. Mertz, Irma Rio de Mertz and Sara Mertz. We don't know if these people were related in any way to Michael Mertz, or Jean Souetre, but it is interesting that these people with the same name were on Pan Am's flight manifest.

After looking into the background of Dominique Roux, an interesting pattern emerges. Dominique Roux was a noted French author and soldier-of-fortune of the day. Dominique Roux was born in Algeria, date not mentioned. He came from a prominent family with his father being the governor of the Bank of France.

Roux was a militant OAS terrorist and served as a member of the Commando Delta unit. He later was one of the founding members of militant terrorist group called Aginter Presse. A further study of the records says that both Jean Souetre and Dominique Roux served together in Aginter Presse. Dominique Roux also had ties with fascist members in Italy under the name of Centro Commerciale Mondial, (a.k.a., Permindex), and had a close relationship with Stefano Della Chaie, and a former intelligence officer called Giannettini. In 1962, Giannettini arrived in the United States on the invitation from General Delvalle, who was the commander of the Marine-Center in Annapolis, Maryland. In Annapolis, he taught a number of courses including "the techniques and the possibilities of a coup d'etat in Europe." By 1964, he founded a European fascist group that later became Aginter. By 1964, the group went by the name AMSAR and was financed by Spanish and Portugese intelligence groups in South Africa and Latin America.[91]

---

91 Fensterwald files at AARC.

Aginter Presse was established in Lisbon, Portugal in 1966 and many disgruntled OAS members flocked to their wings. Roux was described as "A French agent of the Gestapo trained PIDE."

During the proxy war in Angola in the mid 1970s, in which a number of soldiers-of-fortune of the day flocked to, Dominique Roux was the chief advisor to UNITA, along with Stefano della Chaie. Roux was supposed to have fought in such African nations as Mozambique and Guinea-Bissau. Sources said that Dominique Roux died in "a strange automobile accident in the spring of 1978."

There have been allegations that certain elements of the U.S. intelligence community had some knowledge, or had taken part in the assassination attempts on President de Gaulle during the Algerian troubles. There were reports that the secret international business organization called Permindex and its members were involved in the anti-de Gaulle activity (see chapter 1). These allegations took the form of editorials in the leading French newspaper *Le Monde* which, in one of its issues in May, 1961, said that certain American agents encouraged the attacks against de Gaulle. A noted newspaper writer of the time, Marquis Childs wrote that neither the U.S. State Department nor President Kennedy had any knowledge of the assassinations attempts on de Gaulle, but that the Defense Intelligence Agency might have been aware of what was going on. Another newsman who wrote of these events was Crosby Noyes of the old *Washington Star* when he wrote in one column that, "At least a half dozen foreign newsmen were given privately to understand that the generals" plot was backed by strongly anti-Communist elements in the United States Government and military services. The leader of the revolt, General Maurice Challe, was reported to have received assurances that any move to keep Algeria under permanent French domination and out of Algerian hands would be in the interests of the United States. There also was a strong implication that a change in the NATO policies of General de Gaulle would be welcome as one of the results of a successful coup d'etat."[92]

Allegations of possible U.S. interest in the plots against de Gaulle were also reported by newsman Paul Ghali of the *Chicago*

---

[92] Ibid.

Daily News. He wrote that, "French army circles in the French capital made it known that they had irrefutable documents proving that Pentagon agents in Paris and Algiers promised General de Gaulle full U.S. support if the coup succeeded. Simultaneously, the Polish Ambassador in Paris, Stanislaw Gajewski, volunteered the same information with even more precision to colleagues and social acquaintances."

JFK, despite his disagreements with de Gaulle over certain aspects of NATO military policy, had no interest in seeing one of America's most trusted allies be shunted aside in a coup. The president gave de Gaulle his assurances that no one in the U.S. government had taken part in the clandestine plots to kill him.

We now come to a possible Permindex connection to the attempts on de Gaulle's life. From its inception, the U.S. State Department had kept a close eye on the shadowy establishment that had been founded by Ferenc Nagy. In a November 7, 1958 State Department memo they wrote that Permindex had formed an alliance with the Rome World Trade Center (Centro Mondiale Commerciale) and had opened shop in Italy in a building that once held the 1942 Rome World Exhibition. It said that Clay Shaw, the man whom New Orleans DA Jim Garrison had indicted for the Kennedy assassination who was the Managing Director of the International Trade Mart in New Orleans, had been named to the Board of Directors of Permindex.

Certain Italian newspapers such as *Paesa Sera* and *De La Sera,* wrote articles that tried to link the CMC and Clay Shaw as "a creature of the CIA. In 1962, the French newspaper *Les Echos,* wrote a few stories and editorial reports that linked Permindex to the attempts on de Gaulle's life.

One man who was linked to Ferenc Nagy was Jacques Soustelle. Soustelle was once the propaganda chief for de Gaulle but broke with the French government over its Algerian policy. Later, Soustelle had served as Governor-General of Algeria in the 1950s, before becoming an active member of the OAS. Soustelle was opposed to de Gaulle's free Algeria policy and in the 1960s, he went to Washington and met with certain members of the CIA to try and get their support for his cause. He met with CIA officer Richard Bissell who later would become part of the plots to kill Fidel Castro. His arrival in the United States was reported in major

American newspapers of the day, including the *New York Times,* which said that Soustelle had lunch with certain members of the CIA. It was reported that "Soustelle convinced the CIA that Algeria would become, through de Gaulle's blundering, a Soviet base."

The *Chicago Tribune* got wind of the Soustelle story and they reported that, "Congressional leaders have been told of Central Intelligence Agency involvement in a plot by French dissidents to assassinate the late French President, Charles de Gaulle."[93]

Soustelle went into exile in 1962 after numerous allegations of his prior association with the plots to kill de Gaulle and was pardoned in 1968.

In the United States, an anti-Castro organization called MNC, which had offices in both Miami and New Orleans (both places that were violently anti-Castro in the political leanings), was said to have had links with the OAS. A man named Maurice Brooks Gatlin Sr., who was the counsel to a group called the Anti-Communist League of the Caribbean, was said to have delivered the amount of $100,000 in 1962 to a group of individuals in Paris who were going to kill de Gaulle.

The MNC was founded in New York in 1962 by Rosado Tuero and rejected both capitalism and communism "and proclaimed that Christian Nationalism is the only doctrine capable of liberating Cuba and other nations from Communism." They published a four-page newsletter called "Action" which was published in Mexico on a sporadic basis.

U.S. government documents on the MNC said that they boasted of sinking a Cuban patrol boat north of Las Villas Province in Cuba while conducting a raid in late May or early June of 1964. However, U.S. authorities could not confirm that fact. In January 1965, Rosado Tuero said that his organization had joined forces with Emilio Duque's ECA (Anti-Communist Cuban Army) in its fight to topple Castro. In 1962, the MNC was supposed to have had 40 members, most of whom lived in the Miami area. The American government reported that the MNC had no contacts in Cuba, other than people whom they knew.

---

[93]Davy, William, "Through the Looking Glass: The Mysterious World of Clay Shaw". Privately printed. No date. Page 13.

By May 1965, the MNC announced that they had opened a recruitment center in Miami for any Cuban exiles who wanted to fight against the pro-Bosch forces in the Dominican Republic. An article in the *Miami Herald* of May 22, 1965, said that, "five commandos from the MNC's Mexico City cell were responsible for the bombing attack on a building occupied by the Mexican-Russian Cultural Relations Institute in Mexico City in which an explosion broke two glass display cases. No one was in the part of the building were the two homemade bombs landed."

The USG said of the MNC "It appears that the MNC is no more than another insignificant Cuban exile group whose neo-fascist ideology has earned a minium of popular support. The associate Cuban groups of the MNC also appear to be of little importance and lack the necessary funds to carry out militant actions against Cuba. Rosado apparently uses the MNC status as an affiliate of Joven America to impress the Cuban exile community in Miami with MNC's hemispheric contacts."

* * *

The first American news outlet to make mention of Jean Souetre was not any of the mainstream press like the *Washington Post* or the *New York Times* (who refused to believe anything but the "Oswald did it alone theory"), but the not too reliable *National Enquirer,* whose readers were sometimes shown pictures of American politicians meeting aliens, or movie stars wearing little or no clothes.

The tabloid published a commemorative issue on the Kennedy assassination with the headline "Is This the Man Who Killed JFK?' with the accompanying picture of Jean Souetre next to the type. Below the picture was the caption "Notorious Terrorist Was in Dallas on Day of the Shooting." A quote from the article says, "If one believes the CIA and the French secret services, Jean-Rene Souetre used as an alias the name Michael Mertz, was in Dallas the day of Kennedy's murder." If a lot of the story in the *National Enquirer* might have not been the full truth, they did get it right when it came to the use of the Mertz alias that Jean Souetre used during this time.

At the time of the article in the *Enquirer,* Jean Souetre was 53 years old, and was in charge of public relations at Divonne-les-Bains, a casino. Upon reading the article on him, he said that it was "total fabrication."

Jean Souetre was born on October 15, 1930 in the Grionde Department of France. He married a girl from a wealthy family in the Bordeaux region of France, Mile Marcaillou d'Armerie. He served in the French 4th Air Force with the rank of Captain and in 1953 was stationed at Petite Mulioun near Rheims. It was there that he met an American dentist named Dr. Lawrence Alderson whom he kept in contact with after leaving the military. He also befriended Dr. Alderson's successor, an American Captain named Letourneau who was also from Texas (Dr. Alderson was from Houston).

Souetre was sent to Algiers during the years 1955-59 and served with the air commandos in Algeria, until he deserted in February 1961. He then joined the renegade OAS, ant anti-de Gaulle unit of disgruntled French army officers who were opposed to de Gaulle's policy of independence for Algeria. He is alleged to have participated in an attempt on the life of President de Gaulle at Petit Clamart in which de Gaulle escaped unharmed. In May 1963, Souetre was working for the OAS in "foreign affairs." He used a number of false passports in his travels, including a fake U.S. passport. He told his associates that he was documented as a naturalized citizen from the Caribbean island of Martinique.

He was arrested on February 22, 1961 on various charges such as the possession of illegal arms. He was tried in front of a military panel in December 1961, and was sentenced to a detention camp for a three-year period. However, in February 1962, Souetre and 17 other OAS members escaped.

It was during this time that Souetre approached CIA agents and tried to persuade them to have the U.S. give their tacit support to the OAS as the "only viable alternative to communism" in France. The CIA wrote a detailed memo on this affair but bluntly told Souetre they weren't; interested in his offer.

In 1963, Souetre went to Spain, with a number of other OAS deserters, in order to elude the French secret services who were on his tail. In 1966 he was in Lisbon, Portugal where he joined the terrorist group Aginter Press.

Souetre was also involved in a plot to return Moise Tshombe to power in the Congo during the time period 1967-1968. Note that the CIA was tied to attempts to kill Patrice Lumumba in 1960 using two of its most trusted agents, QJ/WIN and WI/ROGUE/1.

One of the men most responsible for the possible return of Moise Tshombe to power in the Congo was Leon Libert. Libert served at one time as Tshombe's pilot. He was recruited by a CIA agent named Ed Rector. Libert and another mercenary named Bracco were hired to train anti-Castro Cuban pilots, as well as former members of the Bay of Pigs invasion who were itching to join a new fight. Libert worked with the CIA until he received a letter from Bracco who was then in Paris, telling him that Tshombe wanted to see him. Libert flew to Paris where he met both Tshombe and Bracco at the Hotel Georges V. During the meeting, both men were hired for a coup attempt that would put Tshombe back in power in the Congo. Tshombe paid Libert $2000 a month and both Libert and Bracco went to Portugal where they met agents from Aginter Press. Libert, Bracco and about 150 other mercenaries waited for nine months in Portugal for the call that never came. It seems that a Belgian newspaper somehow found out about the attempted coup and revealed it.

After the departure of most of the mercenaries, Libert and Bracco remained behind as they were told that group of Frenchmen were attempting to mount a new coup. It was during this time that Souetre met with Libert. Libert was told that, "Souetre was described as the new leader of the coup." Accompanying Souetre was a Frenchman named Alain Bonnet-Gauthier, who was to be his second-in-command… Both Libert and Souetre flew to Luanda and stayed in a hospital while waiting orders. The coup never took place as Tshombe was kidnaped in early 1967 and taken to Algiers and put in jail. (He later died in prison).[94]

Unknown to Jean Souetre during the early 1960s, his escapades in the OAS were to inspire Hollywood to make a major motion picture about him called *The Day of the Jackal*, based on the best selling book of the same name by writer Frederick Forsythe.

Souetre was later pardoned for his crimes by the French government and became a successful businessman. However, his

---

[94]Fensterwald Files: "From Steve Rivele Re: Conversation with Leon Libert and his ex-wife, Dominique Cuypers."

relationship with Michael Victor Mertz (see next chapter) would not go away. Mertz infiltrated Jean Souetre's OAS camp and Souetre later said that, "he and Mertz had served together in two units in Algeria in 1958-59, but had not seen each other after that time." Years later, when interest in the Kennedy assassination was again in the news, Souetre said that Mertz had used his name as an alias, and had used it in 1963, including the time when Mertz was in Dallas on November 22, 1963.

Michael Mertz later went to New Orleans, a hotbed of anti-Castro activity, and the home of many of the prime players in the Kennedy assassination saga; David Ferrie, Guy Bannister, Clay Shaw, and Lee Harvey Oswald. The documents released via the 1992 JFK Records Act, say that at one point a man named Jean Souetre was seen at the Cuban exile training camps outside of New Orleans at Lake Pontchartrain and was helping to train the anti-Castro rebels that flocked to those CIA backed camps.

After the end of the Cuban Missile Crisis in October, 1962, the Kennedy administration decided to crack down on the militant anti-Castro exiles who were carrying out hit-and-run raids into Cuba, not only attacking Cuban military targets, but those of Russia as well. It has been alleged that that Jean Souetre met with the CIA's William Harvey who was in charge of the ZR/RIFLE assassination plots in which both QJ/WIN and WI/ROGUE/1 took part in.

It is believed that Souetre met with Harvey at Plantation Key in Florida to plot strategy. At one point, a number of Cuban exiles were arrested by British police at a training camp in the Bahamas. Souetre was also said to have met with retired Army General Edwin Walker, who was fired by JFK for inciting his troops with right wing propaganda while he was on active duty. After the Kennedy assassination, the FBI would accuse Lee Harvey Oswald of trying to kill General Edwin Walker in his Dallas home by firing a shot through the window. The Walker incident was one of the unsolved mysteries surrounding the Kennedy assassination aftermath.

According to researchers looking into the events at Plantation Key, Souetre told Walker that ten Cuban exiles were to be sent to the Lake Pontchartrain camp from Miami in July 1963, where they were to receive further military training. At the time that the New

Orleans training camps were in existence, David Ferrie, Guy Banister and the other anti-Castro crowd all showed up at one time or another in these camps, and it has been written that at one point, Souetre met Lee Oswald at one of these camps and may have introduced himself to Oswald as "Alfred from Cuba."

An incident that involved the Cuban exiles training in New Orleans was the so-called Houma incident. The story was told to New Orleans DA Jim Garrison by Gordon Novel, who was accused of conspiracy to burglarize the munitions bunker at Houma, LA. The story goes that David Ferrie, Sergio Arcacha Smith, and Gordon Novel, went to the air base at Houma in 1961. They stole land mines, hand grenades, and rifle grenades that belonged to the French oil exploration company called Schlumberger Corporation. The munitions were then divvied up between Banister and Ferrie and were then sent on to the Cuban exiles in Miami.

In an article in the April 25, 1967 issue of the *New Orleans States Item,* Novel "told a number of friends and intimates that he was a CIA operative and will use this role to battle Garrison's charges, if he is returned to New Orleans to face accusations that he burglarized an oil service company's munitions bunker in nearby Terrebonne, Parish."

The article in the newspaper went on to say, "To friends and associates, Novel has said that the munitions burglary was no burglary at all-but a war materials pickup made at the direction of his CIA contact." Novel further said that the munitions held at Houma were supposed to have been used in the upcoming invasion of Cuba at the Bay of Pigs. Novel also boasted that he worked for the CIA in New Orleans before April, 1961 and used as his cover, a job with the Evergreen Advertising Agency which was a CIA front organization."

Other men who took part in the clandestine operations at the New Orleans training camps besides Jean Souetre were Gerry Patrick Hemming and Frank Sturgis. Hemming was an ex-Marine who at one time, worked for the Castro regime before changing sides. He operated his own anti-Castro organization in Florida in the early 1960s and boasted to all who would listen that he was an CIA operative. He also said that he was offered a contract to kill JFK by certain individuals whom he would not name but turned them down. Hemming ran a para-military group called "Interpen," or the Intercontinental Penetration Force" whose members were often times seen taking military training in the Florida Everglades. The FBI closely watched Hemming's Interpen and a number of them were charged with violations of the Neutrality Act.

Frank Sturgis was one of the men arrested for his participation in the Watergate burglary in 1972, as well as a militant anti-Castro organizer in Florida. During the heyday of the 1960s, Sturgis was responsible for many forays into Cuba, along with other militant, anti-Castro exiles who brought the shooting war to Castro's island. Sturgis, who also went by the name "Frank Fiorini," headed up a group called the International Anti-Communist Brigade. He was a prime player in the post-Batista regime in Cuba and did security work for a number of the top casino operators in Havana in the pre-Castro days.

Both Hemming and Sturgis worked in conjunction with the New Orleans branch of the Cuban Revolutionary Council (CRC) which was headed by Sergio Arcacha Smith. Smith's CRC had an office in the same building-544 Camp Street in New Orleans-, as that of Guy Bannister and both men shared their rabid, anti-Castro sentiments. The CRC, along with Hemming and Sturgis set up a military training facility for Cuban exiles in 1962 in the swamps near New Orleans. Other groups which operated in the camps were members of the DRE, the 30th of November Movement and the MIRR.

This camp was located in Lacombe, Louisiana, near Lake Pontchartrain. One of the instructors in the camps was David Ferrie. Another person on whose land was used by the exiles was William McLaney. William McLaney was related to Mike McLaney who owned a casino in Havana called the Nacional. The feds raided the McLaney property on July 31, 1963, and confiscated a large quantity of dynamite, 100-pound aerial bomb casings, and other military equipment. In all, eleven men were arrested in the raid but were not charged and later released.

Another French Connection link to the Kennedy assassination centered around a 24-year-old private in the U.S. Army named Eugene B. Dinkin, serial number RA-76710292, who had quite an interesting story to tell (whether or not it is credible, is another matter entirely). Dinkin told the Warren Commission (which totally ignored his story) that there was a conspiracy on the life of President Kennedy—one week after it actually took place.

Eugene Dinkin was a Private first class who was serving in Metz, France. Before entering the army, Dinkin had studied psychology at the University of Illinois. He enlisted in the army in 1961, and took basic training at Fort Gordon, GA. His job in the army was that of a cryptographic operator, which was actually run by the National Security Agency, the super-secret department which is responsible for communications intercepts for the U.S. intelligence community. By March 1962, Dinkin was sent to the 529th Ordinance Company in France as a "crypto operator." In the military intelligence pecking order, a person with a "crypto clearance" is considered a highly valued commodity.

Private Dinkin did his job well, and it was only in September 1963, that things seemed to go awry. One day during troop formation, Private Dinkin began a long, 25-minute speech on how the U.S. government was stockpiling atomic bombs, a rather strange subject in which a Private First Class was to give. The subject of Dinkin's talk was sent to Lt. Colonel John Lippincott of the Pentagon's Legislative Office. Shortly thereafter, Private Dinkin was given a psychiatric exam after which, it was advised that his access to classified materials should be denied.

But Dinkin had other, more serious matters on his mind than the stockpiling of U.S. atomic weapons: a plot on the life of the president that was being planned by elements of the right wing in the United States.

According to CIA declassified documents released to the public in recent years, Private Dinkin's first allegation was sent to then Attorney General Robert Kennedy in an October 22, 1962 letter.

In his note, Private Dinkin told RFK that his brother was going to be assassinated on November 28, 1963 and if it succeeded, it would be blamed on a "communist or a Negro." Furthermore, said Dinkin, the plot was to be engineered by certain elements in the American military establishment, and that a subsequent coverup would ensue. He closed his letter by pleading with Robert Kennedy that a representative of the Attorney General be sent to Metz, France to talk to him concerning his allegations.

Dinkin had no illusions concerning what might happen once

his letter was sent to Robert Kennedy, and on October 25, he went AWOL and headed for Luxembourg in order to find a representative of the American government to tell his story to. At the American embassy he tried to get an appointment with the U.S. Ambassador but he was out "playing tennis," and could not be reached. He did, however, have a hurried meeting with the U.S. Charge' d' affairs, Mr. Cunningham who promised to relay his message.

On November 3, after briefly returning to his base in Metz, France, Dinkin again went AWOL, this time heading for Geneva, Switzerland where he told his tale to the editor of the *Geneva Diplomat.* What reaction the editor of the paper had is not known. But what is known according to documents on the Dinkin case released by the CIA, and given to the Warren Commission is this.

A memo on the Dinkin case was sent to J. Lee Rankin who was the General Council of the Warren Commission entitled "Allegations of Pfc. Eugene Dinkin U.S. Army, Relative to Assassination Plot Against President Kennedy as transmitted to Warren Commission."

The allegation by Dinkin was sent to the White House, the Department of State and the FBI, along with a copy to the Secret Service.

"On 6 and 7 November 1963, he appeared in the press room of United Nations Office in Geneva and told reporters he was being persecuted. He also wished to alert the world to the U.S. Government "Propaganda Campaign." Army reports show that he voluntarily returned to his unit in Metz on or about 11 November, 1963.

"Around 26 November, after President Kennedy had been assassinated, a Geneva journalist named Alex de Fontaines, stringer for *Time-Life,* and correspondent for Radio Canada, was recounting Private Dinkin's story to the Paris office of *Time-Life* recounting Private Dinkin's visit to Geneva and quoting Dinkin as having said that "they" were plotting against President Kennedy and that "something" would happen in Texas. Des Fontaines had been prompted to do this by an unidentified female reporter who had recalled such statements by Dinkin; des Fontaines thought he recalled he had heard Dinkin say something like that also, and although he did not really believe that Dinkin had grounds for his statements when he made them, he filed the story just to be sure."[95]

The document concludes by saying, "All aspects of this story were known, as reported above, by U.S. military authorities and have been reported by military attache' cable through military channels."

Dinkin was arrested by an officer of the Army's CIC (Counter Intelligence Crop) and put in the brig. On November 13, he was sent to the hospital ward at Landstuhl General Hospital for "examination."

Dinkin was still in the hospital psychiatric ward on November 22, 1963, when he heard the news of President Kennedy's death. He next day he was paid a visit by someone in civilian clothes who said he was with the Secret Service. The agent closely questioned Dinkin about who might have killed JFK, why the day was changed, and other matters relating to the president's death. Dinkin told his questioners that he would not talk further, as long as he was being kept under wraps.

The Warren Commission, in Commission Document 1107, reports "that Colonel W.L. Adams, Jr., of Army Intelligence, stated in 1964 that Dinkin was the subject of a closed investigation by the Office of the Assistant Chief of Staff, G-2, United States Army Communications Zone, Europe."

In early December, Dinkin was sent home to Walter Reed Hospital in Washington, D.C. for further treatment. In his therapy sessions, Dinkin was told that his warnings about the assassination of President Kennedy were really a projection on his part of hostility towards authority figures. Dinkin said that he was drugged and given a test by a doctor who told him to free associate a list of words for a study he was conducting. Shortly after his hospitalization, Dinkin was given a medical discharge from the U.S. Army.

While the Dinkin allegations have nothing to do with either Jean Souetre or Michael Mertz, the story is just one more unexplained event that took place prior to the assassination that still aren't fully answered.

---

[95]RIF No. 1993.06.10.16:04:56:400000 "Allegations of Ffc Eugene Dinkin, U.S. Army, Relative to Assassination." 5/19/1964.

* * *

Unlike the real Michael Mertz who did not like to talk to the press about his past, Jean Souetre surely did. The Souetre story was picked up by a French publication called *Le Quotien de Paris,* on 1 January, 1984. The paper wrote a detailed story about Souetre and Mertz, giving its readers valuable information on both men, and their possible links to the Kennedy assassination.

A reporter from the French paper found the ex-Army paratrooper and had a lengthily conversation with him. It seems that Captain Souetre had read the National Enquirer's story about him and denied most of its charges. "I was very much surprised at the visit of a reporter from the Enquirer," he said. "Their sources are very shaky. They are based on a report written by an American lawyer, B. Fensterwald, a tissue of unlikelihood which blend, in a crafty juggling of names, dates, and other facts from sources devoted to systematic disinformation. That's how this "report" claims that I was in Dallas on the day of the murder under the name of Mertz, whom I knew very well in 59 when he was also a captain in the French army in Algeria where he worked for SDECE before reconverting as a double agent against the OAS, had on the contrary taken over my name. What for? Mertz, who had infiltrated as an agent provocateur in our organization notably as a participant in an abortive attack against de Gaulle could indeed have been in the U.S. in Dallas the day of the murder, and, passing himself off as me, started the rumor that the OAS was in on it just to make things look black for the CNR at a time when Bidault-Soustelle were trying to get help from the U.S. secret services."[96]

Souetre, who knew Michael Mertz said, "It would be very interesting to question Michael Mertz on this matter, a guy who has a lot of publicity in the past, at the time of the discovery of a drug network between France and the U.S."

The article by the French paper, was full of detailed facts regarding the real Jean Souetre and Michael Mertz, and laid out a scenario by which they criticized the investigation done by Bernard Fensterwald on behalf of the Assassination Archives and

96 "This French Terrorist Accused of Murdering Kennedy". *Le Quotien de Paris,* 1 Jan, 1984" located in the Fensterwald Files at AARC.

Research Center. The French paper wrote of the Fensterwald investigation that,

> The Fensterwald report, which admits moreover that the American services, the FBI and CIA, found no trace of Souetre, gets its wires crossed at bit in the narration-deliberate error or accidental-of the "bio" of Captain Souetre who was in Spain, (at the time of the Kennedy assassination), and the "bio" of his counterpart, the very real Captain Mertz, the SDECE agent infiltrated into the OAS and whose role could very well be said to be crucial in this fairy tale of a false conspiracy against Kennedy which may have originated in one of the darker episodes of the struggle against the OAS. Different factions of the French secret services went at it hammer and tongs to produce disinformation and provocation.

In the files on Jean Souetre at the Assassination Archives in Washington, there is a transcript of a conversation that a researcher (not named in the file) who tracked down Souetre in France that relates to his observations on the Kennedy killing. The person who wrote the notes said Souetre was contacted by a unknown person in Divonne-Lef-Baines, about 10 miles from Geneva, Switzerland, and the Frenchman said the evidence compiled by the CIA after the assassination of JFK on him were false. He said he was not in the United States on November 22, 1963 and that the only time he was in America was in 1974 or 1975. At the time of Kennedy's assassination he was Barcelona, Spain as an advisor to General Gardy, a high ranking OAS officer who had fled France. He said that if he was called to testify in any legal situation regarding the Kennedy killing he would be able to bring witnesses to back up his story.

Souetre said that by 1975, he had never been contacted by any law enforcement agency of the United States, the CIA, FBI, until he was visited by two men who were posing as journalists about two years previously whom he believed were really FBI agents in disguise. Souetre said that after the visit by these two men, he made inquiries with friends in French intelligence whom he refers to as "Special Services." They told him that, "another military officer resembling him in physical and facial details, was in fact in Dallas, Texas on the day of the shooting. This man claims that Souetre was traveling under his identity." Souetre said that he knows who this man is, knew that he was still living at the time (1975), knew that this man had committed murders in his career, had served in prison, was expelled from the army, made his way from France to Canada in 1961. He said the man in question was Michael Mertz.

The man who wrote the piece on Souetre said that the Frenchman was a "tall, distinguished looking man with grey hair over his ears and has a manner of a gentleman." He was wearing a double-breasted high-quality grey-striped suit and that he was the Director of the plush Divonne Casino. Their first meeting was on the steps of the casino where Souetre refused to allow a tape recorder to be used. He said that he was aware of the allegations being used against him but would not talk about them at that time. He asked the interviewer if he came back in two days he'd provide more detailed information to him. They met two days later, seated at a bar near the gaming room. Their talk was friendly, but Souetre refused to answer many questions put to him regarding French intelligence sources and about certain aspects of his life.

He did say, however, "My first knowledge of being suspected of involvement in the affair of President Kennedy came a little under two years ago. I was telephoned by someone in the U.S., a friend, you could say, who told me I was a suspect in the assassination. He said he had a document that would surely interest me which had come to him from the FBI. He said I would be interested to read it and sent it to me by mail. When I read it, I could not take it seriously. The allegations were too preposterous."

He then said something that flies in the face of what we know about the real Jean Souetre. He said, "I told them that I am telling you now that I did not know the dentist, Dr. Alderson or any of the other people mentioned in the report. The only person I did know was Michael Mertz, who was suggested in this report and by the "journalists," may have traveled to the USA using my identity. As a result of that revelation, I asked my friends at Special Services in Paris to make me a dossier on Mertz and it is a copy of this dossier that I am giving you now."

If what Souetre said is true, that he did not know Dr. Alderson, then someone is lying. It is a documented fact that the FBI questioned Dr. Alderson after the assassination and he told them that he knew Souetre in Rheims while he was in the French army. Maybe Souetre had forgotten who Dr. Alderson was. It was, after all, twelve years or more since he'd last seen him and maybe he did not remember who he was.

Souetre did have more to say about Michael Mertz. "From the dossier, I learned that Mertz is in fact a very dangerous man. I knew him in the 1950s when he was a fellow Army officer in Algiers before their independence. And then, the formation of the OAS, when he had tried to infiltrate our organization but was disallowed because we thought he was not capable of membership. The last I heard of him was about 1960. However, now I would very much like to ask him what he was doing in Dallas on November 22, 1963 and evidently traveling under my name. The FBI documents say that Michael Mertz was my alias, but it is exactly the other way around-he used my identity to travel to the USA."[97]

Souetre expanded more on Mertz and his involvement in the OAS at the time he knew him.

"For an officer in the Army who was involved in intelligence work, it would not be difficult to obtain a full passport and identity in this way. When he was refused membership in the OAS, I had no idea of what he did, but it is possible that he entered some other organization which among its targets could well have been the OAS and President Kennedy. This type of confusion was common at the time. It is known that among the many attempts (23) to assassinate President de Gaulle, may of them were carried out by French secret service, not only to compromise the OAS, but to make de Gaulle look like a walking miracle, or a superhuman being. It is no secret that the OAS wanted to assassinate de Gaulle, but we were never successful. At the time of the assassination attempt in Petit-Clamart, I was named in all the French newspapers as being the organizer of the attack. But it was not true because it was the OAS interior branch (in France) which organized it. I was a member of the OAS exterior" (outside France).

"I can state categorically that I have never traveled under the

97 Ibid.

name of Michael Mertz. I did use false names as an OAS officer, and during my involvement in the various mercenary soldier operations in Africa... But never Michael Mertz. It is he who used my identity."

Let's back up a minute and remember what Souetre said. He stated that he was a soldier-of-fortune in Africa and used false names at that time. Both QJ/WIN and QI/ROGUE/1 were both soldiers-of-fortune, were both in Africa, and used false names. By his own description, could Souetre have been either QJ/WIN or WI/ROGUE/1?

He then talked about the Kennedy assassination. "In any case, the OAS, of which I was a committed member, have no ambitions to kill President Kennedy. Why should they? They were interested only in France and keeping its territories in Africa. It is possible that there may be other organizations, still in existence today, which were against DeGaulle and Kennedy. It is possible that Mertz may well have been a member of this organization, but if he was in Dallas, I am sure he would have not been there alone. In any case, if he was there, he had gone to a lot of trouble to leave his traces so that if he was discovered, it would look as if it was me."

The writer then said that Souetre spoke to him in French and said, "I would suggest that you go to see Mertz. But he is a very dangerous man who has a criminal record of murder involvement with drug organizations, and violence. He was thrown out of France in 1961 and went to Canada, although since the amnesty against all the OAS and other anti-government terrorists, he has been allowed to live in France. He was sent to prison in 1971 in France for drug trafficking and according to my friends in Special Services, people who have visited him at his home have been known to disappear, never to be seen again. Knowing the man and his record as I do, his answer to the question of whether he killed President Kennedy or not would be no comment. But I believe that certainly *there is a French Connection to the assassination and that Mertz may well have been involved* "(italics by author). "Though if he was, I am sure he was not acting alone."

The writer of this long memo which I have just summarized, ended by saying, "I may be completely wrong, he may have produced a marvelous confidence trick and to the nature of his real personality. But he stuck me as being basically sincere, though I suspect his evasiveness is connected with his enduring connections to French intelligence. Ostensibly, he is extremely experienced in military matters, still fit, and in good form, and I suspect still active in espionage, though not on a permanent basis."

Another person who found, and had an extensive conversation with Jean Souetre was a French researcher named Monique Lajoruande who talked with the Frenchman on June 9, 1999. We learn about his incident in the book *Triangle of Death,* by Brad O'Leary and L.E. Seymour that was published in 2003.

Souetre told Ms. Lajournade that there were some similarities between him and Michel Mertz; they were both parachute captains, and had links with the OAS. However, Mertz was ten years older than Souetre, and noted that Mertz had served in the "Maquis," the French Resistance forces in World War 2.

Souetre said that Mertz infiltrated the OAS and pretended to be an active OAS member. He said his job was to penetrate the OAS and expose what they were doing. Souetre first met Mertz in the late 1950s and still knew him in 1961. After Souetre was arrested, he did not meet with him again. The French Secret Service, according to Souetre, took an active interest in Mertz and wanted to take him on as one of their own for their own reason, to protect President de Gaulle while he went on various international trips. Souetre told Ms. Lajournade that Mertz was a very dangerous man and that, "he also certainly could've been put in touch with the people who were preparing the assassination of Kennedy. Mertz could have been used to inform the French Secret Service about this, and to falsely implicate the OAS."

He talked more about the possible role of Mertz in the Kennedy assassination by telling Ms. Lajournade that, "What I find very strange is the fact that he was there in Dallas the day of the crime and under my identity. What was he doing there that day? It's obvious that he knew that something was going to happen, and that by implicating Captain Souetre he could blame the CNR."

Souetre said that Mertz was a member of the French intelligence service, the SDECE and that he also was a member of the Marseille heroin network headed by Antoine Guerini. He said that Mertz worked for a man named M. Sanguinetti who was against the OAS and that this man had Mertz infiltrate the OAS. When the reporter asked him if he recognized the name Michael Roux, (who was supposed to have been in Dallas on November 22), he said no, and insisted that it was Mertz who was impersonating him in Dallas that day.

Earlier in this book, I described a meeting between certain CIA agents and Souetre in the latter's attempt to get the American government interested in ousting de Gaulle. The CIA agents told Souetre they wanted no part of the deal. When asked about this incident, Souetre gave more details. He said that the meeting was not for anti-De Gaulle purposes, but to ask for CIA assistance in setting up a radio program which was anti-Communist in nature. He only wanted the CIA's financial help in setting up this network, nothing more, nothing less.

Souetre expanded on his reaction to both Mertz and the Kennedy assassination. He questioned why the United States government did not interview Mertz as to why he was in Dallas instead of whisking him out of the country so fast. He hinted that if the FBI had done a full interview with Mertz they could have learned of his association with the mysterious Mr. Sanguinetti of the OAS, of his close ties with the Mafia in the United States, and the totality of his heroin smuggling actions. "He (Mertz) never got interrogated or worried. Instead, he died in a luxurious castle in France with lots of money. I can tell you that as a French military officer, one doesn't earn much money."

"I ask myself why. Why was Mertz protected from the Americans by the French services? Could it be that the French services were afraid the Americans would discover the truth?"

He said that he was convinced that some people in the high echelons of the French intelligence service prepared phony passports for Mertz's use and helped facilitate his trip to the United States in November 1963.

Souetre knew a little about Mertz's heroin connections and was convinced that the French Intelligence Service, the DGSE, received cash to finance their drug business with the drugs that were sold in the U.S. "And Mertz," said Souetre, "particularly could have used the American military services that got sent back to the States to transport in their baggage significant quantities of drugs. I think that at that period the case has been discovered by the narcotic office in the States and that there must have been some echoes in the press. But this is not something that has been exploited. Here too, it wasn't in the interest of the French to make noise about that. Now the Americans and especially those at the narcotic office should have information about that in their archives."[98]

Authors O'Leary and Seymour make the case that Michael Mertz, not Jean Souetre, had the means, motive and opportunity to kill JFK. They also make another interesting observation, one that needs to be analyzed; that the person in the U.S. government responsible for expelling Souetre or Mertz out of the U.S. after the assassination, and not looking further into the case, was none other than the dead president's younger brother, Robert Kennedy.

The authors ask why the French assassin, while he was in custody, was not fully debriefed by the FBI in order to ascertain why he was in the country and for what purpose. This is a reasonable consideration but what the authors say next is open to much debate. They postulate that Robert Kennedy's agenda at that time was to protect the reputation of his deceased brother from political charges that might come to light down the road. They claim that if the facts of the president's knowledge of the CIA-Mafia plots to kill Fidel Castro, (that question is still open to debate, fifty years later), the allegations that Chicago mob boss Sam Giancana had funneled mob money to JFK's 1960 presidential election via his powerful father, former Ambassador Joseph P. Kennedy, and the claim that the president had sanctioned the coup d' etat that resulted in the murder of South Vietnamese president, Diem, were ever exposed, the president's historical reputation would be in tatters. If it were ever absolutely proved that Michael Mertz was the French assassin who killed JFK, a man who had known links to the Marseille mob, and was a noted international heroin dealer who infiltrated the OAS and saved de Gaulle's life, both the long standing reputation of the United States and France would permanently be harmed.

However, what was not known at that time immediately after the assassination was that Robert Kennedy *did* take private

---

[98] O'Leary. Brad & Seymour, L.E., *Triangle of Death*, WND Books, Nashville, TN, 2003, Page 137.

measures to try and find out what happened to his brother. RFK never talked openly about the events on Dealey Plaza, but behind the scenes he was skeptical at best. One week after the assassination, both Robert Kennedy and former CIA Director Allan Dulles (who was a member of the Warren Commission), received a tip that lacked a signature, saying that Jack Ruby was a Mafia "finger man" or a hit man. The source said, that "If my memory services me right, Jack Ruby (the man who killed Lee Oswald in the basement of the Dallas Police Department on November 24, 1963), was visiting Syndicate Members in San Diego between the last months of 1961 and the early months of 1962. The meeting of the Syndicate Members was at the Brass Rail, a bar-restaurant … It was used as a homosexual bar, much as the New York Syndicate under the former Gallo gang used some dozen homosexual bars as 'fronts.'"[99]

Days after Ruby killed Oswald, Bobby sent one of his most trusted aids, Walter Sheridan, to find out as much information as he could on Ruby and his possible mob connections. Years later, Walter Sheridan made an investigation of the efforts by New Orleans DA Jim Garrison in his probe of the assassination of JFK on behalf of NBC news which was doing a show on the assassination, especially as it concerned the New Orleans aspect of the case (Oswald, Ferrie, Shaw, Banister). Sheridan concluded that Garrison's efforts were nothing but a sham investigation, calling it "an enormous fraud" involving, "bribery and intimidation of witnesses." At one point in his career, Sheridan worked closely with RFK in the latter's attempt to investigate mob influence in the United States and was trusted as a loyal lieutenant in the cause by the younger Kennedy.

During his Ruby probe, Sheridan found credible evidence that Ruby had been paid off in Chicago by a friend of Jimmy Hoffa, Bobby's worst enemy. Sheridan said that Ruby had been given cash from Allen Dorfman, who was closely linked with Hoffa and the Chicago mob. One of the men whom the HSCA speculated had the "means, motive, and opportunity" to kill JFK was Sam Giancana, the mob boss of Chicago. After hearing the news from

---

[99] Talbot, David, *Brothers: The Hidden History of the Kennedy Years*, The Free Press, New York, 2007, Page 21.

Sheridan, RFK sent one of his top attorneys in the Justice Department, Robert Peloquin to Chicago to see what he could find.

Another man whom Robert Kennedy dispatched to find out about Ruby's mob links was Julius Draznin, who was a federal labor lawyer and confidant of Kennedy's. Draznin would later write a report saying that Ruby was a mob enforcer and had a penchant for armed violence. When RFK read Ruby's phone records he would comment that, "The list was almost a duplicate of the people I called before the Rackets Committee."

During the Thanksgiving holiday, only one week after the murder in Dallas, the Kennedy family spent a tear filled gathering at Hyannis Port, Massachusetts. Besides the grieving family were some of Bobby's closets friends and colleagues at Justice, including Walter Sheridan. Getting Sheridan alone, Bobby asked him what he'd learned about the assassination. Sheridan reluctantly told Bobby that he suspected that Hoffa was involved in the president's death. He told Bobby that he learned that Hoffa was in Miami, Florida at a restaurant when he heard the news of the president's assassination. Upon getting the news, Hoffa "got up on the table and cheered. At least, that's what we heard."

Bobby later sent Sheridan down to Dallas to poke around and try and find any more leads. Nothing substantial came of out that trip.

A third man whom the Kennedy family trusted to find out about the president's death was an unlikely candidate, the artist, and family confidant of both the president and Jackie Kennedy, William Walton. Walton was a World War 2 veteran who landed at Normandy at D-Day. He was trusted by both the president and his wife who saw in Walton, a man who could be completely trusted. In 1963, the president appointed Walton as the chairman of the Fine Arts Commission.

On November 22, 1963, Walton was supposed to fly to the Soviet Union on an official trip to oversee the opening of a fine arts exhibit for the U.S. Information Agency in Leningrad and Moscow. Upon hearing of the news of the assassination, the trip was cancelled. Later, at Bobby's urging, Walton left the States on November 29, 1963, once again, bound for Russia. However, known to only Bobby and Jackie Kennedy, Walton carried a secret message to the leaders of the Soviet government.

Among the people whom Walton met in Russia was the Soviet journalist Aleksei Adzhubei, who was the son-in-law of Premier Nikita Khrushchev. Adzhubei was also an editor of the Soviet newspaper, *Izvestia.* In their talks, Walton told the Russian that the United States had not been taken over by the far right wing, and that the new president, Lyndon Johnson, would continue with JFK's policy of lessening the tensions with the Soviet's. Before their conversation ended, Walton asked the journalist if he could get him an appointment with a Russian whom Bobby knew quiet well, Georgi Bolshakov. Bolshakov was a Russian intelligence agent who had been stationed in Washington only a few years before and both he and Robert Kennedy became friends, despite their political differences. During the Cuban Missile Crisis of 1962, Bolshakov carried secret messages to and from Washington to Moscow which helped defuse the crisis.

Walton was instructed not to inform the U.S. Ambassador in Russia of the real purpose of his trip and sought out Bolshakov to give a top-secret message to Khrushchev. In complete secrecy, Walton gave the message to Bolshakov in a restaurant in Moscow. Over their meal, Walton told him an incredible story straight from Bobby and Jackie. The message was that JFK had been killed by a wideranging conspiracy in the United States. "Perhaps there was only one assassin, but he did not act alone," was the message given to RFK's friend. Walton said that both Bobby and Jackie believed that there were others behind "Oswald's gun," and that despite the fact that Oswald had defected to the Soviet Union that he was not acting on behalf of any foreign leader. Walton also said that, "Dallas was the ideal location for such a crime."

Walton told Bolshakov some interesting information regarding two of JFK's most trusted people in his administration; Defense Secretary Robert McNamara and National Security Advisor, McGeorge Bundy. He said that on the day after the assassination, with the American government completely paralyzed following the tragic events that had just taken place, that McGeorge Bundy was the defacto head of government, making the decisions until the new president, Lyndon Johnson, could take command.

He said that the only member of the Kennedy cabinet whom the Russians could trust in the days ahead, was Defense Secretary McNamara. JFK had chosen McNamara from the Ford Motor

Company, despite his lack of government experience. During his tenure as Defense Chief, McNamara became close not only to the president, but to Bobby as well. Walton told his Russian friend that McNamara shared the late president's goals of peaceful coexistence with the Soviet Union and told him that Premier Khrushchev would find in McNamara, a receptive person whom he could trust.

Walton however, did not have kind words on the new president, Lyndon Johnson. There was no love lost between the Kennedy's and LBJ, especially as the 1964 re-election campaign neared. There were rumors going around Washington that Kennedy was going to drop LBJ from the 1964 presidential ticket and replace him with someone more attuned to Kennedy's political thinking. He told Bolshakov that Kennedy had made a "dreadful mistake" in choosing Johnson for the VP spot in 1960. Walton described Johnson as "a clever timeserver," "who would be incapable of realizing Kennedy's unfinished plans." He also said that he feared Johnson was tied to closely with big business interests in the United States.

Walton told Bolshakov that RFK planned to stay in his post as Attorney General until the end of 1964 when he would seek the office of Governor of Massachusetts. In time, he intended to run for president to fulfil his brother's unfinished legacy. He also wanted to reassure the Kremlin leaders that if Bobby became president, he'd continue his brother's policy of peaceful coexistence with the Soviet's.

Immediately following his secret meeting with William Walton, Bolshakov informed his superiors in the GRU about what had transpired. After hearing Bolshakov's account of the events in Dallas, an already shaken Kremlin was more worried than usual about what further actions might be taken in Washington. The Kremlin leaders believed that the Kennedy assassination was undertaken by right-wing elements in the United States because of Kennedy's interest in a rapprochement with the Kremlin.

After the assassination, Soviet intelligence did its own digging into the events in Dallas and came up with their own view of what happened that day. In November 1963, a reliable Polish intelligence source, an American who owned some business, said that he learned that the assassination was carried out by three wealthy Texas businessmen, all of whom hated JFK. The men in question were H.L. Hunt, Sid Richardson, and Clint Murchison. All these men hated Kennedy who was instrumental in having a law passed in October 1962, which put new tax provisions on their lucrative oil business.

Further evidence compiled by the KGB, implicated H.L. Hunt in the president's death. Their informant was a reporter for the *Baltimore Sun,* newspaper, Paul Ward. Ward told the KGB that H.L. Hunt was the point man for the group who planned Kennedy's assassination. Ward said that Hunt had instructed Jack Ruby to offer Lee Oswald money to kill JFK. Oswald was instructed not to inform his wife or mother about what he was about to do.

According to the story, "Oswald was a most appropriate figure for staging the terrorist act against Kennedy because of his past—he implicated the USSR, Cuba, and the Communist Party of the U.S." Ward said that after Oswald was arrested, their sources informed them that he was going to spill his guts at trial and he had to be killed before that could happen. Ruby was then dispatched to kill Oswald.[100]

The Russians were not the only ones who believed that a right-wing conspiracy killed JFK. The French also had that same view. The KGB said that their informers in the French government had come to the conclusion that Kennedy had been killed as a result of a right-wing conspiracy because of Kennedy's domestic and foreign policy pronouncements, along with Kennedy's detente with the Soviet Union. The French ambassador to the UN said Soviet intelligence, "believed that the assassination was a carefully organized act by a determined group on the far right of American politics."

There is one more thing to add to the Jean Souetre story. One of the men whom the late Bernard Fensterwald employed on his European trip was Gilbert Le Cavelier, who was a police officer in France and was an ally of de Gaulle. Gilbert Le Cavelier told author Dick Russell, (the author of "*The Man Who Knew Too*

---

[100] Fursenko, Aleksandr, & Naftali, Timothy, *One Hell of A Gamble: The Secret History of the Cuban Missile Crisis: Khrushchev, Castro & Kennedy 1958-1964.* W.W. Norton & Co., New York, 1997. Page 348.

Much"), that Jean Souetre traveled widely throughout Latin America and the Caribbean area from 1962 to 1971. Both locations were the prime staging areas for the CIA's secret bases which were used to train the anti-Castro exiles who would eventually embark on their ill fated invasion of Cuba in April, 1961. One of these countries was Nicaragua whose leader, President Somoza, allowed the CIA to use his land as a staging and training area for Brigade 2506 in their preparations for the Bay of Pigs. Le Cavelier said that Souetre, at that time, lived in Madrid, Spain which was ruled by the fascist dictator, Francisco Franco. Le Cavelier told Fensterwald that there were close ties between the anti-Castro exiles living and training in Florida and members of the French extreme right wing. He then made a startling statement-that Jean Souetre met Howard Hunt in Madrid." Another person who was supposed to have been at that meeting was Jean Claude Perez who was the OAS intelligence chief.

Dick Russell wrote in his book that he had a conversation with Steve Rivele in 1992 concerning Souetre. Rivele told Russell that Souetre had ties with the Corsican mob, and he further said that, "I spoke with an undercover narcotics agent in Marseille who had been following him (Souetre) for years, and there is no question he was on the Paris end of the drug traffic."

Jean Souetre was not the only man to travel throughout Latin American and the Caribbean. Note that both Lucien Sarti and Christian David were in the region during these years, working for Auguste Ricord and Antoine Guerini. Lucien Sarti was a Corsican and Jean Souetre was French. It is not inconceivable, (though there is no positive link between them), that both men may have met each other during their drug smuggling travels in the region. Their areas of expertise were so common, and the men who employed them may very well have known who each of them was.

Jean Souetre was a known French assassin who had links with the anti-de Gaulle OAS. He said he was in Spain at the time of the Kennedy assassination and said that someone else, most likely Michael Mertz, was using his name while the latter was possibly in Dallas at the time of the Kennedy assassination. He took part in at least one attempt to kill de Gaulle, had tenuous links with some members of the radical right wing in the United States-General Edwin Walker, and possibly CIA agent, E. Howard Hunt. He met with some members of the CIA and asked for their help in setting up a radio program which was anti-Communist in nature. He said the only time he was in the United States was in 1974 or 1975. He knew a great deal about Michael Mertz and used his old intelligence connections to get the French secret service files on him (a feat that made him in good standing with at least some part of the French secret services, despite his OAS past). He declared that he never used the alias of Michael Mertz, said that he served in Africa as a soldier-of-fortune, and it is possible that he may have been the elusive QJ/WIN or possibly, WI/ROGUE. He said that they believed there was a French Connection to the Kennedy assassination, and that Mertz may have been involved.

Souetre was also involved in a plot to return Moise Tshombe to power in the Congo in 1967-68 and was said to be the leader of the attempted coup. Souetre's possible involvement in the Kennedy assassination was picked up by news organizations in the United States and Europe, the National Enquirer and the "Le Quotien de Paris. The FBI was interested in who Jean Souetre was, due to an inquiry by a writer named David Duffy who wanted to know if and why Jean Souetre was expelled from Dallas after the assassination of the president.

The CIA also had an interest in Jean Souetre. Sam Papich of the FBI sent a memo to D.J. Brennan on March 9, 1964 regarding a CIA analyst named Jane Roman. They wanted to know about any information her agency had given to the FBI by a letter dated July 12, 1963 to the State Department captioned "OAS Attempt to Enlist the Cooperation of the United States for its anti-de Gaulle Activities." Jane Roman also gave the FBI a picture of Souetre, and a copy of a CIA report dated June 25, 1963 with the caption, "Alleged Plans of Secret Army Organization in Portugal for post de Gaulle Takeover in France."

Besides CIA and FBI interest in Souetre, on March 5, 1964, the INS (Immigration Service) searched its files on Souetre and found nothing on him or his aliases of Mertz or Roux.

The French also were trying desperately to locate Souetre. In 1964, President De Gaulle was planning to make a visit to Mexico and the government put out a worldwide, all points alert for Souetre and any other militant OAS member whom they thought might be a threat to the president. In that vein, the French government asked the U.S. to contact FBI's New York office to see if they had any news on the whereabouts of the elusive Frenchman.

Souetre used another alias of "Eugene Constant," and brought with him to Belgium a group of 50 mercenaries, most of whom were French or Belgium. In the summer of 1967, Souetre and his mercenary friends were given identity papers from an organization called PIDE (Portugese Intelligence), before heading for Luanda, Angola. As mentioned before, Souetre was to be part of a plan to re-instate Moise Tshombe to power in the Congo.

In the years 1962-1971, he lived in Spain but traveled a lot to the Western Hemisphere where he used other aliases. He lived in Martinique where he used the cover as the director of a sugar refinery whose owner lived in France. He was also a director of an industrial development firm in the Caribbean called S.D.D.I.C. Records in Martinique say that Souetre lived on the island from 1972 to 1975 and then went back to Europe in February, 1975, after spending a short period of time in New York.

From July 1970 to October 1971, Souetre was involved with a number of renegade anti-De Gaulle organizations. He was the "section chief" of the ETEC, a "cover operation run by OAS veterans Charles Lascorz and Raymond Courbet." This group consisted of members of various groups including the SDECE (French intelligence), the SAC, and the OAS. Souetre was responsible for ETEC's relations with OAS exiles living in Spain, as well as with the Spanish Secret Police. He subsequently left the group after a falling out.

The OAS at that time was fiercely anti-communist in their political leanings and had similar allies in the United States (Banister, Ferrie, Shaw, General's Willoughby, a member of the John Birch Society, and General Edwin Walker), and the anti-Castro exiles who trained in the swamps near New Orleans where Souetre was supposed to have been.

The OAS's main objective was to keep Algeria in French hands, and deplored with violent acts, de Gaulle's decision to grant the territory is independence.

By the end of 1963, there was an international pool of about 2,000 to 3,000 highly trained and motivated assassins around the world, ready and willing to make a buck for any cause that came their way. If anyone wanted to find an assassin for a mission, this would be a logical area where one would go to find recruits.

The OAS did not like JFK because he backed de Gaulle's free Algeria position. As the late Bernard Fensterwald wrote in his deposition on the French Connection to the Kennedy assassination ("New Shaw/Allen FOIA Litigation" 8-3-82, RIF No. 104-10419-10012), "They believed, and rightfully so, that JFK had vetoed any U.S. help for the OAS. They made 33 attempts on the life of de Gaulle; why not one on the life of JFK?"

Besides the domestic plots to kill de Gaulle in France, their was a plot on his life when he visited New Orleans in May, 1963 (see Shaw/Allen deposition), and in Washington at the time of Kennedy's funeral. Fensterwald wrote that, "the OAS was active in the Western Hemisphere at that time."

What is obvious is that a number of branches of the U.S. government, the CIA, FBI, State Department, and INS, all were interested in Souetre and his possible presence in Dallas on November 22, 1963. It is not known if the U.S. government gave an official answer on the Souetre affair to Paris at that time (If they did, then that report might still be locked up in classified files). Whatever information they did have was not given to the Warren Commission during its 1964 investigation, and if they had done so, would the commissioners have been willing to follow upon that lead?

In his deposition, Bernard Fensterwald summed up the Souetre case by saying:

"According to French intelligence, Jean Rene Souetre, who also used the aliases Michael Mertz and Michael Roux, was in Dallas on the afternoon of November 22, 1963 and was "expelled" by the U.S. Government within 48 hours, possibly to Mexico. The French were concerned because of an up-coming visit by de Gaulle to Mexico, and they considered Souetre a threat to de Gaulle's safety."

"All indications are that Souetre was a trained and experienced terrorist and perfectly capable of murder."

"Equally, if it were in fact Mertz who was in Dallas instead of or in addition to Souetre, he too was a trained and experienced terrorist."

There is no indication that either Souetre or Mertz had any

"legitimate reason" to be in Dallas on that particular day, or why they should be "expelled" by the U.S. Government."

"As to Michael Roux, his story (as told by the FBI) is a bit incredulous. Additionally, the FBI doggedly refuses to identify his two Fort Worth, Texas patrons, hence making it impossible to check his alibi. As to his capacity or incapacity as an assassin, we know only that he too was a deserter from the French Army in Algeria."

The HSCA was going to look into the French Connection to the Kennedy assassination but did not have time to do so before it closed up shop.

All available evidence points to the fact that Jean Souetre would have been a perfect candidate to make an attempt on the life of JFK. He was known by both French and U.S. intelligence services as a man with a dangerous past, despite his attempts to make himself less important. If, what he says is true that he was in Spain at the time of the president's death, then that leaves one huge question. If not Souetre, then who was responsible for the crime of the century?

Chapter 8

Who Was Mertz?

If a poll was taken by the members of the OAS during the early 1960s as to who was the most dangerous leader of the organization, it would probably have been a tie between Jean Souetre and Michael Mertz. Both men came out of the same league of assassins and spies, each well connected with the intelligence networks of France, each man posing a different threat to President de Gaulle and his bid for Algerian independence. However, there was one big difference between both men; Michael Mertz was big time heroin smuggler and dealer, a man well connected to the French Connection heroin ring that operated between Marseille and other points of the world. Unlike Jean Souetre, Michael Mertz was connected with both Santo Trafficante Jr, and Carlos Marcello, both of whom were directly linked in the worldwide shipment of narcotics, and were also prime suspects in the Kennedy assassination. According to authors Lamar Waldron and Thom Hartman in their exhaustive study of the Kennedy assassination called *Ultimate Sacrifice,* Mertz was part of the mob plots to kill JFK. In their research, both authors point to 24 facts that may link Michael Mertz as the infamous CIA assassin, QJ/WIN (more about that later in this chapter).

Michael Mertz was born in 1920 in the Mosellie area of France. Little is known of his early life but he was inducted (forcefully) into the German army in World War 2 in 1941. He was a born gunman and deserted in 1943. He then joined the French Resistance which received tremendous backing from the allies in their secret war against the Germans. It is not known if allied soldiers who secretly worked in France at the time knew, or had been introduced to Mertz, but it is not going out on a limb to say that the answer must have been yes. During his time in the

Resistance, he went by the code name "Captain Bapitise" and became one of its leaders. He operated in the Limoges area of France during the war and soon his reputation went viral. He was captured a number of times by the Germans but always managed to escape. Due to his heroic exploits during the war, he was made Chavalier of the Legion of Honor by de Gaulle in 1945. The citation was signed by de Gaulle himself and it stated that he captured 400 enemy prisoners, killed 20 Gestapo agents, and escaped 4 times. He later received the Liberation Medal and Croix de Guerre.

After the war ended, Mertz served with the Communist Maquis in the northwest of France as a "killer" for Communist chief of F.T.P. in Limoges. Those who were killed were disposed of "legally" for collaboration with the reds. The F.T.P. chief was a man named Guingouin.

In 1946, Mertz was inducted into the French army as a captain and went to Tilberg, Germany and served in the counter-espionage division. He soon applied for a transfer to the SDECE, and between 1946 and 1960 he made several trips to Morocco, Germany, Turkey and the Middle East for the SDECE.[101]

In 1947, Mertz married Paule Scheller Martel, the adopted daughter of Charles Martel, the operator of a famous bordello in Paris by the name of the Sphinx. The Sphinx operated during World War 2 and was operated by George Lemestre and his wife. In 1940, the Resistance smuggled George Lemestre out of Paris to southern France. Martel, who owned part of the Sphinx, remained in charge and often times Lemestre let in German officers. Martel was later captured by the Germans and put in a concentration camp. Charles Martel was a prominent member of the French underworld and drug smuggler (he died in 1966). His marriage to Martel's daughter, brought Mertz smack dab into the world of heroin smuggling that would become a large part of his life. At the time he married Paule, the elder Martel owned a number of brothels in Marseille and Paris and was in cahoots with two of the most noted drug smugglers of the day, named Spirito and Carbone.

101Correspondence from Hilaire du Berrier, Monte Carlo, Monaco, November 25, 1975 letter to "Norman" located at Assassination Archives, Washington, D.C.

Soon after the war ended, the local law closed the bordellos down and Martel switched over to more lucrative areas of income; drug smuggling in which Michael Mertz soon joined his father-in-law.

By 1960, Mertz had become part of two worlds, that of French intelligence in the name of the SDECE and as a up and coming narcotics smuggler who was illegally transporting heroin from France, to Canada, and the U.S.

During his stay with the SDECE, Mertz was introduced, and became quite friendly with a man named Alexander Sanguinetti, a Corsican who was born in Cairo, Egypt. His immediate superior was Jacque Foccart, who was the head of the SDECE. Colonel Foccart was a protégée of de Gaulle and he trusted him immensely. One of the clandestine jobs that de Gaulle gave to him was to seize the broadcast studios in France in case of a coup by rebels who opposed de Gaulle's rule. One of the men whom Col Foccart turned to was Michael Victor Mertz.

Mertz worked closely with a noted heroin dealer named Achilles Cecchini beginning in 1961 and by July 1971, they had both smuggled some $3 billion worth of heroin into the United States. Starting in 1960, Mertz received his heroin from the network owned by Joseph Orcini and Achilles Cesshini in France, and shipped it to North America where it was given to the Orcini group for distribution. On March 11, 1961, Mertz sailed on the ship "Liberte" from La Harve to New York with a Citroen in the ships cargo hold. The car contained 220 pounds of French heroin.

If Mertz thought that his life was nothing but wine and roses, he was in for a rude shock. In April 1961, Mertz was ordered by the SDECE back into military service with a very sensitive job; to infiltrate the OAS, the renegade, anti-de Gaulle organization that was anathema to all that de Gaulle stood for.

He joined an Air Force brigade under Colonel Barberot at the Center for Infantry Coordination, which was part of the French 11th Strike Battalion. It is believed that it was at this time that he first encountered Jean Souetre.

The hatred that most of the top members of the OAS (Algerian Secret Army) had for De Gaulle centered around his policy of independence for the territory of Algeria which had been in French possession for years. Most of the OAS opposition against de Gaulle came from disgruntled Army officers who wanted Algeria to stay part of France. In order to stop the independence of Algeria, they turned to acts of terror in France and its adjoining colonies. These acts of violence by its army leaders would not be tolerated by de Gaulle and he now declared war on them.

Like any good spy, Michael Mertz followed his orders and made his way to Algeria. He had to play his role with extreme caution, not wanting to blow his cover before his mission really began. He infiltrated the OAS in Algiers, fooling even those closets to him. He did his job so well that he was arrested by members of the French secret service (who may, or may not have known who he was) and sent to a detention camp for OAS ringleaders in July 1961.

On July 14, 1961, Mertz managed to get a note to his SDECE chiefs, Jacques Foccart, telling him that he had vital information to reveal. He said that the OAS was planning an attempt on the life of President de Gaulle at Point-sur-Seine, a bridge that the presidential party crossed almost every day. Mertz was told to go back to his camp and try and ascertain just when the assassination attempt would take place. The French security services, with Mertz's knowledge in tow, allowed the presidential motorcade to proceed to Point-sur-Seine as usual. When the convoy was attacked, the president's driver managed to swerve out of the way and avoided the looming catastrophe that almost killed the president and his party.

In the aftermath of the attempt on de Gaulle's life at Point-sur-Seine, all the plotters were eventually captured. They all went on trial with the exception of Michael Mertz. At the time that the other conspirators were facing trial, President de Gaulle owed Mertz his life and he allowed him to be whisked out of France to Canada (at the expense of a grateful nation), out of harms way.

One of the men who was primarily responsible for getting Mertz and his wife out of France was Alexander Sanguinetti of the SDECE. It seems that Mrs. Mertz who was a Canadian, asked Sanguinetti if he could aid her husband after his role in the foiled attempt on de Gaulle. Sanguinetti told her that he would make arrangements for her husband to be sent to Canada to start a new life.

Three months after Mertz fled to Canada, the French Defense Minister got a letter from a General Dodelier, a highranking military official. He wanted to know the whereabout of Mertz. Part of the letter read, "According to your request concerning what happened to Captain Mertz, we have been proceeding to an inquiry led by the Parisian Exelmans Police Headquarters, which revealed that Captain Mertz has been expelled to Canada."

From all the available evidence, it seems that not all parts of the French government were informed of the whereabouts of Michael Mertz. The circumstances of his expulsion from France were kept on a need to know basis, and it seems that a number of highranking members of the government did NOT need to know where he was. Only a few people in the intelligence and presidential palace knew the exact reason why Mertz was sent packing-he was a mole in the OAS-and they wanted to keep that information as safe as possible.

Mertz was now able to proceed in the new phase of his life, one that he'd been doing on and off for years; he used his SDECE connections to go back, full time, in the narcotics trade.

On October 11, 1961, Mertz managed to get back to France without any trouble. For the next eight years, he and his drug smuggling colleagues, were alleged to have smuggled over two tons of heroin to North America. He used the good graces of his father-in-law, Charles Martel to facilitate his thriving business and soon he was the man to be reckoned with in the drug cartel based in Marseille.

One of the men who Mertz worked closely with in the drug trade was Jean Bousquet, "wealthy French contractor," and a colleague of a famous Corsican drug smuggler named Paul Mondoloni, as well as Christian David (both Paul Mondoloni and Christian David would surface in Steve Rivele's investigation of the Kennedy assassination).

The American BNDD (Bureau of Dangerous Drugs) asked its Paris office to have the French government investigate both Mertz and Bousquet and an informer was put in their organization. Bousquet was arrested in France in June 1968 for the arrangement of 112 kilos of heroin bound for the United States. In their investigation of both Bousquet and Mertz, Bousquet said that in 1967, he and Mertz had shipped 730 kilos of heroin to the U.S. in a Citroen.

During the decade of the 1960s U.S. law enforcement

authorities tried in vain to have the French government arrest Mertz for his drug smuggling operation. However, their pleas fell on deaf ears as the SDECE wanted to protect Mertz for his heroics in saving de Gaulle at Point-sur-Seine. Mertz came to be known as one of the "untouchables" in France, a man who was better off on the run then in jail where his true identity and profession, if revealed, would highly embarrass the de Gaulle government.

The similarities between Michael Mertz and Jean Souetre are quite striking and there were reports (unconfirmed) that both men might have been in contract with each other during the Algerian troubles. Souetre said that they served together in the French Army in Algeria in 1958 and 1959. It is also possible that both men were incarcerated together at the Beaujon detention camp (OAS). However, what is not in dispute is that Souetre used Mertz's alias on many occasions.

In the footnote section of Bernard Fensterwald's "New Shaw/Allen FOIA Litigation," he questions the circumstances of Mertz' entering the OAS.

"There is a minority view as to Mertz's political sympathies. A former high official in the anti-OAS ranks that de Gaulle established in 1960 believes that Mertz joined the OAS voluntarily in 1961 and that he was "turned" after he was arrested in June, 1961. He doesn't believe that the SDECE drafted him into the OAS as an agent provocateur."

At one time during the Algerian troubles, Mertz infiltrated the OAS, the group that Souetre belonged to. There is one interesting parallel between the actions taken by Michael Mertz and that of Lee Harvey Oswald in the summer of 1963 in New Orleans. Mertz was arrested for passing out leaflets on a street in Paris, was involved in a brawl, and arrested. This is exactly that happened three months before the assassination in New Orleans when Oswald was arrested for fighting with Carlos Bringueir, a member of the DRE, an anti-Castro Cuban who was friendly with David Ferrie. Oswald had previously gone to Bringuier's store, telling him he was an ex-Marine who wanted to fight against Castro. Bringuier was wary of Oswald and sent him away. Bringueir was shocked when he saw Oswald passing out Fair Play for Cuba Committee leaflets in the city and both men were arrested after a brief scuffle. Many people think that the fight between Oswald and

Bringueir was faked.

Less than one week after the assassination, the U.S. Secret Service got a report from the "Senior Customs Representative, U.S. Treasury Department, Bureau of Customs, Montreal, Canada," from some witnesses who reported seeing Oswald in Montreal passing out leaflets for the FPCC, (the same ones he used in New Orleans earlier in the year). One witness to this event was Jean Paul Tremblay, a Customs Investigator, who swore that the person he saw passing out the literature was Oswald. Tremblay said he knew it was Oswald because he was then working on a Cuba relate case.

At the time of the possible sighting of Oswald in Montreal (if he was indeed there), Mertz had a home in the city. Are all these incidents regarding both Mertz and Oswald passing out literature and getting arrested somehow related? Did the Mertz arrest possibly alert Oswald's handlers in New Orleans that a similar event could be played out in New Orleans? These were just too many coincidences for this to be just a few, random acts

Mertz's ties to the French Connection heroin trade were legion and the drugs he dealt with were picked up in the United States and distributed by both Santos Trafficante and Carlos Marcello, both men who were tied to the Kennedy assassination. Another small cog in the heroin dealership in the United States was Jack Ruby. Ruby, beginning in 1959, had been a low level FBI informant, although just what positive information he provided them is not known. In the 1950s, Ruby made several trips to Havana while Trafficante was in jail. A number of people who were incarcerated with Trafficante in a Havana jail swore that Ruby was allowed in the prison at the same that Trafficante was there. Ruby was also busy running guns to Cuba during those years. Ruby had close ties with many members of the U.S. Mafia, including Marcello, Trafficante, Jimmy Hoffa, and an investigation after the president' death showed Ruby making dozens of phone calls to low, and mid-level Mafia members in the months prior to November 22, 1963.

There is no doubt that the money accumulated by Mertz via his heroin smuggling connection was funneled back to the OAS for their anti-de Gaulle enterprises and other illegal necessities. He even lived in New York City for a while in the 1960s, and used a cover a company that arranged the rebuilding of engines for the

French military.

In 1962, Mertz and Marcello suffered a tremendous blow when a large shipment of heroin bound for Houston, Texas was intercepted. This took place on November 7, 1962, when twenty-two pounds of heroin bound for New York was disrupted.

As Mertz watched from the sidelines, he witnessed the tremendous pressure the Kennedy administration was putting on the narcotics trade, especially that run by Carlos Marcello, Marcello was one of Robert Kennedy's top hoodlums whom he was targeting on an ongoing basis, and it is not a stretch of the imagination to believe that Marcello might have tasked Mertz with the mob of planning, or being part of the attempt on the life of President Kennedy. If Mertz was possibly the rouge, CIA assassin code named QJ/WIN, and took part in the Dallas tragedy, one only has to look backward to the original use of both QJ/WIN and WIROGUE in the plots to kill Patrice Lumumba in 1960.

On November 30, 1964, Mertz suffered a serious blow to his heroin business. A courier whom Mertz employed placed a load of heroin totaling one million dollars inside a Citroen car that Mertz used to smuggle his shipments. The car was parked on a street in Paris near where Mertz lived. The courier disconnected the spark plugs to the car and left it on the street over night. This car was then to be placed on board a ship bound for the United States or another country. When Mertz went down the next morning he was horrified to see that the heroin-laden car had been stolen. After a search, the car was never recovered.

Michael Mertz was arrested for his part in the heroin smuggling business on November 24, 1969. The genesis of his arrest goes back to the Kennedy administration's secret war against Castro. In the early days of 1961, the Kennedy administration hired a number of Cuban exiles who would become officers for the Bay of Pigs invasion contingent. They took their training at Fort Benning, Georgia, a large U.S. Army base that is still operating today. Unknown to most people at Fort Benning was the fact that the military installation was being used as a way station for the shipment of heroin into the United States, run by Santos Trafficante and Carlos Marcello. A number of soldiers at the fort, including some of the Cuban trainees, took part in this scheme. Fort Benning was located in the region that was run by Carlos

Marcello and he had overall control of the heroin shipments that came into and out of the fort.

His arrest came out of the Fort Benning investigation, but his close ties to the French SDECE, proved his free ticket out of jail. He served a partly seven months in jail and was then tried and convicted by a French court. He was given a five-year prison sentence starting in July 1971 on charges of shipping two tons of drugs worth $400 million into the United States over an eight-year period.

Still, the long arm of the SDECE, and an ever-thankful President Charles de Gaulle worked their magic. Mertz served only two months in jail before getting his freedom. He lived the good life in the Loiret region of France near Orleans, a man whose charmed life still had some resonance. It was believed that he had a number of bank accounts in various places in the world, including the United States, Canada, Switzerland, and France. While living in Canada, Mertz owned and operated a series of brothels that were previously owned by his father-in-law, Charles Martel.

What is evident is that Mertz was given protection by the SDECE, his nominal employers who looked the other way as he continued his worldwide heroin smuggling business. Mertz worked in conjunction with the Corsican syndicate lead by the Guerini family in Marseille. Mertz and the Guerini crime family, along with their foot soldiers, had a strong interest in helping the de Gaulle government in its battle against the OAS. As long as the SDECE protected their heroin and drug business, Mertz and the Guerini's had no worry that their golden goose would soon turn to feathers. If and when the OAS took power, they most likely would have shut down the drug business and put them out of work (or in jail).

He died on January 15, 1995.

* * *

Was Mertz QJ/WIN?

One of the enduring questions into the Kennedy assassination and the CIA's two premiere assassins, QJ/WIN and WI/ROGUE, are the identities of both men. Throughout this book, I have postulated a number of people who might have fit either man:

Christian David, Robert Blemant, Lucien Sarti and Charles Siragusa. Now, we add another; Michael Victor Mertz.

This is all speculative, but the parallels between Mertz and QJ/WIN, while never positively confirmed, are numerous. For example, Richard Helms, who ran QJ/WIN, remarked that he was capable of murder. Mertz killed fifteen Germans in World War 11, and later was a hit man for the Corsican mob after the war ended. William Harvey recommended using French Resistance operatives for the ZR/RIFLE project. Mertz worked for the French Resistance during the war. In December 1960, QJ/WIN left the Congo and returned to Europe after his CIA sanctioned mission ended. One month later, Mertz resumed his smuggling activities. Both QJ/WIN and Mertz worked for French intelligence at some point in their careers. Throughout his operational career, Mertz used the alias of two real people; Michael Roux and Jean Souetre, either of whom could have been QJ/WIN.

While drawing up the tenants for the ZR/RIFLE program, William Harvey wrote that they not recommend using Corsicans since "Sicilians could lead to Mafia." Mertz had a long history of working with the French Corsican mob, and was part of the French intelligence service, the SDECE, along with the French Connection heroin network. QJ/WIN was employed by the CIA through the end of 1962. The real Michael Mertz was in the U.S. from January 11, 1962 until February 25, 1962.

A very interesting sidelight regarding the activities of QJ/WIN has to do with the activities of Johnny Rosselli and his ties with CIA activities against Castro. William Harvey wrote in his notes regarding the QJ/WIN file that Rosselli's expenses were paid out of the QJ/WIN program. Now, this just might be a housekeeping matter in order to allocate funds for the operation or it may have a more sinister meaning; that the CIA's mob star, Johnny Rosselli, was somehow working hand in glove with Michael Mertz.

Kennedy assassination researcher Gary Shaw wrote of the similarities between Michael Mertz and QJ/WIN in the now defunct periodical, "*The Continuing Inquiry*." He wrote about the CIA's Executive Action-ZR Rifle program which was directed by William Harvey and their number one assassin, QJ/WIN.

He quotes the Senate Report on "Alleged Assassination Plots Involving Foreign Leaders" as saying that the CIA sought to quash criminal charges that had been brought against QJ/WIN by a foreign government in 1962. Their efforts succeeded and the agent was never tried. It was at this very same time that Michael Mertz and his family moved to Canada after his efforts to prevent the assassination of de Gaulle in a Paris suburb. This man was also France's most notorious heroin smuggler (Mertz).

Richard Helms said of QJ/WIN, that "If you need somebody to carry out murder, I guess you had a man who might be prepared to carry it out." The notes for the ZR/RIFLE team said "former resistance personnel offers possibility" as potential candidates for the team. Mertz worked in the French Resistance in WW2.

Shaw wrote a perfect script relating to Mertz as QJWIN. "The French smuggler was a World War 11 Resistance hero. He was an efficient killer of Germans, acquiring a portion of his reputation by machine-gunning fifteen Germans as they sat drinking in a small French café. After the war, he joined the French Secret Service. While serving in this capacity, he saved the life of President Charles de Gaulle. He accomplished this while on a secret mission during the Algerian strife in 1961. He also had confederates with both heroin and French Secret Service connections."

Shaw also mentioned the names of Jean Souetre and Michael Roux and told the story of Souetre's expulsion from Dallas after the assassination. He concluded by saying, "The Captain Souetre who was so quickly expelled from the Dallas scene is probably described in the previous paragraphs-one Michael Victor Mertz-World War 11 Resistance Hero, French Secret Service agent, heroin smuggler extradinaire and premier assassin. He also matches closely the description of QJ/WIN."[102]

In their 2008 book, *Legacy of Secrecy: The Long Shadow of the JFK Assassination,* authors Lamar Waldron and Thom Hartman give a number of similarities between Michael Mertz and the CIA's QJ/WIN. I will summarize them over the next, several pages.

During World War 2, QJ/WIN was suspected of being a Nazi collaborator. Mertz was also a Nazi collaborator until he switched sides.

When he set up the ZR/RIFLE program, William Harvey

---

[102]Shaw, J. Gary, "QJ/WIN Identified?" The Continuing Inquiry, 1979.

recommended that the CIA use former French Resistance agents. QJ/WIN was in the Resistance movement from 1943-1945. Mertz also worked in the Resistance during the war.

QJ/WIN was recruited in Frankfurt, Germany in 1960, and was contacted by the CIA in "connection with an illegal narcotics operation into the U.S." Michael Mertz made visits to that same city in 1962 and 1963. He was one of the prime operators in the French Connection heroin network that was dominated by his father-in-law, Charles Martel, along with the Guerini family based in Marseille.

The CIA recruited two assassins, QJ/WIN and WI/ROGUE/1 in 1960 for the attempted assassination of Patrice Lumumba. A number of Lumumba's guards were of Moroccan decent, and Mertz had once worked in Morocco for French intelligence.

QJ/WIN ended his mission for the CIA in the Congo in December 1960 and made his way back to Europe. In January 1961, Mertz continued his endeavors in his drug smuggling operation after WIN ended his work for the CIA.

QJ/WIN went to Switzerland and Italy in February 1961. At the same time, Mertz was also in Switzerland where both he and his wife had a bank account. Authors Hartman and Waldron postulate that since Mertz was getting ready to ship 220 pounds of heroin into the United States in March 1961, he made preparations for the shipment from the place (Switzerland) where he had his money.

On March 31, 1961, the CIA gave QJ/WIN a polygraph test to see if he was working for any other foreign intelligence agency (he wasn't). They note that QJ/WIN had previously worked for French intelligence, along with other Western European intelligence services. Mertz was well connected with the SDECE for a long period of time, even infiltrating the OAS on behalf of the SDECE, and foiling a plot to kill de Gaulle.

Both Mertz and QJ/WIN, traveled frequently to Belgium in 1961.

The CIA says that QJ/WIN was a citizen of Luxembourg. Mertz was born on the border of France and Luxembourg (Waldvisse, France). Mertz spoke both German and French, two of the languages used in Luxembourg. He also traveled on false passports which may have allowed him easy access to and from

Luxembourg.

By December 1961 to January 1962, WIN started to create his cover for his future CIA work. At that same time, Mertz had completed his service for the SDECE, and if he was WIN, he was now ready to assume his new relationship with Washington.

During his tenure with the CIA, WIN was supposed to have gone on trial on smuggling charges in Europe. It seems however, that the CIA intervened and no trial was held. At that same time, WIN also worked for other allied intelligence services including Belgium, France, West Germany, and Luxembourg. The authors ask why the CIA had to intervene to stop the trial when his other patrons could have easily pulled some strings to end it before it began. They also point out that a shipment of French Connection heroin was busted in New York and a member of Mertz' group in France was linked to the shipment. However, there was no trial ever held in France, most likely because of U.S. intervention in the matter.

At the beginning of the ZR/RIFLE operation, William Harvey wanted to use Corsicans as agents because, "Sicilians could lead to the Mafia." Mertz belonged to the French Corsican mob, and would have been a perfect candidate if Harvey ever wanted to call on him.

WIN told Harvey that if he needed men to act as assassins for the ZR/RIFLE program, "there were a pool of assassins" located in the Middle East. Mertz had extensive ties for the SDECE in both Turkey and Morocco.

Richard Helms told Harvey to employ WIN through the end of 1962. Mertz was in the United States from January 11, 1962 until February 25, 1962. Recall that William Harvey, when describing the activities of WIN, wrote in his notes that Rosselli's expenses were paid out of the ZR/RIFLE program.

When the ZR/RIFLE program was set up, it was going to be used for the assassination of Fidel Castro, and WIN was to be one of its first agents. Hartman and Waldron say that Mertz had numerous contacts who were still in Cuba who wanted to see Castro dead.

On March 6, 1963, Richard Helms cleared QJ/WIN to be kept on the payroll until the end of 1963. On February 27, 1963, Mertz got his passport renewed in New York. It is not known whether it was a French or U.S. passport that he used. If he was going to be put into service until the end of that year, then it would have been much easier for Mertz to operate in the U.S., unencumbered, from any outside players. [103]

* * *

If Mertz was QJ/WIN, and he was one of the shooters in the Kennedy assassination, his role as one of the most notorious heroin dealers in the world at the time might not have been the only reason why he had a motive to kill the president. Besides the fact that the Kennedy administration was doing its best to disrupt the global drug trade which would have put Mertz and his patrons such as Carlos Marcello, Santos Trafficante and Jimmy Hoffa out of business, the administration was also at war with the Mafia in the United States. For years, J. Edgar Hoover, the Director of the FBI, did not even acknowledge the existence of the Mafia in this country. His original mandate was to stop domestic subversion in the U.S. and during the 1930s and 1940s, the FBI went after the most notable mobsters of the day such as Al Capone, Bonnie and Clyde, John Dillinger, Pretty Boy Floyd, etc.

During World War 2, Hoover's G-men went after German agents who somehow managed to land on our shores (in Long Island and Florida), and kept a watch on a number of double agents who decided it was better to work with the United States then with their one time, German backers.

There were also persistent rumors that Hoover was in bed with a number of the top Mafia dons in the United States who had been able to blackmail Hoover due to his supposed homosexual behavior over the years.

When Jack Kennedy was elected president, he appointed his younger brother Robert, to be the Attorney General. The younger Kennedy had never even tried a case in court but the president knew he needed someone whom he could trust completely in the new administration and, with little encouragement from his powerful father, the former ambassador to England, Joseph P. Kennedy, he chose Bobby. Bobby had run his brother's successful

---

[103] www.legacyofsecrecy.com/documents.html.

1960 presidential campaign and he knew he could help him immensely as he settled down in the White House.

Bobby did not lobby for the job and many of the Kennedy family and political allies did not believe Bobby was ready for the job. Bobby even met with J. Edgar Hoover who told him that he'd make a good attorney general (Hoover must have regretted that statement as time went on). Bobby at first told his brother that he wouldn't accept the job as attorney general; he wanted to go back to Massachusetts and do other things. However, family considerations came first and Bobby accepted in the end.

When Ben Bradlee of *Newsweek* asked the president-elect how he was going to make the announcement, Kennedy said, "Well, I think I'll open the front door of the Georgetown house some morning about 2:00 A.M., look up and down the street, and, if there's no one there, I'll whisper, 'It's Bobby.'"

When the announcement was about to be made, Bobby recalled his brother saying, "Go upstairs and comb your hair to which I said it was the first time the President had ever told the Attorney General to comb his hair before they made an announcement. And then when we were outside he said, "Don't smile too much or they'll think we're happy about the appointment."

Robert Kennedy's first foray into the world of law and politics came in December 1952, when he was appointed as an assistant counsel for the Committee on Government Operations by the co-chairman of the committee, Senator Joseph McCarthy, a long time ally of the elder Kennedy (Joseph P. Kennedy—JFK would later be taken to task when he failed to vote in the censure motion against McCarthy in the 1950's). Bobby resigned his job in July 1953, but returned to the committee as the chief minority counsel in February, 1954. RFK became the committee's chief counsel in 1955. Some time later, a Permanent Subcommittee on Investigations of the U.S. Senate Committee on Government Operations (the so-called McClellan Committee), under the directorship of Democratic Senator John L. McClellan, was opened. The purpose of the committee was to look into labor racketeering in the United States.

The focus behind the McClellan committee hearings was a scandal that began in 1956 in the union, the International Brotherhood of Teamsters which was then headed by Jimmy

Hoffa. Hoffa, it seems, wanted the powerful union to himself, and he tried to muzzle out Dave Beck, who was the union's international president. Hoffa and his pal Johnny Dio, met in October, 1955 and set up fifteen dummy unions in order to gain more votes for Hoffa when the balloting for a new union president came due. These fake unions then asked for charters from the international union, and when Hoffa's enemies found out, all hell broke loose. In time, the union feud was noticed by the Department of Justice and an official investigation was launched.

An internal battle broke out in the congress as to which committee would investigate the case, and on January 30, 1957, a new committee named the Select Committee on Improper Activities in Labor and Management, was given the task of looking into Hoffa, Beck and the Teamsters. Among the members of the committee were powerful senators such as Joseph McCarthy, Sam Ervin, Carl Mundt, Barry Goldwater, and John F. Kennedy. Bobby Kennedy served as the subcommittee's chief counsel and lead investigator. Soon, both Kennedy brothers were in the forefront of the investigation, with JFK, making it his prime objective to get Jimmy Hoffa at all costs, and root out all mob connections in the Teamsters Union.

Bobby hired a number of his close associates, people who would later play a role in the Kennedy administration, and remain part of the extended Kennedy political machine; Kenneth O'Donnell, Pierre Salinger, Walter Sheridan.

JFK took on Dave Beck in the hearings and gave the committee irrefutable facts concerning Beck's swindling of the union to the tune of hundreds of thousands of dollars. Beck was ultimately convicted of larceny and income tax evasion. While JFK was in the public spotlight, a newspaper reporter wrote of Bobby's work, saying, "It is plain that this is Bob Kennedy's show so far."

As the proceedings went on, Beck admitted to receiving an interest-free loan of $300,000 from the Teamsters which he never repaid. Beck appeared before the committee and invoked his 5th amendment right not to incriminate himself. He again testified before the committee in May 1957 and a grand jury later indicted him on tax evasion charges on May 2, 1957.

Senator McClellan let Bobby have free reign when it came to calling witnesses, testimony of witnesses, areas of investigation, and the questioning of witnesses. Soon, both he and Jack were the rising stars of the committee and their names were constantly in the nation's newspapers. The Kennedy dynasty had just begun, but no one at the time knew just how far they'd go.

After successfully indicting Beck, the committee, and Bobby Kennedy in particular, lined up their next opponent, James Hoffa. That first encounter between the younger Kennedy and the tough, street-smart Hoffa, was the beginning of a decades long blood feud between the two men. Each were in their own way, the almost the mirror image of the other; tough, relentless, independent minded, stubborn, and willing to go to considerable lengths to outdo the other. Hoffa's goal was to unite all the Teamsters into one union with him as its leader. In order to gain that result, Hoffa made a deal with the Mafia, and soon the two men were hip deep in league with each other. The mob used terror tactics to intimidate those in the Teamsters who balked at their demands and soon Hoffa began paying off the mob via hundreds of thousands of dollars that he extorted from the Teamsters pension funds.

On February 19, 1957, with the use of an intermediary, both Hoffa and Bobby Kennedy sat down for their first, face-to-face meeting. Both men came ready for combat and Hoffa told Kennedy that ' I do to others what they do to me, only worse."

Bobby won the first round as Hoffa was arrested for allegedly trying to bribe a New York attorney by the name of John Cye Cheasty. It seems that Hoffa had offered him a bribe to work for Kennedy and then give the Teamsters whatever evidence he gained. Hoffa went on trial on bribery charges but was acquitted. In September 1957, through threats and intimidation, Hoffa was elected president of the Teamsters Union.

After Hoffa's acquittal, Bobby began a second round of hearings against Hoffa. Bobby sent Pierre Salinger to Detroit to pursue a lead and in time, five subpoenas were filed on five Teamster locals. Hoffa found out that Salinger was in town and he had his Teamster pal, Frank Fitzsimmons (who would later become Teamster president) made contact.

The next day, Salinger and Carmine Bellino had a meeting with Hoffa. The five men who had been subpoenaed were in the room and when Hoffa saw them, he went crazy. Hoffa stood up and yelled at the men in the room, "You can tell Bobby Kennedy for me that he's not going to make his brother President over Hoffa's dead body."

Hoffa appeared at the Senate hearing on August 20, 1957 in a less combative mood. Bobby began questioning Hoffa on his knowledge of various mobsters including Johnny Dio who was suspected of blinding newspaper columnist Victor Riesel. This time, Hoffa did not plead the Fifth Amendment, instead, saying on numerous occasions that he could not remember. Hoffa was now in hot water, having been indicted in New York on charges of illegal wiretapping. He was subsequently indicted again in New York for making perjured testimony before a grand jury.

Hoffa lucked out again when his wiretapping case was dismissed in the spring of 1958. In an awkward moment, Bobby and Hoffa met by accident in the federal courthouse in New York. Bobby said hello and then asked him how the trial was going. Hoffa replied, "You never can tell with a jury. Like shooting fish in a barrel." Hoffa was acquitted once again, making Bobby even more determined to get his new foe.

The acquittal of Jimmy Hoffa was the first shot in Kennedy's war on the Teamster leader. As the years passed, Bobby would pull out all punches in order to harass, and generally make life as hard on Hoffa as possible. It was during this time on the McClellan Committee that Bobby began to earn the reputation as being "ruthless" to his enemies, especially those men in the Mafia. When the mobsters came before his committee, Bobby turned on them like bats on hell, ridiculing their clothes, their demeanor, and their refusal to answer his questions. For example, on March 24, 1959, the committee called as its witness, Carlos Marcello. The mob don took the 5th amendment fifty-six times. Sam Giancana also testified before Bobby's committee and he too took the 5th over forty times. When Giancana snickered at one of Bobby's questions, the younger Kennedy remarked, "I thought only little girls giggled, Mr. Giancana."

For his part, Senator John F. Kennedy stood by the side, letting Bobby take the lead against the nations mobsters, and Hoffa in particular. If Bobby did his job the way he was supposed to, any positive national publicity would begin to effect not only Bobby, but Jack as well. As time went on, both brothers took the credit for successfully taking on the mob, with the positive publicity that went along with it.

The hearings before the McClellan Committee, not known at the time, would pit three of the top mobsters in the United States against the Kennedy brothers; Jimmy Hoffa, Carlos Marcello, and Sam Giancana. All three men were linked in some way (Marcello and Giancana in particular), to the Kennedy assassination, with the HSCA saying that both Marcello and Giancana had the "means, motive, and opportunity" to kill the president.

On September 11, 1962, a meeting was held at the home of Carlos Marcello on his 3,000-acre plantation near New Orleans. In attendance were three of Marcello's friends, including Edward Becker, a man with mob ties. The meeting concerned the Kennedy administrations war against the mob, including Marcello who had been deported to South America on Bobby's orders and had slipped back into the country.

At that meeting, as reported years later, Marcello lashed out at the Kennedy brothers saying, "Take the stone out of my shoe." Don't worry about that little Kennedy son of a bitch. He's going to be taken care of."

In 1969, Becker told writer Ed Reid who wrote about the incident in his book *The Grim Reapers* the following story. Marcello wanted revenge against Bobby after his deportation to Guatemala. He knew that to get rid of Bobby he'd have to remove Jack Kennedy himself. If RFK *was* killed, there would be a nation-wide manhunt until the man was apprehended.

As the HSCA later reported in its findings:

> No one in the meeting had any doubt about Marcello's intentions when he abruptly arose from the table. Marcello did not joke about such things. In any case, the matter had gone beyond mere "business'; it had become an affair of honor, a Sicilian vendetta. Moreover, the conversation at Churchill Farms also made clear that Marcello had begun to plan a move. He had, for example, already thought of using a "nut" to do the job.
>
> Roughly one year later President Kennedy was shot in Dallas—Two months after Attorney General Robert Kennedy had announced to the McClellan Committee that he was going to expand his war on organized crime. And it

is perhaps significant that privately Robert Kennedy had signaled out James Hoffa, Sam Giancana, and Carlos Marcello as being among his chief targets.[104]

Becker told the HSCA that "Marcello was very angry and had clearly stated that he was going to arrange to have President Kennedy murdered in some way." Becker stated that Marcello made some kind of reference to JFK being a dog and RFK as the dog's tail and said, "the dog will keep biting you if you cut off its tail, but that if the dog's head were cut off, the dog would die."

Another of Bobby's nemeses, who was planning JFK's murder was Santos Trafficante. Jose Aleman, a leading Cuban exile, told the HSCA that he had a meeting with Trafficante in which JFK's name came up. When Aleman told Trafficante that JFK was a shoe-in for re-election in 1964, Trafficante said, "You don't understand me. Kennedy's not going to make it to the election. He is going to get hit." (hit, meaning killed). Aleman told the congress that he believed that Trafficante was actively planning the president' assassination, and that "Trafficante had given him the distinct impression that Hoffa was to be principally involved in the elimination of Kennedy."

Michel Mertz was actively involved in the heroin trafficking network set up by Santos Trafficante and it is not too much of a stretch of the imagination that Trafficante might have thought of using Mertz as the gunman to kill the president when the time came.

Little publicity was given to the public by the press to the fact that in 1963, the Kennedy administration had began a war on narcotics with the creation of a "Presidential Advisory Commission on Narcotics and Drug Abuse" in the United States. It was to be the new policy of the administration to recommend "rehabilitation for addicts rather than imprisonment" for their offenses. The Kennedy's targeted both Marcello and Trafficante for their heroin smuggling operations, a fact that Michael Mertz surely did not miss.

The HSCA also looked into the telephone calls that Jack Ruby,

---

[104] Duffy, James, *Who Killed JFK? The Kennedy Assassination Cover-Up, the Web.* Shapolsky Publishers, New York, 1988, Page 213.

the man who shot Lee Harvey Oswald in the basement of the Dallas Police Department on November 24, 1963, made before the president's murder. What they found was a man who was linked to many people who were associated with both Carlos Marcello and Santo Trafficante. From May to September 1963, Ruby placed a number of calls to Mafia linked people to the tune of 25-35 per month to almost 75 in October, 1963, and 96 during the first 3 weeks of November (prior to the assassination). Among the people whom Ruby called were: Irwin Weiner of Chicago who was a bondsman and a man linked to the Teamsters Union, Robert "Barney" Baker, a close associate of Jimmy Hoffa's, Nifio Pecora, a lieutenant in the Marcello organization, Harold Tannenbaum, who owned a number of night clubs in New Orleans, Lewis McWillie, one of Ruby's closets friends who was widely linked to gambling interests in Havana during the 1950s, and Murray "Dusty" Miller, a deputy of Hoffa's in the Teamster's Union.

Ruby said that all the calls he made to these people had to do with his nightclub activities in order to settle a labor dispute. The HSCA, in their report on Ruby's phone calls said, "In particular, the Committee was not satisfied with the explanations of three individuals closely associated with organized crime who received telephone calls from Ruby in October or November 1963."

They further wrote that, "In assessing the significance of these Ruby contacts, the Committee noted, first of all, that they should have been more thoroughly explored in 1964 when memories were clearer and related records were available. Further, while there may be persuasive arguments against the likelihood that the attack on Oswald would have been planned in advance on the telephone with an individual like Ruby, the pattern of contacts did show that individuals who had the motive to kill the President also had knowledge of a man who could be used to get access to Oswald in the custody of the Dallas police. In Ruby, they also had knowledge of a man who had exhibited a violent nature and who was in serious financial trouble. The calls, in short, established knowledge and possible availability, if not actual planning."[105]

* * *

[105] Ibid. Page 229.

Another person who was linked to Michel Mertz, Santo Trafficante and possibly Jack Ruby, was a petty criminal based out of Montreal, Canada, by the name of Lucien Rivard. His name came up in the HSCA's investigation of the Kennedy assassination but, like so many other possible leads, this one went nowhere.

Lucien Rivard was born in 1914 in Canada and was a small time ciminal who operated out of Quebec. Beginning in the 1940s, Rivard had been engaged in the profitable drug smuggling trade. Like many other gangsters of the time, Rivard, in the 1950s, headed for the sunny climes of Havana, Cuba where the American mob had taken root under the protective umbrella of President Batista who got kick backs from the profitable casino's that flourished in Havana. In 1958, two of Rivard's partners in the heroin trade were Michael Victor Mertz and Paul Mondoloni who had close ties with Santo Trafficante. Rivard was put in prison for a brief period of time in Cuba while he was the co-owner of the El Morocco club with gangster, Norman Rothman.

It may be just coincidence but Lucien Rivard was in jail in Cuba at the same time that Santo Trafficante was also serving a brief prison term. Santo Trafficante was detained in Cuba on June 6, 1959 as a result of a request by the Bureau of Narcotics as part of an INTERPOL investigation. He was put in Trescornia jail more for protective purposes that for anything else. The HSCA said that among Trafficante's mob associates in Cuba at that time were Charles Tourine Jr, Jake Lansky, Dino Cellini, Henry Saavedra, and Lucien Rivard.

The U.S. Bureau of Narcotics wrote a memo dated November 24, 1958 saying that, "Mondoloni's operation in Cuba, which had begun in 1955 with Norman Rothman and Trafficante, poses a most serious threat to the suppression of the illicit heroin traffic at the present time."

Rivard belonged to the Cotroni family that operated out of Montreal, Canada (this was a branch of the organized crime family of Joseph Bonanno which operated out of New York). In 1958, after leaving Cuba, he returned to Quebec and began dealing drugs for the gang. He was arrested in 1964 as a result of a heroin bust. The drugs were part of a shipment that came out of Mexico City that was given to Rivard by Paul Mondoloni.

In 1965, in what turned out to be a media sensation of the time, Rivard escaped from a Montreal prison by using a water hose to climb a wall gain his freedom. He was on the lamb for a period of four months before being re-captured and sent back to the United States.

The sensational escape of Lucien Rivard from prison became a national scandal that went up to the office of the Prime Minister, Lester Pearson. The Canadian Press voted Rivard the title of "Canadian News maker of the Year" for 1965.

Another coincidence that involved Lucien Rivard was an incident that took place in October 1963, the same time that Lee Oswald (or someone impersonating him) was in Mexico City. Rivard knew a man named Michel Caron who was also a small time criminal. Caron was a family man with a wife and four children. He needed money, and he asked Lucien Rivard if he could help. Rivard obliged his friend and asked him if he would act as a courier for him on a small matter. Caron agreed, and on September 26, 1963, Michel Caron and his wife made plans to go to Mexico City to retrieve a packet that Rivard asked him to bring back. Caron and his family arrived in Mexico City in late September and made plans to pick up the package.

At the same time that Michel Caron was in Mexico City, another person was also in the Mexican capitol, on another, strange mission. Lee Oswald had arrived in Mexico City around the same time supposedly to get a visa from the Cuban embassy in order to travel back to Cuba and then to the Soviet Union. While in Mexico City, Oswald appeared at both the Soviet and Cuban consulates, making his presence known to all who saw and came in contact with him. Both the Warren Commission and the HSCA did an exhaustive study of Oswald's activities in Mexico City and came away with more questions than answers. What is undeniable is that a mystery man was impersonating Oswald while he was in Mexico City, a man whose identity is still not known to this day. The CIA had a large contingent of assets in Mexico City and were aware of his presence in the city at that time. The CIA also had photographic surveillance at the Cuban and Soviet embassies but when it came to time see if they could identify Oswald as being the person who entered the buildings, the cameras were not working that day.

While in the city, Caron turned his car over to a contact of Rivard's and something was placed inside. On October 10, 1963, Caron and his family are stopped at the US-Mexican border for a routine search. While checking the car, U.S. Customs police found an astonishing site; 35 kilos of heroin. Caron and his family were placed under arrest and an intensive period of questioning began. Caron spilled the beans and told U.S. authorities that the person who asked him to bring the heroin into the country was Lucien Rivard. Caron was shown a number of photographs and identified the people in Mexico City whom he met on his brief trip. He later identified them as, Paul Mondoloni, Santos Trafficante, Michael Mertz, and other members of the gang belonging to Carlo Gambino.

The Rivard-Caron operation got the attention of Attorney General Robert Kennedy, whose office was briefed on the matter. This was a just another link in the chain that joined Santos Trafficante, one of Bobby's prime suspects in the world of organized crime, one, that he had been pursing for his entire term as AG.

The Rivard case connects indirectly a number of people who played a role in the planning of the Kennedy assassination; Santos Trafficante, Michael Mertz (if he was QJ/WIN), Jack Ruby, as well as the French Connection heroin network that was operated by Marcello, Trafficante, Mertz, and Christian David. All this information, of course, was not investigated by either the Warren Commission (which knew nothing of it), or the HSCA which did not have the time or the monetary resources to make any further inquiries. This is just another piece of the puzzle that needs to be followed up in the future if any headway is to be made of this intriguing case.

The story of Michael Mertz is culled from a variety of sources that have been compiled over the years by dogged researchers, without the benefit of official government documents. What little information that has been disseminated on Mertz fills in the background, but not the entire picture.

However, from what we know of his life in the shadows, one can make the following observations from the available evidence and make the following conclusions.

Michael Mertz was one of the topnotch assassins and drug

dealers of the day, the perfect man to call on when a clandestine operation was needed. He was closely associated with a number of men who were implicated in the plots to kill JFK; Santos Trafficante, Carlos Marcello, and to a much lesser degree, Jack Ruby. He was most likely in Dallas and Fort Worth, Texas on the day before, and on the day of the assassination. He used the aliases of two real people, both associated with French intelligence and drug running, Jean Souetre and Michael Roux. He was most likely deported from Dallas two days after the assassination and went either to Canada or Mexico. He had a reputation for violence, both with the Corsican drug network, as well as with the SDECE (French intelligence). He was protected by the French government for his part in saving the life of President de Gaulle. He was given the specific job of infiltrating the OAS, a dangerous job that if he were made, would have meant his instant death. He worked for both sides of the political establishment, the SDECE, as well as the French Connection heroin network run the Guerini family.

Mertz was seen in Montreal in the months prior to the assassination passing out Fair Play for Cuba literature on the streets of the city (as did Oswald in New Orleans). There is a considerable body of evidence as shown in this chapter that makes a strong case that Mertz was indeed the CIA's prime assassin, QJWIN. QJWIN was attached to the ZR/RIFLE assassination program and Mertz certainly filled the bill in that regard. Mertz was a French Corsican by heritage and was a perfect candidate as called for by William Harvey to be used for the purpose of political assassination. Finally, Mertz was part of the heroin network that ended in the arrest of Lucien Rivard in 1963 at the border between Mexico and the United States in what was then, one of the largest heroin busts up to that time.

It is the job of the historian to tell the story as per the available evidence. Until the time comes when the classified documents on Michael Mertz are released, the whole story will not be complete.

Chapter 9:

The Steve Rivele Investigation

In 1988, the Arts and Entertainment Channel in the United States aired for the first time a six part controversial documentary called "The Men Who Killed Kennedy." The second episode was called "The Forces of Darkness," which talked about the second assassin on the grassy knoll in Dallas on November 22, 1963. The last part of the episode featured for the first time on national television, the story of Steve Rivele's private investigation of the Kennedy assassination, featuring the so-called "French Connection" to the president's murder. When the hour was up, Rivele, a California based writer and investigator, described the plot to kill JFK, and the men who were behind it. The documentary was quickly debunked by many skeptics in both the media and in the anti-conspiracy crowd as just another questionable theory, one, that had no basis in fact. However, as more facts surrounding the story became known, the more plausible the theory became.

Rivele's thesis said that the assassination was planned by the Corsican network based in Marseille, France, headed by Antonie Guerini, one of the world' most wanted heroin dealers of the day. The man who gave Rivele the background was none other than Christian David, whose story has been told in these pages. At the end of the hour-long telecast, Rivele gave the names of the three men who were allegedly supposed to have killed the president, and the entire backstory to the event. Besides Antoine Guerini, both Carlos Marcello and Santos Trafficante were also involved in the assassination planning.

Rivele told how he traveled around Europe, mostly on his own, and at his considerable expense, to try and track down JFK's killers. His was a story of dogged persistence, one whose outcome was in doubt from the start.

Steve Rivele's efforts to find JFK's assassins had an unexpected benefactor in the late Bernard Fensterwald, the president of the Assassination Archives and Research Center located in Washington, D.C. (The firm is now operated by attorney Jim Lesar). When I met Bernard Fensterwald in Washington when I was starting "Back Channels" magazine, we had conversation regarding the French Connections and his thoughts on it. He told me that he believed there was a French back up team in Dallas on November 22, 1963 but that they took no part in the President's death. With his passing, Mr. Lesar teamed up with Steve Rivele and offered the services of his company in his efforts. There are numerous files in the AARC's office regarding the French Connection investigation and they give the researcher a good glimpse as to how the probe was carried out.

In one of the files on the French Connection in the AARC that I obtained on my visit in the 1990s were notes regarding the investigation. One sentence read, "Fensterwald thinks that the attempts on de Gaulle were made by the same crowd that shot JFK, the ex-OAS. He is skeptical about the Christian David connection. Fensterwald admits that the whole subject is very complicated and thought it would be very difficult to do on the box."

So, who was the man who took it upon himself to find JFK's assassins and postulate another theory in the Kennedy assassination?

Steve Rivele was born in May 6, 1949 and is a writer by profession. He is the co-author of *The Plumber: The True Story of How One Good Man Helped Destroy the Entire Philadelphia Mafia (*1991*), The Mothershed Case (*1992*), and Lieutenant Ramsey's War: From Horse Soldier to Guerilla Commander* (1996). He also wrote the screenplays for *Nixon* (1995) and *Ali* (1996). He said he got interested in the Kennedy assassination when he picked up a paperback copy of the "Warren Commission" which was published to an eager American audience after its findings were released in September 1964. The Commission, which was widely flawed, did not have the time nor the inclination to look deeply into the circumstances of the Kennedy assassination; they wanted to reassure a grieving nation that there was not a conspiracy, domestic or foreign, in the murder of the president. The Warren Commission held the view that Lee Harvey Oswald killed JFK and that he acted alone. For a time, the American public took the commission's findings to heart.

However, only a few years later, the facade of the Warren Commission's findings began to become unraveled as a few, intrepid authors had the gumption to challenge the WC's findings. Among the books that debunked the WC's conclusions were Mark Lane's *Rush To Judgement* and Edward Jay Epstein's *Inquest.* Early researchers like Harold Weisberg and Vincent Salandria added their own interpretation to the events of November 22, 1963 and wrote about the case in lesser-known magazines and on talk radio which was then, just beginning to take off in the Untied States. In time, the public began to take notice and demand more answers than what their government had told them.

Rivele traveled to Dallas to begin his nascent investigation and try and put some of the pieces of the puzzle together. One of the first people whom he met was Gary Shaw, one of the first researchers to delve into the varied pieces of the Kennedy assassination. Rivele asked Shaw if he could provide him with any names of people who would be willing to speak about a conspiracy in the president's death. Shaw gave Rivele three names; two Americans and one Frenchman. The name of the Frenchman was Christian David.

Shaw could not find the two Americans whom he named but they had better luck with Christian David. David was then serving time in jail in Atlanta for his part in the French Connection heroin business. Rivele took a chance and wrote a letter to David who was now transferred to a jail in Levaneworth, Kansas. Much to his surprise, David responded and a two-way conversation had begun. Rivele contacted Bernard Fensterwald and they both made the trip to see David.

David was 53 years old when they first met and was fit, despite his living conditions. In their preliminary talks, Fensterwald told David that for his own sake he should be given something that he could use in return from the government for his cooperation with them, i.e, anything he knew about the Kennedy assassination. Fensterwald said that he'd wait for David to talk about the assassination, if he wanted to. Much to his surprise, David said,

"There was a conspiracy." When asked how he knew, David replied, "The contract was offered to me." During that first conversation, both researchers said, "It is impossible to say whether he was bluffing or if he (David) was revealing a secret he had hidden for a long, long time."

When asked who offered him the contract, David responded by saying, "An important man from Marseille. He made all the decisions, He was the only one who could take on a contract like that one." David gave the name of the man who offered the contract. "It was Antoine Guerini."

David then elaborated further on his conversation with Antonie Guerini. "It was May or June 1963. I was in Marseille. Each evening I went into Guerini's mailbox to see if the man who owed me money were sending it. One evening Guerini asked me to go to his office. He told me he had an important contract. He wanted to know if it would interest me?" I asked Guerini, who was the contract out on? An American political man, he told me. A government Senator, I wanted to know? No, he said, much higher up. The big cheese. I felt that he wanted me to reveal more. I asked him where this (contract) would take place, and when? In America, he advised. No thank you, I replied. It's too risky. Not just because of where. I have taken chances (in my life) but in these conditions, I'm not that foolish."[106]

Steve Rivele translated what David said to Jim Lesar who then said "that he (Lesar) knew of someone who had accepted the contract. David looked at me with an air of fatigue and resignation. Lucien, he remarked slowly. However the family name of Lucien, David pretended not to know."

In what turned out to be a cat and mouse game between Rivele and David, the Frenchman finally gave in, and supplied the last name of Lucien. When pressed by Rivele that he (David) really knew of Lucien's last name, David admitted that the man he was referring to was Lucien Sarti. David said he was reluctant to reveal Lucien's last name because, even though he was dead, the man still had family to consider. He hinted that if Sarti's family learned he had revealed Lucien's last name, they might take revenge on him.

---

[106]"Assassination of Kennedy: Another Theory on the Three Vagrants From Marseille." *L'Express* (translation) 4 November 1988.

Rivele now had confirmation that the man who took the contact to kill the president of the United States was Lucien Sarti.

Upon further questioning by Rivele, David gave more details regarding the circumstances of the assassination. Sarti told David that about two months prior to the assassination he left France bound for Mexico. He spent three weeks there, and then traveled by car to Brownsville, Texas. Sarti used an Italian passport to enter the States and upon arriving in Texas, he was met by a "soldier" from the Chicago Mafia (which was run by Sam Giancana) who picked him up. They then drove to Dallas and stayed in a private residence so as not to leave any trace of their being in the city.

David said that Sarti was paid for the assassination not in cash but in heroin. Rivele asked if he was paid because Sarti was a drug dealer and he said no.

Rivele then asked David about the circumstances of the assassination. He wanted to know where Sarti was positioned when he killed the president. "On the bridge on Elm Street," he said. David then said that Sarti wanted to use the bridge but it was too heavily guarded. He then moved on to small knoll before the bridge that had the wooden fence. Sarti was positioned behind the fence, waiting for the motorcade to pass by. How many shots were fired?, asked Rivele. David replied that the president was shot in the front and the back. "It was a crossfire. They had someone in a building behind there." David said that before the assassination, the team researched Dealey Plaza, making themselves acquainted with the entire area. "I know only that Sarti was not in the building. He was outside, on the knoll."

Rivele then showed David a picture taken moments before the assassination by a bystander with a camera, Mary Moorman. David said, pointing to the picture, "Look, a silhouette behind the fence. Here is Sarti. He is easy to recognize." The photo that was shown to David was the so-called "Badgeman" picture, a grainy photo of a man wearing some type of uniform, and held what looked like a gun in his hand.

David said that Sarti used a rifle, not a pistol and that he used only one eye to train the rifle on the motorcade. "You know," he said, "you shoot much better with one eye than two. A one-eye shot is better because it is not distracted by the vision of the other eye."

David was then shown an aerial view of Dealey Plaza and studied it before answering. He said that Sarti was not in a building, but outside, on the knoll. "It was a crossfire, with three gunmen." David said that two of the shooters were in a building (he did not mention which one), "One up high, the other down low—nearly horizontal."

Rivele asked if David knew the particulars of what happened during the assassination. "Absolutely. Listen, the wounds, they couldn't tell which of the bullets was shot horizontally. You couldn't look at the wounds. Without that gun wounds were incomprehensible."

Kennedy was hit by three gunshots. The first came from behind and hit him in the back. The second also was fired from the back and hit Governor Connally. The third shot was fired from the front. The fourth came from behind and the shooter missed. "Two of the bullets were simultaneous, or almost." Sarti used an "explosive "bullet. "He was the only one to have this kind of ammunition."

In the tumult of the assassination, said David, "There was naturally a felling of panic. Sarti protected himself by hiding. But there was one thing to avoid, the roads. So they returned to their hiding place, where they stayed for about two weeks. After that, they quietly left the country."[107]

After the heat was off, the assassins left for Montreal, Canada where they had contacts who would protect them (remember, Mertz was seen in Montreal passing out FPCC pamphlets).

Rivele now had the scoop of a lifetime, but was it real? He knew he had to verify David's story. But where would begin?

Following their meeting with Christian David, both Jim Lesar and Steve Rivele knew they had to at least try and get someone in the American government to listen to their story. At the time of their meeting, David's term in jail was rapidly coming to a close and he faced extradition back to France for the murder of a policeman in 1966. They approached Congressman Thomas "Tip" O'Neill to try and arrange a judge's stay of extradition. The stay was granted but David was forcibly drugged and taken back to France.

Once back in France, David grew a long beard and his life was

---

[107]Ibid.

made miserable. Rivele told David that Bernard Fensterwald would act as his attorney, and try to get him returned back to the United States. David, in return, would disclose what he knew of the assassination.

In notes found at the AARC on the French Connection case is the following story regarding the Rivele investigation:

> "The Background"
>
> He (Rivele) has clearly done some dogged research work, though has become very nervous about his own safety since the revelations have emerged in the course of four interviews last week. Summers (most likely author Anthony Summers) had advised Rivele that he should attempt to build on his personal relationship with David and continue to see him. He has also told him to be very sensitive to the atmosphere and release his story at the right time. David's credibility would clearly be damaged if he were revealing the identity of JFK's killer from inside a lunatic asylum. Acting I believe in our own interests, he has advised Rivele to release his article in conjunction with our program and Rivele seems very happy about this. But we are being very definitely told that we cannot move independently of the assassinations bureau and Rivele. In addition, changing circumstances many mean the release of the story before November 22.
>
> "The Assessment"
>
> It's a fascinating story though it may prove very difficult to stand up. David appears to have everything to gain by spinning a yarn which will get him out of his nasty French jail and over to America where technically he can live a free man. He may of course be totally mad; Rivele is a graduate of the Paris Film School and not the Institute of Psychiatry. Sensational though it may be, it is rather difficult to illustrate dramatically. We are not likely to get him on film and may have at best to rely on affidavits and Rivele as our reporter of his words. Affidavits themselves may prove difficult, through the non-cooperation of either David himself or more likely the French authorities.
>
> My view is that we must stay with this and request

immediate sight of the documentation. Even if it is a load of rubbish it's interesting rubbish and will attract a lot of attention. We will not be presenting it as unassailable truth, as the lawyers will have the opportunity to tussle over it in court. I have no doubt that it will be royally scorned, dismissed and even debunked, but it should add some new color and may win us the congressional medal of honor. But whatever happens we should be flexible to enable us to take advantage of our "in."[108]

After his initial meeting with Christian David, Rivele went back to Washington where he met with Jim Lesar and Bud Fensterwald concerning their next move. It was decided that Rivele would travel to Europe to try and make as many personal contacts as he could in tracking down David's story. Rivele departed the U.S. for Europe in June 1985.

His primary interest was to find out as much information as he could on the mysterious assassin "Lucien" who was based in Marseille, France. He also wanted to identify the Mexico City "Mystery Man," the person whom the CIA misidentified as being Oswald. David told Rivele in their conversation that he believed the mystery man was a Belgian gunrunner and former mercenary named Vic. Vic was identified by a former mercenary by the name of Dutcher, as a Belgian named Nick or Nicolai.

His goals, as he wrote in his memo for the file, "were to determine the full identities of Lucien and Vic/Nick, find out more about Antonie Guerini and the Marseille mob of the early 60s and meet Vic/Nick, if I could. I also plan to meet once with David at the prison at Fresnes, where he is waiting trial for the 1966 murder of a policeman."

He arrived in Paris on June 2 and began laying out his research trip. He was given the names of contacts by Bud Fensterwald and Rivele began tracking them down. His second week was spent in Marseille where he spoke to as many people as he could, trying to find the elusive Lucien. From Marseille, Rivele traveled to Paris for one night, then on to Brussels for three days, then on to Liege,

108"Mark's Meeting With Summers," January 20, 1986. Found at the AARC, Washington, D.C.

Belgium, and returned to Paris to meet with David. Rivele's contacts were of particular help in providing the information he needed. It seems the only entity that would not help him was the American Consulate in Marseille, who refused to talk with him.

Upon his return home, Rivele wrote a report on his trip, including summarizing the information he received from his sources. He met with a wide range of people, including journalists, policemen, judges, and mercenaries who were active in the 1960s. Here is a synopsis of the most interesting information he was given.

A number of journalists said they believed Lucien was Lucien Sarti who had worked for the French Connection/Auguste Ricord network. A writer by the name of Alain Dugrand told Rivele that the U.S. Mafia might have gotten in touch with the Guerini family through their Sicilian-Corsican mob war, when they had good relations. When Rivele mentioned Lucien, he "was not surprised to be told that Lucien might be Sarti." Lucien Aime-Blanc, the Chief Inspector of the Lille Police Department, and a former chief inspector in Marseille, replied straight out that Lucien was Sarti. "No doubt or hesitation. Said Sarti was a leading and well-known killer."

Journalist Karl Van Meter believed that Nick was J-P Vanderberhe, and said that he: "thought that the CIA would have gone through its connections to hire Guerini to engage assassins. Why Marseille? 1) needed white men who could blend-in in Dallas, 2) needed a closed leak-proof milieu, 3) needed people who were not known to the American police, 4) needed experienced professional killers. Cubans, Asians, Middle Easterners and Americans would not do. Marseille mob offered pool of suitable assassins. CIA had long-standing relations with the Guerinis."[109]

Rivele met with Judge Biswang, the Investigating magistrate in the David case. At first the judge refused to give Rivele permission to visit David, but he was able to get his secretary to give him special permission to see David outside the normal visiting hours.

An interesting sidelight on Sarti was provided by Alex Panzani, a writer who told Rivele that Lucien might be Sarti for the

---

[109]From Steve Rivele, Re: "European Trip, June, 1985," Page 3, At AARC, Washington, D.C.

following reasons: "Said every drug trafficker had to act as a hired killer at some point in his career. Sarti had been a killer at one time." Judge Patric Guerin replaced the murdered judge Michel who was killed in the 1980s while investigating the Marseille mob. He said that he found the idea of a possible Marseille-Sicilian contract interesting. This was what Michel was looking into when he was murdered."

Rivele struck pay dirt when he met Commissioner Bezert, the retired head of a major crime section of the Marseille police force. He spent 31 years in the department and knew all the principal mob figures, including the Guerini family and all those who served with them. He did not recognize Nick but said that he was not based in Marseille. He said that only two killers who were based in Marseille at the time would have been offered the contract (to kill JFK) by Guerini were Lucien Sarti and Christian David.

He told Rivele this before Rivele mentioned their names: "Said that no Marseille based killer would have accepted such a contract because in those days there were rules. One contract you did not kill 1) a cop, 2) a judge, 3) a politician above a certain level. Said several times contract had been proposed on Feferre, the Mayor of Marseille and all the local killers had refused. Said the highest-ranking person ever killed on contract by Marseille killers was ex-inspector Robert Blemant who was working for the mob at the time. Said only Sarti and David would have been offered the contract and would have accepted because they were not Marseille killers. Sarti was from Nimes and David, from Paris. Also Sarti and David would have been crazy enough to have done it. Pointed out that David was the premier sniper in Marseille at the time. Emphasized that no one else in Marseille at the time would have been offered the contract because they would have refused. He said it he and Domenech did not know Nick, Nick was not in Marseille for any substantial period. Told me that A. Guerini was the biggest gangster in France, and gave me to understand that if he offered you a big contract, you did not refuse. Impressed me strongly as a man who knew what he was talking about and who was being frank and open with me. Left me with the conviction that if what David said was true, about the contract, about Antoine and Lucien, that he was probably lying when he said he turned it down."[110]

Commissioner Barbazin, a 31-year veteran narcotics cop on the Marseille police force, could not identify Nick but he did have some useful information on Michael Mertz. He said that it was he who arrested Mertz "on the heroin-in-the-refrigerators scam." He said there was a connection between Mertz and Guerini through Achille Cecchini who worked with Mertz and was under the orders of the Guerini's."

Another person who provided Rivele with valuable information was Charles May, a former mercenary in the Congo, and at the time, the owner of a bar. He was shown a picture of Nick and identified him as Edmond Meunier, a former Congo mercenary under his command. They served together in Katanga in 1961-62 and then from 64-65. Said he did not know his whereabouts in 1963. "Said Meunier was a good soldier but not too bright." His nickname was "Le Manou," and that he believed he lived in Ledge.

Another person who talked about Edmond Meunier was Roger Bracco, a former mercenary pilot in Katanga. Bracco trained anti-Castro Cuban pilots in the Congo as a contract agent for the CIA. He identified the photos of Nick, but said (like May) that close ups were not the same person, or were taken years later. He said Meunier was a petty crook in Liege, and he had a reputation as a killer.

He described him as "a big, brutal man who would not scruple to walk up to someone and shoot him." He said that the CIA were looking for people just like Meunier in the Congo at the time, "able to kill in cold blood, French speaking, knowledgeable about Congo and too stupid to ask embarrassing questions. What was more, Meunier would do anything for money, always needed money." Rivele told him that the photos were taken in Mexico and he replied that he couldn't imagine what Meunier was doing in Mexico or how he got there.

Before heading home, Rivele met for two hours with Christian David in his prison cell in Fresnes. He did not answer the questions that were not related to his case and Rivele states that David was very angry. David knew he was in serious legal trouble and realized that the chances of him being convicted of murder were

---

110 Ibid Page 6-7.

increasing by the day. Rivele told him that the only way he could possibly get a lesser sentence was to tell all he knew of the Kennedy assassination.

He then told him about his trip to Marseille and the contacts he made. He emphasized the point that the only two people who would have accepted the Kennedy contract offered by Antoine Guerini were Sarti and him:

> At this he turned pale and left the room. When he came back, I told him frankly that I did not think he was going to get out of his spot. He asked me to tell him the story. He listened in silence and totally absorbed as I explained what I thought. When I mentioned Sarti he said, "I don't know anything about that! I had a strong impression that I was right about Sarti. When I came to Meunier, although he said nothing, he clearly recognized the name and was disturbed that I knew it. I asked if he knew Meunier and he said, "Go on with your story." When I said that Antoine had hired Sarti and perhaps Meunier and one other assassin, I paused and asked if I was right so far. He said, "Go on with your story." I said I thought the assassins got to Dallas on November 18 or 19, did the job, and left the country. I added that I did not think they knew who they were really working for. I then said to him, "You told me that when Antonie offered you the contract, you turned it down. Was that true?" David gave me a long, hard stare and said, "You do something to help me, and I'll tell you what you want to know.

What Christian David really wanted, according to Rivele, was to have his story published in the French and American press. Rivele wrote in his notes regarding the meeting with David that, "To sum up the trip and the information acquired: I believe that Antoine Guerini hired Lucien Sarti and Christian David and perhaps Edmond Meunier for a contract which came either from the American Mafia or the CIA or both. I am satisfied that Meunier was the Mexico City man, though until I get another photograph of Meunier I cannot be certain.

I do not know whether Meunier had anything to do with the

assassination, but if it is he, someone went to the trouble to bring him from Katanga to Mexico City at the same time that Oswald was there, and he made several visits to the Soviet Embassy. In short, I now believe that Sarti and David were the assassins and Meunier was the mystery man, pending further or better information… It may be that only David and Meunier can tell us the truth now. The ultimate goal should be to get it from one or both of them. Meunier may be willing to talk for money; David may be willing to talk in exchange for relief from his current condition. In either case, we have a chance."

Rivele made a second trip to Europe and met with Christian David on January 15, 1986, and this meeting turned out to be more fruitful. Rivele gave David a letter from Congressman Dellums who wanted to know what David knew. The Dellums letter implied that if David gave verifiable information on the assassination, he would try and persuade the HSCA to look into his case. However, David was reluctant to go along with the offer. After a while of face-to-face talk, David dropped a bombshell; he said that the Lucien he had talked about taking the Kennedy contract was indeed, Lucien Sarti.

He said that two weeks before the assassination, Sarti flew from France to Mexico City, and then drove across the border to Brownsville, Texas, where he was met by a member of the Chicago mob. They then stayed at a private residence. He said that Sarti probably traveled on an Italian passport. At that point, David refused to say any more about the assassination.

He did, though, admit that he was working for the CIA in the Congo in 1960-61, to kill Lumumba (like QJ/WIN): "Admits he discussed intelligence network with a man in a hotel in Leopoldville but would not say who initiated the conversation. Refuses to say who it was, though said he could say, but is terrified of CIA. Repeated that everyone who has expressed knowledge of the assassination has been killed, and he will be killed if he goes back to the U.S. to testify. Said he would talk if released and in Mexico."[111]

Rivele met with various other people in his search for

---

111 "First Meeting with Christian David," January 15, 1986. AARC records, Washington, D.C.

information regarding the French Connection. Pierre Lemarchand, a lawyer, and an organizer of the SAC, and a Gaullist deputy, said that he never knew David, but that the CIA did recruit members of the Guerini gang in Marseille through the DEA office there. At the mention of QJ/WIN, he said that he may have known a person going by that cryptonym in Algiers. The man's name might have been "Georges," who was 30 years old in 62, a former OAS agent. He was arrested for smuggling in central France sometime in the 1960s. "He said that the Guerini family had an unwritten agreement with the police which was ruptured when Antoine helped David and Sarti. Has never understood why."

Alain Jaubert, a journalist, verified Lemarchand's story about the CIA hiring mercenaries out of Marseille, and said that why Antonie Guerini decided to help both Sarti and David in 1966, "remains a major mystery."

Two former mercenaries, a Colonel Tavernier and Joseph Smal, who served in the Congo, provided tantalizing information on Nick, Lumumba and WIN and ROGUE. Col. Tavernier said Nick, whom Rivele believed might have been the Mexico City mystery man, said he saw him in the Congo and that he worked for the CIA in the Congo and in Belgium for fifteen years until he was "purged" during Watergate. He said he worked for CIA agent Devlin who was involved in the Lumumba case and "would have killed Lumumba himself if he was asked to." He said that a Belgian officer killed Lumumba. "Said CIA had plenty of people in Congo who would gladly have done it."

Joseph Smal, the former Congo mercenary, said that WIN and ROGUE most likely stayed at either the Hotel Memling or Regina when they were in Leopoldville. He said he knew Devlin and that Devlin went to Thailand after leaving the Congo and got involved in the drug trade there. Devlin worked with an American gangster named Peters in Singapore. He thought that Peters supplied Devlin with drug money for the CIA. Said that Devlin hired a French gangster named Francis Bodenan in 1967 to kidnap Tshombe. He said that Tshombe was killed by being injected with two substances, one of which resulted in a heart attack, and one that caused him to lapse into a coma.

A Colonel Lahaye, who served as the former chief of internal security in the Congo (for Mobutu), added more to the story of the mysterious CIA agent Devlin. He said Devlin was parachuted into France in WW2 and married a French woman. “Said Leopoldville in 60-61 was chaotic, many plots going.” He was aware of Devlin’s plot to kill Lumumba but he refused in order to protect the lives of Europeans from retaliation. He said there was never any serious attempt to kill Lumumba by any foreigner. Said that Devlin did bring Marseille gangsters to Leopoldville to kill him. He related that he deported at least one of these Marseille gangsters into the hands of the SDECE in Brazzaville. He said that Devlin’s agents stayed in the Hotel Regina (where WIN and ROUGE/1 stayed).

Germain Bezert, the former police commissioner of Marseille, talked freely to Rivele about many different subjects. When Rivele told him his thesis on the Kennedy case and what David told him, Bezert confirmed a lot of what Rivele believed. He said he thought there was a contract and that David and Sarti were involved. He did not know who Meunier was. When questioned about whom he thought might have been the third Dealey Plaza assassin, he said it might have been Michel Nicoli. He said that Nicoli was a killer and was then under a death sentence for murder. Bezert warned Rivele about the risks of his continuing investigation into the Kennedy case. He said, “I was onto a very explosive affair.”

During one of his meetings with Christian David in prison, David said that his appearance had never been changed surgically, but also said that all the photographs of him that were in public hands were faked. When Rivele showed him a picture of Sarti he said that Sarti was bald and always wore a wig when his picture was taken. He refused to answer when asked if Sarti’s face were retouched. Rivele said that he got the impression from David that the photo of Sarti was not genuine, or did not really look like him. Regarding Oswald (whom he never met), David said “the CIA manipulated Oswald and him in the same way, and would be killed in same way if he was not careful.”

It was during this trip that Rivele managed to track down the elusive Edmond Meunier at his home in Liege, Belgium. Rivele was desperate to find out the identity of the mysterious man in Mexico and at that time, the only lead to the person’s identity was that of Edmond Meunier. They talked in his apartment for an hour and Rivele recognized Meunier from the photos he’d seen previously. The one difference was that his hairline was not as sparse as Nick's was in 1963. Meunier showed Rivele pictures of him taken in Rhodesia in 1963 and he looked younger than Nick in the shots. At the time of their meeting, Meunier was 53 years old and when he showed him a picture of Nick, he had no visible reaction. Meunier said that he'd never been to North America, said that he was absent from Africa between February, 1963 and September 1964. He said that he was unaware of the any CIA recruitment among "ground troops in the Congo, though pilots were recruited." He showed Rivele one picture of the only American mercenary he ever met, a man who was killed in the Congo. He also gave Rivele a phone number of a military officer who was present when Patrice Lumumba was killed. Much to Rivele's disappointment, he soon came to realize that Edmund Meunier was not the mystery man in Mexico who impersonated Oswald. "Despite striking resemblance," wrote Rivele, "reluctantly concluded Meunier was not Nick."

Rivele spoke a number of times with Christian David in his prison cell during the month of January, 1986, in which David provided him with additional information regarding the background of the Kennedy killing.

In a meeting on January 17, 1986, Rivele said that David's lawyer had been in to see him that morning to tell him that the French government was attempting to have him committed, and upon hearing the news, David went into a frenzy, fearing for his life. Hoping to get any leverage he could regarding his impending jail term, he gave more information to Rivele during that session. He said that Lucien Sarti was in Mexico several weeks before going to the United States, but not more than a month. When Rivele asked him where Sarti stood on the day of the assassination he first said from the bridge over Dealey Plaza, but soon, corrected himself and said that he moved to the area of the wooden fence on the hill and that Sarti fired from behind the wooden fence (picket fence).

When Rivele mentioned that the president was shot from the front, he replied that he was shot from in front and behind. "It was a crossfire," David said. He said there was a person in an office building but could not recall where it was. He said that his team cased Dealey Plaza several days before the assassination in order to get accumulated to their surroundings when the day of the assassination came. He said that he could not remember how much heroin Sarti received for payment but noted that Sarti was not in the drug trade at the time, "but heroin was the liquid currency of the time."

He said that Antoine Guerini was the only intermediary between Sarti and the Chicago Mafia which was run by Carlos Marcello, "but that once he had put them in touch, he withdrew from the affair." Sarti made his own arrangements with the Chicago mob, deciding it was better for his own security if he did not include anyone else in the affair.

He startled Rivele by saying that Sarti was in the Congo at the same time he was. When Rivele told him that Sarti was only 23 or 24 at the time, he replied that he was there at the same time. "At the end of the conversation, in discussing Sarti," wrote Rivele, "he mentioned that you can shoot better with one eye than with two; that when you have only one eye you are a better shot than someone with two eyes. Said there was no comparison since you're not distracted by the sight in the other eye. This statement recalled the "France Sori" article which said that Sarti had lost the sight in his left eye in a car accident."

They met the next day for another hour of fruitful conversation. He said that he believed Antoine Guerini was involved in the plots to kill Castro but he would not elaborate, that Paul Mondoloni was the intermediary who set up the assassination, and that he spent much time in the U.S. He mentioned in passing that he knew Tommy Davis (who was sprung from a jail in Morocco, possibly by QJWIN), but refused any more comment on him. Rivele then showed David an aerial photo of Dealey Plaza and asked him where Sarti had shot from? He said again that Sarti fired from the front (the grassy knoll area), David then asked him to show him a picture of the buildings in Dealey Plaza.

David said the shooting happened in the following manner:

> Three gunmen, very definite on this point. Said that it was a crossfire with three guns, two behind, one in front. Of the two behind, one was high and one was low. Repeated this several times. Said you can't understand the wounds if you don't realize that one gun was low, almost

on the horizontal. Said if not, the wounds would have been impossible. First shot fired from behind and hit Kennedy in the back. Second shot fired from behind and hit the other person in the car. Third shot fired from in front. Fourth shot fired from behind a missed because the car was too far away. Said that two shots were almost simultaneous. Said the official investigation was faked. Said Kennedy was killed for revenge and money. Said CIA was incapable of killing Kennedy but did cover it up. Says he believes the gunmen went to Canada, that there were people in Canada who had the ability to fly them out of the US. Said they had important contacts in Montreal. Refused to answer any more questions. Insisted that we find Nicoli who was informed on the plot. Refused to comment on whether was he involved in plot, but also refused to deny that he was.[112]

David related that he saw Sarti two months after the assassination and that only a handful of people knew that Sarti had taken part in the president's death. He stated that Sarti was "assassinated" in Mexico, and that there was no reason for the Mexican police to kill him. He believed that Sarti's death was deliberate and that it was ordered by the CIA. While he knew Sarti for a long period of time, David said he was not a real friend of his, only that they worked together and "but he would not have chosen Sarti as friend." He said he was quite bitter about Sarti but would not give any further explanation as to why. He also emphasized that Sarti killed for money, not for any political cause.

Sarti, according to David, first accepted heroin as payment for any job when he took part in the Kennedy hit. David said that one of his former associates in the criminal underworld saw Sarti in Argentina in late 1963 or early 1964 with a large quantity of heroin.

Regardless of David's assertions that the CIA was involved in the Kennedy assassination, that entire part of the story is still in doubt. The one real link in David's story concerns the CIA and its relationship with Antoine Guerini. That relationship went back to

---

112 "Fourth Meeting with David," January 18, 1986. Rivele file, AARC, Washington, D.C.

World War 11 when the OSS, the CIA's predecessor, supported Guerini and his allies who were fighting with the French Resistance in Southern France. When the war was over, the CIA funneled millions of dollars to Guerini crime organization who were fighting to prevent the communist labor unions in Marseille from getting a solid hold of the movement. One ex-CIA officer said of the Guerini-CIA connection that, "the first battles of the Cold War were fought on the Marseille docks, and Guerini's thugs were in the front lines." Guerini had solid connections with the American Mafia, especially through Mexico City and Montreal where their illegal drugs were trans-shipped from France to North America. Two of Guerini's most supportive American mob allies were Carlo Gambino of the powerful New York crime family, and Florida mob boss, Santo Trafficante.

According to Christian David, the real reason that Antonie Guerini offered the plot to kill JFK was because of Guerini's hopes of re-establishing his lost gambling interests in Cuba that had been shut down after Castro came to power. David asserts that this was to come about by making Oswald a convenient patsy—Castro agent—in Kennedy's death, thus, making necessary an American lead invasion of Cuba in retaliation. Once Castro was overthrown, then the mobsters would once again have free reign in operating the casinos in Havana.

Rivele summed up his talk with David in "notes" that he wrote on his talk with the French gangster.

He said the chief accomplishment of the trip was that he had gotten from David, the essentials of the assassination namely, the names of the gunmen, dates, routes of entry and escape, place names and other vital indications. David said that he would not spend one more year in jail under his present circumstances and if he were not freed, then he'd make an attempt on his life.

Rivele believed that David was telling the truth for the most part, but was keeping a sizable chunk of information from him. Rivele believed that David was not involved in the assassination, "but the nature of what he has said suggests that he was... I accept the idea that Sarti was the man on the grassy knoll, and it strikes me as quite possible that Nicoli was another of the gunmen. The careers of the three men-David, Sarti and Nicoli-are parallel, their names almost always appear together, so that there seems to have been some sort of link among them. However, for the first time we have substantial reason to think we know the identity of one of the gunmen, and we have been given the name of another man who apparently knows a great deal about the assassination, namely, Nicoli. We must now make a major effort to locate and interview Nicoli, I believe. At the very least he can corroborate the essentials of what David has said, specifically, that there was a contract in Marseille in May of 1963, that David was solicited for it and that Sarti accepted it. With such corroboration we would have more than a line of enquiry; we would have a case. It would then remain to connect this case up with what we know about U.S. intelligence and Mafia operations of the era. The priority, then, is to find Nicoli at any cost."

Their conversation of January 25, according to the notes, was not very profitable. David refused to answer any questions put to him, but said that he could not reveal any of the names of the dead gunmen who killed the president because this man still had family alive. He said that he could positively identify the "other man" in the Congo but refused. "Said there were documents, statements made under torture which proved he was telling truth. Assume he was referring to Sarti's Argentine statement." When asked if he could name the other people who had knowledge of the Kennedy assassination who had been killed to stop them from talking he said, "I knew better then he who they were; people in the U.S… Asked for examples, he refused, but repeated they were killed in the U.S."

Their seventh meeting was both worthwhile, as well as frustrating. David met with his lawyer the day before and told him not to cooperate any more with Rivele and Jim Lesar because he would soon be getting out of jail. David said that he'd write down what he knew of the assassination and would give it to his Corsican lawyer. He said he'd give all the details he knew, but that the lawyer would have possession of that information, and that his lawyer would contact Jim Lesar. In return, David wanted Jim Lesar and his organization to appeal David's sentence to the International Criminal Court in The Hague. If they succeeded in getting David out of jail, his lawyer would provide them with all the information David had written down. If David somehow managed to get out of jail, he would sell the information in order to provide for his family. If he died, then David's lawyer would sell the information as payment for his family. He said that he'd also write down what he knew of the Congo operation under separate cover and give it to his attorney. In the afternoon session, David told Rivele that that he'd be getting out of jail soon, or if not, he'd be placed under psychiatric observation for a few months and then be released. If neither of these things happened, then he'd kill himself before the year ended. David reported in that same conversation that all the gunmen were Corsican. When Rivele observed that Sarti was born in Marseille, David countered by saying that Sarti's mother was Corsican, thus, making him Corsican. He said that all the three gunmen still had living relatives "who would revenge them if he told, and that they would trace the information back to him. Said Sarti had an explosive bullet and only Sarti was paid in heroin. Would not explain the difference. Said find out who Sarti's contacts in U.S. were and I will know who was involved."

After considerable time and effort traveling through Europe on Rivele's part (and with the backing of the Assassinations Archives and Research Center), Rivele now believed he had the rudimentary knowledge of just how the assassination of JFK took place. The hit was offered by Antoine Guerini to Christian David who refused to take part in it. Lucien Sarti, a member of the Ricord gang, a man who was connected to both U.S. and French intelligence, as well as the Corsican Mafia, was one of the assassins in Dealey Plaza on November 22, 1963. Sarti was paid in heroin—something that he'd never consented to do before. He said a man named Nicoli knew a great deal about the assassination but he refused to say more. Once Nicoli was found, said David, the story would come full circle.

In a recent e-mail chat with Jim Lesar, he told me that Christian David was finally released from prison, (he didn't know when), and that he did not know if David is still alive at this writing.

The stage was now set for the murder of a president. Dealey Plaza would be the spot, all played out in advance.

Chapter 10:

The Guns of Dallas

The president of the United States, John F. Kennedy, went to Texas in November, 1963 for two reasons, one, to raise money for the Democratic party and two, to heal a rift in the state Democratic party, and to beef up his chances in Texas in the upcoming 1964 presidential election. Despite having his vice president, Lyndon Johnson who was a Texan on the ticket, Kennedy was not as popular as he was in 1960 when he and Johnson won the state by 46,233 votes over Richard Nixon. The reason for Kennedy's political slide in Texas was due to a number of factors, including his more liberal stance on such high octane topics as the civil rights bill which would have outlawed segregation in public places, a bill the president had sent to congress, and the president's decision to ask the national legislature to cut the oil depletion allowance for the rich, Texas oil companies that dominated politics in that state.

The two most popular politicians in Texas in November 1963 were Vice President Lyndon Johnson and Governor John Connally. Both men represented the more conservative wing of the Democratic Party in Texas and they reflected the majority political opinion in the state as opposed to Kennedy's more liberal New Frontier. When Kennedy came to power, he appointed Connally as Secretary of the Navy, a post for which he was not really qualified, and which he did not last long in. Connally quit and ran successfully for Governor of Texas (critics called him "Lyndon's Boy John"). Connally went so far as to criticize JFK's civil rights bill, a position that was gaining more traction in the state.

On the other side of the political fence was Texas Senator Ralf Yarborough, who represented the more "liberal" wing of the party, and a stalwart Kennedy man. Since Yarborough ran for Senator in

1957, both Johnson and Connally supported Yarborough's primary opponent, a move that the senator never forgot, nor forgave. The president faced a political dilemma as he planned his Texas trip; how to reconcile the rift between Connally and Yarborough, both of whom he'd need in 1964. Johnson, Kennedy decided, would play middleman.

Johnson, himself, was not interested in taking sides, as his stock in the administration waned since the day both men took office. The President did not like nor trust the powerful, ex-Majority Leader of the Senate and he gave Johnson little of substance to do in the White House. Kennedy's aides called both Johnson and his wife, Lady Bird, derogatory nicknames behind their backs, word of which reached Johnson's ear. There was even quiet talk within the administration that the president was considering dumping LBJ from the ticket in 1964. However, he put aside his differences with the president and agreed to help him with his Connally-Yarborough problem.

The original decision to make the Texas trip came in June 1963 when JFK was in El Paso, Texas. There, he met with Gov. Connally and LBJ and said he wanted to make a campaign swing through Texas in order to raise money for the party. He wanted to make four fund-raising events in Houston, San Antonio, Fort Worth and Dallas. It was suggested that the trip be made in the last week of August, but the date was opposed by Connally, saying the fall would be better. Neither Connally nor Johnson really wanted JFK to come to Texas, seeing his presence in the state as detrimental to both of their political standings, as well as being seen as interfering in domestic Texas politics.

On October 4, Gov. Connally met privately with JFK in the White Hose, a meeting at which Johnson was not invited. The topic got down to the president's trip to Texas and the governor recommended that the president make a two day, four city trip to the state. They agreed to the new schedule that called for the president to leave Washington on November 21st, in order to dedicate a $16-million aerospace medical center in San Antonio, then to Houston where he'd honor a dinner for Congressman Albert Thomas. That same night, the party would head to Fort Worth where, the next day, a breakfast for the presidential party would be hosted by the chamber of commerce.

They'd then fly to Dallas for a luncheon speech at the Trade Mart before their last stop in Austin where a fund raising event was to be held,, and a reception at the governor's mansion. The president and his wife, Jacqueline, would spend the night at the LBJ ranch before flying back to Washington.

The president asked his wife if she'd accompany him on the Texas trip and she reluctantly agreed. Jackie did not like the art of politics and only did so because she knew her husband would really wanted her along. The presidential couple had recently lost their infant son Patrick who had died shortly after his birth and this would be her first political trip since the tragic event. Jackie told a friend shortly before the trip was planned that, "I know I'll hate every minute of it." She'd go because, "It's a tiny sacrifice on my part for something he feels is very important to him."

Even before the president's trip was announced, there were certain misgivings from a number of people who thought that the political atmosphere in Texas, and especially in Dallas, was not be conducive to a visit by the president at that time. One of these men was Byron Skelton who was a Democratic National Committeeman from Texas. Kennedy knew Skelton well; he was instrumental in arranging then candidate Kennedy's talk with the Greater Houston Ministerial Association during the 1960 presidential campaign. He especially didn't want the president to make a stop in Dallas, saying that the city was on edge, and the extreme right wing elements in the city were making threatening noises about Kennedy and his national policies.

On November 4, Skelton wrote a letter to Robert Kennedy telling of his concerns. He wrote that, "I am worried about President Kennedy's proposed trip to Dallas." He mentioned in his letter about a leading citizen of the city who wrote that, "Kennedy is a liability to the free world." Skelton said that, "A man who would make this kind of statement is capable of doing harm to the president." He finished by recommending that the Dallas trip be canceled.

Skelton further wrote a letter to LBJ's top aid Walter Jenkins, repeating his concerns and urging that both JFK and LBJ skip Dallas entirely. Skelton then flew to Washington where he met with John Bailey and Jerry Bruno of the Democratic National Committee. He told them of his worries.

Bobby Kennedy then sent a letter on November 8 to Kenny O'Donnell, telling of Skelton's worries. Skelton's misgivings went nowhere and the Dallas trip went on as planned.

JFK knew of the risks he was facing as president but never let those fears stop him from doing his job. In the time between his election and inauguration on January 20, 1961, a man named Richard Paul Pavlick wired seven sticks of dynamite to his body in an effort to kill both himself, the president-elect and Mrs. Kennedy at the president's father's home in Florida.

In the past, Dallas had a penchant for violence against its public officials. During the 1960 campaign, a number of women shot saliva on both LBJ and his wife. Shortly before the Texas trip, U.N. Ambassador Adlai Stevenson had been attacked in Dallas while he was in the city on UN Day. Ambassador Stevenson later told the White House that he was horrified about the hatred toward him and the president that he encountered in Dallas and wondered if the president would be better off if he canceled the trip to the city. Both Dallas newspapers published editorials asking for calm in the city when the president arrived. The *Times,* wrote, saying, "both the world and John F. Kennedy will like what is seen here."

The right-wing *News* opined that, "another incident similar to the one involving Stevenson could lead Dallas on a deadly blow on the national level, particularly from a political standpoint."

At the time of Kennedy's proposed trip to Dallas, the city was known for his radical right-wing politics and the people who supported them. Dallas was the home of right-wing former Army general Edwin Walker, a member of the John Birch Society, and a decorated World War 2 army officer. Walker once called President Eisenhower "a dedicated, conscious agent of the Communist conspiracy." While he was on active duty, General Walker, in a speech, told his troops how to vote and openly attacked the president. When Kennedy heard of Walker's statements, he was relieved of his command. After the assassination, it was reported that Lee Oswald took a shot at Walker's home in which a bullet was fired into his window. However, there was no positive proof that Oswald took part in the incident.

In the city, signs that called for the impeachment of Chief Justice Earl Warren were common. Dallas was the home of such radical groups as the John Birch Society, the Minutemen, the

Christian Crusaders, and the Patrick Henry Society. It was also the home of such rightwing, and anti-Kennedy leaders such as oil man H.L. Hunt and Clint Murchison Sr.

In an interesting aside, a letter that was supposed to have been written by Lee Oswald on November 8, 1963, read:

> *Dear Mr. Hunt.*
>
> *I would like information concerning my position. I am asking only for information. I am suggesting that we discuss the matter fully before any steps are taken by me or anyone else.*
>
> *Thank you,*
>
> *Lee Harvey Oswald.*

It is now known if Oswald was writing the letter to H.L. Hunt or to Watergate burglar, E. Howard Hunt and if so, why?

H.L. Hunt had a covert relationship with Sergio Arcacha-Smith, the head of the Cuban Revolutionary Council which was located in New Orleans in the summer of 1963. The CRC was closely linked with Guy Banister's private detective agency and were located in the same building at 544 Camp Street. Oswald was connected with Banister and was passing out Fair Play for Cuba literature in the city (one leaflet had the 544 Camp Street address written on it).

On November 23, 1963, one day after the assassination, H.L. Hunt met with Jack Crichton, a member of Army intelligence, and other Army intelligence officers, to discuss the first meeting with Marina Oswald, Lee's wife. Why?

Dallas was not the only place that was a hot bed of conspiracy and hatred towards JFK. Unknown to most Americans of the day, there was a plot to kill Kennedy that was hatched in Chicago and was to have taken place on November 2, 1963 during a scheduled presidential visit to the city. The plot was discovered by local police and reported up the chain of command. In light of the plot, the president's motorcade to Chicago was cancelled at the last possible moment.

Two people who had knowledge of the plot to kill JFK in Chicago played a prominent part in the story, one, a CIA affiliated mobster, and ex-Chicago policeman named Richard Cain, and the first African American Secret Service Agent, Abraham Bolden.

According to the testimony of Abraham Bolden, who a few years later, would break FBI protocol and try to contact the Warren commission regarding the lax behavior of a number of Secret Service agents guarding JFK, the CIA had known before had that an attempt to kill the president was in the works. Bolden said that on October 30, 1963, the FBI sent a teletype to the Chicago Secret Service Office saying that an attempt to kill the president would take place in Chicago on November 2 by a four man hit team using a high powered rifle. He said the message was given to Maurice Martineau, the Special Agent in Charge. On the morning of November 2, SAC Martineau told his fellow agents the details of the plot, saying that the attack would take place as the motorcade traveled from O'Hare airport across the Northwest Expressway and down the famous loop.

The shooters were supposed to be a group of "right-wing para-military fanatics." The source on these men was an informant named "Lee." No one knows who this "Lee" person was.

Abraham Bolden would later be arrested for trying to sell a file to a man indicted for counterfeiting. He spent time as a prisoner at the Federal Medical Center in Springfield, Missouri, Bolden always said that he was arrested and framed because he tried to tell the Warren Commission about the "general laxity among Secret Service agents assigned to President Kennedy."

The other person who had knowledge of the plot in Chicago was Richard Cain, a man with little formal education, yet he became a high ranking Chicago police official, as well as a hit man for the Chicago mob. During his life, he aided the anti-Castro cause in Chicago, meeting with a number of high-ranking anti-Castro Cubans, making several trips to Cuba on behalf of these people, and at the same time, offering his services to the CIA, who read his reports, yet did not want to formalize their relationship with him. Cain, in the company of an unidentified woman, was sent to Cuba to kill Fidel Castro. According to Cain's account, he made it into the office of Fidel Castro but was not able to hide the poison that he was going to use.

From May 16, 1956 until May 16, 1960, Cain worked for the Chicago Police Department and rose to the rank of detective in February 1958. He resigned from the police force in May 1960 because of an investigation that was started against him by the police. At the time of his arrest, he was working for the Police Sex Bureau Squad. He was accused of spying on City Commissioner Irwin Cohen, and was alleged to have been paid $1,700 by the State's Attorney's Office.

Richard Cain's violent end came on December 20, 1973 when he was having a meal at Rose's Sandwich Shop in Chicago with mobster Marshall Caifano. Dick Cain unexpectedly left the restaurant at around 12:30 p.m. He returned one hour later and found Caifano gone. Suddenly, two men wearing ski masks burst into the diner, and lined Cain up against the wall. He was shot point blank with a shotgun and died instantly.

Another person who was interviewed by the police in the wake of the president's canceled trip to Chicago was Thomas Arthur Valle. On October 30, 1963, the Secret Service was told that Valle, an outspoken opponent of JFK, owned a number of weapons and might pose a threat to the president. The FBI went to his residence and found that he had in his apartment two M-1 rifles, a 22-caliber revolver, and almost 1,000 rounds of ammunition. Vallee also worked in a building overlooking the Jackson Street ramp where Kennedy's motorcade would travel.

The Secret Service told the Chicago P.D. about Vallee and they decided to put a surveillance team on him to monitor his activities. Two members of the Chicago police department, Daniel Groth and Peter Schurla followed Vallee around the city and took him into custody on the morning of November 2, the day of Kennedy's trip. Both officers stopped Vallee in his car for making an improper turn signal. They found a hunting knife in the car, as well as ammunition stored in the trunk. If Vallee planned to harm the president, he did not now pose a threat.

It seems that Vallee had no connection to the four-man sniper team that the Secret Service was following. The Secret Service picked up the trail of two of the four men and traced their location to a rooming house where they were staying. While following them in an unmarked car, two of the suspects suddenly reversed their direction and passed the approaching agents who saw them drive by. The agents were able to catch up with the fleeing men and they were taken back to the office of the Chicago Secret Service. The agents did not find any weapons in their car, nor at their place of residence.

Abraham Bolden would later say that the men who were taken into custody at the Secret Service headquarters at that time did not look like Thomas Vallee. Bolden testified years later that the men taken in for questioning gave their names as "Gonzales and Rodriguez." While they were being questioned, the other two shooters quietly slipped out of town. Soon, both men were also released and the feds were never able to determine just who these two suspicious men were, or what, if anything, they were planning, vis-a-vi, JFK's trip to Chicago.

By sheer luck, the plot to kill JFK in Chicago never took place. However, Dallas, the next city of opportunity awaited.

The presidential party departed the White House for the last time on, Thursday, November 21, en-route to San Antonio. Senator Yarborough was still feuding with Governor Connally, because he was not invited to a reception at the Governor's official residence. The motorcade passed by thousands of happy, eager fans who lined the route into the city. The president made a speech about the America's planned program to land a man on the moon by saying that,"This nation has tossed it's cap over the wall of space-and we have no choice but to follow it. With the help of all those who labor in the space endeavor, with the help and support of all Americans, we will climb this wall with safety and with speed-and we shall then explore the wonders on the other side."

The next stop was Houston, where the president and his wife stayed at the Rice Hotel. The president made a speech at the Houston Coliseum and then they departed for Fort Worth. They stayed at the Hotel Texas, one of the oldest establishments in the city. That night, while the Kennedy's slept, nine members of the president's secret service detail spent the wee hours of the morning drinking and taking in the show at "The Celler" a nightclub that they shouldn't have been in the first place.

On the morning of the 22nd, JFK was supposed to make a speech in front of the Fort Worth Chamber of Commerce. Before the speech, the president, Gov. Connally and Vice President Johnson made an impromptu address in a misty rain to a crowd of people in a parking lot near the hotel. Wen the president began to address the crowd, they wanted to know where Mrs. Kennedy was. The president jokingly said, "Mrs. Kennedy is busy organizing herself. It takes longer, but of course, she looks better than we do when she does it."

The party then arrived at the main event; a talk to 2,500 awaiting guests at the Chamber. Before leaving the event, one of the hosts presented JFK with a Stetson hat and asked if he would put in on. Kennedy, who did not usually wear hats, told the crowd that he'd "put in on at the White House on Monday."

At 10:37 a.m. they left for Carswell Air Force base for the very short ride to Dallas and the presidential speech at the Trade Mart.

At Love Field in Dallas, Lyndon Johnson was waiting for the president to deplane with Mrs. Johnson. After a perfunctory hello, the first couple strode over to the fence and began shaking hands with the waiting crowd. As the motorcade began to form up, Senator Yarborough rode with Johnson and his wife Lady Bird. Governor Connally and his wife rode in the presidential limousine. At 11:55. A.M., the presidential party began the 9 mile trip to downtown Dallas. The presidential limousine was dubbed SS 100X, a twenty-one foot long, midnight blue color with Agent Bill Greer driving and Agent Roy Kellerman beside him. The Connally's rode in the jump seats, with JFK sitting behind Connally and Jackie next to him.

There were estimated to be at least 150,000 people who thronged the streets of Dallas to see the president and his young wife, Cheers and friendly shouts were heard along the way, and as they neared downtown, the crowds grew even greater. The presidential limousine did not have the bubble top up, due to the sunny, warm weather that greeted them in Dallas. The president waved to the crowd, enjoying the adulation that they gave him.

At 12:29 p.m., the motorcade made a right hand turn onto Houston Street, approaching a tiny area known as Dealey Plaza. They could see, in the short distance, the shade of an underpass that would give them temporary shelter from the hot sun. They were looking forward to getting near it. Near the underpass, a resident named James Teague loitered, waiting to see the passing limousine. Standing on a perch in Dealey Plaza was businessman Abraham Zapruder and his secretary. Zapruder was holding a movie camera that was trained on the street right in front of him. He hoped to film the president as he went by. In the Texas School Book Depository overlooking Dealey Plaza, a window on the sixth floor was open, an obvious breach of security.

Lee Oswald, a former-Marine who had defected to the Soviet Union and then came back to the Untied States under mysterious circumstances was working in the building. He was supposed to have been lining up his old, Italian 6.5 rifle, a Manlicher Carcano, at the motorcade below. On the grass in the plaza, Mary Moorman had her camera ready to film the motorcade… The photo she took of the assassination was never returned to her. On grassy knoll, right in front of the picket fence, was Gordon Arnold, a serviceman who was home on leave. He too readied his mother's camera for a shot at history.

The motorcade made a sharp turn onto Elm Street, at a very slow rate of speed. All had gone surprisingly well, The Trade Mart loomed ahead.

According to Christian David, Lucien Sarti, in disguise, took aim at the president's car as it came into view. Using an explosive bullet, he, and the other snipers who were stationed in a triangular crossfire, opened fire.

But who were the other snipers in Dealey Plaza that day? In order to find out, Rivele would have to find Michel Nicoli.

During Rivele's discussions with Christian David in his French prison cell, Rivele told him that he had quiet a story, but if he were to tell the world about it, there was one huge doubt that would surely come out; his personal credibility. Rivele wanted to know if there was any other person who could confirm his story. David thought a minute and gave him a name, Michel Nicoli. He now had to find this elusive man who could, one way or another, either confirm or deny David's astonishing story.

Michel Nicoli had been a confidant of August Ricord's drug business and was suspected of being the leader of one of Ricord's five subgroups. Over the years, both Nicole and Christian David worked closely together in Ricord's organization and the dossier on both men were piled high. After Ricord's 1971 arrest in Paraguay, both David and Sarti moved their drug operation to Brazil's Ilha Bella Island where David now took the reigns as the number one man in Brazilian connection, along with Michel Nicoli. Nicoli was arrested by Brazilian police in October, 1972 in Sao Paulo and he was subsequently sent to the United States for trial. Brazilian police were not kind to Nicoli and he said that he was tortured by them while he was in custody. David was also captured and they were both subsequently sent to the Untied States where they faced years in jail for drug smuggling. At trial, both men plead guilty to conspiracy charges (Nicoli was later reindicted on his narcotics charge, and for bail jumping). In time, Nicoli proved to be an intelligence find of the first order for the United States government and in return for his cooperation, he was placed in the Federal Witness Protection Program for his own safety.

Rivele struck pay-dirt, when, in June, 1986, quite by accident, he found the one person who was able to put him in touch with Michel Nicoli, a highly placed member of the Drug Enforcement Administration, Michael Tobin. Rivele persuaded Tobin to put him in touch with Michel Nicoli without telling him the real reason why he wanted to speak with him. In their talks, the DEA official told Rivele that in his thirty years experience in the DEA, that Nicoli was the most reliable witness he'd ever come across and that if Nicoli told him anything about the crimes or people he'd been involved with, "You could go to the bank on it."[113]

Nicoli said that the last time he saw David was in 1972 when both men were in a court in Brazil, waiting trial. Nicoli agreed that the assassins who killed Kennedy were paid in heroin, and that it was he who converted the heroin payment into cash for the assassins. He said that the three assassins were in his apartment in Buenos Aires, Brazil a few months after the assassination, with, "a substantial quantity of heroin." Nicoli was surprised because no previous assassin had dealt in heroin. He said that he did not want to ask any more questions and he agreed to convert the heroin into cash for them. Nicoli said that he did see Christian David in a bar in Argentina in 1966 with at least six other men (the bar might have been the Maison de Anciens Combattants Francais. This bar was a favorite of Auguste Ricord when he was in Argentina). In his talks with Nicoli, he told Rivele that one of the killers in Dealey Plaza was Lucien Sarti. When questioned how he knew this, Nicoli said that he learned about it from the same source, at the same time that Christian David had.

In subsequent conversations, Nicoli told Rivele the names of the two other assassins who worked with Sarti, one of whom was

113 "The Corsican Connection," world-wide web.

Roger Bocognani. He said that at the time that this interview took place, Bocognani was still alive and that he was a member of Lucien Sarti's group. Bocognani was a childhood friend of Sarti's and he was also involved in the drug trade. He said that the third person was known to him as "Le Blanc" (the white one) and noted that: "I was never certain he was real" (could be trusted or relied upon). You don't ask questions, you know. If someone doesn't want to tell you his name, you don't get to know."

"Le Blanc" was "a big shot, very dangerous, He was not in the drug trafficking in South America. He lived in Europe. He was in Sarti's gang, and he was one of Sarti's friends since childhood."

When asked if "Le Blanc" was still alive, Nicoli replied, "I have not heard any word that he is dead. For all I know, he is alive and living in Marseille."

Rivele questioned Nicoli how he knew that these three men actually were the ones who killed Kennedy. According to Nicoli:

> One evening we were together. It was in a bar in Buenos Aires at the end of 1965. Present at the bar were David, Sarti, Bocognani and myself. The conversation was about Kennedy's assassination. Sarti gestured toward Bocognani and said, "you know where he was? David asked him "where." And Sarti responded, "in Dallas." Me, I didn't ask any questions. It was none of my business, added Nicoli. However, David-who was a blabbermouth-started asking details. I listened, and that is how I got the information.

When asked how he knew that "Le Blanc" was the third killer, Nicoli responded by saying that he had separate business to conduct with him "and from the things he said, his facial expressions and his gestures, I concluded that he was the third (conspirator) Also, they (Sarti, Bocognani, and "Le Blanc" were always together. They made all of their "hits" together."

Nicoli subsequently asked David if "Le Blanc" was involved in the Kennedy assassination "and David responded that he thought so."

Steve Rivele believes that the contract to kill the president started with Carlos Marcello who placed it in Marseille via Santo

Trafficante Jr. who was close to Antoine Guerini. He also thinks that Sam Giancana was also involved in the affair because the shooters were met at the US-Mexico border by members of the Chicago mob. He then asked Nicoli why the conspirators went so far away to find the assassins. "In my opinion" replied Nicoli, "to obliterate any traces; to fool the government. It's more difficult to find foreign killers. It's more difficult, in my view."

In his appearance in the tv documentary "The Men Who Killed Kennedy," Rivele stated that "The Mafia had to hire white men for the job since it was to take place in the American South, which meant that they could not go to the other two centers where one found assassins at that time, namely Beirut and Hong Kong. Secondly, they needed assassins who, if they were caught, could not directly be tied to the American Mafia, also who were not known to the American police. And fourthly, once again, if they were caught, assassins who could be counted on not to talk."

When asked why the assassins took such a risk in targeting the American president Nicoli said:

> When someone has a contract to kill someone, he is not rubbing out the name; he is rubbing out the person. You just have to kill him, that's all. And according to who it is, you get paid more; according to who it is, and that's all…
>
> Question: But after all, it was the president of the United States they were talking about.
>
> Nicoli: If they did it, it's because they didn't give a damn. There are people like David who refused to do it. There were others who didn't refuse.
>
> Question: But Sarti, would he have been capable of that?
>
> Nicoli: Oh yes. As a killer, he's capable of anything. It's not a question of sentiment. No sentiment with him.

Rivele then asked him to expound on the fact that Sarti used an explosive bullet:

> Nicoli said: Oh yes, it's Lucien Sarti. Me too. I sometimes carried them with me, but I didn't use them.

Question: What was the advantage of having bullets like that?

Nicoli: It makes a larger hole in the body. When the bullet flattens out, there aren't any traces. No marks. Nothing.

In the papers at the Assassination Archives in Washington is a sworn affidavit that was signed by a notary public of a conversation that Rivele had with Michel Nicoli. Some of the major points are:

Rivele asked him if Sarti and or David were working for the CIA in the Congo. He said he didn't know. He described David's tale about his part in the plot to kill Kennedy as follows:

That Christian David used to hang out at Guerini's club in Marseille to collect money. Said that Guerini offered him the contract to kill JFK. He said that he believed that one of the men who killed the president was named Lucien and thought it was Lucien Sarti. The three Corsicans went to Mexico City where they stayed for about two weeks, then came to the U.S. on Italian passports. They were met at Brownsville, Texas and all their subsequent talks were in Italian. He said that this is what he had heard, but that it may have been in the Corsican dialect, which is close to Italian. Said the assassins staked out Dealey Plaza, taking many pictures of the entire area. He said there was one shooter in front and two behind. Rivele told him that the shooter in the front, most likely Lucien, used an explosive bullet. "He sighed and said that was so, of course."

He said that he didn't know if Sarti was paid in heroin, that the killers left via Montreal after a short while in Dallas. When asked if David was in Austria (as he indicated) during "these events," he said he thought that was so."

I asked him if he knew where Sarti was in November 1963. He replied that he was supposed to have been in Marseille, but that, as he, Nicoli left Europe in September 1963, he couldn't be sure. He confirmed the fact that Sarti had only one eye and that fact made him a better shot. He boasted that Sarti was known as the best shot in Marseille. Rivele asked him if he could identify the unknown American who saw David in Guerini's club, and while he could not, he said that the man was probably from the U.S. Mafia. When asked why Guerini would take such a high risk in taking on the contract he said that Guerini was the number one Mafia figure in France and had strong connections with the U.S. Mafia (Trafficante, Marcello, Hoffa), and that he would have had no problem in doing the job for them. When asked who his contacts were in 1963, he refused to answer. He said again that Christian David had refused to take on the Kennedy contract, but gave no further clue as to why. He did, however, say that David was afraid of going to the United States to carry out such a high profile mission because it was too dangerous.

Their talk now turned to the CIA. Nicoli said he had no idea if Guerini had any ties with the CIA, and said that David was afraid of the French Secret Service but not the CIA. When asked if he ever heard of Lucien Sarti's involvement in the Kennedy assassination, "He said he had not heard that he was, but that he and his friends discussed many things, though in a kind of code, so not one actually said anything directly. I asked how he knew these things. He said they were always together, spent a lot of time together, and such things came up. They were discussed indirectly, but if you don't need to know, you didn't ask questions."

Nicoli said that he did not know the identities of the three Corsicans in Dealey Plaza, but knew of their Corsican heritage.

Rivele asked him if he believed that David's story might not be true. "He said he heard that such things had happened and while he did not have all the details, the story is true as David has told it."[114]

For all intents and purposes, Michel Nicoli had backed up the incredible story that Christian David gave to Steve Rivele in their meetings in France. If this was true, it would shed an important new light on the Kennedy assassination and possibly turn the Warren Commission's investigation on its head. But what could Rivele do now?

Rivele gave all his information that he'd collected from Christian David and Michel Nicoli to his DEA source who found it credible. He then forwarded it to the FBI which, to this date, almost 50 years later, decided not to follow up on any of the leads.

---

114 From: Steve Rivele. "Conversation with Michel Nicoli," 9-4-86. Document at AARC, Washington, D.C.

The French Connection theory as postulated by Christian David and backed up by Michel Nicoli, took a pounding in the press when the "Men Who Killed Kennedy" was aired on the A&E network in the United States. When the identity of the other man who was supposed to have been one of the assassins, Sauveur Pironti, was revealed, both men (Pironti and Bocognani) gave airtight alibis as to their location on November 22, 1963.

Rivele later admitted that he was wrong as to the roles of Pironit and Bocognani and said that if he were still looking into the case, he'd concentrate more on Paul Mondoloni, a Mafia figure from Montreal, and mysterious figure know as "Le Blanc."

Rivele summed up his work on the French Connection by saying,

"I've become convinced that Oswald had nothing to do with the assassination, and that he was very carefully chosen and very carefully set up to take the blame. Based on what I've learned, it seems to me that all the principles involved in the plot to kill the President had ties of one kind or another with U.S. intelligence agencies. There was Trafficante and Giancana who had been conspiring with the CIA to assassinate Fidel Castro; Antonie Guerini who had a relationship with both the OSS and the CIA dating from 1943; and there was Oswald whom I'm satisfied had ben used as a low level intelligence operative.

So even though I don't think that the CIA, for example, had anything directly to do with the assassination; on the day of after the assassination, they found themselves in a horribly compromised position, a position in which they could very easily have been blackmailed by the plotters into covering up whatever they knew about the assassination."

While it seems a fact that neither Sauveur Pironti and Roger Bocognani were not part of the hit team in Dealey Plaza, one eye-witness to the crime, a man named Gordon Arnold, was standing on the grassy knoll when, according to Christian David, when the shots were fired, by Lucien Sarti.

Gordon Arnold was interviewed in the A & E Special, "The Men Who Killed Kennedy." On November 22, 1963, Gordon Arnold was on leave from the Army and decided to come down to Dealey Plaza where he wanted to see the presidential motorcade as it came by. He had with him a camera which his mother had given to him. He wanted to film the motorcade at the railroad bridge that spanned Dealey Plaza. As he was making his way there, a man came up to him, showed him some kind of identification and told him to leave the area. Arnold said he wouldn't leave when the unidentified man told him he was with the Secret Service. (There were no official Secret Service Agents in Dealey Plaza at that time) He then made his way across the length of Dealey Plaza and wound up on the grassy knoll, not too far from where Abraham Zapruder was standing. As soon as the presidential limousine came into view, Arnold put the camera to his face and began filming, he said he felt a shot come whizzing by his head. He had just come from basis training in the army and knew what the sound of rifle fire sounded like. Reacting instantly, Arnold ducked for cover, fearing for his life. He later said that he heard two shots coming by his head, inches from his ear.

In the immediate seconds after the assassination, Arnold said that that someone came next to him and began kicking his body. Arnold got up and saw a policeman standing, menacing, next to him. The cop then asked him where the shots had come from and Arnold replied from the rear (behind the picket fence on the knoll). The cop then demanded that he give him his film. Terrified, and fearing for his life, Arnold handed over the film, (but not the camera). Arnold also said that while the policeman was wearing a uniform, his hands were dirty (most cops have clean hands), and that he was not wearing a hat (most real cops wear hats).

Two days after the assassination, Arnold was back in the Army, headed for a duty station in Alaska. He never knew what happened to the film that was confiscated from him that day and never asked that it be returned.

Arnold was never interviewed by the Warren Commission nor the HSCA, but he did, however, give his story to the *Dallas Morning News* in 1978. He also told his story to two writers who were doing books on the Kennedy assassination, Jim Marrs (Crossfire) and Henry Hurt (Reasonable Doubt). In his appearance on "The Men Who Killed Kennedy," Arnold said that the Secret Service man "pulled out an identification card." He told Earl Golz of the "Morning News" and author Henry Hurt that the man had a badge with him. In the A&E special, Arnold said the man who told him to get off the bridge was a CIA officer. Upon hearing that,

Arnold said, “Well, that’s enough muscle. I’ll leave.”

While there were numerous on site witnesses in Dealey Plaza that day, there no one else who came up to support Arnold’s claims. However, there was one person who backed up Arnold’s story. That man was Texas Senator Ralph Yarborough who was riding in the presidential motorcade when the shots were fired. Yarborough later told the *Dallas Morning News* that when the first shot rang out, he saw a man in a uniform immediately hit the dirt at the same point where Arnold said he was. Yarborough also said that upon seeing the man drop so fast to the ground, he immediately knew that he had some sort of military training.

Another person who reported a similar story as that of Gordon Arnold’s was Lee Bowers who worked in a railroad tower overlooking Dealey Plaza on the afternoon of the assassination. While observing the scene before the motorcade arrived, Bowers said that he saw three cars entering the parking lot near the picket fence area. He also said that he saw two men standing near the picket fence on the knoll. He said, “These men were the only two strangers in the area. The others were workers whom I knew.” Bowers confirmed that these two men were there when the shots rang out.

He was interviewed by author Mark Lane in the book, *Rush to Judgement* (1966). Bowers said that, “At the time of the shooting, in the vicinity of where the two men I have described were, there was a flash of light or, as far as I am concerned, something I could not identify, but there was something which caught my eye in this immediate area on the embankment. Now, what this was, I could not state at that time and at this time I could not identify it, other than there was some unusual occurrence-a flash of light or smoke or something which caused me to feel that something out of the ordinary had occurred there.”

Lee Bowers died under mysterious circumstances. On August 9, 1966, he was killed when his car left the road and crashed into a concrete abutment in Midlothian, Texas. Author Robert Groden wrote that Lee Bowers was driving west on highway sixty-seven from Midlothian to Cleburne, Texas. An eyewitness said that he was driven off the road by a black car, into a bridge abutment.

In “The Men Who Killed Kennedy,” Gordon Arnold was interviewed on camera and was shown the picture of the assassination that was taken by Mary Moorman. The interviewer showed him an artist's rendition of the picture that he began to study. He said that he saw a picture of a person in a summer uniform with an overseas cap and said that it looked like his own uniform. He commented that there was a camera or something like it near the persons face. He said he saw a white spot or a white spot on the picture.

"If it's a flash it would be like off of a muzzle flash," said Arnold. "This looks like a police officer. Because if that would be the badge, that would be the arm emblem. Would, would this fellow back here be the railroad man I asked you about this morning? Because when I was walking to the sight and I had never told anybody that I had when we were out there filming, it reminded me that there was a railroad worker just standing out there by the railroad tracks. Could that, it looks like somebody's taking a picture. Yeah. I couldn't figure out why would I be standing crooked until I flipped that up (the artists sketch) and, if that's a muzzle blast or flash, then whomever's standing there would have been a fool to stand up straight, he'd be trying to get away from harm's way is what it boils down to. And that could very well be me. Son of a gun."[115]

What Arnold was taking about was the so-called "Badgeman" picture that was brought to the Kennedy assassination debate by filmmaker, Jack White. Over the years, White was able to re-create the photo of the shooter on the knoll whom he dubbed "Badgeman," showing what looked like a puff of smoke coming from a rifle, a police emblem on the man's jacket, and the outline of a rifle on the person. Could "Badgeman" be Lucien Sarti?

While many researchers into the Kennedy assassination have found fault with Gordon Arnold' story, he may be the only one who was in the direct line of fire from the shooter on the grassy knoll. It would have been better for the Arnold case if just one other witness who was standing in the same, general proximity of where he was, backed up his story. Since no one has done so in the past fifty years (and his film had never surfaced), his story will have to stand on its own merits.

---

115 Excerpt from "The Men Who Killed Kennedy," A& E Network.

So, who was Badgeman? If Gordon Arnold's story is true, that someone fired two or more shots from behind his standing position on the knoll—that makes conspiracy. Let's remember what Christian David and Michel Nicoli told Rivele during their interviews. David said that Sarti used disguises when he conducted his "hits," depending on where he was, and what his local environment was. If there was a military base nearby, then he (or others who were working with him), would be wearing military style uniforms. Dr. Cyril Wecht, a medical doctor who had once been the President of the American Academy of Forensic Sciences, and the Coroner of Allegheny County in Pittsburgh, and a noted JFK assassination critic, said that the bullets that hit the president were "frangible," that its, they broke up in his body and could not be traced. Dr. Wecht debunked the single bullet theory at many conferences and in the medial community, and received almost no backing from his medical colleagues.

Speaking about the "single bullet theory," and the gunshots that hit Kennedy and Gov. Connally, Dr. Wecht said, "The angles at which these two men were hit do not permit a straight line trajectory (or near straight line trajectory) of Commission exhibit 399 (the so-called magic bullet that was brought to life by ex-Senator Arlen Spector) to be established. Indeed, quite the opposite is true. In order to accept the single-bullet theory, it is necessary to have the bullet move at different vertical and horizontal angles, a path of flight that has never been experienced or suggested for any bullet known to mankind."[116]

Both David and Michel Nicoli said that Sarti used an explosive bullet, one that makes a larger hole in the body and leaves no traces. The wounds on the president's head were massive, not the small, regular sized hole that the Warren Commission said were the wounds that were seen on JFK's body during the autopsy. Most of the president's head was blasted away, most likely from an explosive bullet that came from the front (some people who were in Dealey Plaza that day said that they heard two shots coming almost simultaneously, thus, making the use of an explosive bullet, with its major impact upon entering the body, more probable).

---

116 Fonzi, Gaeton, *The Last Investigation*, Thunders Mouth Press, New York, 1993, Page 216.

Arnold said that he encountered a man wearing a policeman's uniform after the assassination who took away his film. Lucien Sarti used disguises when he took on his assassination projects.

Both Roger Bocognani and Sauveur Pironti had alibis when the events in Dealey Plaza took place and most objective researchers are in agreement that they had nothing to do with the assassination. However, there were two other men, Jean-Paul Angeletti and Francisco Chiappe, both whom worked at one time for Auguste Ricord, the French Connection kingpin, and were big-time heroin dealers, were mentioned by writers researching the Kennedy assassination as possibly being involved in the murder.

The activities of Auguste Ricord have been documented throughout this book and it is not necessary to retell his story at this point. Ricord, nevertheless, needed trusted men who worked as conduits between his French-Corsican heroin network and his customers in the United States. Among those he trusted the most in handling his narcotics shipments were Christian David, Michel Nicoli, Lucien Sarti, and to a lesser extent, Jean-Paul Angeletti and Francisco Chiappe. These men were to become Ricord's main lieutenants in the decade of the 1960s.

Jean-Paul Angeletti was thirty years old in 1971, was a Corsican, a man of danger, who showed up each year at the most plush casinos in Argentina, Brazil, Paraguay, and Uruguay. Like Lucien Sarti, Jean-Paul was wanted for murder and he went by the nickname of "Big Lips." Besides working for Ricord, Angeletti was also associated with Antoine Guerini and it has been speculated that since David turned down the Kennedy hit, it might have been offered (and accepted) by Angeletti. Both Ricord and Guerini were in the heroin smuggling business, illegally transporting opium that was produced in the Golden Triangle area of Southeast Asia, back to the United States. Angeletti and Chiappe were both well connected with both Guerini and Ricord, were of Corsican heritage, and both could very easily have been aware of, or asked to participate in the Kennedy assassination.

Francisco Chiappe was wanted on two counts of murder by the French police, was six-feet tall, and weighted 210 pounds, not a man to be trifled with under any circumstances. Both he and Angeletti were extremely violent men and Chiappe and Sarti were known in the Corsican underworld as "pistoleros."

When William Harvey was setting up the ZR/RIFLE assassination program, one of his conditions for recruiting agents was as follows: "Cover: planning should include provision for blaming Sovs (Soviets) or Czechs in case of blow… organization criminals, those with record of arrests, those who have engaged in several types of crime. Corsicans recommended. Sicilians could lead to Mafia." Another recommendation said, "Former resistance personnel a possibility. Period of testing, surveillance, etc for each selection. All Kubark (code name for CIA) personnel should have some CE (counter-espionage) experience."

If we are to take William Harvey's recommendations seriously, (and there is no reason not to), these two men of Corsican descent, Francisco Chiappe and Jean-Paul Angeletti, were perfect candidates for the CIA's use in their assassination program, and ideal candidates for any attempt on JFK's life.

Steve Rivele, the Mob, and the CIA

In his comments in the "Men Who Killed Kennedy," Steve Rivele said, "I don't think that the CIA, for example, had anything directly to do with the assassination." Be that as it may, Rivele failed to look at the numerous connections of the CIA to Lee Oswald, as well the Kennedy's administration's various actions against Castro that may have led to his own death. Rivele, along with other writers and researchers into the Kennedy assassination, like Lamar Waldron, Thom Hartman, the late John Davis, Robert Blakey, and David Scheim, have pinned the blame for the president's murder squarely on the head of the American Mafia, almost to the exclusion of all other players in the drama. While there is no doubt that four of the most powerful mob figures of the day, Carlos Marcello, Santos Trafficante Jr, Jimmy Hoffa, and Johnny Rosselli, were all in league against the Kennedy brothers in one form or another, they could not have been responsible for the massive cover up following the president's death. The possible mob involvement in the assassination was not looked into by the Warren Commission, despite direct information to the contrary. The HSCA did however, look into the possible mob involvement and said that Marcello and Trafficante had "the means, motive, and opportunity" to kill the president.

What rankles this writer is the penchant for some in the

Kennedy assassination research community to disregard all those who disagree with their own conclusions, i.e., the Mafia killed Kennedy. All writers bring some knowledge to the table on the assassination and their viewpoints should not be pushed aside for one's own petty grievances.

It would take an entire book to describe the possible involvement of the CIA in the Kennedy assassination, as well as the wealth of information on Oswald's connections to the U.S. intelligence community and the people in that area who came in direct contact with him in the months leading up to Dealey Plaza. Here then, is a short course in CIA 101 that Rivele did not look into.

John Kennedy came to office as president of the United States at the height of the cold war, with the United States and the Soviet Union staring each other down the barrel of possible nuclear war. In his inaugural address, Kennedy asked for sacrifice, saying, he would "support any friend, oppose any foe to assure the survival of liberty." He retained Eisenhower's choice as Director of the Central Intelligence Agency, Allen Dulles. He also continued Ike's secret plan to overthrow the Castro regime in what would turnout to be the ill fated Bay of Pigs invasion of Cuba in April, 1961.

Kennedy was given assurances by the CIA that the invasion would succeed, and that Castro would be overthrown in the ensuing battle. Their assumptions were completely wrong, as the invasion was doomed from the start. The CIA was mad at Kennedy's cancellation of a second air strike against Castro's air force when the invasion got bogged down, and also when he refused to allow U.S. combat forces to join the rebels in invading Cuba. While the president took personal responsibility for the failure of the Bay of pigs invasion, certain individuals at the CIA were deeply wounded regarding what they believed was Kennedy's betrayal of the brigade and were very vocal in their criticism. After the invasion, Kennedy fired Dulles and his deputy, Charles Cabell and replaced Dulles with John McCone, a Republican businessman.

The next phase in the CIA's secret war against Castro was Operation Mongoose that was run entirely by the CIA, eventually becoming the largest covert war in the agency's history. The entire Kennedy administration took part in Operation Mongoose, including State, Defense, Justice, the Army, CIA, Voice of America, among others. Newly declassified reports show that Defense Secretary Robert McNamara urged that Castro be removed even if it meant killing him. The man put in overall charge of Operation Mongoose was Attorney General Robert Kennedy. RFK ran rough shod over the CIA, pelting them with daily calls about what they were doing that particular day to get Castro. While Bobby was in command of the plan, there were other members of the government who formed a secret group that monitored the CIA's activities, including General Edward Lansdale, General Maxwell Taylor, presidential advisor McGeorge Bundy, Roswell Gilpatrick, Arthur Schlesinger Jr, Richard Goodwin, and military men such as Defense Chief McNamara, and General Lyman Lemintzer of the Joint Chiefs of Staff.

One of the CIA officers who ran right into trouble with RFK was William Harvey, would wind up running the CIA's covert assassination unit called Executive Action-ZR/RIFLE, which would later employ two of the CIA's most elusive assassins, QJ/WIN and WI/ROGUE. During the height of the Cuban Missile Crisis, Harvey and a group of his men made their way into Cuba to try to ferment hit and run raids against Cuban military targets, just at the time when the president was trying to defuse the situation that might have lead to nuclear war. Harvey was subsequently fired and sent to a post in Europe where he would be out of the line of fire. The CIA set up their own secret base in South Florida called JMWAVE where its agents trained in all aspects of warfare to topple Castro.

A document released via the "JFK Records Act" dated November 5, 1962, sums up the Kennedy administration's attitude toward Castro. "Looking back to the origins of Mongoose, one finds the AG (Attorney General) and Mr. McNamara seeking primarily to remove the political stain left on the President by the Bay of Pigs failure. Both the AG and the Secretary of Defense felt it necessary for political reasons that some action with respect to Cuba to ensure the president's future. In a nutshell, they were out to dump Castro or made him cooperate."

Looking back at the Cuban Missile Crisis with 50 years of hindsight, it seems that JFK's actions in managing the thirteen-day crisis, stopped the world from a nuclear holocaust. Kennedy's use of a naval quarantine to stop the flow of Soviet missiles from arriving in Cuba, plus the back channel diplomacy with Khrushchev and his personal representatives in Washington at the time ended the threat before all hell broke loose. During the thirteen day crisis, there were certain forces, primarily the Joint Chiefs of Staff, who were urging Kennedy to attack Cuba with an all out invasion to stop the missiles from being completed. They were furious when Kennedy refused to retaliate against a missile site that downed an American U-2 spy plane that was taking pictures over Cuba. After the crisis, the Chiefs believed that Kennedy lacked guts and was selling out Cuba to the Russians at American expense. Their resentment at what they believed was Kennedy's lack of will against the Russians in Cuba boiled up after the crisis ended and never waned.

While Operation Mongoose continued into 1963, the Kennedy administration, contrary to CIA objections, began secret peace feelers towards the Castro regime in the hope of easing the tensions between each country. Castro initiated the idea and the administration asked their good friend, William Atwood, a former diplomat, to work on their behalf. Atwood was, at that time, part of the U.S. delegation to the United Nations. He told the president that his contacts told him that Castro was disillusioned with Khrushchev and wanted more freedom to run his own country. Atwood asked JFK if he could put out feelers to the Cuban Ambassador to the UN, Carlos Lechuga. He also asked the president if he could persuade Lechuga to gain an invitation for him to go to Cuba, could he do it? The president gave his permission and soon, a chance encounter was arranged. Journalist Lisa Howard, who had interviewed Castro in the spring, hosted a dinner party at her home. Among those attending the party were William Atwood and Carlos Lechuga.

The day afer the party, Atwood reported to the White House where he met with both JFK and RFK. While nothing of substance took place, Robert Kennedy thought Atwood's contacts with Castro were "worth pursuing."

Lisa Howard's covert contacts with top ranking Cuban's continued, and she had a good discussion with Dr. Rene Vallejo, Castro's friend and private doctor. On October 31, 1963, Vallejo told Howard that Castro was ready for a meeting with a high-ranking American diplomat. JFK was informed and told Atwood to go to Cuba.

But the Atwood-Vallejo channel was not the only one burning. Another man to be used as in intermediary between the U.S. and Castro was French journalist Jean Daniel of *L'Express*. Daniel met with JFK before his trip to Cuba to interview Castro. The president asked Daniel to pass along a message to Castro, the gist of what would become U.S. conditions for better Cuban-American relations. While Atwood never got to Cuba himself, Daniel was with Castro when news of the president's assassination was announced. These covert discussions between the Kennedy administration and the CIA's number one enemy, Fidel Castro, must have been seen by certain circles in the agency as another betrayal by the weak, Kennedy administration.

When one studies the history of the Kennedy-Cuba relationship, one is struck with the contradictory viewpoints that were trending at the time. At the same moment that Operation Mongoose was going on, the Kennedy team was seeking a modus vivendi with Castro. What is also not known is to what extent did the Kennedy brothers know or authorize the plots to kill Castro. That topic is still undetermined, nearly 50 years after the fact, and historians are still puzzled as to exactly what was authorized or not.

What is not in dispute is the fact that the CIA made a secret pact with certain members of the U.S. Mafia to kill Castro. The Castro plots began in 1960, and finally ended in the early years of the Johnson administration. Most of the activity to kill Castro took place during the Kennedy administration and involved the use of the Mafia. There has been considerable speculation in the past 49 years that the CIA-Mafia plots to assassinate Castro might have been linked in some way to the assassination of JFK, and to further tie in the president's alleged assassin, Lee Harvey Oswald as a pro or anti-Castro operative in the assassination.

What is known is this. When the CIA proposed a plan to eliminate Castro in 1960, all they were interested in at the time was to discredit his regime and lay the groundwork for his eventual downfall. The later stages of the plot involved extensive military planning, culminating in the Bay of Pigs invasion that took place in April 1961.

One of the early schemes to kill Castro involved spraying LSD on the radio station that Castro was to speak at, poisoning his cigars, his food, exploding sea shells that would be put in an area where Castro liked to dive, and later, the use of assassins inside of Cuba to kill Castro.

But the most ambitious plan to kill Castro took place in the summer of 1960 which directly involved the CIA and Organized Crime. Richard Bissell, then Deputy Director of Plans for the CIA asked Sheffield Edwards, Director of Security at CIA, if he could make contact with certain members of organized crime which had its own extensive gambling interests in Cuba. The mob suffered hundreds of millions of dollars in losses from the casinos when Castro shut them down and were anxious to get back in business.

J.C. King, the head of the CIA's Western Hemisphere Division, originally gave Bissell the idea of contacting the"Gambling Syndicate." Edwards then turned to Robert Mahue, a former FBI agent who had numerous contacts with the mob. Mahue contacted Los Angeles crime boss Johnny Rosselli and told him that certain "business interests" wanted to eliminate Castro. Could Rosselli help in any way?

In September 1960, CIA agent James O'Connell met with Rosselli in New York and formally asked for his help. Rosselli agreed and passed word along to two of his pals in the mob, Sam Giancana and Santos Trafficante. Bissell then reported on his meetings with the mob to CIA Director Allen Dulles, deliberately avoiding any mention of any "bad words," instead, telling Dulles that they were taking on an "intelligence operation." It should be noted that while all this was going on, Vice President Richard Nixon was actually in charge of the administration's plans to get rid of Castro. Whether or not Nixon knew of the CIA-Mafia plots is still unknown, but all evidence points to that fact. In November 1960, JFK won the election and became president. Once he took office in January 1961, the CIA-Mafia plots began in earnest. Unknown to Kennedy, the Cuban connection would haunt his presidency and its aftermath would forever change the way historians would look at his assassination, two years later.

The name of E. Howard Hunt is well known to those people interested in the Kennedy assassination as someone who knew more about the event than he ever revealed. Shortly before his death in 2007, Hunt wrote a memoir called *An American Spy: My Secret History in the CIA*. If anyone really believed that Hunt would reveal something earth shattering about the Kennedy assassination, they were wrong. That task would fall on the shoulders of his son, St. John Hunt who had a rather adversarial, so to speak, relationship with his father.

In the months before Hunt's death, he called St. John to his bedside to tell him what he knew of his life in the CIA and more importantly, his knowledge of the Kennedy assassination. St. John Hunt took notes, as well as recording the conversations. The elder Hunt mailed the tape to his son in January 2004, and asked that he keep it safe until after he died. In the tape which was aired in 2007 via a radio interview, and which was given wide spread publicity on the web, Hunt revealed the names of the men whom he alleged took part in the planning of JFK's murder. The names Hunt revealed were: Frank Sturgis, David Morales, David Atlee Phillips, Antonio Veciana, William Harvey, Cord Meyer, a French gunman on the grassy knoll, and LBJ.

Hunt said that he played no active role in the assassination planning but was just a "bench warmer" in their discussions. During his confession, Hunt wrote down the names of the people who were involved in the plot like a flow chart, connecting each dot as it went along its natural path. He wrote down "LBJ" first, followed by lines for each of the other players; Cord Meyer, who became the second highest ranking member of the CIA's Clandestine Service (also, JFK was having an affair with Cord Meyer's wife, Mary), Bill Harvey, who ran the Cuban plots and nurtured a bitter hatred towards the Kennedy brothers, David Morales, a tough, CIA agent who worked in Havana and later in the CIA's JMWAVE station in Miami, Frank Sturgis, of Watergate fame, and a member of Gerry Hemming's IFP, David Phillips, a CIA propaganda officer who was stationed in Mexico City at the same time that Oswald was supposed to have been in the city, Antonio Veciana, the leader of the militant, anti-Castro organization, ALPHA 66, and finally, the so-called French Connection gunman on the grassy knoll, none other than Lucien Sarti.

The scenario that Hunt laid out was that LBJ ordered the assassination of the president and passed on his instructions to the rest of the group. By implying that Lucien Sarti, a member of the Corsican underworld was on the grassy knoll, firing at the president (as depicted by Nicoli and David), disproves the Oswald as the lone gunman theory into a conspiracy involving at least two people, possibly more. Saint John further states that his father gave him a document that spelled out how the conspiracy unfolded. Cord Meyer discussed the plot with David Atlee Phillips, who then met with William Harvey and Antonio Veciana, Oswald had a meeting with the above mentioned men in Mexico City. Veciana then met with Frank Sturgis in Miami who brought David Morales into the plot. There is a change in the location of the assassination plot and it is finally agreed that Dallas is the city where the event will take place.

Hunt goes on to describe his involvement in the assassination planning. In 1963 he met with Morales and Sturgis in a Miami hotel room. Morales takes his leave and in comes Frank Sturgis who talks about a "Big Event" and wants to know if Hunt is willing to go along with their plans. Hunt asks Sturgis what the plan is and Sturgis replies, "Killing JFK." Hunt then asks Sturgis why he needs him. Hunt tells him that he wants no part in the deal.

St. John writes that he was shocked to hear of his father's confession, believing that he had been lied to over the decades by him and his constant denials that he had anything to do with the assassination.

Can Howard Hunt's deathbed confession be believed? If it is true, then Hunt was a participant after the fact, knowing just what was going to happen, and did nothing to stop it. What is most relevant in the Hunt-death-bed story, is the fact that most of the people alleged to have been part of the plot had ties to the CIA.

New, bombshell information on the covert relationship between Lee Oswald and the CIA revolves around a now deceased, former CIA officer named George Joannides. After postings overseas, he was returned to the United States and become an integral player in the Kennedy administrations's secret war to topple the Castro regime. Unknown to Joannides at the time was that his role as the liaison between the D.R.E. the militant anti-Castro organization, would put his Cuban benefactors in touch with an ex-Marine named Lee Harvey Oswald, prior to the assassination.

The organization that George Joannides was assigned to watch was the D.R.E., one of the most militant, and one of the largest anti-Castro groups in the United States. It was founded in Havana only a few years before and immediately became the beneficiaries of CIA largess, in the form of money, training and other assistance. The CIA sent one of its top officers, David Atlee Phillips, to work closely with the Cuban students.

As the CIA cemented its relations with the D.R.E., they named George Joannides as their representative to that group. Joannides' cover name was "Howard" as he was known to many in the group. Joannides was the intermediary between the CIA and the D.R.E., getting them guns, money, and any other assistance they needed. He earned their trust and the young Cubans liked him immensely.

Joannides served for seventeen months as the contact officer between the D.R.E. and the CIA. According to the few records that the public was allowed to see on Joannides ties with the D.R.E., his job was to pay for "intelligence and propaganda" from the Cuban group. He instructed the D.R.E. to clear any public announcements that they made with him. Along with giving money to the members of the D.R.E., Joannides also dispensed funds to D.R.E members in New Orleans. The CIA's relationship with members of the D.R.E. in New Orleans during the summer of 1963, let them have a unique perspective when Oswald tried to make contact with certain members of the group that summer. When the Warren Commission was investigating the Kennedy assassination, the CIA failed to inform them of Joannides's relationship with the D.R.E., nor the fact that he was aware (or should have been aware) that Oswald had been in touch with certain members of the New Orleans group.

When Oswald arrived in New Orleans during the summer of 1963, he began handing out pro-Castro leaflets on the streets of the city on behalf of the FPCC. He subsequently got into an altercation with an anti-Castro shopkeeper named Carlos Bringuier whom Oswald previously had met and offered his services as an ex-Marine who wanted to help the anti-Castro cause. Bringuier said that Oswald had tried to worm his way into the D.R.E. in New Orleans in August 1963 but that he gave Oswald no reason to believe that he would take up his offer.

It is unclear whether or not the leadership of the D.R.E. told their CIA bosses (as well as George Joannides) about their confrontation with Oswald in New Orleans. It seems logical that if Joannides was the action officer with the D.R.E., the paymaster, the babysitter for their group, then he would have been privy to all the information coming from the D.R.E.

George Joannides would, years later, be thrust back into the Kennedy assassination case when the congress began their own probe of both the Kennedy and King assassinations. The House panel demanded that the CIA provide them with as much of their secret information held in their vaults on Lee Oswald and any other pertinent information. In a move that he did not expect, Joannides was recalled by the CIA (he had retired and was in a private law practice for some time) to act as their liaison with the HSCA. The House committee especially wanted to see what information the CIA had on Oswald's possible connections with Cuba, one area that the Warren Commission did not even look into.

Joannides was in a unique position, if he truly wanted, to enlighten the HSCA on his relationship with the D.R.E. in Miami during the summer of 1963, and his knowledge (if any), on the CIA's relationship with Oswald in New Orleans. Instead, he kept quiet, never revealing what he knew about these tumultuous times.

Joannides filtered the HSCA's request for documents, only giving the committee what he thought would not hurt the CIA's reputation. He also did not tell Robert Blakey, the HSCA's chief counsel, about his relationship with the D.R.E. Blakey, a former Notre Dame law professor, had gone into his job with the perception that the mob was responsible for the president's assassination. Years later, when he learned of Joannides secret relationship with the anti-Castro group he said, "I was not told of Joannides ties with the DRE, a focal point of the investigation. Had I known who he was, he would have been a witness who would have been interrogated under oath by the staff or by the committee. He would never have been acceptable as a point of contact with us to retrieve documents. In fact, I have now learned, as I note above, that Joannides was the point of contact between the Agency and the DRE during the period Oswald was in contact with the DRE."

After Joannides's relationship with the D.R.E. was made public, the CIA went into its protective shield. They stated in no uncertain terms that Joannides had no relationship with the D.R.E.

whatsoever. Journalist Jefferson Morley, who took an active interest in the Joannides story, said that when he asked J. Barry Harrelson who worked in the CIA's Office of Historic Review, if the CIA had any relationship with the D.R.E. in 1963, he gave this answer, "We think the record speak for themselves."

What is not in question is that the CIA had an important asset, George Joannides, inside the D.R.E. in 1963. By all accounts, the D.R.E. had information on the activities of Lee Oswald in New Orleans that summer, information that was withheld from the Warren Commission.

Reporter Morley had filed a legal suite against the CIA asking them to release all their files on George Joannides. The motion was denied by the court. Joannides died on March 9, 1990, age 67.

Newly released documents describe a frantic investigation of the assassination by the CIA, only days after the president's murder. The man who was given the job of probing the assassination for the agency was John Whitten, a.k.a. "John Scelso." Whitten' role in the CIA's investigation of Oswald's activities are paramount in our understanding of how the agency fudged its conclusion and decided not to let Whitten and his thirty trained analysts learn all they could about what transpired on November 22, 1963. If Whitten had been provided with all the detailed information available to him at the time, it is possible that the Warren Commission may have come to a different conclusion about Oswald and his possible association with the Castro government.

Less than twelve hours after the president was killed, the CIA was alive with activity as analysts were called in to learn all they could about the alleged assassin, Lee Harvey Oswald. Whitten, at 43-years old, was the chief of the covert operations branch for Mexico City and Central America. Whitten had been on the phone with CIA Mexico City Chief Winston Scott when Scott told him that the CIA had on file a photograph of Lee Oswald entering the Cuban consulate that October. Whitten asked Scott to send him the picture as soon as possible. What the picture showed was that Oswald had visited both the Cuban consulate and the Russian embassy. What was Oswald, a former Marine, doing at the embassies of America's enemies?

As Whitten began his investigation, it soon became apparent

that he was being stymied in his search by none other than Richard Helms who stopped him from looking into Oswald's Cuban related activities in New Orleans in the summer of 1963, information that the FBI had on hand for months. In the end, Helms's decision to withhold vital information from John Whitten forced him to end his probe and stop an avenue of activity that may have altered what the public knew about the activities of Lee Oswald, and have clouded the investigation of the JFK case for decades that followed.

On December 6, 1963, Whitten was sent to the White House to look at an FBI report that had been prepared on Lee Oswald. To his shock, he found out that Helms had not been forthcoming with him about all of Oswald's activities. The most important information that Helm's withheld from him dealt with Oswald's association with anti-Castro people in New Orleans, as well as his membership in the Fair Play for Cuban Committee. Whitten was shocked to learn of Oswald's Cuban connections and he voiced his objections to Helms. To his amazement, Helms relieved Whitten of his duties and the investigation was turned over to the office of Jim Angleton, the head of the Counter-intelligence division at CIA. Years later when his almost 200 page deposition was released, Whitten said that his opinion of Oswald's guilt or innocence was subject to change. He said that he changed his mind about Oswald's guilt by saying, "it is obviously, completely irrelevant in view of all this Bureau information."

As Whitten began his investigation, he was immediately held up on two fronts, one, from Angleton, and two, from the FBI. The Bureau sent his team thousands of documents that they knew Whitten and his staff could never read. Whitten called the information given him by the FBI as "Weirdo stuff." Among the information that he was not told by the FBI was Oswald's association with both pro and anti-Castro people in New Orleans, his alleged attack on right wing General Edwin Walker in Dallas in 1963, and the contents of Oswald's "historic diary" which he supposedly penned while he lived in the Soviet Union. Even more surprising was the fact that Whitten, who was supposed to have been knowledgeable of all CIA activities in Latin America, and Mexico, had never been made aware of Oswald before November 22, 1963, even though the various U.S. intelligence agencies had a file on him since his defection in 1959.

When he later testified before the HSCA in 1979, Whitten said that if he had been informed of Oswald's Cuban ties he would have focused his investigation on the "possible involvement of the (CIA's) Miami station." He told the HSCA that he did not believe that Oswald was in any way connected to the CIA, but after he learned of the Executive Action operation, he remarked that he could not rule out any agency ties to Oswald.

More important to his investigation, Whitten was not told of the identity of George Joannides, who took over as the CIA's liaison with the DRE in Miami in 1963. Joannides was the paymaster to the anti-Castro group and followed closely Oswald's activities in New Orleans, including his meeting with Carlos Bringuier and other DRE members in the Crescent City. It was Richard Helms who deliberately withheld the Joannides file from Whitten so the latter could not delve into Oswald's anti-Castro activities. Both Angleton and Helms desperately wanted to keep any mention of the Castro-Oswald connection secret, and put the blame on the assassination of the president squarely on the shoulders of the men in Moscow.

Whitten also commented on the famous "mystery man" photograph that the CIA took in Mexico City (and whom Rivele was desperately trying to find) that proved not to have been Oswald. He told his interviewer (in the Scelso report) that the CIA had not received this picture prior to the assassination, and when it was finally received, he did not know if the picture was the real Lee Oswald.

Whitten had stinging remarks regarding Richard Helms. Whitten said that he was surprised that he had appointed Bill Harvey to create the secret assassination plots called "Executive Action."

"I think, continued Whitten, "on the fact that Helms did not inform the Warren Commission on the Castro assassination plots, that was a morally highly reprehensible act, which he cannot possibly justify under oath of office, or any other standard of professional public service."

Asked why he thought Helms failed to tell the Warren Commission about the Castro plots he said that, "I think that Helms withheld the information because he realized it would have cost him his job and would have precipitated a crisis for the agency, which could have a very adverse effects on the agency."

After departing the CIA, Whitten and his family left the United States and moved to Vienna, Austria. There, he took up opera and joined the Vienna Men's Coral Society. In Vienna, he never revealed his secret past.

On the weekend of the assassination, New Orleans District Attorney James "Jim" Garrison, began an investigation of Oswald's associates in New Orleans, namely David Ferrie, and Guy Bannister. Garrison heard reports that Ferrie, a former pilot who had close ties to the anti-Castro underground in the city, might have been associated with Oswald prior to the assassination. The FBI was informed of Garrison's Ferrie probe and the feds shortly cleared him of any knowledge of Oswald or any role in the assassination.

Not satisfied with the Warren Commission's report that Oswald was the lone assassin, Garrison, in late 1966, secretly began his own, internal probe of the Kennedy assassination, focusing on Oswald's associates in New Orleans in the summer of 1963. The CIA soon began to learn of Garrison's investigation and began a large scale, internal effort to block his work.

In a memorandum for the "Director, Domestic Contact Service" of the CIA, dated April 28, 1967, "subject: Garrison Investigation in New Orleans" is a list of the names of "the principal persons whom Jim Garrison has involved or sought to involve in ths investigation of his alleged assassination plot." Among the names were, Attorney Dean Andrews, Sergio Arcacha Smith, Carlos Bringuier, Edward Butler, William David Ferrie, James Garrison, Layton Martens, Gordon Novel, Perry Russo, Clay Shaw, and Miguel Torres. Many of these people had ties, one way or another, with the CIA and have been depicted in the pages of this book.

It was requested by Washington that the New Orleans office send "Any information that is holds on any of the above-named except SHAW, on whom the office has already reported… " It is suggested that the New Orleans office co-ordinate closely with the New Orleans office of the FBI in reporting to investigations by Garrison or his staff of any person known to have or to have had a tie to CIA. Finally, it is suggested that the New Orleans office be alert to the possibility that Garrison may tap, or may have tapped home or office telephone."

The CIA took an active interest in Garrison's investigation and the documentation on him is large. On September 15, 1967, in a memorandum for the Director of the CIA, subject, "Garrison's Charges Against CIA," is a detailed description of the names of the principal persons whom Garrison was looking into and the facts of the CIA relationship. For example for Clay Shaw, the "Facts re CIA say, "Contract of DCS office, New Orleans, 1948-1956. Source of several DCS reports, chiefly on Latin America. Introduced the then DCCI, Gen. Charles P. Cabell, who addressed its members, on 9 May 1961, to the New Orleans Foreign Policy Association."

Clay Shaw, who was the head of the International Trade Mart in New Orleans, was indicted by a grand jury in New Orleans and was the only person to be put on trial for his alleged participation in the Kennedy assassination. Garrison had a hard time convincing a jury of Shaw's guilt and he was ultimately acquitted in the JFK assassination plot. Shaw's possible role in the Kennedy assassination was brought to a nation-wide audience with the release of Oliver Stone's blockbuster movie, *JFK*. The fallout of the movie was so stunning that the congress approved a measure called the "JFK Records Collection Act "which allowed thousands of previously classified materials on the JFK assassination that had been withheld since 1963 to be released (thousands of more files are still classified as of this writing, and are not to be released in full until 2017-if ever).

Another of Garrison's persons of interest was Gordon Novel, whom Garrison alleged was a CIA agent. Novel said that he ran the Evergreen Advertising Agency in New Orleans that was supposed to have been a CIA front. On May 28, 1967, Novel sent a telegram to the CIA regarding Garrison's investigation and said that he would try and keep the CIA from becoming involved in Garrison's investigation. The CIA wrote about Novel saying, "All of Novel's claims about association with CIA are lies. His motives remain obscure. One possibility is that he is in collusion with Garrison."

Garrison tried to link the CIA directly to the assassination by connecting the dots from Clay Shaw, David Ferrie, and Guy

Bannister in which they all conspired to kill JFK, using Oswald as a scapegoat.

In May 1967, the CIA received a call from a lawyer named Jack Miller who said he had information regarding the Garrison probe. Miller said that Garrison was going to subpoena an FBI agent and a former FBI agent. "The thesis he is attempting to develop is that Oswald was a CIA agent, violently anti-Communist, recruited by the Agency for an operation approved by Robert Kennedy to kill Castro. When Oswald killed President Kennedy, the thesis is, it was necessary to show Oswald as a Communist in order to cover up the original plan.

"Garrison says he has letters signed by CIA or Robert Kennedy which authorize certain Americans to work with the Cubans for the assassination of Castro."

Miller's source was Walter Sheridan, an investigative reporter for NBC television. "NBC has done a thirty-minute program on Garrison and plans another one of an hour for a few weeks from now. It is expected to "bury" Garrison because everyone is convinced that Garrison is a wild and dangerous man."

Why the CIA was so paranoid regarding Garrison, a man with limited means to subpoena anyone in the national security apparatus who may have known anything about the assassination, must have had their own reasons regarding this "wild and dangerous man."

Another possible CIA connection to Lee Oswald was given to the U.S. government in one of the most audacious spy cases in history, one that almost turned the Warren Commission on its knees, regarding a possible Soviet connection to the Kennedy assassination, that might have involved Lee Oswald himself. On January 20, 1964, a KGB officer named Yuri Nosenko decided to defect to the U.S. At the time of his "defection," Nosenko was one of the highest-ranking Russian intelligence officials to come westward. Nosenko worked for the second directorate of the KGB's Seventh Department-the section that oversaw all visiting American tourists to the Soviet Union. At the time that Nosenko was monitoring the few Americans to set foot on Russian soil, his branch was keeping tabs on a recent American defector, a former Marine radioman named Lee Harvey Oswald.

The Oswald case would come to haunt the CIA when Nosenko

arrived in the U.S. for good in January 1964. The Warren Commission that was investigating the Kennedy assassination, knew of Nosenko and his revelations concerning Oswald but they did not pursue the matter. His other bombshell was the fact that the CIA was infested with "moles" which were feeding the KGB with all sorts of topsecret information coming out of Langley headquarters. For the members of James Angleton's Counterintelligence Staff, Nosenko was the devil incarnate, a man who came to destroy the CIA. Furthermore, he was the man whom, a former KGB defector, Anatoly Golitsin, said would follow him in a massive disinformation program.

Nosenko first made contact with the CIA in 1962 while he was in Geneva, Switzerland in his capacity as chief of security for the Soviet delegation to the disarmament talks. The CIA was very much interested in what he had to say and he was soon debriefed by two topnotch agency officials, Pete Bagley and George Kisvalter.

CIA officials decided to recruit Nosenko and determined to let him alone for further intelligence purposes. Nosenko said that he did not wish to defect at that moment because of family considerations. As time went on, Nosenko told the CIA that he received a note from his Soviet controller saying that he was being ordered back to Moscow for "consultations." Nosenko, now fearful for his life, demanded to be granted political asylum in the U.S. After much debate, the CIA made arrangements for him to come to the U.S. For better or worse, Yuri Nosenko and his "secrets" had arrived.

As Nosenko began to be quizzed by the CIA, his story was met with deep suspicion by the one man in the Agency whose opinion mattered the most; James Angleton. From the beginning of the Nosenko saga, Angleton was deeply suspicious of the newest Russian defector, certain beyond any doubt that he was on a disinformation mission, as spelled out by Anatoly Golitsin.

As the Nosenko interrogations began in earnest, he dropped a bombshell that only made Angleton even more distrustful of him. He said that while he was in Moscow monitoring American tourists, he had seen the KGB file on Lee Oswald. Under further questioning, Nosenko said that there was no connection between the Russians and the assassination of President Kennedy. Nosenko said that the Russians had no interest whatsoever in a loner like Oswald, and the only reason why they allowed him to say in the country was his attempt to commit suicide.

But that was not good enough for Angleton. Despite the fact that the Warren Commission decided that there was no conspiracy, foreign or domestic in the Kennedy assassination, Angleton was convinced that Oswald was a "dispatched agent," sent to the United States to absolve the Soviet Union in any plot to kill Kennedy. Furthermore, Angleton believed that Oswald was groomed as an assassin by the KGB during his three year stint in the Soviet Union, that he was sent to the U.S. to kill Kennedy, and lastly, that the Nosenko mission was to excise any possible connection by the Soviet's in the president's death. The culprit in the whole, sordid mess, was none other than Yuri Nosenko.

Nosenko's revelations fit right in with the mid set of FBI Director J. Edgar Hoover who laid a trail from the beginning that Oswald was the lone assassin of JFK. But if Hoover's FBI was taken in by Nosenko's shocking surprise, others in the CIA did not. From April 1964 to September 1967, Nosenko was put in solitary quarters in a CIA safe house and would undergo "hostile interrogation" in order to find out the truth behind his defection.

The differences over whether or not Nosenko was or was not a real defector lead the CIA to write a report stating that he was the real thing, and he was eventually brought into the CIA mold. He worked for the CIA as a "consultant," and was paid $16, 5000.

Nosenko's startling news regarding the KGB and Oswald was given to the Warren Commission via Richard Helms and alarm bells began to ring almost immediately. If Oswald was working for the Soviet's in any capacity, then the Warren Commission's entire characterization of him as being the lone assassin of the president would be in tatters.

On July 8, 1964, a memo for the CIA's Deputy Director for Plans, "Subject: Discussion with Mr., Dulles Re; the Nosenko Information on Oswald" was sent by the Chief, SR Division. The pertinent passages is as follows: "Mr. Dulles, with whom I spoke today, recalled his earlier conversation with you on this subject and said that there were still some members of the Commission who were concerned rest they suppress the NOSENKO information now only to have it surface at a future date. They expressed concern that this could possibly prejudice the entire Warren Commission report. I told Mr. Dulles that this concern was understandable but that we still felt the best course by far would be to omit any reference to the NOSENKO information in the final report. While it is conceivable that NOSENKO might someday be in a position to claim that he provided information on the KENNEDY assassination, I said that the difference between NOSENKO's situation and that of other bona fide defectors was such that it would be less likely that NOSENKO would be allowed to surface in this way…"[117]

Yuri Nosenko died a number of years ago and the jury is still out on whether or not his claims of his reviewing the Oswald file in the Soviet Union are true or not. Instead, the Nosenko story is just one other item in Oswald's association with the CIA and the people who inhabited it that demand a clearer answer.

Another person in the intelligence arena whom Oswald associated with in Dallas was George de Mohrenschildt, a rich nobleman who came from a distinguished Russian family, a member of the Dallas Petroleum Club and the World Affairs Council. He was a petroleum engineer, having worked around the globe, traveling extensively in all the hot spots of the cold war, and accumulating a rather large FBI and CIA file along the way. Just why the rich, suave de Mohrenschildt would make friends with Lee Oswald, the complete opposite, boggles the mind.

Among the places that de Mohrenschildt and his wife traveled during the days of the cold war were Yugoslavia, Haiti, Africa, and Latin America and South America. In 1961, he and his wife took a seven thousand mile walking tour of Latin America, and wound up not too far from the CIA's covert training base for the Bay of Pigs invasion in Guatemala. In September 1962, the de Mohrenschildt's arrived back in Dallas and their fateful meeting with the young Oswald couple.

His links to various countries' intelligence services go back to the days prior to Pearl Harbor. In 1941, he worked as an agent of the French counter intelligence corps, helping to run an agent network in the U.S. to monitor the shipment of oil to Europe. He was also working at the same time for the German secret service

[117] JFK Exhibit F-529.

and his activities were being watched by the FBI. While he was en-route to Mexico he was stopped by the Bureau while sketching near a Texas Coast Guard base. Despite all his questionable behavior, in the summer of 1942, he applied for a job with the wartime OSS. His application was turned down because of the OSS's belief that he was a Nazi agent.

When de Mohrenschildt was questioned by Counsel Jenner of the Warren Commission if he had worked for any other intelligence agency, he said no.

When George de Mohrenschildt returned to Dallas from his South American sojourn, he was met by a member of the CIA's domestic contact division, J. Walton Moore. Moore questioned de Mohrenschildt on his travels and sent the news back to Washington. These "informal contacts" between de Mohrenschildt and the CIA, and its links to Lee Oswald, get more interesting. Shortly before his death on March 29, 1977, de Mohrenschildt told author Edward Jay Epstein that he had met with Moore in Dallas over a lunch date. During their meeting, the name of Lee Oswald came up. This was in 1961, and took place shortly after the Oswald's had returned from the Soviet Union. De Mohrenschildt told Epstein that Moore told him that Oswald had lived in Minsk, was an ex-Marine, and that the CIA had an interest in him; could he, de Mohrenschildt, "look after" Oswald, possibly meet him, and do the agency a big favor? De Mohrenschildt said that Moore replied that Oswald was "ok." In return, said Moore, the CIA would help him in his oil business.

Moore and de Mohrenschildt had been in contact with each other since 1957 and Moore de-briefed him upon his return from Yugoslavia for the International Cooperation Administration. In a 1964, memo, Moore said that he was in contact with de Mohrenschildt in both 1958 and 1959. When he was interviewed by the HSCA in 1978, Moore said that he did interview de Mohrenschildt in 1957 and that they had met periodically in the ensuing years. Moore however said that in their conversations they did not talk about Lee Oswald.

In his book, *The Man Who Knew Too Much,* author Dick Russell tells of a conversation he had with Richard Case Nagell that concerned George de Mohrenschildt and his Oswald-CIA connection. Nagell said of the de Mohrenschildt-Oswald story,

"Now, there's a relationship to pursue. I'm surprised Jim Garrison never really got into that." Later, Nagell said that, "there was enough of intermittent surveillance on Oswald by other people whose reports I read, that I have intimate knowledge who he was associating with. De Mohrenschildt's name popped up, not in connection with the CIA, though he might have been."

George de Mohrenschildt is one of the many people associated with the Kennedy assassination whose death is still unexplained. After a strange trip to Europe that he made in connection with an investigation into the Kennedy assassination by Dutch writer, Willem Oltmans, George de Mohrenschildt suddenly arrived at his daughters home in Palm Beach, Florida, It was at this time that de Mohrenschildt contacted the staff of the House Select Committee on Assassinations in Washington that was conducting its probe of the Kennedy murder. He said that he had information that might be useful in their investigation and would someone like to come down to see him? The HSCA sent down Gaeton Fonzi who was stationed in Miami, and who was tasked with the job of investigating the Cuban link to the assassination. When Fonzi arrived at de Mohrenschildt's daughter's home, she told him that her father was out and would be back later that day. Fonzi left his card and departed, never having a chance to hear what the baron had to say. Later that afternoon, in circumstances that have never been satisfactorily been explained, George de Mohrenschildt was dead. The coroner said that the cause of death was suicide by putting a 20-gauge shotgun to his mouth.

Whatever information he was about to tell went with him to the grave. But in a later interview with his wife Jeanne, author Russell said that she was certain that her husband did not kill himself, and furthermore, that Oswald did not kill the president.

While there is no solid proof that the CIA as an organization ordered the assassination of the president of the United States, there is a solid connection to Oswald and various persons in the U.S. intelligence community as a whole that link the two together. From the CIA-mob plots to kill Castro, George Joannides and the Oswald linked DRE, to John Whitten's probe of the assassination on behalf of the CIA, to Yuri Nosenko's allegation that he handled the KGB's Oswald file, to the links between de Mohrenschildt and Oswald, and finally, Howard Hunt's confession in which he mentioned a number of prominent names affiliated with the CIA, as well, and more importantly, his allegation that there was a Corsican-French Connection gunman on the grassy knoll, make Oswald the perfect patsy in the killing of the president, as well as creating a foundation for him being a low level asset. in one form or another, to U.S. intelligence.

Starting with the 1961 allegation by Jose Luis Romero who said he was offered $460,000 to kill JFK by an American named "Mike" (which he refused) and throughout the rest of this book, the blame for the assassination of JFK points, in one form or another, to the OAS, the anti-de Gaulle organization of the 1960s. A number of people who were prominently mentioned in the book; Robert Blemant, Christian David, Lucien Sarti, Michel Mertz and Jean Souetre were all associated, one way or another, with the OAS and tangentially, the CIA. We have seen the roles played by both QJ/WIN and WIROGUE in the assassination plots to kill Patrice Lumumba in the Congo, their relationship with the CIA, and whom they might have been. We saw Senator Gary Hart desperately looking for the elusive QJWIN in Amsterdam, only to be left out in the cold.

From all the available evidence, it seems clear that Jean Souetre was not in Dealey Plaza on November 22, 1963, and that he was most likely being impersonated by Michael Mertz, a big-time heroin dealer and assassin and the most likely candidate for being the CIA's elusive assassin, QJWIN. We have tried to pin-point the most likely candidates for both WIN and ROGUE as being either, Robert Blemant, Charles Siragusa, Christian David or Lucern Sarti. The use of men of Corsican decent in the CIA's assassination program ZR/RIFLE is a common thread in the narrative and could point to David, Sarti, Souetre, and Mertz. The fact that Christian David said that both he and Sarti were in the Congo at the same time puts them in a direct line to the ZR/RIFLE project.

If one is to believe Howard Hunt's deathbed confession, then a Corsican gunman, most likely to be Lucien Sarti, was on the grassy knoll at the time of the assassination. The fact that Sarti used an explosive bullet such as the one used to kill the president from the front, was something that Sarti would have used. The fact that Michel Nicoli backed up Christian David's story, without having seen him in years, points to someone with inside knowledge of the affair. Gordon Arnold's story of a shot coming from behind him, means that a second shooter was behind the knoll, thus, making a conspiracy in the president's death.

A number of police, judges and writers tacked down by Steve Rivele in Europe, including Alan Dugrand, Alex Panzani, Commissioner Bezert, all pointed, one way or another, to Lucien Sarti as being part of the plot to kill Kennedy, starting with Antoine Guerini in Marseille, and backed by Santo Trafficante and Carlos Marcello (with considerable help in the coverup by unknown people in the CIA and the military).

Steve Rivele tried and failed to find the elusive Mexico City mystery man, finally excluding Edmond Meunier. Future researches should also look into the backgrounds (if one can find them) of both Francisco Chiappe and Jean-Paul Angeletti as possibly being the other two men on the knoll.

The French Connection to the assassination of President Kennedy is not the end of the story. It is just one more nail in the coffin of the Warren Commission and its findings of a lone assassin.◊

Jean Souetre: A rare photo of him in the 1950s.

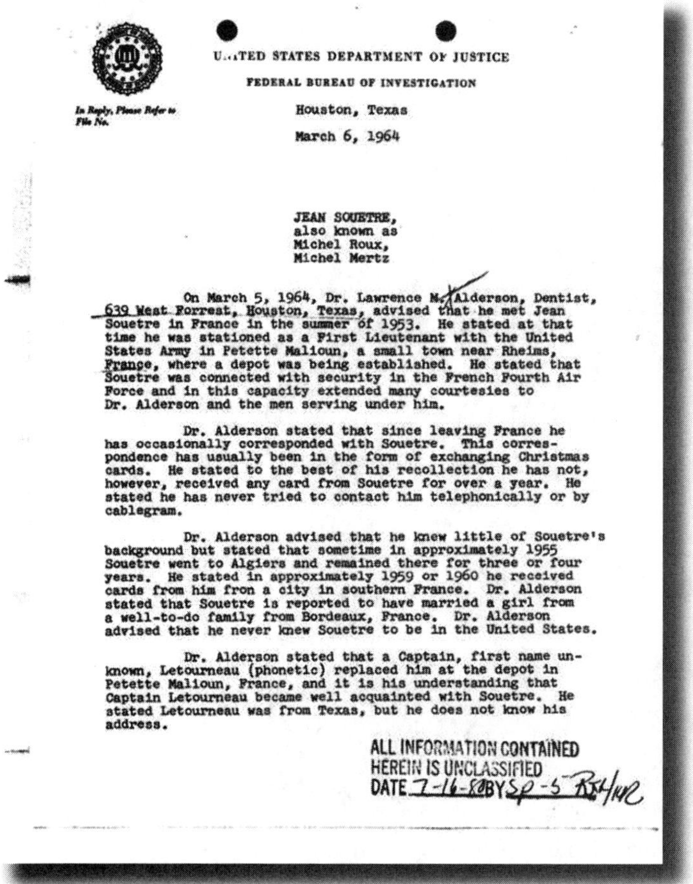

UNITED STATES DEPARTMENT OF JUSTICE

FEDERAL BUREAU OF INVESTIGATION

In Reply, Please Refer to File No.

Houston, Texas

March 6, 1964

JEAN SOUETRE,
also known as
Michel Roux,
Michel Mertz

On March 5, 1964, Dr. Lawrence M. Alderson, Dentist, 639 West Forrest, Houston, Texas, advised that he met Jean Souetre in France in the summer of 1953. He stated at that time he was stationed as a First Lieutenant with the United States Army in Petette Malioun, a small town near Rheims, France, where a depot was being established. He stated that Souetre was connected with security in the French Fourth Air Force and in this capacity extended many courtesies to Dr. Alderson and the men serving under him.

Dr. Alderson stated that since leaving France he has occasionally corresponded with Souetre. This correspondence has usually been in the form of exchanging Christmas cards. He stated to the best of his recollection he has not, however, received any card from Souetre for over a year. He stated he has never tried to contact him telephonically or by cablegram.

Dr. Alderson advised that he knew little of Souetre's background but stated that sometime in approximately 1955 Souetre went to Algiers and remained there for three or four years. He stated in approximately 1959 or 1960 he received cards from him fron a city in southern France. Dr. Alderson stated that Souetre is reported to have married a girl from a well-to-do family from Bordeaux, France. Dr. Alderson advised that he never knew Souetre to be in the United States.

Dr. Alderson stated that a Captain, first name unknown, Letourneau (phonetic) replaced him at the depot in Petette Malioun, France, and it is his understanding that Captain Letourneau became well acquainted with Souetre. He stated Letourneau was from Texas, but he does not know his address.

ALL INFORMATION CONTAINED
HEREIN IS UNCLASSIFIED
DATE 7-16-80 BY SP-5 RSH/KR

FBI document concerning Jean Souetre.

Right: Fidel Castro: Fidel Castro was the target of numerous assassination plots by the CIA, including the use of the Mafia. The ZR/RIFLE program targeted him but it was never carried out.

One of the "Hands off Cuba" flyers that Oswald gave out in New Orleans under the curious alias: A J Hiddel.

Bibliography

Books

Benson, Michael, *Who's Who In The JFK Assassination,* Carol Publishing Group, N.Y., 1993.

Clark, Evert, & Harrock, Nicholas, *Contrabanista*, Praeger Publishing Co., New York, 1973.

Davy, William, "Through The Looking Glass: The Mysterious World of Clay Shaw." Privately Printed, No date.

Douglas, James, *JFK and the Unspeakable: Why He Died & Why It Matters*. Orbis Books, Maryknoll, N.Y., 2009

Duffy, James, *Who Killed JFK?: The Kennedy Assassination Cover-up, The Web*. Shapolsky Publishers, New York, 1988.

Emery, Fred, *Watergate: The Corruption of American Politics and the Fall of Richard Nixon*. Times Books, New York, 1994.

English, T.J., *Havana Nocturne*, William Morrow & Co., New York, 2008.

Epstein, Edward Jay, *Legend: The Secret World of Lee Harvey Oswald*, McGraw Hill Book Co., New York, 1978.

Fonzi, Gaeton, *The Last Investigation*, Thunders Mouth Press, New York, 1993.

Furiati, Claudia, *ZR Rifle: The Plot to Kill Kennedy and Castro*. Ocean Press, Melbourne, Victoria, Australia, 1994.

Fursenko, Aleksandr, & Naftali, Timothy, *One Hell of A Gamble: The Secret History of the Cuban Missile Crisis*. W.W. Norton & Co., New York, 1997.

Gillon, Steven, *The Kennedy Assassination: 24 Hours After.* Basic Books, New York, 2009.

Hinkle, Warren & Turner, William, *Deadly Secrets: The CIA-Mafia War Against Castro and the Assassination of JFK*. Thunders Mouth Press, New York, 1992.

Hougan, Jim, *Spooks: The Haunting of America—The Private Use of Secret Agents*. William Morrow & Co., New York, 1978.

Hurt, Henry, *Reasonable Doubt*. Holt, Rinehart & Winston, New York, 1985.

Kross, Peter, *Spies, Traitors and Moles: An Espionage and Intelligence Quiz Book*, Illuminet Press, Lilburn, Ga., 1998.

Ibid, *Oswald, The CIA and the Warren Commission: The Unanswered Questions*, Bridger House Books, Hayden, ID. 2011.

Ibid, "Target Fidel: A Narrative Encyclopedia on the US Government's Plots to kill Fidel Castro-1959-1965", Privately Printed, 1999.

Lacouture, Jean, *De Gaulle: The Ruler, 1945-1970*, W.W. Norton Co., New York, 1991.

Mahoney, Richard, D., *Sons and Brothers: The Days of Jack and Bobby Kennedy.* Arcade Publishing Co., New York, 1999.

Manchester, William, *The Death of a President, November, 1963*, Galahad Books, New York, 1967.

Marrs, Jim, *Crossfire: The Plot that Killed Kennedy*, Carroll & Graf, New York, 1989.

Mellen, Joan, *A Farewell to Justice*, Potomac Books, Dulles, VA, 2005.

McCoy, Alfred, *The Politics of Heroin in Southeast Asia*, Harper Publishers, New York, 1973.

Moran, A.G.D., *Mafia: Inside the Dark Heart*, Thomas Dunne Books, New York, 2008.

Newark, Tim, *Mafia Allies*, Zenith Press, St. Paul, MN, 2007.

Ibid, *Lucky Luciano: The Real and the Fake Gangster*, Thomas Dunne Books, New York, 2010.

O'Leary, Brad & Seymour, L.E., *Triangle of Death*, W.N.D. Books, Nashville, Tn., 2003.

Ranelagh, John, *The Agency: The Rise and Decline of the CIA*, Simon & Schuster, New York, 1986.

Riebling, Mark, *Wedge: The Secret War Between the FBI and CIA*, Alfred Knopf, New York, 1994.

Russell, Dick, *The Man Who Knew Too Much*, Carroll & Graf Publishers, New York, 1992.

Russo, Gus, *Live By the Sword: The Secret War Against Castro and the Death of JFK*, Bancroft Press, Baltimore, Md., 1998.

Scheim, David, *Contract on America: The Mafia Murder of President John F. Kennedy*, Shapolsky Publishers, New York, 1988

Schlesinger, Arthur, Jr., *Robert Kennedy And His Times*. Houghton Mifflin Co, Boston, MA, 1978.

Sifakis, Carl, *The Mafia Encyclopedia: From Accardo to Zwillman*, Facts on File Publishers, New York, 1987.

Stockton, Bayard, *Flawed Patriot: The Rise and Fall of CIA Legend Bill Harvey*, Potomac Books, Washington, D.C., 2006.

Summers, Anthony, *Conspiracy*, McGraw Hill & Co., New York, 1980.

Talbot, David, *Brothers: The Hidden History of the Kennedy Years*, The Free Press, New York, 2007.

Trahair, Richard, *Encyclopedia of Cold War Espionage, Spies and Secret Operations*, Greenwood Press, Westport, CT, 2004.

Twyman, Noel, *Bloody Treason: The Assassination of John F. Kennedy*, Laurel Pub. Co., Rancho Santa Fe, CA, 1997.

Valentine, Douglas, *The Strength of the Pack*, Trine Day, Walterville, OR, 2008.

Waldron, Lamar, & Hartmann, Thom, *Legacy of Secrecy: The Long Shadow of the JFK Assassination*, Counterpoint, Berkeley, CA, 2008.

Ibid, *Ultimate Sacrifice: John and Robert Kennedy, the Plan for a Coup in Cuba, and the Murder of JFK*, Carroll & Graf Publishers, New York, 2005.

No author, *It's A Conspiracy*, Earth Works Press, Berkeley, CA, 1992.

New York Times, *Final Assassinations Report*, Bantam Books, 1979.

No author, *CIA Targets Fidel: The Secret Assassinations Report*, Ocean Press, Melbourne, Australia, 1996.

Magazines and Government Reports, etc.

Anderson, Jack & Whitten, Les, "Watergate Plotters Reportedly Market Torrijos For Assassination," *Kentucky New Era*, December 16, 1977.

Anderson, Jack, "Watergate Plotters Set Assassination of Torrijos," *Times Daily*, December 16, 1977.

Bardach, Ann Louise, "Vesco's Last Gamble," *Vanity Fair*, March, 1996, Pg 76-103.

Crille 3rd, George, "The Colonel's Secret Drug War," *The Washington Post*, June 13, 1976.

Kross, Peter, "Project ZR/RIFLE & JFK," *Back Channels Magazine*, Vol. 3, No 1 & 2, Fall-Winter, 1993-94, Page 9-11.

Ibid, "The Plumbers and the Torrijos Assassination," *Back Channels Magazine*, Vol. 4, No. 1.

Ibid, "The Vesco Capers," *Back Channels Magazine*, Vol. 4, No. 1, Page 8-12.

Ibid, "JFK and the French Connection," *Back Channels Magazine*, Vol. 1, No. 1, October 1991, Page 3-4.

Ibid, "The Assassination Archives," *Back Channels Magazine*, Volume 1, No. 1, October, 1991, Page 23-24.

Rivele, Steve, "The Plot to Kill Lumumba" The Corsican Connection," *The National Reporter*, Fall, 1987.

Ibid, "Trajectory of an Unguided Missile," Files of the Assassination Archives & Record Center, Washington, D.C.

Rosen, James, "Rogue on the Run," *Conde Nast's Portfolio*, Feb, 2008.

No Author, "International Heroin Ring Smashed," *Eugene Register Guard*, November 18, 1972.

AP "20 Persons linked to 2 heroin rings," *The Free Star*, November 18, 1972.

Select Committee-Assassination Report, 9-1-75.

Steve Rivele Collection at AARC, Washington, D.C.

"The Men Who Killed Kennedy" DVD, The History Channel, A&E Network.

Mary Ferrell Foundation on the worldwide web.

The New York Times.

KENNEDY IS KILLED BY SNIPER AS HE RIDES IN CAR IN DALLAS; JOHNSON SWORN IN ON PLANE

Gov. Connally Shot; Mrs. Kennedy Safe

Why America Weeps

Get these fascinating books from your nearest bookstore or directly from: Adventures Unlimited Press

www.adventuresunlimitedpress.com

LBJ AND THE CONSPIRACY TO KILL KENNEDY
By Joseph P. Farrell

Farrell says that a coalescence of interests in the military industrial complex, the CIA, and Lyndon Baines Johnson's powerful and corrupt political machine in Texas led to the events culminating in the assassination of JFK. Farrell analyzes the data as only he can, and comes to some astonishing conclusions. Chapters include: Oswald, the FBI, and the CIA: Hoover's Concern of a Second Oswald; Oswald and the Anti-Castro Cubans; The Mafia; Hoover, Johnson, and the Mob; The FBI, the Secret Service, Hoover, and Johnson; The CIA and "Murder Incorporated"; Ruby's Bizarre Behavior; The French Connection and Permindex; Big Oil; The Military; Disturbing Datasets, Doppelgängers, Duplicates and Discrepancies; Two (or is that Three?) Faces of Oswald; Too Many (or Was That Too Few?) Bullets; The Dead Witnesses: Jack Zangretti, Maurice Gatlin, Guy Bannister, Jr., Mary Pinchot Meyer, Rose Cheramie, Dorothy Killgallen, Congressman Hale Boggs; LBJ and the Planning of the Texas Trip; LBJ: A Study in Character, Connections, and Cabals; LBJ and the Aftermath: Accessory After the Fact; The Requirements of Coups D'État; more.

342 Pages. 6x9 Paperback. Illustrated. $19.95 Code: LCKK

ROSWELL AND THE REICH
By Joseph P. Farrell

Farrell here delves ever deeper into the activities of this nefarious group. In his previous works, Farrell has clearly demonstrated that the Nazis were clandestinely developing new and amazing technologies toward the end of WWII, and that the key scientists involved in these experiments were exported to the Allied countries at the end of the conflict, mainly the United States, in a move called Operation Paperclip. Now, Farrell has meticulously reviewed the best-known Roswell research from UFO-ET advocates and skeptics alike, as well as some little-known source material, and comes to a radically different scenario of what happened in Roswell, New Mexico in July 1947, and why the US military has continued to cover it up to this day. Farrell presents a fascinating case that what crashed may have been representative of an independent postwar Nazi power—an extraterritorial Reich monitoring its old enemy, America, and the continuing development of the very technologies confiscated from Germany at the end of the War.

540 pages. 6x9 Paperback. Illustrated. $19.95. Code: RWR

THE MYSTERY OF U-33
By Nigel Graddon

The incredible story of the mystery U-Boats of WWII! Graddon first chronicles the story of the mysterious U-33 that landed in Scotland in 1940 and involved the top-secret Enigma device. He then looks at U-Boat special missions during and after WWII, including U-Boat trips to Antarctica; U-Boats with the curious cargos of liquid mercury; the journey of the Spear of Destiny via U-Boat; the "Black Subs" and more. Chapters and topics include: U-33: The Official Story; The First Questions; Survivors and Deceased; August 1985—the Story Breaks; The Carradale U-boat; The Tale of the Bank Event; In the Wake of U-33; Wrecks; The Greenock Lairs; The Mystery Men; "Brass Bounders at the Admiralty"; Captain's Log; Max Schiller through the Lens; Rudolf Hess; Otto Rahn; U-Boat Special Missions; Neu-Schwabenland; more.

351 Pages. 6x9 Paperback. Illustrated. $19.95. Code: MU33

REICH OF THE BLACK SUN

Nazi Secret Weapons & the Cold War Allied Legend

by Joseph P. Farrell

Why were the Allies worried about an atom bomb attack by the Germans in 1944? Why did the Soviets threaten to use poison gas against the Germans? Why did Hitler in 1945 insist that holding Prague could win the war for the Third Reich? Why did US General George Patton's Third Army race for the Skoda works at Pilsen in Czechoslovakia instead of Berlin? Why did the US Army not test the uranium atom bomb it dropped on Hiroshima? Why did the Luftwaffe fly a non-stop round trip mission to within twenty miles of New York City in 1944? *Reich of the Black Sun* takes the reader on a scientific-historical journey in order to answer these questions. Arguing that Nazi Germany actually won the race for the atom bomb in late 1944,

352 PAGES. 6X9 PAPERBACK. ILLUSTRATED. BIBLIOGRAPHY. $16.95. CODE: ROBS

THE GIZA DEATH STAR

The Paleophysics of the Great Pyramid & the Military Complex at Giza

by Joseph P. Farrell

Was the Giza complex part of a military installation over 10,000 years ago? Chapters include: An Archaeology of Mass Destruction, Thoth and Theories; The Machine Hypothesis; Pythagoras, Plato, Planck, and the Pyramid; The Weapon Hypothesis; Encoded Harmonics of the Planck Units in the Great Pyramid; High Fregquency Direct Current "Impulse" Technology; The Grand Gallery and its Crystals: Gravito-acoustic Resonators; The Other Two Large Pyramids; the "Causeways," and the "Temples"; A Phase Conjugate Howitzer; Evidence of the Use of Weapons of Mass Destruction in Ancient Times; more.

290 PAGES. 6X9 PAPERBACK. ILLUSTRATED. $16.95. CODE: GDS

THE GIZA DEATH STAR DEPLOYED

The Physics & Engineering of the Great Pyramid

by Joseph P. Farrell

Farrell expands on his thesis that the Great Pyramid was a maser, designed as a weapon and eventually deployed—with disastrous results to the solar system. Includes: Exploding Planets: A Brief History of the Exoteric and Esoteric Investigations of the Great Pyramid; No Machines, Please!; The Stargate Conspiracy; The Scalar Weapons; Message or Machine?; A Tesla Analysis of the Putative Physics and Engineering of the Giza Death Star; Cohering the Zero Point, Vacuum Energy, Flux: Feedback Loops and Tetrahedral Physics; and more.

290 PAGES. 6X9 PAPERBACK. ILLUSTRATED. $16.95. CODE: GDSD

THE GIZA DEATH STAR DESTROYED

The Ancient War For Future Science

by Joseph P. Farrell

Farrell moves on to events of the final days of the Giza Death Star and its awesome power. These final events, eventually leading up to the destruction of this giant machine, are dissected one by one, leading us to the eventual abandonment of the Giza Military Complex—an event that hurled civilization back into the Stone Age. Chapters include: The Mars-Earth Connection; The Lost "Root Races" and the Moral Reasons for the Flood; The Destruction of Krypton: The Electrodynamic Solar System, Exploding Planets and Ancient Wars; Turning the Stream of the Flood: the Origin of Secret Societies and Esoteric Traditions; The Quest to Recover Ancient Mega-Technology; Non-Equilibrium Paleophysics; Monatomic Paleophysics; Frequencies, Vortices and Mass Particles; "Acoustic" Intensity of Fields; The Pyramid of Crystals; tons more.

292 pages. 6x9 paperback. Illustrated. $16.95. Code: GDES

SECRETS OF THE UNIFIED FIELD
The Philadelphia Experiment, the Nazi Bell, and the Discarded Theory
by Joseph P. Farrell

Farrell examines the now discarded Unified Field Theory. American and German wartime scientists and engineers determined that, while the theory was incomplete, it could nevertheless be engineered. Chapters include: The Meanings of "Torsion"; Wringing an Aluminum Can; The Mistake in Unified Field Theories and Their Discarding by Contemporary Physics; Three Routes to the Doomsday Weapon: Quantum Potential, Torsion, and Vortices; Tesla's Meeting with FDR; Arnold Sommerfeld and Electromagnetic Radar Stealth; Electromagnetic Phase Conjugations, Phase Conjugate Mirrors, and Templates; The Unified Field Theory, the Torsion Tensor, and Igor Witkowski's Idea of the Plasma Focus; tons more.

340 pages. 6x9 Paperback. Illustrated. Bibliography. Index. $18.95. Code: SOUF

NAZI INTERNATIONAL
The Nazi's Postwar Plan to Control Finance, Conflict, Physics and Space
by Joseph P. Farrell

Beginning with prewar corporate partnerships in the USA, including some with the Bush family, he moves on to the surrender of Nazi Germany, and evacuation plans of the Germans. He then covers the vast, and still-little-known recreation of Nazi Germany in South America with help of Juan Peron, I.G. Farben and Martin Bormann. Farrell then covers Nazi Germany's penetration of the Muslim world including Wilhelm Voss and Otto Skorzeny in Gamel Abdul Nasser's Egypt before moving on to the development and control of new energy technologies including the Bariloche Fusion Project, Dr. Philo Farnsworth's Plasmator, and the work of Dr. Nikolai Kozyrev. Finally, Farrell discusses the Nazi desire to control space, and examines their connection with NASA, the esoteric meaning of NASA Mission Patches.

412 pages. 6x9 Paperback. Illustrated. References. $19.95. Code: NZIN

ARKTOS
The Polar Myth in Science, Symbolism & Nazi Survival
by Joscelyn Godwin

Explored are the many tales of an ancient race said to have lived in the Arctic regions, such as Thule and Hyperborea. Progressing onward, he looks at modern polar legends: including the survival of Hitler, German bases in Antarctica, UFOs, the hollow earth, and the hidden kingdoms of Agartha and Shambala. Chapters include: Prologue in Hyperborea; The Golden Age; The Northern Lights; The Arctic Homeland; The Aryan Myth; The Thule Society; The Black Order; The Hidden Lands; Agartha and the Polaires; Shambhala; The Hole at the Pole; Antarctica; more.

220 Pages. 6x9 Paperback. Illustrated. Bib. Index. $16.95. Code: ARK

PARAPOLITICS!
Conspiracy in Contemporary America
by Kenn Thomas

From the Kennedy assassination to 9/11, Thomas examines the underlying parapolitics that animate the secret elites and the war-ravaged planet they manipulate. Contents include: Octopus Redux; Previously unpublished interview with the girlfriend of Octopus investigator Danny Casolaro; Orgone; Wilhelm Reich: Eisenhower's secret ally against the aliens; Clinton era conspiracies; You Too Can Be a Researcher: How to use the Freedom of Information Act; Anthrax Terrorists; Media Mindwash; 9/11 Commission Omission, and much, much more.

340 Pages. 6x9 Paperback. Illustrated. $20.00. Code: PPOL

ATLANTIS & THE POWER SYSTEM OF THE GODS

by David Hatcher Childress and Bill Clendenon

Childress' fascinating analysis of Nikola Tesla's broadcast system in light of Edgar Cayce's "Terrible Crystal" and the obelisks of ancient Egypt and Ethiopia. Includes: Atlantis and its crystal power towers that broadcast energy; how these incredible power stations may still exist today; inventor Nikola Tesla's nearly identical system of power transmission; Mercury Proton Gyros and mercury vortex propulsion; more. Richly illustrated, and packed with evidence that Atlantis not only existed—it had a world-wide energy system more sophisticated than ours today.

246 PAGES. 6x9 PAPERBACK. ILLUSTRATED. $15.95. CODE: APSG

THE ANTI-GRAVITY HANDBOOK

edited by David Hatcher Childress

The new expanded compilation of material on Anti-Gravity, Free Energy, Flying Saucer Propulsion, UFOs, Suppressed Technology, NASA Cover-ups and more. Highly illustrated with patents, technical illustrations and photos. This revised and expanded edition has more material, including photos of Area 51, Nevada, the government's secret testing facility. This classic on weird science is back in a new format!

230 PAGES. 7x10 PAPERBACK. ILLUSTRATED. $16.95. CODE: AGH

ANTI–GRAVITY & THE WORLD GRID

Is the earth surrounded by an intricate electromagnetic grid network offering free energy? This compilation of material on ley lines and world power points contains chapters on the geography, mathematics, and light harmonics of the earth grid. Learn the purpose of ley lines and ancient megalithic structures located on the grid. Discover how the grid made the Philadelphia Experiment possible. Explore the Coral Castle and many other mysteries, including acoustic levitation, Tesla Shields and scalar wave weaponry. Browse through the section on anti-gravity patents, and research resources.

274 PAGES. 7x10 PAPERBACK. ILLUSTRATED. $14.95. CODE: AGW

ANTI–GRAVITY & THE UNIFIED FIELD

edited by David Hatcher Childress

Is Einstein's Unified Field Theory the answer to all of our energy problems? Explored in this compilation of material is how gravity, electricity and magnetism manifest from a unified field around us. Why artificial gravity is possible; secrets of UFO propulsion; free energy; Nikola Tesla and anti-gravity airships of the 20s and 30s; flying saucers as superconducting whirls of plasma; anti-mass generators; vortex propulsion; suppressed technology; government cover-ups; gravitational pulse drive; spacecraft & more.

240 PAGES. 7x10 PAPERBACK. ILLUSTRATED. $14.95. CODE: AGU

PRODIGAL GENIUS: The Life of Nikola Tesla

by John J. O'Neill

This special edition of O'Neill's book has many rare photographs of Tesla and his most advanced inventions. Tesla's eccentric personality gives his life story a strange romantic quality. He made his first million before he was forty, yet gave up his royalties in a gesture of friendship, and died almost in poverty. Tesla could see an invention in 3-D, from every angle, within his mind, before it was built; how he refused to accept the Nobel Prize; his friendships with Mark Twain, George Westinghouse and competition with Thomas Edison. Tesla is revealed as a figure of genius whose influence on the world reaches into the far future. Deluxe, illustrated edition.

408 pages. 6x9 Paperback. Illustrated. $18.95. Code: PRG

GRAVITATIONAL MANIPULATION OF DOMED CRAFT
UFO Propulsion Dynamics
by Paul E. Potter

Potter's precise and lavish illustrations allow the reader to enter directly into the realm of the advanced technological engineer and to understand, quite straightforwardly, the aliens' methods of energy manipulation: their methods of electrical power generation; how they purposely designed their craft to employ the kinds of energy dynamics that are exclusive to space (discoverable in our astrophysics) in order that their craft may generate both attractive and repulsive gravitational forces; their control over the mass-density matrix surrounding their craft enabling them to alter their physical dimensions and even manufacture their own frame of reference in respect to time. Includes a 16-page color insert.

624 pages. 7x10 Paperback. Illustrated. References. $24.00. Code: GMDC

TAPPING THE ZERO POINT ENERGY
Free Energy & Anti-Gravity in Today's Physics
by Moray B. King

King explains how free energy and anti-gravity are possible. The theories of the zero point energy maintain there are tremendous fluctuations of electrical field energy imbedded within the fabric of space. This book tells how, in the 1930s, inventor T. Henry Moray could produce a fifty kilowatt "free energy" machine; how an electrified plasma vortex creates anti-gravity; how the Pons/Fleischmann "cold fusion" experiment could produce tremendous heat without fusion; and how certain experiments might produce a gravitational anomaly.

180 PAGES. 5x8 PAPERBACK. ILLUSTRATED. $12.95. CODE: TAP

QUEST FOR ZERO-POINT ENERGY
Engineering Principles for "Free Energy"
by Moray B. King

King expands, with diagrams, on how free energy and anti-gravity are possible. The theories of zero point energy maintain there are tremendous fluctuations of electrical field energy embedded within the fabric of space. King explains the following topics: TFundamentals of a Zero-Point Energy Technology; Vacuum Energy Vortices; The Super Tube; Charge Clusters: The Basis of Zero-Point Energy Inventions; Vortex Filaments, Torsion Fields and the Zero-Point Energy; Transforming the Planet with a Zero-Point Energy Experiment; Dual Vortex Forms: The Key to a Large Zero-Point Energy Coherence. Packed with diagrams, patents and photos.

224 PAGES. 6x9 PAPERBACK. ILLUSTRATED. $14.95. CODE: QZPE

DARK MOON
Apollo and the Whistleblowers
by Mary Bennett and David Percy

Did you know a second craft was going to the Moon at the same time as Apollo 11? Do you know that potentially lethal radiation is prevalent throughout deep space? Do you know there are serious discrepancies in the account of the Apollo 13 'accident'? Did you know that 'live' color TV from the Moon was not actually live at all? Did you know that the Lunar Surface Camera had no viewfinder? Do you know that lighting was used in the Apollo photographs—yet no lighting equipment was taken to the Moon? All these questions, and more, are discussed in great detail by British researchers Bennett and Percy in *Dark Moon,* the definitive book (nearly 600 pages) on the possible faking of the Apollo Moon missions. Tons of NASA photos analyzed for possible deceptions.

568 PAGES. 6x9 PAPERBACK. ILLUSTRATED. BIBLIOGRAPHY. INDEX. $32.00. CODE: DMO

LOST CITIES & ANCIENT MYSTERIES OF THE SOUTHWEST
By David Hatcher Childress

Join David as he starts in northern Mexico and searches for the lost mines of the Aztecs. He continues north to west Texas, delving into the mysteries of Big Bend, including mysterious Phoenician tablets discovered there and the strange lights of Marfa. Then into New Mexico where he stumbles upon a hollow mountain with a billion dollars of gold bars hidden deep inside it! In Arizona he investigates tales of Egyptian catacombs in the Grand Canyon, cruises along the Devil's Highway, and tackles the century-old mystery of the Lost Dutchman mine. In Nevada and California Childress checks out the rumors of mummified giants and weird tunnels in Death Valley, plus he searches the Mohave Desert for the mysterious remains of ancient dwellers alongside lakes that dried up tens of thousands of years ago. It's a full-tilt blast down the back roads of the Southwest in search of the weird and wondrous mysteries of the past!

486 Pages. 6x9 Paperback. Illustrated. Bibliography. $19.95. Code: LCSW

TECHNOLOGY OF THE GODS
The Incredible Sciences of the Ancients
by David Hatcher Childress

Childress looks at the technology that was allegedly used in Atlantis and the theory that the Great Pyramid of Egypt was originally a gigantic power station. He examines tales of ancient flight and the technology that it involved; how the ancients used electricity; megalithic building techniques; the use of crystal lenses and the fire from the gods; evidence of various high tech weapons in the past, including atomic weapons; ancient metallurgy and heavy machinery; the role of modern inventors such as Nikola Tesla in bringing ancient technology back into modern use; impossible artifacts; and more.

356 Pages. 6x9 Paperback. Illustrated. Bibliography. $16.95. Code: TGOD

VIMANA AIRCRAFT OF ANCIENT INDIA & ATLANTIS
by David Hatcher Childress, introduction by Ivan T. Sanderson

In this incredible volume on ancient India, authentic Indian texts such as the *Ramayana* and the *Mahabharata* are used to prove that ancient aircraft were in use more than four thousand years ago. Included in this book is the entire Fourth Century BC manuscript *Vimaanika Shastra* by the ancient author Maharishi Bharadwaaja. Also included are chapters on Atlantean technology, the incredible Rama Empire of India and the devastating wars that destroyed it.

334 Pages. 6x9 Paperback. Illustrated. $15.95. Code: VAA

LIQUID CONSPIRACY
JFK, LSD, the CIA, Area 51 & UFOs
by George Piccard

Underground author George Piccard on the politics of LSD, mind control, and Kennedy's involvement with Area 51 and UFOs. Reveals JFK's LSD experiences with Mary Pinchot-Meyer. The plot thickens with an ever expanding web of CIA involvement, from underground bases with UFOs seen by JFK and Marilyn Monroe (among others) to a vaster conspiracy that affects every government agency from NASA to the Justice Department. This may have been the reason that Marilyn Monroe and actress-columnist Dorothy Kilgallen were both murdered. Focusing on the bizarre side of history, *Liquid Conspiracy* takes the reader on a psychedelic tour de force. This is your government on drugs!

264 Pages. 6x9 Paperback. Illustrated. $14.95. Code: LIQC

THE TESLA PAPERS

Nikola Tesla on Free Energy & Wireless Transmission of Power

by Nikola Tesla, edited by David Hatcher Childress

David Hatcher Childress takes us into the incredible world of Nikola Tesla and his amazing inventions. Tesla's fantastic vision of the future, including wireless power, anti-gravity, free energy and highly advanced solar power. Also included are some of the papers, patents and material collected on Tesla at the Colorado Springs Tesla Symposiums, including papers on: •The Secret History of Wireless Transmission •Tesla and the Magnifying Transmitter •Design and Construction of a Half-Wave Tesla Coil •Electrostatics: A Key to Free Energy •Progress in Zero-Point Energy Research •Electromagnetic Energy from Antennas to Atoms •Tesla's Particle Beam Technology •Fundamental Excitatory Modes of the Earth-Ionosphere Cavity

325 PAGES. 8X10 PAPERBACK. ILLUSTRATED. $16.95. CODE: TTP

UFOS AND ANTI-GRAVITY

Piece For A Jig-Saw

by Leonard G. Cramp

Leonard G. Cramp's 1966 classic book on flying saucer propulsion and suppressed technology is a highly technical look at the UFO phenomena by a trained scientist. Cramp first introduces the idea of 'anti-gravity' and introduces us to the various theories of gravitation. He then examines the technology necessary to build a flying saucer and examines in great detail the technical aspects of such a craft. Cramp's book is a wealth of material and diagrams on flying saucers, anti-gravity, suppressed technology, G-fields and UFOs. Chapters include Crossroads of Aerodymanics, Aerodynamic Saucers, Limitations of Rocketry, Gravitation and the Ether, Gravitational Spaceships, G-Field Lift Effects, The Bi-Field Theory, VTOL and Hovercraft, Analysis of UFO photos, more.

388 PAGES. 6X9 PAPERBACK. ILLUSTRATED. $16.95. CODE: UAG

THE COSMIC MATRIX

Piece for a Jig-Saw, Part Two

by Leonard G. Cramp

Cramp examines anti-gravity effects and theorizes that this super-science used by the craft—described in detail in the book—can lift mankind into a new level of technology, transportation and understanding of the universe. The book takes a close look at gravity control, time travel, and the interlocking web of energy between all planets in our solar system with Leonard's unique technical diagrams. A fantastic voyage into the present and future!

364 PAGES. 6X9 PAPERBACK. ILLUSTRATED. BIBLIOGRAPHY. $16.00. CODE: CMX

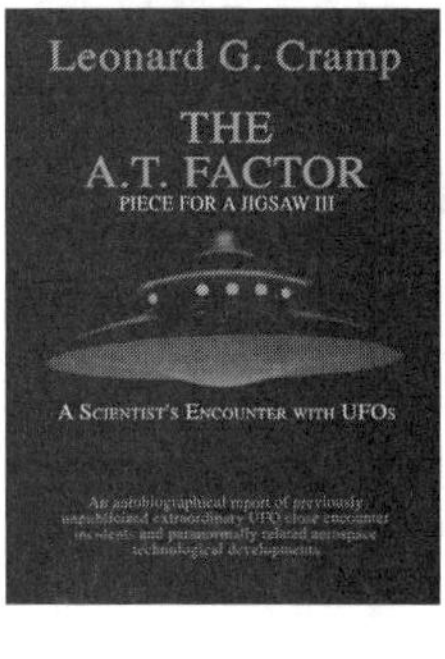

THE A.T. FACTOR

A Scientists Encounter with UFOs

by Leonard Cramp

British aerospace engineer Cramp began much of the scientific anti-gravity and UFO propulsion analysis back in 1955 with his landmark book *Space, Gravity & the Flying Saucer* (out-of-print and rare). In this final book, Cramp brings to a close his detailed and controversial study of UFOs and Anti-Gravity.

324 PAGES. 6X9 PAPERBACK. ILLUSTRATED. BIBLIOGRAPHY. INDEX. $16.95. CODE: ATF

ORDER FORM

10% Discount When You Order 3 or More Items!

One Adventure Place
P.O. Box 74
Kempton, Illinois 60946
United States of America
Tel.: 815-253-6390 • Fax: 815-253-6300
Email: auphq@frontiernet.net
http://www.adventuresunlimitedpress.com

ORDERING INSTRUCTIONS

- ✓ Remit by USD$ Check, Money Order or Credit Card
- ✓ Visa, Master Card, Discover & AmEx Accepted
- ✓ Paypal Payments Can Be Made To: info@wexclub.com
- ✓ Prices May Change Without Notice
- ✓ 10% Discount for 3 or more Items

SHIPPING CHARGES

United States

- ✓ Postal Book Rate { $4.00 First Item; 50¢ Each Additional Item
- ✓ POSTAL BOOK RATE Cannot Be Tracked!
- ✓ Priority Mail { $5.00 First Item; $2.00 Each Additional Item
- ✓ UPS { $6.00 First Item; $1.50 Each Additional Item

NOTE: UPS Delivery Available to Mainland USA Only

Canada

- ✓ Postal Air Mail { $10.00 First Item; $2.50 Each Additional Item
- ✓ Personal Checks or Bank Drafts MUST BE US$ and Drawn on a US Bank
- ✓ Canadian Postal Money Orders OK
- ✓ Payment MUST BE US$

All Other Countries

- ✓ Sorry, No Surface Delivery!
- ✓ Postal Air Mail { $16.00 First Item; $6.00 Each Additional Item
- ✓ Checks and Money Orders MUST BE US$ and Drawn on a US Bank or branch.
- ✓ Paypal Payments Can Be Made in US$ To: info@wexclub.com

SPECIAL NOTES

- ✓ RETAILERS: Standard Discounts Available
- ✓ BACKORDERS: We Backorder all Out-of-Stock Items Unless Otherwise Requested
- ✓ PRO FORMA INVOICES: Available on Request

ORDER ONLINE AT: www.adventuresunlimitedpress.com

Please check: ☑

☐ This is my first order ☐ I have ordered before

Name

Address

City

State/Province | Postal Code

Country

Phone day | Evening

Fax | Email

Item Code	Item Description	Qty	Total

Please check: ☑

	Subtotal ▸	
	Less Discount-10% for 3 or more items ▸	
☐ Postal-Surface	Balance ▸	
☐ Postal-Air Mail (Priority in USA)	Illinois Residents 6.25% Sales Tax ▸	
	Previous Credit ▸	
☐ UPS (Mainland USA only)	Shipping ▸	
	Total (check/MO in USD$ only) ▸	

☐ Visa/MasterCard/Discover/American Express

Card Number

Expiration Date

10% Discount When You Order 3 or More Items!